Placenames of
the Civil War

ALSO BY JOHN D. BENNETT
AND FROM McFARLAND

*The London Confederates:
The Officials, Clergy, Businessmen and Journalists
Who Backed the American South
During the Civil War* (2008; paperback 2012)

PLACENAMES OF THE CIVIL WAR

Cities, Towns, Villages, Railroad Stations, Forts, Camps, Islands, Rivers, Creeks, Fords and Ferries

John D. Bennett

McFarland & Company, Inc., Publishers
Jefferson, North Carolina, and London

LIBRARY OF CONGRESS CATALOGUING-IN-PUBLICATION DATA

Bennett, J.D. (John D.), 1937–
Placenames of the Civil War : cities, towns, villages, railroad stations,
forts, camps, islands, rivers, creeks, fords and ferries / John D. Bennett.
 p. cm.
Includes bibliographical references.

ISBN 978-0-7864-7009-9
softcover : acid free paper ∞

1. United States—History—Civil War, 1861–1865—Miscellanea. 2. Names,
Geographical—United States. 3. Historic sites—United States. I. Title.
 E468.B45 2012   973.7—dc23   2012008627

BRITISH LIBRARY CATALOGUING DATA ARE AVAILABLE

© 2012 John D. Bennett. All rights reserved

*No part of this book may be reproduced or transmitted in any form
or by any means, electronic or mechanical, including photocopying
or recording, or by any information storage and retrieval system,
without permission in writing from the publisher.*

Front cover images: *clockwise from top left* Potomac River, Harpers Ferry, West Virginia;
Scrub oak trees, Fort Fisher, North Carolina; Historic Burnside's Bridge, Antietam, near
Sharpsburg, Maryland; Site of Battle of Bull Run, Manassas, Virginia © 2012 Shutterstock

Manufactured in the United States of America

*McFarland & Company, Inc., Publishers
Box 611, Jefferson, North Carolina 28640
www.mcfarlandpub.com*

Contents

Preface 1

Introduction 3

THE PLACENAMES 7

Appendix 1: United States Census of 1860 169

Appendix 2: Towns by State 173

Bibliography 183

"There is no part of the world where nomenclature is so rich,
poetical, humorous and picturesque as in the United States of America."
— Robert Louis Stevenson, *Across the Plains* (1892)

Preface

"The Civil War was fought in 10,000 places, from Valverde, New Mexico, and Tullahoma, Tennessee, to St. Albans, Vermont, and Fernandina on the Florida coast," wrote Geoffrey C. Ward in the book accompanying the documentary film *The Civil War*, made for public television by Ric and Ken Burns.* In spite of the enormous number of books about the Civil War, there does not seem to be one which explains the origins of the names of those places. There are, of course, a number of reference books on American placenames, but those associated with the Civil War are not always to be found there. In writing this book I set out to remedy this, bringing together information about the most important and interesting of them from a wide range of sources, including not only guidebooks, dictionaries and gazetteers, but also histories of uniforms and weapons, prisons and hospitals, shipbuilding and railroads.

This is not a dictionary of battles, nor is it a guidebook. Though most places which were the scene of significant military events are included, so too are the sites of military academies, arsenals, factories, iron works and navy yards, as well as supply depots, prison camps and hospitals. Some of these were behind the lines, often far from the fighting but part of the economic and industrial infrastructure, both North and South.

Choosing these places has often been difficult. Sometimes significant events occurred in places whose names are not very interesting; on other occasions, places with fascinating name origins were the scene of minor, relatively unimportant skirmishes. There were inevitably many borderline cases as well. Since the Civil War, some placenames have changed, been absorbed by larger communities, or in a few instances, disappeared altogether. When possible, I have used placenames in use during the 1860s rather than modern versions, with a note indicating any variations.

I performed my research in London, at the British Library, the Institute of Historical Research and Senate House Library (University of London), at Birmingham Reference Library, Leicester University Library and Leicester Reference Library. Valuable information also came from the Ohioana Library in Columbus,

---

*Geoffrey C. Ward with Ric Burns and Ken Burns. The Civil War: An Illustrated History. New York: Alfred A. Knopf, 1990, xix. Professor E.B. Long gives the total number of "fights" of one kind or another as 10,455, the greatest number taking place in the states of Virginia, Tennessee and Missouri. It is a figure which he readily admits can be disputed.

Ohio; the South Carolina Department of Archives and History in Columbia; and the Virginia Historical Society and the Library of Virginia in Richmond. John Cox and Muireall Sperrings obtained important books for me and Charles Priestley, a fellow member of the American Civil War Round Table (UK), read and commented on parts of the manuscript.

The information is presented in the form of a gazetteer, which explains the origin of each placename and provides a note of its Civil War connections. Counties, and parishes in Louisiana, are given in brackets after each placename. Also included are islands, rivers and creeks, fords and ferries, railroad stations, army camps and forts. A population table from the Eighth United States Census (1860) provides an indication of the size of cities, towns and villages on the eve of civil war and a state index brings together the entries for each state. The enormous disparity in population between Northern and Southern cities helps to reinforce the late Shelby Foote's remark that "the North fought that war with one hand behind its back."*

To avoid a plethora of dates, I have limited them to the month in question. Similarly, for reasons of simplicity, all general officers are described as "General," regardless of their actual rank. Because of the complexities surrounding the use of brevet ranks in the Union Army, I have omitted references to these altogether. For more information on dates and ranks, the various chronologies and biographical dictionaries listed in the bibliography provide full details.

The American Civil War was unusual in the use of alternate names for some battles and engagements. The Federals often called them after rivers, creeks or other geographical features, while the Confederates preferred the names of nearby towns or villages. Bull Run, for instance, was known to the Confederates as Manassas, and Antietam as Sharpsburg; these are entered in the gazetteer under their various names, and cross-referenced (q.v.). I have used the usual two-letter postal abbreviations for states, with the exception of New Mexico, then part of New Mexico Territory (NMT), and Oklahoma, which was known as Indian Territory (IT). Places marked with a diamond (♦) are independent cities; i.e., not administratively part of the surrounding counties.

*Ward, 272.

Introduction

In his book *Names on the Land*, the historian George R. Stewart gives a flavor of Civil War placenames: "They were the names of little towns with familiar endings—Gettysburg and Vicksburg, Chancellorsville and Murfreesboro. Or they were those the Indians left, like Antietam and Chickamauga; or of the little country churches of the South—Shiloh and Bethesda and Big Bethel … Or else they were the names of plantations and taverns and crossroads—Five Forks and Yellow Tavern … Or again, they were the names that the English had brought into the land—Winchester, Malvern Hill and Cold Harbor. When they fought two bloody days at Fredericksburg, few remembered it was named for an English prince. The names of those battles had the true flavor of the land—Wilson's Creek and Bull Run … Pea Ridge, the Wilderness and Chickasaw Bayou."*

The familiar, and less familiar, placenames of that war can be divided into a number of categories. Early settlers sometimes chose Indian or Native American names, or their version of them, though the original meanings were sometimes misunderstood or lost in translation, and even the actual language may have been uncertain. Transplanted English placenames were frequently used in the original thirteen colonies and replicated many times as settlers moved further west. French settlement, particularly in what became known as the Louisiana Purchase, influenced placenames in the states of Louisiana, Arkansas and Missouri, as did Spanish exploration and conquest of Florida and the Southwest, including the future states of Texas and New Mexico.

The names of English royalty, aristocrats, politicians and generals naturally fell out of favor after the American Revolution, though few existing ones seem to have been changed.† Those commemorating national celebrities like Benjamin Franklin, and presidents, vice-presidents and military heroes, became popular in the early 19th century. At a more local level, the names of territorial and state governors, senators and representatives were often commemorated. Then there were biblical names, saints' names (often originating with Spanish or French

---

*George R. Stewart. *Names on the Land: An Historical Account of Place-naming in the United States*. New York: Random House, 1945, 298–9.

†*Two exceptions were Charles Town, South Carolina, named for King Charles II and renamed Charleston, and Kingston, North Carolina, named for King George III and renamed Kinston.*

missionaries) and even literary ones. There were also some invented names and occasionally promotional names, intended to encourage development.

Just as there are fashions in given names, so there were fashions in placenames. French names tended to displace English ones for a while after the American Revolution because of the assistance given by France. The Marquis de La Fayette, a hero of the Revolution who revisited America in the 1820s, gave his name to a number of places, while the unfortunate King Louis XVI was commemorated by several towns and cities. What might be described as exotic names, from both the ancient and modern world, were often derived from books or newspapers and enjoyed a vogue in the early 19th century.

The given or family names of town founders or early settlers, combined with "town" (often contracted to "ton") or "borough" (frequently shortened to "boro") together with the French "ville" and the German or Dutch "burg" or "burgh," became one of the most common forms of placenames across America.

Not all were named for men: a number of towns honored the wives or daughters of early landowners or settlers; a town in Arkansas was named for Jenny Lind, one of the most famous international singers of her day who visited America at the beginning of the 1850s; and at least two towns were named for the 17th century Indian princess Pocahontas.

Names which recur in different states sometimes have quite different origins. Florence, Alabama, was named after the city in Italy by the Italian surveyor who laid it out, while another Florence in South Carolina commemorated the daughter of a local railroad director. Names given to early settlements were often changed, sometimes more than once, as communities which were growing and becoming more prosperous and sophisticated, sought out less mundane and more dignified names.

During the Civil War, obscure towns and villages, often previously known only to those in the locality, became household names through newspaper reports, not only across America, but also in Europe and even further afield. How many people had even heard of places like Manassas, Gettysburg or Appomattox Court House before the war? Appomattox Court House, the scene of Lee's surrender, which for a while became the most famous village in America, was a county seat, though it is one no longer. Counties are not the subject of this book — they are dealt with elsewhere — but there are inevitable parallels between their names and some of the towns and villages within their boundaries, deriving as they often do from common origins.*

For both sides, railroads played an important part in the Civil War, enabling troops, ordnance, supplies and foodstuffs to be moved long distances relatively easily, hospitals to be transported and battlefield casualties to be evacuated. In the South, stations and depots, named for company directors or line engineers, state governors or other local personalities, were often the scenes of military engagements.

The North had a much more comprehensive network of railroads than the South, with two and a half times as many miles of track and the resources to maintain them. Furthermore, the Railways and Telegraph Act of January 1862

The origins of county names are described in Joseph N. Kane's The American Counties; *3rd ed. Metuchen, NJ: Scarecrow Press, Inc., 1972.*

gave the Federal government unprecedented powers over railroad companies, their lines and employees, and created the United States Military Railroads, which as well as requisitioning or building rolling stock, constructed two new lines, from Washington to Alexandria and Petersburg to City Point.

The Confederate government, on the other hand, was never able to exercise the kind of authority it needed over Southern railroads, whose directors proved reluctant to co-operate with either them or other companies. With just under 9,000 miles of railroad track in the entire Confederacy, about one quarter of it in Virginia, and hardly any in the huge state of Texas, many lines, often short, poorly constructed, with differing gauges and deteriorating rolling stock, were intended for the transportation of staple crops rather than people.

The Civil War also produced a huge crop of temporary placenames in the form of camps and forts. Recruitment and training camps were established in both North and South in 1861 for the floods of volunteers, though disillusionment with military life had already set in by the time conscription was introduced in the South in 1862 and in the North in 1863. Later, there were exchange and parole camps, contraband camps, set up to house the many thousands of freed and runaway slaves, and prison camps, some of which became notorious for the sufferings of their unfortunate inmates and for their high mortality rates.

Some camps were only in existence for a short time, while others remained in operation for most of the war, in the North sometimes serving as rendezvous points for the disbanding of volunteer regiments in 1865. Because of their transitory nature, information about their origins and even their locations has sometimes proved elusive, though we know what some of them looked like from contemporary photographs.

Lithographic publishers, mostly in the North where the printing industry was more widespread and there was no shortage of materials, also issued views of army camps which usually gave details of the occupying regiments and their commanding officers. In many cases these lithographs were probably commissioned, to send to the folks back home. They were produced by firms like August Hoen & Co. and Edward Sachse & Co., both of Baltimore; John H. Bufford of Boston; Middleton, Strobridge & Co. of Cincinnati; L. Pessou & B. Simon of New Orleans; Sarony, Major & Knapp of New York; and Thomas S. Sinclair of Philadelphia. One of the most prolific publishers was Louis N. Rosenthal, also of Philadelphia, who issued a large number of colored lithographic prints of Union army camps, mostly in Maryland and Virginia.*

Most camps were named for army officers, and a few for state governors, politicians or landowners. One in Pennsylvania for the training of African American recruits was named for the Quaker William Penn, the founder of the "City of Brotherly Love," and at least two, in Florida and Virginia, for women, rare examples of Civil War nomenclature.

---

*He is known to have issued at least 74 between 1861 and 1863, though his output may have been much greater, perhaps as many as 150, according to Harry T. Peters, from information derived from Albert Rosenthal, a descendant. Harry T. Peters. America on Stone: The Other Printmakers to the American People. New York: Arno Press, 1976 [1931]. Both the Historical Society of Pennsylvania in Philadelphia (Collection 3128) and the Special Collections Department, University of Delaware Library in Newark (GRA 106) have collections of Rosenthal lithographs.

Many of the forts which existed at the outbreak of the Civil War had been built to defend ports and coastal cities. Some of these, constructed over a number of years, were not yet complete in 1861. Others had been built to protect the expanding frontier from Indian attacks. A number were established from the second quarter of the 19th century onwards in Kansas, the Indian Territory (present-day Oklahoma), Texas and New Mexico Territory. Most of these frontier forts were abandoned by their United States garrisons in 1861 as troops were ordered east.

Many more were built during the Civil War. Washington, which at the start of the war had only one neglected and largely abandoned fort, became the most heavily fortified city in North America, surrounded by more than 60 forts, constructed in the District of Columbia, Virginia and Maryland, but it was never under siege. Suffolk, Virginia; Knoxville, Tennessee; and Louisville, Kentucky, were also defended by Union-built forts.

As soon as the Confederate capital was moved from Montgomery, Alabama, to Richmond, Virginia, in May 1861, work started on defensive fortifications there. Various forts were also built along the Mississippi, of which those defending Vicksburg, the "Gibraltar of the Confederacy," were the most extensive, withstanding two Federal assaults and a 47-day siege. Petersburg, Virginia, during the siege of June 1864 to April 1865, was surrounded by a number of forts called the Dimmock Line after Confederate Colonel Charles H. Dimmock who supervised their construction; these were opposed by a ring of Union ones. Savannah's Confederate fortifications succumbed to General Sherman's troops in December 1864, fresh from their march to the sea, but Galveston's forts remained in Confederate hands till the beginning of June 1865.

Antebellum coastal and frontier forts were often named for army officers, sometimes quite junior ones, and this practice was continued during the Civil War, new ones often commemorating men killed in recent combat. During the war a number of forts changed their names, usually when they changed hands. They are entered here under their later name, with references from earlier ones.

THE PLACENAMES

Abbeville (Wilcox) GA
On the Ocmulgee River, it was named either for the wife of David Fitzgerald who gave land for the town site, or for Abbeville, South Carolina. Jefferson Davis stopped here in May 1865, only days before he was captured near Irwinville.

Abbeville (Abbeville) SC
French Huguenots settled here in 1764 and named their town after Abbeville in northern France. On the Greenville & Columbia Railroad, it is sometimes called the "Cradle and the Grave of the Confederacy"—a secessionist meeting was held here in November 1860, and Jefferson Davis, who stayed here in May 1865 on his flight south, conferred with the officers commanding his escort in what has been described as "the last Confederate council of war held east of the Mississippi River."

Aberdeen (Monroe) MS
First settled in 1834, it was originally called Dundee by Scotsman Robert Gordon, who established a trading post on the Tombigbee River, but the name was changed in 1837, apparently because local people had difficulty with the pronunciation. A former cotton gin factory and iron foundry owned by Beckett & Tindall was converted into a gun and cannon factory in 1861, but was destroyed by fire in March 1862. There was also skirmishing here in February 1864.

Abingdon (Washington) VA
First settled c.1770, it was named in 1778 after Abingdon, Oxfordshire, the English ancestral home of Martha Washington's family, the Dandridges. A finishing school for young ladies became the Washington Hospital during the Civil War and is now the Martha Washington Hotel. A popular center for Confederate refugees, Abingdon was also an important supply depot on the Virginia & Tennessee Railroad; an accident here in September 1861 resulted in the death of a number of Louisiana soldiers. General John H. Morgan, retreating from Kentucky, made his headquarters here in June 1864, but the town was recaptured and much of it burned by General Stoneman's cavalry in December of that year.

Acworth (Cobb) GA
Was named by Western & Atlantic Railroad engineer Joseph L. Gregg in 1843 after his hometown of Acworth, New Hampshire. There was skirmishing in and around here on a number of days in June 1864 during the Atlanta campaign, and General William T. Sherman made his headquarters here during the battle of Kennesaw Mountain. There was fighting on the Western & Atlantic Railroad in October, involving General Hood's retreating Army of Tennessee, which succeeded in breaking the track. The town was burned in November by Federal troops who called it "Little Shanty" (as opposed to Big Shanty, present-day Kennesaw).

Adairsville (Bartow) GA
It was established in 1847 as the northern terminus of the Western & Atlantic Railroad on the site of a Cherokee village and named for Walter S. Adair, a Scotsman married to a

Cherokee woman, who had been the first settler here. It saw fighting in the Atlanta campaign: the Georgia state arsenal was destroyed by General Sherman's troops in May 1864 as they pursued General Johnston's retreating forces, and there was more fighting in early July.

Aiken (Aiken) SC

Laid out in 1834, it was named the following year for Irish-born William Aiken (1779–1831), president of the South Carolina Canal & Railroad Co. who had been killed in a Charleston carriage accident. There was fighting here in February 1865 during General Sherman's drive through the Carolinas, when Union cavalry commanded by General H. Judson Kilpatrick, on their way to destroy the mills at Graniteville, were defeated by a force under General Joseph Wheeler.

Albany (Dougherty) GA

The site was purchased and laid out on the Flint River by Alexander Shotwell, a New Jersey Quaker, in 1836 and named after Albany, New York. The Confederate Navy had a storehouse here, a meat-packing plant was opened in 1863, and the following year a flour mill and bakery were established.

Albany (Clinton) KY

What began as a tavern owned by Benjamin Dowell was named in 1837, also after the capital of New York state. There was fighting here in September 1861 and near here in August 1863, and it was occupied by Federal troops for most of that year.

Albany (Albany) NY

Originally a Dutch trading post on the Hudson River and then a fort, a village established in 1652 was named in 1664 for James, Duke of York and Albany (1633–1701), later King James II. It became the state capital of New York in 1797, and developed after the opening of the Erie Canal in 1825 and the Albany-Schenectady Railroad in 1831. During the Civil War the firm of Corning, Winslow & Co. made rifled cannon here for the Union Army and Albany Penitentiary housed Confederate prisoners in 1862–1863. It was also one of a number of rendezvous points for New York troops being mustered out at the end of the war.

Albuquerque (Bernalillo) NMT

A Spanish settlement, founded in 1706 on the Rio Grande, it was named in honor of Francisco, Duque de Alburquerque (d.1733), viceroy of Mexico, 1702–1711, whose name appears to have been confused with that of the Portuguese soldier Afonso de Albuquerque, hence the absence of the first "r." In turn a Spanish, a Mexican, then a U.S. army post (1846), it was abandoned in March 1862 and briefly occupied by General Sibley's Confederate troops in April during the New Mexico campaign before they were forced to evacuate it.

Aldie (Loudoun) VA

Was named after the former home of Charles F. Mercer (1758–1857), a member of the Virginia House of Delegates, called *Aldie* after a village in Italy. There was skirmishing near here in June 1863 and in February and July 1864.

Alexandria (Rapides) LA

Was laid out in 1810 by Alexander Fulton, on whose land on the Red River it was originally founded in 1785, and named for his infant daughter. Evacuated by the Confederates in May 1863 and occupied by Rear Admiral Porter's flotilla, it was the scene of fighting between March and May 1864 during General Banks' unsuccessful Red River campaign. The last Confederate ironclad, the CSS *Missouri*, surrendered here at the beginning of June 1865.

Alexandria (♦) VA

On the Potomac River, it was originally settled by Scottish merchants in 1695, and named in 1748 for John Alexander, the first settler and owner of much of the land. It was part of the District of Columbia, 1791–1847. During its occupation by Federal troops in May 1861, it was the scene of the shooting at the Marshall House Tavern of Union Colonel E. Elmer Ellsworth. His assailant, James W. Jackson, in turn shot dead, is described on a plaque on the site as "The first martyr to the cause of Southern independence." Alexandria remained in Union hands for the rest of the war and became the terminus of a specially constructed U.S. Military Railroad, linking it with Washington. Twenty Federal soldiers were killed and 14 injured when a powder magazine near here exploded in June 1863. That same year, Francis H. Pierpont, previously provisional governor of the pro-Union counties that became West Virginia, moved his headquarters here as the would-be future governor of the Old Dominion.

Allatoona (Bartow) GA

Probably derives from a Cherokee word, though its meaning is uncertain. It developed in the early 1830s when gold was discovered nearby. During a determined attack by Confederate troops on a Union supply depot here in October 1864, General Sherman's flag signal to General John M. Corse—"Hold fast; we are coming"—was later interpreted by journalists as "Hold the fort; I am coming," inspiring Philip P. Bliss's famous revivalist hymn, *Hold the Fort, For We Are Coming*.

Alleyton (Colorado) TX

On the Colorado River, it was first settled in 1821–1822 by Rawson Alley (c.1793–1833) and his four half-brothers. In 1860 it became the western terminus of the Buffalo Bayou, Brazos & Colorado Railroad, and during the Civil War was an important communications hub for troops, outgoing cotton and incoming weapons, clothing and medicine. It was also the site of a Confederate quartermaster depot.

Alton (Madison) IL

It was first settled in 1783 and laid out in 1816–1818 by Colonel Rufus Easton who apparently named it for one of his sons, though its height above the Mississippi River has also been suggested as the origin of the name. The original Illinois state prison, built in 1831, had been abandoned by the start of the Civil War, but was re-opened as a military prison at the request of General Henry W. Halleck, the first Confederate prisoners arriving early in 1862. Some of them took the oath of allegiance to the Union in 1865 to become galvanized or recoated Yankees, for frontier service against the Indians.

Altoona (Blair) PA

The name probably derives from Altona, a German river-port in Schleswig-Holstein, though it may also have been an invented name, deriving from its high situation. It was laid out in 1849 by the Pennsylvania Railroad when that was being driven across the Alleghenies and their workshops were built here in the 1850s. The governors of 14 Northern states met here in September 1862, approved President Lincoln's preliminary Emancipation Proclamation and pledged their support with a centralized policy.

Amelia Court House (Amelia) VA

Was named for Princess Amelia (1710–1786), a daughter of King George II. At the beginning of April 1865 General Lee's remaining forces, retreating westwards from Petersburg, headed in the general direction of Amelia Court House, on the Richmond & Danville Railroad, hoping to follow this into North Carolina and join up with General Johnston's Army of Tennessee. The rations they expected to find were not here, causing unexpected delays while desperate foraging took place, and some skirmishing occurred.

Amelia Island FL

Off the east coast of Florida, it was originally Spanish, but under British control, 1763–1783, and may also have been named for Princess Amelia. The United States took possession of the island in 1821. Built at its northern end in 1847–1861, **Fort Clinch** was named for General Duncan L. Clinch (1787–1849), a hero of the Seminole War. Still unfinished at the start of the Civil War, it was seized by Confederates but evacuated with the rest of the island in March 1862 and occupied by Federal troops the next day. **Fernandina** (now called Fernandina Beach), named for Don Domingo Fernandez, who received a land grant from Spain in 1785, was the scene of a skirmish in April 1862.

Amelia Springs (Amelia) VA

A well-known country resort before the war and also named for Princess Amelia, it became popular with Confederate refugees. During General Lee's retreat, fighting occurred here, in an engagement also known as Jetersville (q.v.).

Americus (Sumter) GA

Was founded in 1832 and named for Amerigo Vespucci (1454–1512), the Italian-born Spanish explorer who gave his name to the continent of America, the Latinized version of whose first name was Americus. The Foard and Newsom Hospitals were located here, and a former college building was turned into the Bragg Hospital in late 1863. The jail was used as a military prison in 1863, and possibly also in 1861 and 1864.

Anderson (Grimes) TX

Was named for Kenneth L. Anderson (1805–1845), vice-president of the Republic of Texas. It was the site of a Confederate quartermaster depot, and J.H. Dance & Bros. who made revolvers, carbines and bayonets for the Confederate Army moved here from Columbia on the Brazos in 1864. There was also a munitions factory near here by then.

Andersonville (Sumter) GA

Originally called Anderson for John W. Anderson, superintendent of the Southwestern Railroad when that was extended from Oglethorpe to Americus in 1854, it was subsequently renamed Andersonville by the U.S. Post Office Department, to avoid confusion with Anderson, South Carolina.

"The place is set down as *Anderson* on maps and in guidebooks; and that is the name by which it was known to the inhabitants of the country, until the ... war dignified it with the title of *ville*," observed a Northern writer who visited it in early 1866. "It is a disagreeable town with absolutely no point of interest about it except the prison. Before the war it had but five buildings: a church without a steeple, a small railroad depot, a little framed box in which was the country post office and two dwellings. Such was Anderson. *Andersonville* contains some forty additional, cheap-looking, unpainted buildings of various sizes, all of which were constructed with reference to the prison, such as officers' houses, government storehouses, hospital buildings (for troops on duty), and so forth."

The Confederate military prison was originally called Camp Sumter (q.v.) but soon became known as Andersonville. An open stockade, it received its first prisoners in February 1864 and became the largest and most notorious prison camp in the South, a byword for suffering and death. Malnutrition, poor sanitation, overcrowding, disease and exposure, exacerbated by the Federal government's halt to the exchange of prisoners, all contributed to the high death rate. The approach of General Sherman's army in the fall of 1864 caused most able-bodied prisoners to be moved elsewhere. It ceased to exist in May 1865.

That summer, nurse Clara Barton came here to help identify and mark the graves of some 12,000 Union prisoners who had died. The prison commandant, Swiss-born Captain Henry Wirz, who protested that conditions at Andersonville were beyond his control, was nevertheless hanged at Washington in November 1865.

Annandale (Fairfax) VA

The name may derive from Annandale, one of the divisions of the old Scottish county of Dumfriesshire. Skirmishing took place here in December 1861, in August 1863, when a Union wagon train was captured by Confederates, in October 1863 and in March and August 1864.

Antietam (Washington) MD

The battle took its name from Antietam Creek rather than this village a few miles further south. It stands at the mouth of the creek, on the Potomac River, and developed around the Antietam Iron Works established in 1765 by Joseph Chapline, the founder of Sharpsburg. It was the scene of skirmishing in August 1861 and there was more fighting here in July 1864 during General Early's raid into Maryland.

Antietam Creek (Washington) MD

A branch of the Potomac, Antietam Creek comes from an Algonquin word of uncertain meaning. The battle fought here in September 1862, on the bloodiest single day of the Civil War, ended General Lee's first attempt to invade the North. Confederate casualties numbered 13,724, among them Generals Lawrence O. Branch, William E. Starke and George B. Anderson, who died of his wounds the following month; Union losses were 12,410 and included Generals Joseph K.F. Mansfield, Israel B. Richardson and Isaac P. Rodman, killed or mortally wounded. The Confederate name for the battle of Antietam was Sharpsburg (q.v.).

Apalachicola (Franklin) FL

On the Apalachicola River, a name which derives from a Hitachi word meaning "people on the other side," it was founded c.1821 and named in 1831. The arsenal here was seized by state forces in January 1861. Blockaded by the Union Navy in June 1861, Apalachicola surrendered the following April.

Appomattox Court House (Appomattox) VA

Originally called Clover Hill after a nearby farm, with a tavern which was a stopping-off point on the Richmond-Lynchburg stage road, it was renamed in 1845 when Appomattox County was formed and became the county seat. It takes its name from the Appomattox River. General Robert E. Lee surrendered the remainder of the Army of Northern Virginia to General Ulysses S. Grant here in April 1865, the beginning of the end of the Civil War. It ceased to be a county seat in 1892.

Appomattox River VA

Was previously called Apumetec's River, from an Indian word meaning either a "sinuous tidal estuary" or "tobacco plant country." General Lee's retreating troops crossed it in April 1865, two days before their surrender.

Appomattox Station (Appomattox) VA

Also takes its name from the Appomattox River. There was fighting here on the South Side Railroad in April 1865 during General Lee's retreat, when trains containing supplies for the Army of Northern Virginia were captured by Union cavalry.

Aquia Creek (Stafford) VA

A pseudo-Latin name, derived from an Algonquin word meaning "bush nut." The Richmond, Fredericksburg & Potomac Railroad terminated here, on a tributary of the Potomac. Confederate batteries were unsuccessfully bombarded from the sea in May and June 1861 before being voluntarily withdrawn, and this important rail and port facility came under Federal control; Aquia Landing became an important supply depot for the campaigns of 1862–1864. President Lincoln made several visits here, conferring with Generals Irvin McDowell in May 1862 and Ambrose E. Burnside in November.

Aransas (Aransas) TX

Is called after the Aransas River which flows into Aransas Harbor. This derives from *Nuestra Senora de Aranzazu* (Our Lady of Aranzazu), a name given it by Spanish explorers in 1746, from Aranzazu in Spain. The USS *Arthur* captured the CSS *Breaker* in Aransas Pass in August 1862 and a Confederate battery here was captured in November 1863. The Aransas Saltworks near here were raided by Federal troops in 1864. (Now called Port Aransas.)

Arkadelphia (Clark) AR

Was first settled on the Washita River c.1811. Arkansas became a state in 1836, and Arkadelphia, founded in 1839, was a combination of its first syllable + *adelphia*, Greek for "brother-place." The arsenal made copies of the British Enfield rifle, repaired arms and manufactured ammunition. There was skirmishing here in February 1863, and after the fall of Little Rock in September, Confederate General Sterling Price briefly made it his headquarters, but the following month it was occupied by Federal cavalry. Salt works, which had operated 1811–1850, were re-opened during the Civil War, but working ended when the Federals reoccupied the town in March 1864.

Arkansas Post (Arkansas) AR

A fort built on the Arkansas River in 1686 became the residence of French and Spanish governors, and after the Louisiana Purchase (1803), was the first capital of Arkansas Territory, 1819–1821. The oldest white settlement in Arkansas, it was captured in January 1863 when Union troops under General John A. McClernand sailed up the river.

Arkansas River AR

Both the state and river take their name from a tribe called *Arkansea*, whom the French called Arkansa(s). The CSS *Pontchartrain* was burned in the river in October 1863 to prevent its capture. A Federal steamer, the USS *Miller*, was captured in August 1864 and another steamer, the *Alamo*, was attacked by Confederate guerrillas in November.

Arlington (Arlington) VA

Overlooking the Potomac River, the estate of the Custis family, which they bought in 1778, took its name from Henry Bennet, Earl of Arlington (1618–1685), who had received a land grant in Virginia from King Charles II in the 17th century. This became the home of Robert E. Lee after his marriage to Mary Custis, but after he resigned from the U.S. Army in April 1861, was occupied by Union soldiers and then confiscated. The Freedman's Village established here became a wartime showpiece, attracting many visitors. It is now the site of Arlington National Cemetery, established in 1864.

Arrow Rock (Saline) MO

A town on the Santa Fe Trail and a river port on the Missouri, it was apparently so called because Indians came here in search of material for their arrowheads. It was laid out as New Philadelphia in 1829 but this was thought too pretentious and it reverted to its old name in 1833. There was skirmishing in July and October 1862, and in October 1863 General Shelby's Confederate cavalry was defeated here. It was also attacked by Confederate guerrillas in July 1864.

Asheville (Buncombe) NC

Was first settled in 1794 on the French Broad River and called Morristown, for Robert Morris, a Revolutionary War financier and politician, but three years later renamed in honor of Samuel Ashe (1725–1813), governor of North Carolina, 1795–1798. The armory, originally a private arms factory, was taken over by the Confederate government in 1861 and manufactured rifles until the operatives and machinery were moved to Columbia, South Carolina, in late 1863. The Sorrel Hospital was also located here. By the last winter of the war, Asheville was full of Confederate refugees.

Ashland (Hanover) VA

It originated in 1848 as a health resort, and by 1855 was named for *Ashland*, the Lexington, Kentucky, home of politician Henry Clay. On the Richmond, Fredericksburg & Potomac Railroad, this village was a convenient location for Confederate refugees, who found it a cheaper and more congenial place than the overcrowded capital; among them was Judith W. McGuire, author of *Diary of a Southern Refugee* (1867). Confederate supplies here were destroyed in May 1862, there was skirmishing near here in June, in May 1863 during General Stoneman's central Virginia raid, when a hospital train full of Confederate wounded from Chancellorsville was captured, in May and June 1864, and finally in March 1865.

Ashley (Pike) MO

General William H. Ashley (1778–1838), for whom it was named, was a prominent fur trader who came to Missouri from Arkansas in 1803. Skirmishing broke out here in August 1862.

Astoria (Queens) NY

Now part of the borough of Queens, New York City, it was first settled in the mid–17th century, but only began to develop in the early 19th century. It was named for John Jacob Astor (1763–1848), America's first multi-millionaire; by the 1830s he was starting to invest in New York real estate and it was hoped to interest him in this area. In 1863 Federal Surgeon General William A. Hammond established a U.S. Army Laboratory here, testing and manufacturing drugs and also making sheets, pillow cases, towels and hospital clothing. It was one of two such government-operated laboratories (the other was at Philadelphia).

Atchafalaya River LA

The name comes from a Choctaw word meaning "long river." There was skirmishing here in September 1863, and Federal troops crossed it at the end of the Red River campaign in May 1864.

Atchison (Atchison) KS

Was founded in 1854 by pro-slavery settlers and named for their leader, David R. Atchison (1807–1886). A stopping place for westbound wagon trains, it was the scene of skirmishing in January 1862. It later became the northern terminus of the Atchison, Topeka & Santa Fe Railroad, which received its first land grant in 1863.

Athens (Limestone) AL

Founded in 1818 as Athenson, it became Athens, one of several towns named after the ancient Greek city. In May 1862, Russian-born Union Colonel John B. Turchin invited his men to loot and burn the town in retaliation for the actions of local guerrillas, remarking, "I shut mine eyes for von hour." Turchin was court-martialed and dismissed for this, but his wife not only persuaded President Lincoln to pardon him, but promote him as well. There was more fighting here in August, and in January and September 1864, and it was captured by General Forrest's cavalry that month.

Athens (Clarke) GA

Though founded in 1785 on the Oconee River as the site of the future University of Georgia, building did not begin till 1801. By 1806 it had "538 free people, 26 four-wheeled carriages and 26 widows," and the coming of the Georgia Railroad in the 1850s encouraged its development. Ferdinand W.C. and Francis L. Cook (Cook & Brother), who made rifles and carbines, moved here from New Orleans in 1862, but their armory ceased operations in 1864 because work done for the Confederate Ordnance Bureau to the value of $250,000 had gone unpaid. F.W.C. Cook, who had raised an infantry regiment, was also killed in action in that year. The members of the Lucy Cobb Institute, an early women's college founded in 1858, raised money during the war to help the South.

Athens (Clark) MO

There was an unsuccessful Confederate attack on Athens at the beginning of August 1861, a few days before the engagement at Wilson's Creek. It was the northernmost Civil War battle fought west of the Mississippi.

Athens (McMinn) TN

Was founded in 1821 and originally called Pumpkintown before acquiring its present name. There was skirmishing here on several days in September 1863. At the beginning of August 1864 the Confederate garrison was pursued across the state line into North Carolina, but in February 1865 the Confederates attempted to retake the town.

Atlanta (Fulton) GA

Established in 1837 as the terminus of the Western & Atlantic Railroad and given the prosaic name of Terminus, this was changed to Marthasville in 1843 in honor of Martha Lumpkin, daughter of Wilson Lumpkin, a former governor of Georgia. Two years later the name of Atlanta, thought to be the feminine form of Atlantic, was coined by railroad engineer J. Edgar Thomson and it was officially adopted.

By the start of the Civil War, Atlanta was the meeting place of four different railroads—the Western & Atlantic, the Georgia, the Macon & Western and the Atlanta & West Point—and with its railroad workshops and the Atlanta Ordnance Works, became an important manufacturing center for war materials—the "Citadel of the Confederacy." The Atlanta Arsenal, established in 1862, repaired arms and supplied ordnance stores to the Army of Tennessee; it was moved to Columbus, Georgia, in 1864. The Scofield & Markham Iron Works (subsequently known as the Atlanta Rolling Mill) made armor plate for the Confederate Navy. Ordnance and laboratory stores, moved here from New Orleans in 1862, formed the Atlanta Naval Ordnance Works; they were moved to Augusta, Georgia, in 1864. The Spiller & Burr pistol factory, which had been making weapons for the Confederate Army since 1862, was purchased by the government in 1864 and its machinery transferred to Macon.

Confederate military hospitals located here included the Gate City, the Empire, Fair Ground Nos. 1 and 2, Polk and Brown, this last one set up by Governor Joseph E. Brown. The Fulton County Jail was used as a military prison in 1861–1864.

The approach of General Sherman's army in May 1864 caused widespread panic in Atlanta. It was "utterly demoralized ... confused, bewildered; a whole city like one moving household, hurried, up-torn, panic-stricken," declared a reporter from the *Mobile Register*. The battle for Atlanta began in July. Among the Confederate casualties in the fighting around the city were Generals William H.T. Walker killed, and Samuel Benton mortally wounded. At the beginning of September General John B. Hood, who had replaced General Joseph E. Johnston as commander of the Army of Tennessee, withdrew from the city. The following day Sherman entered, and telegraphed President Lincoln: "Atlanta is ours, and fairly won."

Later that month, he ordered the expulsion of all residents not authorized to remain. Those going south went by road to Rough and Ready Station, those heading north by rail from the Western & Atlantic depot. Sherman's final act, before he began his march to the sea in November, was to order the destruction of "all storehouses, machine shops, mills, factories, &c." and "all buildings and works of any military importance," and there was more unauthorized burning of property in revenge for the destruction of Chambersburg, Pennsylvania.

Its condition was recorded early in 1866 by a Northern visitor: "Everywhere were ruins and rubbish, mud and mortar and misery. The burnt streets were rapidly rebuilding; but in the meanwhile hundreds of the inhabitants, white and black, rendered homeless by the destruction of the city, were living in wretched hovels...."

Atlee's Station (Hanover) VA

Was probably named for Jacob S. Atlee, a delegate to the state legislature in the 1850s. There was a skirmish here, on the Virginia Central Railroad, in June 1862 and track was damaged during General Stoneman's raid in May 1863. (Now called Atlee.)

Augusta (Richmond) GA

Was founded in 1735 by General James Oglethorpe as a trading post on the Savannah River, and named for Princess Augusta (1719–1772), the future mother of King George III. It was the state capital of Georgia, 1786–1796, and by the time of the Civil War, an important market for tobacco and cotton.

The arsenal, established in 1819, was seized by state forces in January 1861, and construction of a gunpowder works began later that year; the Confederate States Powder Works began operation in April 1862. Both were to be of major importance to the Confederate war effort: at its peak, the powder works was capable of turning out 75,000 cartridges a day. A foundry and machine shops also produced cannon, and naval ordnance works were transferred here from Atlanta in June 1864.

In addition, naval clothing and shoe factories were established here. The Bellville Factory, owned by George Schley, made uniforms for Georgia troops, and Jones & Davenport manufactured military clothing and equipment in waterproof cloth. The Ladies' Volunteer Association of Richmond County, established in May 1861, produced clothing for local troops. The jail was used as a military prison in 1863 and possibly also in 1861 and 1864.

Augusta filled with refugees during 1864, many hoping for employment in the factories and ordnance plants. Against a background of military disintegration, a conference of state governors meeting here in October adopted a resolution calling for "the arrest and return to their commands of all deserters and stragglers"; it was wishful thinking. Earlier that month, President Davis, in a remarkably upbeat speech, had assured a cheering Augusta crowd that the Confederacy was a "free and independent people." Six months later it had collapsed and he was a fugitive.

Austin (Travis) TX

Was founded in 1835 on the Colorado River as Waterloo but four years later renamed for Stephen F. Austin (1793–1836), the "father of Texas." It was the capital, 1839–1842, and again from 1845. A Ladies' Needle Battalion was formed here in June 1861 to make clothing for Texas troops; George Todd manufactured Colt revolvers; the Texas Military Board established an ordnance works at the state foundry in 1862; and the Austin Iron Co. was set up in 1864. A Confederate quartermaster depot was also located here.

Averasboro (Harnett) NC

On the Cape Fear River, it was named for William Avera, a prosperous planter and landowner, who in 1791 gave 120 acres for a town site. It was originally called Averasburg. Confederate troops under General William J. Hardee fought a delaying action here in March 1865, the first attempt to halt General Sherman's relentless progress through the Carolinas.

Avery Island (Iberia) LA

The existence of salt wells here had been known since the 1790s. The island passed by marriage to Judge Daniel D. Avery in 1855. His son, John M. Avery, developed the workings, and huge deposits of rock salt were discovered in May 1862. Of great importance to the Confederate Army, production was under way by August, and in November Commissary General Northrop's agent reported: "The mine is getting out nearly 100,000 pounds of salt per diem, with a prospect of largely increasing production. The salt is of the very best description...." An attempt by a Federal gunboat to bombard the mine failed, but production ended in April 1863, when it was captured and destroyed by General Banks' Union troops.

Baldwin (Duval) FL

It was named for Dr. Abel S. Baldwin (1811–1905?), who led the move for the building of the Florida, Atlantic & Gulf Central Railroad in 1860, between Jacksonville and Lake City. Federal troops from Jacksonville raided in the direction of Baldwin in July 1864, and there was skirmishing here the following month.

Baldwyn (Lee) MS

It came into being with the building of the Mobile & Ohio Railroad in 1848–1861 and was named for a railroad engineer. Skirmishing near here occurred in June and October 1862, and the battle of Brice's Crossroads took place in June 1864.

Baltimore (♦) MD

Was founded in 1729 and named in honor of Cecilius Calvert, Baron Baltimore (1605–1675), who had received a charter granting him possession of Maryland.

A plot to assassinate Abraham Lincoln in February 1861 as he changed stations here *en route* for Washington was foiled with amended travel plans.

Rioting occurred in April that year when Pennsylvania and Massachusetts militia passing through the city were attacked by secessionists; several soldiers and a number of citizens were killed. Federal troops under General Benjamin F. Butler occupied the city the following month. A Sanitary Fair was held in April 1864, to raise funds for the U.S. Sanitary Commission, and Republican and War Democrat delegates to the National Union Convention, meeting here in June, chose Lincoln as their candidate for the forthcoming presidential election. In July, troops from the Army of the Potomac arrived to protect the city from General Early's raiders, though the threat never materialized.

In June 1861 the Federal authorities took possession of the gun factory of Merrill, Thomas & Co. which subsequently produced carbines and rifle muskets for the Union Army. There was an ordnance depot here, and the railroad engineering workshops of Ross Winans made muskets and pikes for Maryland militia. Charles & John Wethered manufactured cloth for military uniforms, Joseph Bernhard made hats and caps and E.W. Briding, cavalry saddles and harness. The Baltimore & Ohio Railroad workshops built locomotives, and the Abbott Iron Co. made armor plate for monitors. The City Jail was used to house Confederate prisoners in 1861–1863. At the end of the war Baltimore was a state rendezvous point for the mustering out of Maryland troops.

Barboursville (Cabell) WV

Was established in 1813 and named for Philip P. Barbour (1783–1841) of Virginia who held a number of important offices at both state and Federal level. There was fighting near here in July 1861.

Barbourville (Knox) KY

Founded in 1800, it was named for James Barbour (1775–1842) who gave the land for its site c.1800. Fighting took place here in September 1861 when Confederate troops burned a Federal recruiting camp, and there was further skirmishing in September 1862, April 1863 and February 1864.

Bardstown (Nelson) KY

Founded in 1778, it was named for William Bard of Pennsylvania, one of the original landowners, and laid out in 1785. It was the scene of skirmishing in October 1862 during General Bragg's Kentucky campaign, and in July 1863, when it was captured by General John H. Morgan, and again in August 1864.

Barhamsville (New Kent) VA

Took its name from the Barham family who settled here c.1654. An engagement here in May 1862 during the Peninsula campaign is also known as Eltham's Landing or West Point (q.v.).

Barnesville (Lamar) GA

Was founded in 1826 by Gideon Barnes (1791–1871), a tavern keeper and landowner. At the beginning of September 1864, a passenger train packed with Confederate wounded being evacuated from Atlanta, ran into another train near here carrying commissary stores, on the Macon & Western Railroad; about 30 men were killed and many more were injured. The Erwin Hospital was located at Barnesville, which was the scene of a skirmish in April 1865 involving General Wilson's Union cavalry.

Barnwell (Barnwell) SC

Was named in 1798 for Revolutionary War hero General John Barnwell (1748–1800). Skirmishing took place near here in February 1865 as Confederate forces tried to impede General Sherman's advance through the Carolinas, and it was burned.

Barton's Station (Colbert) AL
On the Memphis & Charleston Railroad, it was the scene of skirmishing in April and October 1863. It was possibly named for William Barton (1748–1831), a general in the Revolutionary War. (Now called Barton.)

Bastrop (Bastrop) TX
Was re-established on the Colorado River in the 1830s, after an earlier colony of Germans founded in 1823 by Felipe Enrique Neri, Baron de Bastrop (d.1828), had been abandoned because of Indian troubles.

The Bastrop Military Institute, established in 1858, closed in 1861 as instructors and cadets left to join the war. N.B. Tanner had a bayonet and rifle factory here and contracted with the Texas Military Board to supply Mississippi rifles, though they were of poor quality. The Bastrop Iron Manufacturing Co. produced pig and bar iron, and the Bastrop Cotton & Wool Manufacturing Co. made cotton and woolen fabrics.

Batesville (Independence) AR
A port on the White River, it was founded in 1812 as a trading post and named for territorial judge and congressman James W. Bates (1788–1846) when laid out in 1821–1822. It was later the site of a ferry and steamboat stop. The scene of considerable military activity, there was skirmishing in May and July 1862, and General Marmaduke's Confederate troops were driven out in February 1863.

Baton Rouge (East Baton Rouge) LA
There have been several attempts to explain the origin of this placename. In French it means "red post" and is thought to refer either to a post erected by French colonists to mark the boundary between their land and that of the Indians, or between the hunting grounds of two tribes. First established in 1699 as a French military outpost on the Mississippi, the settlement dates from 1719, and became in turn British, Spanish, then French again, before becoming American following the Louisiana Purchase in 1803. It was the state capital in 1849–1861, then again from 1882.

The arsenal here, established in 1810, came under state, and then Confederate control in 1861 and produced small-arms ammunition. Works belonging to Major W.F. Tunnard, leased to the Confederate government, produced cartridge and cap boxes. Workshops at the state penitentiary, established in 1832, manufactured cloth for uniforms for local troops in 1861–1862. The Ladies' Campaign Sewing Society, formed in April 1861, also made uniforms for Louisiana soldiers. A converted building was used as a military prison in 1861–1862.

Baton Rouge was first occupied by Federal troops in May 1862, then re-occupied in July. An attempt by Confederates under General John C. Breckinridge to retake it the following month was unsuccessful; Union General Thomas Williams was killed during the engagement.

Baxter Springs (Cherokee) KS
Was named for squatter John L. Baxter who was killed in a land dispute. After an assault on the small Federal garrison at Baxter Springs in October 1863, Quantrill's Confederate guerrillas, many wearing captured blue uniforms, mounted a surprise attack on Federal soldiers escorting a wagon train transporting General Blunt's headquarters from Fort Scott to Fort Smith, Indian Territory, inflicting heavy casualties.

Bean's Station (Grainger) TN
A hamlet by the Holston River, it was named for William, Robert, George and Jesse Bean who built a fort here in 1787. On the Virginia & Tennessee Railroad, it was the scene of fighting in December 1863, in an unsuccessful attempt by General Longstreet's troops to capture three Union cavalry brigades, towards the end of the Knoxville campaign. There was more skirmishing here in June 1864 and nearby in October. (Now called Bean Station.)

Beaufort (Carteret) NC
It was named for Henry Somerset, Duke of Beaufort (1684–1714) and laid out in 1722. After the surrender of Fort Macon, the port of Beaufort was opened to commerce in May 1862. The U.S. Navy vessels designated for the attacks on Fort Fisher rendezvoused off here in December 1864 and January 1865. Mary Ann ("Mother") Bickerdyke arrived here in April 1865, describing the hospital as "in bad shape and honored by … the greatest lot of pimps it has ever been … my [mis]fortune to meet."

Beaufort *see* **Port Royal Island**

Beaumont (Jefferson) TX

The original settlement established in 1825 here on the Neches River was called Tevis Bluff, after Noah and Nancy Tevis. Beaumont was founded in 1835 by Henry Millard and laid out in 1837. Though this is a descriptive name — "beautiful hill" in French — it may commemorate Jefferson Beaumont, Henry Millard's brother-in-law. The depot here, at the junction of the Texas & New Orleans and Eastern Texas Railroads, was destroyed by Federal troops in October 1862.

Beaver Dam Creek (Hanover) VA

The battle here on a branch of the Chickahominy, during the Peninsula campaign in June 1862, is also known as Mechanicsville (q.v.). It was a Confederate victory. Beavers are skilled at constructing dams to preserve their supply of water.

Beaver Dam Station (Hanover) VA

On the Virginia Central Railroad, it took its name from Beaver Dam Creek. It was an advance supply depot for General Lee's army, and stores there were destroyed by Federal cavalry in July 1862. John S. Mosby, then serving as a scout for General J.E.B. Stuart, was captured here while waiting for a train to take him home, briefly imprisoned, then exchanged. The station itself was burned by General Kilpatrick's cavalry during their raid on Richmond in February 1864. During General Sheridan's Richmond raid in May 1864, it was again attacked, this time by General Custer's cavalry, when warehouses containing food rations and medical supplies were burned, and locomotives, railroad cars and track destroyed. (Now called Beaverdam.)

Bedloe's Island NY

In New York harbor, and also sometimes called Bedlow's Island, it took its name from Isaac Bedlow (d.1673?), a French-born merchant and one-time owner. **Fort Wood**, built here in 1811, was named for Lieutenant Colonel Eleazer Wood (1783–1814), a hero of the War of 1812, and was a military prison in 1861 and again in 1863–1864. Renovated, this later became the base of the Statue of Liberty on what is now called Liberty Island.

Beersheba Springs (Grundy) TN

Though the name of an ancient Israelite city, this is thought to originate with a man called Beersheba P. Cain, who discovered Beersheba Springs in 1833. There was a skirmish near here in October 1863 and another in March 1864.

Belle Grove (Frederick) VA

Is another name for the battle in October 1864 better known as Cedar Creek (q.v.). Belle Grove Plantation, near Middletown, the home of the Hite family, was used as General Sheridan's headquarters.

Belle Isle VA

In the James River, its name means "beautiful island" in French and it had been a favorite resort of the citizens of Richmond since c.1815. It contained the Old Dominion Iron and Nail Works, and in 1862–1864, a prison camp housing Federal enlisted men, at times one of the largest in the South. An attempt to rescue the Federal prisoners held in Richmond at the beginning of March 1864 (the Kilpatrick-Dahlgren Raid) was a costly failure. By then the prisoners were starting to be moved to other prisons further south, particularly Andersonville.

Bellona (Goochland) VA

On the James River, 15 miles from Richmond, it was named for the Roman goddess of war. The foundry here, converted from an old U.S. arsenal and owned by Dr. Junius L. Archer, was taken over by the Confederate government and became a major source of cannon, particularly for the C.S. Navy, second only to Tredegar.

Bellville (Austin) TX

Was named for Thomas Bell who gave the land for the town site. A Ladies' Aid Society, organized in July 1861, made clothing, knapsacks and tents; Harigal & Co. made canteens for Texas troops; and H. Trotter and H.S. Hubby opened a gunshop in 1862. Bartlett's Mills, a large cotton factory, was destroyed by Unionists in August of that year.

Belmont (Mississippi) MO

Is on the Mississippi, opposite Columbus, Kentucky. Though once a common English place, locality and street name meaning "fine hill," this was apparently named for August Belmont of New York. There was fighting here in September 1861, but it is remembered now for the inconclusive battle fought in November 1861, Ulysses S. Grant's first command as a brigadier general.

Benton (Saline) AR

Both this and the following were named for politician and newspaper editor Thomas H. Benton (1782–1858). First settled c.1815, the town was founded in 1837. There was fighting here in July and August 1864.

Bentonville (Johnston) NC

Thomas Benton was born in North Carolina. The three-day battle fought here in March 1865, the largest in the state, was the last serious attempt to stop General Sherman's advance through the Carolinas, and was remarkable for the large number of Confederate generals involved. As one historian observed: "There was never a battle line where so much of 'rank' commanded so little of 'file.'" In the event, Sherman proved unstoppable. It is regarded as the last major battle of the Civil War.

Berryville (Clarke) VA

Laid out in 1798, it was named in 1803 for settler Benjamin Berry. It was the scene of skirmishing in May 1862, June and October 1863, and July and August 1864, as well as an indecisive, two-day engagement in September. In November 1864, seven of General Custer's cavalrymen were executed near here in retaliation for the hanging of an equal number of Colonel Mosby's rangers at Front Royal.

Berwick (St. Mary) LA

Was named for Thomas Berwick, a surveyor from Pennsylvania, who settled on the banks of the Atchafalaya River in the late 1700s. There was fighting here in May and June 1863, and April and May 1864.

Bethesda Church (Hanover) VA

A popular 19th century name for churches and chapels, it was a Hebrew biblical term meaning "house of mercy." Confederate Generals George P. Doles and James B. Terrill, were killed during fighting here at the end of May and beginning of June 1864, and Colonel Edward S. Willis, who had been recommended for general's rank, was mortally wounded leading an assault.

Bethlehem (Northampton) PA

Founded in 1741 as a Moravian settlement on the Lehigh River, it was named for the birthplace of Christ. By the time of the Civil War it had become an industrial town where the Bethlehem Iron Co., founded in 1857, manufactured railroad rails and armor plates for the U.S. Navy.

Beverly (Randolph) WV

First settled in 1753, then resettled in 1774 after an Indian attack, it was originally called Edmundton, for Edmund J. Randolph, governor of Virginia, 1786–1788, but renamed Beverly in 1790 for his mother, Beverly Randolph. There was some military activity around here in June and July 1861. It was captured by Confederates during the Jones-Imboden raid in April 1863, along with large quantities of ammunition and rations, and there was further skirmishing in June, July and November 1863. It was raided by Union cavalry in December 1863, there was fighting here in October 1864, and in bitter winter weather the small Federal garrison was surprised by a Confederate raiding party under General Thomas L. Rosser in January 1865.

Beverly Ford (Culpeper) VA

Was probably named for Robert Beverly and his son William, 18th century landowners along the Hazel and Rappahannock Rivers. August 1862 saw skirmishing here on the Rappahannock. Federal cavalry operations in April 1863 were followed in June by the battle better known as Brandy Station (q.v.).

Big Bethel (York) VA

Bethel is a Hebrew word meaning "house of God" and it became a popular name for chapels and meeting houses from c.1840 onwards. The engagement here in June 1861, an early Confederate victory, was described by one Union officer as "the disastrous *fight* at Big Bethel—battle we scarce may term it."

Big Black River MS

A tributary of the Mississippi, the name probably derives from the color of the water or clay lining its banks (cf. Red River). It witnessed fighting in May-July 1863 during General Grant's second Vicksburg campaign, and skirmishing in February 1864 in the Meridian campaign.

Big Shanty (Cobb) GA

A shanty is a roughly constructed hut, and this station on the Western & Atlantic Railroad took its name from a two-story eating house. It is remembered now for its part in the raid in April 1862, when James J. Andrews and 24 Union Army volunteers stole a train, in an attempt to cut the line between Marietta and Chattanooga, at the start of what subsequently became known as the Great Locomotive Chase. There was also skirmishing here in June, July and October 1864, and the station was burned by General Sherman's troops in November. (Now called Kennesaw.)

Biloxi (Harrison) MS

This coastal town was founded in 1699 and was the first permanent white settlement in the Mississippi Valley. *Biloxi* is a Choctaw name, possibly meaning "broken pot" or "worthless." It was captured by Federal troops on the last day of 1861, though no attempt was made to hold it.

Binghamton (Broome) NY

At the confluence of the Chenango and Susquehanna Rivers, on the site of an Iroquois village, it was first settled in 1787. Laid out in 1800, it was named for William Bingham (1752–1804), a Philadelphia merchant and politician who founded the Bank of North America and owned land here. During the Civil War the Starr Arms Co. made revolvers for the Union Army and Navy.

Blacksburg (Montgomery) VA

Originally spelt Blacksburgh, it was named for William Black, a son of the original landowner, who laid out the town in 1797. There was a Federal raid on the railroad here in May 1864.

Blackshear (Pierce) GA

Founded in 1859, it commemorates General David Blackshear (1764–1837) of North Carolina who served in the War of 1812. A Confederate prison stockade was in use here in 1864.

Blackville (Barnwell) SC

Was named in 1832 for Scotsman John Alexander Black (1810–1875) of the South Carolina Railroad which created this town. There was skirmishing here in February 1865 during General Sherman's march through the Carolinas.

Bloomfield (Stoddard) MO

So called from the fields of flowers that were here when Bloomfield was founded in 1835, on the site of a Shawnee village. It witnessed much military activity during the Civil War, with fighting in May, July, August and September 1862, January and March 1863, when it was captured by Federal troops, April and May 1863, and April and July 1864. It was the scene of a mutiny by the 6th (U.S.) Missouri Cavalry in October 1863, and was attacked by Confederates the following month.

Blountstown (Calhoun) FL

Was founded in 1823 and named for Seminole chief John Blount, who died in 1834 while en route to Texas. The Confederate gunboat *Chattahoochee* exploded near here on the Apalachicola River in May 1863, killing 18 of her crew.

Blountsville (Blount) AL

On the Black Warrior River, it was settled after 1813–1814 and named for Willie Blount (1768–1835), governor of Tennessee, 1809–1815. There was skirmishing here at the beginning of May 1863 involving Colonel Streight's Federal raiders and General Forrest's cavalry.

Blountville (Sullivan) TN

William Blount (1749–1800), territorial governor of Tennessee, 1790–1795, is commemorated here; it developed after 1792. Skirmishing just west of the East Tennessee & Virginia Railroad took place in September and October 1863, prior to the Knoxville campaign.

Bluffton (Beaufort) SC

Is a descriptive name, from high bluffs overlooking a stream, in this case the May River. It gradually developed in the first half of the 19th century and was well established by 1852. Salt workings here were destroyed by the Federals in September 1862, and it was shelled and burned by them in June 1863.

Bogue Island NC

Situated off the North Carolina coast, this was the site of **Fort Macon**, built 1826–1834 to protect Beaufort harbor and named for North Carolina politician Nathaniel Macon (1758–1837), an early defender of states' rights. It was taken over in April 1861 and remained in Confederate hands till April 1862, when it fell to a combined army and navy bombardment following a siege. *Bogue* is a Choctaw word meaning "stream" or "creek."

Bolivar (Hardeman) TN

It was named in 1825 for Simon Bolivar (1783–1830), the South American soldier, statesman and revolutionary leader who gave his name to Bolivia. There was considerable military activity around Bolivar between July 1862 and May 1864, including an attack by Confederate guerrillas on a train between there and Grand Junction on the Mississippi Central Railroad. A camp for contrabands was also established here.

Bolivar Heights (Jefferson) WV

Was established in 1825 and also named for Simon Bolivar. There was skirmishing here near Harpers Ferry at the beginning of July 1864 during General Early's Washington raid.

Bolton Depot (Hinds) MS

Was named for the promoter of the line from Vicksburg to Jackson (the Southern Railroad of Mississippi). It was the scene of fighting on several days in July 1863 and in February 1864.

Bonham (Fannin) TX

Started life as Fort Inglish, named for Bailey Inglish. This became part of a nearby settlement named for Colonel James B. Bonham who died fighting at the Alamo in 1836. It was the headquarters of the Northern Military Sub-District of Texas and a Confederate quartermaster depot was also located here.

Boone (Watauga) NC

Legendary pioneer Daniel Boone (c.1734–1820) is commemorated by a number of places in the South and West. He moved to North Carolina c.1760 and this town was named for him. There was a skirmish here in March 1865.

Booneville (Owsley) KY

Daniel Boone guided settlers into Kentucky in 1775. Booneville developed after 1844. There was fighting here in April 1864.

Booneville (Prentiss) MS

Was also apparently named for Daniel Boone. The town was captured by the Federals at the end of May 1862. There was skirmishing near here in June and a cavalry engagement at the station on the Mobile & Ohio Railroad in July. Colonel Philip H. Sheridan's success in defeating the Confederates earned him a brigadier general's star, and he was reported to be "worth his weight in gold."

Boonsboro (Washington) MD

Settled in 1774, it takes its name not from Daniel Boone but from pioneers George and William Boone. There was fighting here during the Antietam campaign in September 1862, when General Thomas J. "Stonewall" Jackson narrowly escaped capture.

Boonville (Howard) MO

Some of the settlers who came here in 1810 were from Kentucky and named their new town on the Missouri River for Daniel Boone, who by then had come to live in what is now Missouri. The first battle in Missouri, fought near here in June 1861, was only a minor engagement but it kept the state in the Union. Boonville was occupied by Federal troops, but in October 1863 was captured by General Shelby's Confederates. There was further skirmishing near here in October 1864 and as late as May 1865.

Boston (Suffolk) MA

Many of the people who established a settlement here in 1630 came from the English town of Boston, Lincolnshire. By 1700 it was the largest city in British North America. The state capital of Massachusetts, it saw rioting against the draft in July 1863, though nothing like that which swept New York.

The ironclad monitor USS *Monadnock* was built in the Charlestown Navy Yard. Henry N. Hooper and the Revere Copper Co. manufactured smoothbore cannon for the Union Army; Cyrus Alger & Co., which started life as the South Boston Iron Co., produced cannon for both the Union Army and Navy; Hinkley,

Williams & Co. built locomotives for Northern railroads and also made naval cannon; and the American Powder Co. manufactured gunpowder for the Union Navy. Spencer carbines, widely used by the Union cavalry, and rifles were also manufactured here by Christopher M. Spencer of the Spencer Repeating Rifle Co.

Bowling Green (Warren) KY

On the Barren River, was first settled in 1780 by immigrants from Virginia led by Robert and George Moore. The name may derive from Bowling Green Square in New York City where a lead statue of King George III was used to make bullets during the American Revolution, or simply be from the local custom of playing bowls. It became the Confederate state capital of Kentucky when occupied by Confederate forces from September 1861 to February 1862, but was evacuated after the fall of Forts Henry and Donelson.

Brandenburg (Meade) KY

Colonel Solomon Brandenburg, for whom it was named in 1825, was an early settler who had bought land here in 1804. It witnessed skirmishing in September 1862, and General Morgan's Confederate raiders crossed the Ohio River near here in July 1863 on their way into Indiana.

Brandon (Rankin) MS

Was named for Gerard C. Brandon (1788–1850), governor of Mississippi, 1825–1831. It was the site of the Brandon State Military Institute and the scene of fighting in July and December 1863 and February 1864.

Brandy Station (Culpeper) VA

When the Orange & Alexandria Railroad was built in 1854, this station took its name from a nearby crossroads tavern known as Brandy House from the potent liquor it sold. There was fighting here in August 1862, then in June 1863 occurred the largest cavalry engagement of the war, involving Federal troops under General Alfred Pleasanton and Confederates under General J.E.B. Stuart. It is regarded as a Confederate victory, but was a close-run thing. Brandy Station "*made* the Federal cavalry," wrote one Confederate; it was their coming-of-age. Union General Benjamin F. "Grimes" Davis was among those killed. The engagement is also known as Beverly Ford (q.v.). There was further skirmishing here in August 1863.

Brattleboro (Windham) VT

On the Connecticut River, it was settled in 1724 and named for Colonel William Brattle (d.1776), a Boston land speculator and donor of the town site. There was a large recruiting camp for the Union Army here, as well as a military hospital, and the town was a state rendezvous point at the end of the war for the mustering out of Vermont troops.

Breckenridge (Caldwell) MO

Was laid out in 1858, one of a number of places, with variant spelling, commemorating John C. Breckinridge (1821–1875), vice-president under James Buchanan, 1857–1861, and subsequently a Confederate general and the last secretary of war in 1865. It witnessed fighting in June 1864.

Brice's Crossroads (Prentiss) MS

Was named for the Brice family house. An attempt to destroy General Forrest's raiders failed when a Federal force was defeated here by less than half that number in June 1864; they lost most of their artillery, wagons and supplies and the Union commander, General Samuel D. Sturgis, spent the rest of the war "awaiting orders." It is also known as the battle of Guntown or Tishomingo Creek (q.v.).

Bridgeport (Jackson) AL

First settled in the 1830s, it was named in 1854, apparently for town developer John Bridges, but also because of a new railroad bridge across the Tennessee River. There was skirmishing here in April and August 1862, and the town was occupied by Federal troops in July 1863. General Ulysses S. Grant, recovering from a fall from his horse in New Orleans, arrived here in October 1863, and General Hooker's troops crossed the river, on their way to Chattanooga. What became known as the "Cracker Line," a water-borne supply route up the Tennessee, for the besieged Federal garrison in Chattanooga, was also instituted here that month. In November, Federal forces were reinforced with the arrival of General Sherman's divisions.

Bridgeport (Fairfield) CT
Originally settled in 1639, its present name dates from 1800, when the first drawbridge across the Pequonnock River was opened. The Sharps Rifle Manufacturing Co. had a factory here. A Sanitary Fair was held on behalf of the U.S. Sanitary Commission but succeeded in raising only $200.

Brierfield (Bibb) AL
May have been named in honor of *Brierfield*, Jefferson Davis's plantation, which supplied the Bibb County Ironworks, founded in 1860 by Caswell Huckabee and Jonathan Smith, with machinery. The ironworks were purchased for the Confederate Navy Department in 1863 but were badly damaged in a raid by Federal cavalry at the end of March 1865. After the war they were bought by a company formed by Josiah Gorgas, the former head of the Confederate Ordnance Bureau.

Bristol (Bristol) RI
Was settled in 1680 and named after the English port city of Bristol. The Bristol Fire Arms Co. was established in 1855 by Ambrose E. Burnside, who patented his breech-loading carbine in 1856. It was manufactured in large numbers for the Union cavalry, both here and at Providence, by the Burnside Arms Co. which took over after the original firm had failed. As a general, Burnside commanded the Army of the Potomac in 1862–1863.

Bristol (Sullivan) TN
Originally established as a trading post in 1771, it had several names before a new town was laid out c.1852 by Joseph R. Anderson and became a railroad junction; it was also named after Bristol, England. The Hood Hospital was located here. It was the scene of skirmishing in November 1861, September 1863 and December 1864.

Brookhaven (Lincoln) MS
Though first settled in 1818, it did not develop until it became the first northern terminus of the New Orleans & Great Southern Railroad in 1851. The name chosen was a euphonius one. Colonel Grierson's cavalry skirmished here in April 1863 during their raid through Mississippi.

Brooklyn (Kings) NY
Was first settled by the Dutch in 1636–1637 and called Breuckelyn ("broken land") in 1645, after a place in Holland, which gradually evolved into Brooklyn. Thomas F. Rowland's Continental Works at Greenpoint, which produced floating batteries for the Union Navy, built and launched the USS *Monitor*, the "Yankee cheese box on a raft," in January 1862, prior to its encounter with the CSS *Virginia* in Hampton Roads. The Morgan Iron Works of George W. Quintard also built monitors as well as sloops-of-war. A submarine, nicknamed "Halstead's Folly" for one of its builders, was constructed in the Brooklyn Navy Yard in 1864, one of several built in the North. There was also a naval hospital here, founded in 1834. Brooklyn became part of New York City in 1897.

Brooksville (Bracken) KY
It was named in 1839 for Congressman David Brooks (1756–1838) when it became a county seat. There was a skirmish here in September 1862.

Brown's Island VA
At Richmond, between the James River and the Haxall Canal, it was named for Elijah Brown, a Rhode Island gunsmith who came here in 1811 and bought the land in 1826. During the Civil War it was the site of a Confederate ordnance laboratory; an explosion here in March 1863 killed 46 workers, mostly women.

Brownsville (Cameron) TX
Was first settled by the Spanish in 1772. A U.S. Army fort, built here in 1846, was named Fort Brown for Major Jacob Brown (1788–1846), a hero of the Mexican War. Brownsville was founded in 1848. Just across the Rio Grande from Matamoros, it became an important place for blockade runners during the Civil War. It was captured by Federals in November 1863, then reoccupied by Confederates in July 1864. The two days of skirmishing near here on the banks of the Rio Grande in May 1865 at Palmito Ranch are regarded as the last engagement of the Civil War; ironically, it was a Confederate victory.

Brunswick (Glynn) GA
On the Georgia coast and founded in 1771, it was laid out from 1772 onwards and named for

the House of Brunswick (King George III was also Elector [Prince] of Brunswick-Luneberg in present-day Germany). Occupied by Federal forces early in 1862, it was reoccupied by Confederates in June the following year.

Brunswick (Chariton) MO

Laid out in 1836, the name apparently derived from Brunswick Terrace, London, the home of its founder, the Rev. James Keyte. Skirmishing occurred here in August 1861 and again in September and October 1864.

Buchanan (Botetourt) VA

Established in 1811, it was named for Colonel John Buchanan who was deputy surveyor of Augusta County. It was the scene of a skirmish in June 1864.

Buckhannon (Upshur) WV

Takes its name from the Buckhannon River, which derives from a Delaware chief called *Buck-on-ge-ha-non*. First settled in 1770, the site was bought in 1806 by Elizabeth Jackson, whose son, Colonel Edward Jackson, the grandfather of "Stonewall" Jackson, laid it out in 1815. There was skirmishing near here in July 1861, and a Federal force under General Benjamin S. Roberts retreated from here in April 1863 during the Jones-Imboden West Virginia raid. There was more skirmishing in September 1864.

Buffington Island OH

Its name derives from Joel Buffington (d. 1821), who purchased this island in the Ohio River, near the present town of Portland, in 1787. During his Indiana and Ohio raid in July 1863, Confederate General John H. Morgan was defeated by Federal troops and local militia near here when trying to cross over into West Virginia. Three future American presidents— James A. Garfield, Rutherford B. Hayes and William McKinley— apparently took part in the battle, and among the Union casualties was Major Daniel McCook, one of the "Fighting McCooks" of Ohio. It was the only one fought on Ohio soil.

Bull Run Creek (Prince William) VA

Takes its name from the Bull Run Mountains in Loudoun County. A tributary of the Potomac, flowing into the Occoquan, Bull Run Creek, which forms the boundary between Fairfax and Prince William Counties east of Manassas, gave its name to the two battles known as First and Second Bull Run in July 1861 and August 1862. They were both victories for the Confederates who called them First and Second Manassas (q.v.).

Bunker Hill (Jefferson) WV

Established between 1726 and 1732, it took its name from the site of the first important battle in the American Revolution (1775), now part of Boston, Massachusetts. It was the scene of considerable military activity, with skirmishing occurring in September 1862, June 1863, and January, July and September 1864. General Robert E. Lee was here in July 1863, only a fortnight after Gettysburg, and wrote President Davis: "The men are in good health and spirits, but want shoes and clothing badly.... As soon as these ... are obtained, we shall be prepared to resume operations," a remarkably optimistic letter in the circumstances.

Burkesville (Cumberland) KY

Was founded in 1798 and named for Samuel Burke, an early settler. It was the scene of a skirmish in November 1862, and General John H. Morgan crossed the Cumberland River here during his Indiana and Ohio raid in July 1863.

Burkeville Junction (Nottaway) VA

Was named for landowner Colonel Samuel D. Burke (1794–1880). At the meeting point of the Richmond & Danville and South Side Railroads, it was originally called Burke's Junction. It was the scene of skirmishing in December 1861 and August 1863. During the Appomattox campaign in April 1865 there was a major Union field hospital here, where Irish-born General Thomas A. Smyth died from wounds received at Farmville.

Burlington (Mineral) WV

The Earls of Burlington have links with Yorkshire, the former English home of many of the settlers here. This may also explain its original name of New Beverly, probably called after the Yorkshire town of Beverley. On the Ohio River, it was established in 1833. A number of skirmishes occurred here, in September 1861, and April, August, October and November 1863.

Burning Springs (Wirt) WV

On the Little Kanawha River, its oil deposits were known about as early as the 1770s, but extraction only began in 1860. An "oil rush" then developed in what became popularly known as Oiltown, and continued until its oil wells and storage tanks were set on fire in May 1863 by General "Grumble" Jones' Confederate cavalry during their raid into West Virginia, in a spectacular act of destruction. "Great pillars of flame ... rose to a prodigious height in the air from the burning wells, lighting the surrounding country for miles," one soldier recalled.

Butler (Bates) MO

Was named for William O. Butler (1791–1880), a general in the Mexican War. It was burned in November 1861 by Federal cavalry from Kansas. There was an engagement in October 1862 between men of the 1st Kansas Volunteer Colored Infantry and Confederate troops under Colonel Francis M. Cockrell, near Island Mound, just outside Butler. It is thought to have been the first time black soldiers were in combat in the Civil War.

Byhalia (Marshall) MS

Founded in 1838, the name derives from a creek called *Bihalee*, a Chickasaw word meaning "standing white oaks." It was in use by 1846. There was fighting near here in October 1863 and February 1864.

Cabin Creek (Mayes) IT

A fairly self-evident name for a branch of the Neosho River. It was the scene of fighting in July 1863 when Confederate Cherokees under the command of Colonel Stand Watie attacked a Union wagon train. The escort included men of the 1st Kansas Volunteer Colored Infantry commanded by Colonel James M. Williams, whose coolness in battle impressed their white colleagues. The attack was unsuccessful, but a second one, in September 1864, resulted in the capture of more than 200 wagons and equipment.

Cahaba (Dallas) AL

At the confluence of the Alabama and Cahaba Rivers and founded in 1819, it was the state capital of Alabama till 1826. *Cahaba* is a Choctaw word meaning "water-above." It became a center for Confederate refugees, and the town's population was further increased early in 1864 when an unfinished cotton warehouse on the Alabama River was turned into a prison, which the locals nicknamed "Castle Morgan" (q.v.). An attempted uprising by the prisoners in January 1865 was soon quelled and it remained in use for the rest of the war. Flooding, which had already reduced the population of Cahaba by the time of the Civil War, caused it to be eventually abandoned.

Cairo (Alexander) IL

The Mississippi was often called the Nile of America and this town, at its confluence with the Ohio, was named after Cairo, Egypt. First projected in 1818, it was permanently established in 1837 with the founding of the Cairo City & Canal Co. but only really began to develop with the coming of the Illinois Central Railroad in 1855.

During the Civil War it was the site of a Union military supplies depot. A naval station was also established here in 1861, where river gunboats could put in for repairs. "Four of these gunboats were still lying in the Ohio, close under the terminus of the railway, with their flat, ugly noses against the muddy bank.... They certainly seemed to be formidable weapons for river warfare," observed English novelist Anthony Trollope, when he visited Cairo in February 1862. The rest of them, together with troops under General Ulysses S. Grant, had gone up the Ohio and the Tennessee, and while he was there Fort Henry was captured. Trollope was less impressed by what he calls "the sheds of the soldiers ... bad, comfortless, damp and cold," but at least they "did not stink like those of Jefferson Barracks at St. Louis."

Mary Ann ("Mother") Bickerdyke began her tireless work for soldiers at the Union Hospital in June 1861, at first working independently, then for the U.S. Sanitary Commission. Cairo was General Grant's headquarters in September 1861 prior to the Fort Henry and Donelson campaign, and again in October 1863 when he was ordered here from Vicksburg. During the war there were also many Confederate prisoners here, often en route to Northern prison camps.

Calhoun (Gordon) GA

It was named in 1850 for John C. Calhoun (1782–1850), secretary of war under James

Monroe, 1817–1825, vice-president under both John Quincy Adams and Andrew Jackson, 1825–1832, and finally secretary of state under John Tyler, 1844–1845. There was fighting here in June 1864 during General Sherman's advance towards Atlanta and the town was largely destroyed.

Camden (Ouachita) AR

First established on the Ouachita River in 1783, it was refounded in 1824 and named in 1844 by General Thomas Woodward, either for his home town of Camden, Alabama, or for Camden, South Carolina. The woolen mill here made cloth for Confederate uniforms and the arsenal repaired arms and manufactured ammunition. It became a refugee center after the fall of Little Rock in September 1863. There was considerable fighting in and around Camden during the Red River campaign in March and April 1864.

Camden (Kershaw) SC

Settled in 1733–1734 along the Wateree River by English colonists and Irish Quakers, it was named in 1768 for the English lawyer Charles Pratt, Earl of Camden (1714–1794), a champion of colonial rights. It became a center for Confederate refugees from Charleston. There was skirmishing near here in February 1865, and a supply depot was burned by General Sherman's troops when they occupied the town.

Camp Abraham Lincoln see Camp Berry

Camp Alcorn (Christian) KY

Near Hopkinsville, it was named for General James L. Alcorn (1816–1894) who commanded Mississippi state troops in Kentucky. It was probably abandoned in February 1862 after its troops were sent to Fort Donelson.

Camp Allegheny (Pocahontas) WV

Built in the summer of 1861 to protect the Staunton-Parkersburg turnpike, its site in the Alleghenies was the highest in the eastern theater of the war. Named for Confederate Colonel Edward "Allegheny" Johnson (1816–1873) of the 12th Virginia, it was the scene of an engagement in December 1861, the success of which earned him general's rank. The Confederates abandoned it in April 1862.

Camp Allen (Warren) KY

A Confederate camp near Woodburn, possibly named for Colonel William W. Allen (1835–1894), who commanded the 1st Alabama Cavalry during the invasion of Kentucky in 1862.

Camp Ammen (Brown) OH

Near Ripley, it was probably named for Colonel Jacob Ammen (1808–1894) of the 24th Ohio. Later a brigade and divisional commander in the Army of the Ohio, he also served as commandant of Camp Douglas, the prison camp at Chicago, in 1863.

Camp Amory (Craven) NC

Established in 1862, it was named for Colonel Thomas J.C. Amory (c.1830–1864) of the 17th Massachusetts who died of yellow fever while commanding the defenses here at New Bern. He also gave his name to Fort Amory (q.v.).

Camp Anderson (Mobile) AL

Named for Colonel Charles D. Anderson of the 21st Alabama, it was near Mobile.

Camp Anderson (LaPorte) IN

In existence in 1863–1864 at Michigan City, it was probably named for the Rev. Edward Anderson, colonel of the 12th Indiana Cavalry.

Camp Anderson (Monroe) KY

May be named for Major Robert Anderson (1805–1871), the "Hero of Fort Sumter" who as General Anderson subsequently commanded the Department of Kentucky.

Camp Anderson (New Hanover) NC

Established near Wilmington in February 1862, like Fort Anderson (q.v.) it was named for George B. Anderson (1831–1862), who was colonel of the 4th North Carolina and later commanded a brigade; he was mortally wounded at Sharpsburg.

Camp Anderson see Camp Stillwell

Camp Andrew (Suffolk) MA

John A. Andrew (1818–1867), for whom this was named, was governor of Massachusetts,

1860–1866, and an anti-slavery campaigner whose organization of the state militia was exemplary. It was at West Roxbury.

Camp Andrew Johnson (Knox) KY
Was named for Andrew Johnson (1808–1875), who was military governor of Tennessee, 1862–1865, before becoming Abraham Lincoln's second vice-president and successor as 17th president of the United States.

Camp Andrews (Knox) OH
Colonel Lorin Andrews (d.1861), for whom this was named, commanded the 4th Ohio. It was near Mount Vernon.

Camp Andrews (Fairfax) VA
The camp of the 128th Pennsylvania Volunteers, it was named for Captain W.H. Andrews, who was their commanding officer when a Rosenthal lithograph was published in 1862.

Camp Armstrong (Bryan) IT
A Confederate camp and hospital near Bokchito, in existence 1862–1865, it was named for General Frank C. Armstrong (1835–1909), who commanded the cavalry at Iuka and Corinth.

Camp Arnold (Providence) RI
This was a recruitment and training camp at Pawtucket, in existence 1861–1862. The origin of the name is uncertain: it may have been for Captain Richard Arnold (1828–1882), who was chief of artillery in the Peninsula campaign, or Samuel G. Arnold (1821–1880), three times lieutenant governor of Rhode Island.

Camp Astor see Riker's Island

Camp Asylum (Richland) SC
Union prisoners from Camp Sorghum were moved to a more secure location in the grounds of the South Carolina State [Mental] Hospital at Columbia in December 1864. This new prison camp became known as Camp Asylum but was only in use till February 1865, by which time its inmates had been moved again, to North Carolina and Georgia.

Camp Austin (Travis/Matagorda) TX
There were two camps of this name in Texas. The first one, originally established in 1848 on the outskirts of the state capital, named for Texan hero Stephen F. Austin (1793–1836), was used as a muster station when the Civil War broke out. The second, established near the coastal town of Matagorda in 1863, may have been named for William T. Austin (1809–1874), wartime inspector general of Texas.

Camp Averell (Frederick) VA
Near Winchester, it was named for Union General William W. Averell (1832–1900), who commanded the 2nd Cavalry Division.

Camp Badger (Wake/New Hanover) NC
Two camps were named for George E. Badger (1795–1866), a North Carolinian who was secretary of the navy in 1841 under William Henry Harrison and John Tyler. They were near Raleigh and Fort Fisher.

Camp Banks (Wayne) MI
A training camp established at Detroit in 1862, it was named for General Nathaniel P. Banks (1816–1894), remembered now for his part in the Red River campaign of 1864.

Camp Barclay DC
Was established in December 1861 for the 6th Pennsylvania Cavalry and named for Clement C. Barclay of Pennsylvania.

Camp Barker DC
Was a contraband camp in downtown Washington, established in a former barracks and perhaps named for Colonel A.S. Barker who had employed several hundred African Americans to construct formidable defenses at Stevenson, Alabama.

Camp Barnard Bee (Brazoria) TX
On the Brazos, it was in use 1864–1865. General Barnard E. Bee (1824–1861), whose father had been secretary of state for the Republic of Texas, was an early Confederate hero; he was mortally wounded at First Manassas where he commanded a brigade.

Camp Barry DC
An instruction camp probably named for General William F. Barry (1818–1879), who was

chief of artillery for the defenses of Washington, 1862–1864.

Camp Barstow (Rock) WI
Was established at Janesville in October 1861 and named for Colonel William A. Barstow (1813–1865) who commanded the 3rd Wisconsin Cavalry.

Camp Barton (Highland) VA
Was named for Lieutenant Colonel (later General) Seth M. Barton (1829–1900) of the 3rd Arkansas who was "Stonewall" Jackson's chief engineer in the first winter of the war.

Camp Bartow (Dallas) TX
Near Lancaster, it was named for Colonel Francis S. Bartow (1816–1861) of the 8th Georgia, who commanded a brigade at First Manassas where he was killed. His last words were: "They have killed me, boys, but never give up the field."

Camp Bartow (Pocahontas) WV
Constructed in August 1861, it was also named in honor of Francis Bartow, killed the previous month. There was a skirmish nearby at Greenbriar River in October and the camp was abandoned the following month when the troops moved to Camp Allegheny.

Camp Bass (Bowie) TX
Was named for Colonel Thomas C. Bass, whose 20th Texas Cavalry were camped here in 1862.

Camp Baxter (Caledonia) VT
At St. Johnsbury, it was established in April 1861 and named for Portus Baxter (1806–1868), Vermont's adjutant general. It was also called Baxter Barracks.

Camp Beall (Chesterfield) VA
Recruits to the Confederate States Marine Corps were trained here at Drewry's Bluff overlooking the James River, at a camp named for their commandant, Colonel Lloyd J. Beall (1808–1887).

Camp Beauregard (Lee) AL
A number of Confederate camps were named for General Pierre G.T. Beauregard (1818–1893), the "Hero of Sumter." This one was near Auburn.

Camp Beauregard (Graves) KY
Was a recruitment and training camp established in September 1861 at Water Valley, 20 miles south-east of Columbus. In November an outbreak of disease, exacerbated by bad weather and poor diet, caused many deaths among Alabama, Georgia, Louisiana and Tennessee troops and it was evacuated the following March.

Camp Bee (Guadalupe) TX
Was named for General Barnard E. Bee (1824–1861), the originator of General Jackson's nickname of "Stonewall" at First Manassas, where he was mortally wounded.

Camp Belknap (Young) TX
Named for General William G. Belknap (1794–1851), it was merged with Fort Belknap (q.v.) in March 1864.

Camp Ben Butler (Cherokee) KS
A Union camp at Baxter Springs, named for Benjamin F. Butler (1818–1893), an incompetent but influential general.

Camp Ben McCulloch (Greene) MO
Near Springfield, it was named for Confederate General Ben McCulloch (1811–1862) who was killed at Pea Ridge.

Camp Benjamin (New Orleans) LA
Established in 1861 near New Orleans, this was named for Judah P. Benjamin (1811–1884), Confederate secretary of war, 1861–1862, and secretary of state, 1862–1865. It was also sometimes called Camp Jerusalem, perhaps a humorous reference to Benjamin's Jewish origins.

Camp Benton (Loudoun) VA
Near Edwards Ferry on the Potomac, it was the camp of the 7th Michigan, commanded by Colonel I.R. Grosvenor, in the winter of 1861. It may have been named for Thomas H. Benton (1782–1858), who lost his seat in the Senate because of his opposition to the extension of slavery to the new territories.

Camp Berry DC
Was an artillery instruction camp north of

the Potomac. Both this and the following were named for General Hiram G. Berry (1824–1863) who was killed at Chancellorsville.

Camp Berry (Cumberland) ME
This was established in 1861 as Camp Abraham Lincoln, but renamed in 1863. It was situated between Cape Elizabeth and South Portland.

Camp Bissell (St. Clair) IL
Between Belleville and Caseyville, it was established in 1861 and named for William H. Bissell (1811–1860), the first Republican governor of Illinois, 1857–1860.

Camp Blair (Jackson) MI
This camp at Jackson was named for Austin Blair (1818–1894), the wartime governor of Michigan.

Camp Bliss (Providence) RI
Named for Colonel Zenas R. Bliss (1835–1900), it was established at Providence in 1862 as the camp of the 7th Rhode Island Volunteers.

Camp Boggs (Rapides/Caddo) LA
There were two camps called this, one near Lecompte, in existence in July 1864, and the other near Shreveport in 1864–1865. Both were named for Confederate General William R. Boggs (1829–1911), who served as chief of staff in the Trans-Mississippi.

Camp Boone (Jefferson) KY
A Union camp at Louisville, this and the following probably commemorated legendary pioneer Daniel Boone (c.1734–1820) who lived in Kentucky in the 1770s and 1780s.

Camp Boone (Montgomery) TN
Near Clarksville and the Memphis branch of the Louisville & Nashville Railroad, this was a Confederate recruitment and training camp established in July 1861 and commanded by Colonel William T. Withers.

Camp Boyle (Adair/Columbia) KY
There were two Union camps in Kentucky named for General Jeremiah T. Boyle (1818–1871), who helped organize its defenses and was military governor, 1862–1864.

Camp Bradford (Baltimore) MD
Was named for Augustus W. Bradford (1805–1881), governor of Maryland, 1862–1866, who worked to keep his state in the Union.

Camp Bradley (Rutherford) TN
At Murfreesboro, it was established in 1863 and named for Colonel Luther Bradley of the 31st Illinois who was killed at Stones River.

Camp Bragg (Lonoke) AR
Was erected near Woodlawn in 1863 for Confederate General Price's troops and named for General Braxton Bragg (1817–1876).

Camp Bragg (Winnebago) WI
Named for General Edward S. Bragg (1827–1912), who was previously colonel of the 6th Wisconsin and went on to become a prominent Democrat after the war; it was at Oshkosh.

Camp Branch (Craven) NC
A Confederate camp established near New Bern in 1862, like Fort Branch (q.v.) it was named for General Lawrence O. Branch (1820–1862) who was killed at Sharpsburg.

Camp Brandywine (New Castle) DE
The name derives from Brandywine Creek, north of Wilmington. There were two camps called this, one in existence May-September 1861 and the other, September-October 1862.

Camp Breaux (East Baton Rouge) LA
Near Port Hudson, it was in existence August 1862-May 1863, and named for Colonel Gus A. Breaux of the 30th Louisiana.

Camp Breckinridge TN
On the Memphis, Clarksville & Louisville Railroad, this was an instruction camp named for John C. Breckinridge (1821–1875), who had been vice-president under James Buchanan. He served as a Confederate general and was the last secretary of war.

Camp Bridgeland (Marion) IN
Established in November 1861 near Indianapolis, on the banks of Fall Creek, it was originally called Camp Bullock, but renamed for a Colonel J.A. Bridgeland. It was occupied by

the 20th Indiana Infantry, then by the 2nd U.S. Cavalry.

Camp Brightwood DC

New York, Rhode Island and Massachusetts regiments were housed at this camp in Washington, which took its name from the nearby Brightwood Hotel.

Camp Brown (Cobb) GA

An instruction camp four miles south of Marietta, it was set up in April 1861 by General William Phillips and named for Governor Joseph E. Brown (1821–1895) of Georgia, one of Jefferson Davis's fiercest opponents. Cadets from the Georgia Military Institute came here to train the officers and N.C.O.s of the 4th Brigade of Georgia Volunteers.

Camp Brunson (Montague) TX

Was named for Captain Allen Brunson of the Texas Rangers.

Camp Buchel *see* Camp Wharton

Camp Buckingham (Richland) OH

Established in September 1861 at Mansfield, it was named for General Catharinus P. Buckingham (1808–1888), at that time adjutant general of Ohio.

Camp Buckner (Talladega) AL

At Talladega, it was named for Confederate General Simon B. Buckner (1823–1914), who was a corps commander at Chickamauga.

Camp Buell (Johnson) KY

Was named for Union General Don Carlos Buell (1818–1898), whose career stalled after the indecisive battle of Perryville in October 1862.

Camp Bullock *see* Camp Bridgeland

Camp Burgwyn (New Hanover) NC

Sometimes spelt "Burgwin," Camp Burgwyn was named for a Lieutenant Colonel Henry K. Burgwyn. Near Wilmington, it was in existence throughout the war.

Camp Burnett (Houston) TX

Near Crockett, it was in existence February–June 1862 and despite the variant spelling, may have been named for David G. Burnet (1788–1870), interim president of the Texas Republic in 1836 and vice-president, 1838–1841.

Camp Burnham (Warren) KY

A Union camp at Bowling Green named for General Hiram Burnham (d.1864), who was killed at the battle of Chaffin's Farm.

Camp Burnside (Polk) IA

A training camp at Des Moines established in 1862, it was one of a number named for General Ambrose E. Burnside (1824–1881), who was relieved of his command of the Army of the Potomac after Fredericksburg.

Camp Burnside (Lincoln/Pulaski) KY

There were two camps in Kentucky named for General Burnside.

Camp Burnside (Providence) RI

Was established in 1861.

Camp Butler (Sangamon) IL

Named for William Butler (1797–1876), the state treasurer of Illinois, it was a training camp for Illinois militia near Springfield, established in August 1861, but used as a military prison in 1862–1863.

Camp Butler (Macomb) MI

One of several camps named for General Benjamin F. Butler (1818–1893), this was at Mount Clemens (now part of Detroit); it was in existence throughout the war

Camp Butler (York) VA

Was established at Newport News in May 1861 and also named for General Butler. A Federal prison camp was in use here, April–July 1865.

Camp Cadwalader (Baltimore) MD

Situated at Locust Point, this was the first Union camp in Maryland. This and the following were named for General George Cadwalader (1803–1879), who commanded Pennsylvania troops in the early months of the war.

Camp Cadwalader (Philadelphia) PA

Was on the outskirts of Philadelphia. The

32nd U.S. Colored Infantry was one of the units raised and mustered out here.

Camp Cameron DC
At Georgetown, it was named for Simon Cameron (1799–1889), President Lincoln's first secretary of war, 1861–1862, and was the base of the elite 7th New York Infantry, one of the first militia regiments to answer President Lincoln's call for troops.

Camp Cameron (Middlesex) MA
Barracks built at North Cambridge near Boston in 1862 housed two Massachusetts regiments, the 1st and 38th. Often called Camp Day because it was on land owned by the Day family, it was officially Camp Cameron, also named for Secretary Cameron.

Camp Carondelet (Prince William) VA
Louisiana troops were quartered here, near Manassas, in the winter of 1861–62, and held a "Grand Military Ball" in February 1862. It was probably named for Francisco Luis Hector de Carondelet (c.1748–1807), the Spanish governor of Louisiana, 1791–1797.

Camp Carrington (Marion) IN
A training camp at Indianapolis, established in 1862 at the request of Governor Morton and named for General Henry B. Carrington (1824–1912), who had been in command of a regular army camp in Ohio.

Camp Carter (Waller) TX
Near Hempstead, was named for Lieutenant Colonel John C. Carter, 2nd Cavalry, Texas state troops.

Camp Casey (Prince Georges) MD
This was occupied by regiments from Massachusetts, New Hampshire, New York and Rhode Island. Near Bladensburg, it may have been named for General Silas Casey (1807–1882), the author of a standard work on infantry tactics.

Camp Cass (Arlington) VA
On Arlington Heights, this was named in honor of Colonel Thomas Cass (1822–1862) of the 9th Massachusetts Volunteers, who was mortally wounded at Malvern Hill.

Camp Cavender (St. Louis) MO
Was a major Union training camp at St. Louis, named for Major John S. Cavender (d.1886) of the 1st Missouri Artillery, who later commanded the 29th Missouri Infantry.

Camp Chalmers (Escambia) FL
At Warrington, it was named for Confederate General James R. Chalmers (1831–1898), who had fought at Santa Rosa Island.

Camp Charles Russell (Nueces) TX
This was named for Major Charles Russell, General Hamilton Bee's quartermaster. It was near Corpus Christi.

Camp Chase (Franklin) OH
Near Columbus, it was named for Salmon P. Chase (1808–1873), governor of Ohio, 1855–1859, and President Lincoln's secretary of the Treasury, 1861–1864. Originally a training camp for state troops, its barracks were turned into a military prison in 1862, initially housing both officers and enlisted men; it became very overcrowded and the former were transferred to Johnson's Island. It was also used as a parole camp when prisoners were being exchanged. Some Confederate prisoners were recruited into the 6th U.S. Volunteers here as galvanized Yankees for service on the frontier.

Camp Cheatham (Robertson) TN
It was established near Cedar Hill in 1861 and named for General Benjamin F. Cheatham (1820–1886), who served as a brigade, division and corps commander in the Army of Tennessee.

Camp Claassen (Craven) NC
At Bachelor's Creek, near New Bern, it was named for Colonel Peter J. Claassen of the 132nd New York Volunteers who were here in 1863–1865.

Camp Clark (East Baton Rouge) LA
Was established at Baton Rouge in August 1862 after its occupation by Federal troops and named for Lieutenant Colonel T.S. Clark of the 6th Michigan.

Camp Clark (Caldwell) TX
A camp of instruction in 1861–1862 on the San Marcos River near Martindale, it was

named for Edward Clark (1815–1880), governor of Texas, 1859–1861.

Camp Clingman (Buncombe/Wayne) NC

There were two Confederate camps of this name in North Carolina. One was established at Asheville in August 1861, the other near Goldsboro in October 1862. They were both named for General Thomas L. Clingman (1812–1897), originally colonel of the 25th North Carolina, who took part in the defense of Goldsboro and New Bern.

Camp Cobb (Gadsden) FL

Florida was the third Southern state to secede, and Camp Cobb, established at Quincy, was named for General Howell Cobb (1815–1868) who was commander of the District of Middle Florida.

Camp Cole (Cole) MO

Cole County was named for Stephen Cole, an Indian fighter. There was skirmishing at this Union camp in June 1861 when it was attacked by secessionists, and further military activity in October 1862, and June and October 1863.

Camp Colfax (LaPorte) IN

At LaPorte, it was named for Congressman Schuyler Colfax (1823–1885), speaker of the House, 1863–1869, and later Ulysses Grant's first vice-president, 1869–1873.

Camp Collier (Brown) TX

With the departure of so many men for the war, this was established in 1862 to protect this part of Texas from Indian attack. It was named for a Captain Frank M. Collier.

Camp Connelly (Socorro) NMT

Was named for Henry Connelly (1800–1866), territorial governor of New Mexico, 1861–1866. In early 1862 it was the scene of a mutiny by two companies of Union volunteer militia over government failures to pay and clothe them.

Camp Constitution *see* Camp Fry

Camp Cooper (Nassau) FL

One of several camps named for General Samuel Cooper (1798–1876), the highest ranking officer in the Confederate Army, who served as adjutant and inspector general throughout the war. It was captured by Federal troops in February 1864.

Camp Copeland (Allegheny) PA

Near Pittsburgh, it was originally called Camp Reynolds but renamed in 1863 for the new post commander, General Joseph T. Copeland (1830–1893), a cavalry officer who later commanded the military prison at Alton, Illinois.

Camp Crittenden (Fayette) KY

At Lexington, it was named for Union General Thomas L. Crittenden (1815–1893) of Kentucky, who was a divisional and corps commander in the Army of the Tennessee.

Camp Crump (Marion) TX

This camp was named for Colonel Philip Crump of the 3rd Texas Cavalry who were here in 1862. It was near Jefferson.

Camp Curry (Talladega) AL

Was named for Jabez L.M. Curry (1825–1903), on whose land near Talladega it was established. A Confederate States congressman, the Richmond *Whig* described him as "a polished gentleman ... [and] a gifted orator." In 1864, as a lieutenant colonel of Confederate cavalry, he became an aide-de-camp to Generals Joseph E. Johnston and Joseph Wheeler.

Camp Curtin (Dauphin) PA

Established near Harrisburg in April 1861, it was reputedly the first and certainly the largest Union training camp in the Civil War. It was named for Andrew G. Curtin (1815–1894), governor of Pennsylvania, 1860–1866, who made a major contribution to the Northern war effort, raising regiments and organizing relief for soldiers' families. During General Stuart's Chambersburg raid in October 1862, he tried to set up state defenses and organize a pursuit of the raiders.

Camp Daly (Harris) TX

Constructed alongside the Galveston, Houston & Henderson Railroad, this was named for a Lieutenant Colonel Andrew Daly.

Camp Darnell (Dallas) TX

Was named for Nicholas H. Darnell (1807–

1885), a Dallas man who raised the 18th Texas Cavalry, sometimes known as "Darnell's Regiment."

Camp Davidson (Chatham) GA

A prison camp at Savannah, in use in 1864, it was possibly named for General Henry B. Davidson (1831–1899), who commanded a brigade of Confederate cavalry in Georgia.

Camp Davis (Alcorn) MS

May be named for Union General Jefferson C. Davis (1828–1879), who commanded a division in the Army of Mississippi here at Corinth in 1862.

Camp Davis (Harrison/Gillespie) TX

There were two camps of this name in Texas. One, established in 1862 near Marshall, was named for a Captain Jack Davis; another, at the confluence of White Oak Creek and the Perdinales River, was named for a Captain H.T. Davis.

Camp Day *see* Camp Cameron

Camp Dennison (Montgomery) OH

An important mobilization and training camp on the Little Miami River established in the spring of 1861, it was named for William Dennison (1815–1882), governor of Ohio, 1859–1864, and postmaster general in Lincoln's second administration. At Germany, 17 miles northeast of Cincinnati, it was also in use as a prison camp in 1862 and later housed convalescent soldiers. There was a skirmish here during General Morgan's Ohio raid in July 1863.

Camp Dick Robinson (Garrard) KY

Established in August 1861 near Lancaster, on land belonging to farmer Richard M. Robinson, a staunch Unionist, it was the main Federal recruitment and training camp in Kentucky. General George H. Thomas took charge in September 1861, by which time four Kentucky regiments and nearly 2,000 men from Tennessee were here. In October 1862 it was occupied by General Polk's Army of Mississippi at the time of the battle of Perryville, but subsequently re-occupied by Union troops for the rest of the war.

Camp Doubleday DC

North of the Potomac, it was named for General Abner Doubleday (1819–1893) who took part in the defense of Fort Sumter and is also credited with the invention of baseball.

Camp Douglas (Cook) IL

Was built in 1861 on land near Lake Michigan on the outskirts of Chicago belonging to statesman Stephen A. Douglas (1813–1861). It was originally intended as a training camp for Illinois volunteers, but after the fall of Fort Donelson in 1862 it became a prison camp, one of the largest in the North. Like Elmira, it became a visitor attraction for local people, some of whom came by street car to stare at the prisoners. It had a succession of commandants, some of whom seem to have been particularly vindictive, and it acquired the nickname of "80 acres of hell." More than 5,000 Confederates may have died here from neglect, disease, ill treatment and even torture. A plot to free the prisoners in November 1864 at the time of the presidential election and then capture Chicago was foiled. Some Confederate prisoners from here became galvanized Yankees in 1865 for frontier service against the Indians.

Camp Dumont (Shelby) KY

At Shelbyville, it was named for Union General Ebenezer Dumont (1814–1871), a brigade and divisional commander in the Armies of the Ohio and the Cumberland.

Camp Du Pont (Arlington) VA

An unusual example of an army camp named for a naval officer, in this case Rear Admiral Samuel F. Du Pont (1803–1865), who was much acclaimed for his part in the Port Royal expedition in November 1861.

Camp Ellis (Wake) NC

Established at Raleigh in May 1861, it was named in honor of John W. Ellis (1820–1861), governor of North Carolina, who died two months later of strain and overwork.

Camp Ellsworth (Lee) IA

At Keokuk, it was a training camp established in 1861 and named for Colonel E. Elmer Ellsworth (1837–1861) of the 11th New York ("Ellsworth's Zouaves"). The first Union martyr, he was killed at Alexandria when removing a Confederate flag from the roof of a tavern. Fort Ellsworth (q.v.) was also named for him.

Camp Emerson (Jefferson) IN

This camp at Madison was named for Colonel Frank Emerson of the 67th Indiana Infantry. It was also the home of the 82nd and 100th Indiana.

Camp Fenton DC

Reuben E. Fenton (1819–1885), a leading New York Republican who became governor in 1865 gave his name to this camp on Meridian Hill. It was the home of the 9th New York Cavalry.

Camp Finegan (Duval) FL

Was named for Irish-born General Joseph Finegan (1814–1885), commander of the District of Middle and East Florida. There was skirmishing here in February 1864 when it was abandoned by the Confederates, but reoccupied the following month, and there was further skirmishing in May. It was near Jacksonville.

Camp Fisher (Davidson/Craven/ Rowan) NC

Three camps in North Carolina were named for Colonel Charles F. Fisher (1816–1861) of the 6th North Carolina, who was also commemorated by Fort Fisher (q.v.). They were established at High Point (September 1861), near New Bern (February 1862) and near Salisbury (June 1862).

Camp Fisher (Prince William) VA

At Dumfries, it was established in September 1861 and also called after Colonel Fisher, who had been killed at First Manassas. It was abandoned in March 1862.

Camp Fisk (Warren) MS

Was probably named for Union General Clinton B. Fisk (1828–1890), who had commanded troops in Missouri. It was established near Vicksburg in 1865 for the exchange of prisoners captured during the operations of the western armies.

Camp Fiske (Shelby) TN

A camp for contrabands near Memphis, established early in 1863. It was named for Chaplain Asa S. Fiske, assistant to John Eaton, chaplain of the 27th Ohio and General Grant's superintendent of freedmen.

Camp Flournoy (Wood) TX

Was named for Colonel George M. Flournoy (1832–1889) of the 16th Texas Infantry. He was the pre-war attorney general of Texas.

Camp Ford (Smith) TX

Colonel John S. Ford (1815–1897), for whom it was named, was known as "Rest in Peace" or RIP Ford, a nickname he acquired from the letters he wrote to soldiers' next-of-kin while serving as a regimental adjutant in the Mexican War. At Tyler, it was originally a Confederate training camp, but turned into a prison stockade in August 1863 for both officers and enlisted men. Conditions were initially good, but after the Red River campaign of 1864 there was serious overcrowding and disease. The largest Confederate prison camp west of the Mississippi, it was closed in May 1865.

Camp Forney (Conecuh) AL

Almost certainly named for one of the Forney brothers, either John H. (1829–1902) or William H. (1823–1894), who grew up in Alabama and became generals in the Confederate Army.

Camp Franklin DC

A labor camp for men working on the forts east of the Anacostia River, it was probably named for General William B. Franklin (1823–1903), a brigade, divisional and corps commander who saw no further war service after he was wounded at Sabine Crossroads in 1864.

Camp Frémont (Johnson) IA

A training camp for state troops was established at Iowa City in 1861 and named for General John C. Frémont (1813–1880), commander of the newly created Western Department. As a pre-war explorer he was known as the "Pathfinder."

Camp Frémont (Marion) IN

Was established at Indianapolis in December 1863. The 28th Indiana Colored Infantry, the state's only black regiment, was formed here in March 1864. It was also named for General Frémont.

Camp French (New Hanover) NC
General Samuel G. French (1818–1910) assumed command at New Bern in March 1862 when this Confederate camp was set up near Wilmington.

Camp Fry DC
Both this and the following were probably named for Colonel James B. Fry (c.1827–1894), who became assistant adjutant general and then provost marshal general in Washington.

Camp Fry (Cook) IL
A training camp on the outskirts of Chicago established in 1864. Some Confederate prisoners from Camps Chase, Douglas and Morton who became galvanized Yankees trained here in 1865 before their departure for the West.

Camp Fry (Rockingham) NH
Was established at Portsmouth in 1861 for the 2nd New Hampshire. It was originally called Camp Constitution before being renamed.

Camp Gamble (St. Louis) MO
Near St. Louis, it was named for Hamilton R. Gamble (1798–1864), the Union governor of Missouri, 1861–1864.

Camp Garnett (Randolph) WV
Named for Confederate General Richard S. Garnett (1819–1861) who was mortally wounded at Corrick's Ford, it was near Beverly.

Camp Gaston (Craven) NC
A short-lived Confederate camp in existence near New Bern, October 1861–February 1862. It was named for a local landowner, Judge William Gaston.

Camp Gatlin (Craven) NC
Established near New Bern in February 1862, it was named for General Richard C. Gatlin (1809–1896) who began the war as adjutant general of the North Carolina militia and later commanded coastal defenses.

Camp Gilbert (Jefferson) KY
At Louisville, it may have been named for Union General Charles C. Gilbert (1822–1903), who served in Kentucky in 1862.

Camp Goddard (Muskingum) OH
Various Ohio regiments assembled at this camp near Janesville, named for Colonel C.B. Goddard of the Ohio militia.

Camp Goldthwaite (Talladega) AL
Was named for George Goldthwaite (1809–1879), a lawyer who was adjutant general of Alabama for three years during the Civil War. It was near Talladega.

Camp Gould (Smith) TX
Colonel Nicholas Gould commanded the 23rd Texas Cavalry, who were here briefly in 1862, and this camp was named for him.

Camp Grant (Coles) IL
Ulysses S. Grant (1822–1885) was colonel of the 21st Illinois in June 1861 when this training camp was established near Mattoon. Two months later he was a brigadier general of volunteers.

Camp Griffin (Fairfax) VA
Near Lewinsville, it was the camp of the Vermont Brigade which suffered the greatest number of casualties of any in the Union Army. It may have been named for General Charles Griffin (1825–1867), an artillery officer who commanded a battery at Washington early in the war.

Camp Grinnell (Fairfax) VA
A short-lived camp near Alexandria, it was occupied in June-July 1861 by the 39th Infantry—the "Garibaldi Guard"—from New York City, composed of companies of Hungarians, Germans, Swiss, Italians, French, Spanish and Portuguese. It was probably named for Josiah B. Grinnell (1821–1891), an abolitionist and politician.

Camp Groce (Waller) TX
Established near Hempstead, on the Liendo Plantation owned by Leonard W. Groce, it was a training camp for Confederate soldiers, then in 1863 became a prison camp for both officers and enlisted men; the first Federal prisoners arrived in June, some transferred from the state penitentiary at Huntsville. It became very overcrowded, but was abandoned in 1864 when the prisoners were paroled.

Camp Halleck (Lee) IA
A training camp at Keokuk named for General Henry W. Halleck (1815–1872) who served mainly as President Lincoln's military advisor and chief of staff.

Camp Hallett (Providence) RI
At Cranston, it was established in October 1861 and named for Colonel George W. Hallett of the Providence Horse Guards, a pre-war volunteer militia unit.

Camp Hamilton (York) VA
Originally called Camp Troy when established in May 1861 near Hampton and Fort Monroe, this was the first U.S. army camp in post-secession Virginia. It was used as a prison camp for Confederate officers and may have been named for General Schuyler Hamilton (1822–1903), brother-in-law and assistant chief of staff to General Henry W. Halleck.

Camp Hamilton *see* Camp Wood

Camp Hammond (Kane) IL
Near Aurora, it was established in 1861 and named for the president of the Chicago, Burlington & Quincy Railroad.

Camp Hampton GA
An instruction camp named for General Wade Hampton (1818–1902) who raised and outfitted the Hampton Legion. Cadets from the South Carolina Military Academy came here in June 1861 to help with the training. Its location has not been established.

Camp Harker (Davidson) TN
Near Nashville, it was named for Union General Charles G. Harker (1837–1864), killed during the Atlanta campaign.

Camp Harlan *see* Camp McKean

Camp Harrison (Hamilton) OH
Six miles north of Cincinnati, on the Cincinnati, Hamilton & Dayton Railroad, it was established in 1861 and named for William Henry Harrison (1773–1841) who was president in 1841 for only one month.

Camp Harvey (Kenosha) WI
Like the Harvey Soldiers' Hospital at Madison, it was named for Governor Louis P. Harvey (1820–1862) who was drowned on an errand of mercy on his way to Shiloh.

Camp Hawley (Warren) MS
Was a contraband camp at Vicksburg in 1865, named for its superintendent, Chaplain James A. Hawley of the 63rd U.S. Colored Infantry.

Camp Hébert (Waller) TX
Like Fort Hébert (q.v.), it was named for General Paul O. Hébert (1818–1880), who commanded the District of Texas.

Camp Heffren (Jackson) IN
At Seymour, it was established in September 1861 for the 50th Indiana Infantry and named for Lieutenant Colonel Horace Heffren. He was later arrested and tried for membership of the Knights of the Golden Circle, a secret organization of Peace Democrats or Copperheads.

Camp Heintzelman (Montgomery) MD
Was named for General Samuel P. Heintzelman (1805–1880), who commanded the Military District and Department of Washington when this camp was in existence at Poolesville in 1862–1863.

Camp Henry McCulloch (Victoria) TX
A camp of instruction, situated near Victoria, in existence September 1861-May 1862, it was named for General Henry E. McCulloch (1816–1895), brother of General Ben McCulloch and commander of the Department of Texas.

Camp Herron (Scott) IA
Was established at Davenport in 1862 and probably named for General Francis J. Herron (1837–1902), who had served with Iowa regiments.

Camp Hicks (Frederick) MD
Near Frederick, this was the camp of the 12th Massachusetts and named for Governor Thomas H. Hicks (1798–1865) of Maryland, who succeeded in keeping his state in the Union.

Camp Hill (Northampton/New Hanover) NC
There were two Confederate camps called

this, one near Garysburg, the other at Wilmington, both named for General Daniel H. Hill (1821–1889), who had been superintendent of the North Carolina Military Institute before the war.

Camp Hoffman (St. Marys) MD

Was the official name of what was often called Point Lookout (q.v.), a Union prison camp at the junction of the Potomac River and Chesapeake Bay. It was named for Colonel William H. Hoffman (c.1808–1884) of the 3rd U.S. Infantry, who was himself briefly a prisoner-of-war in 1861. Exchanged, he became commissary-general of prisoners in October of that year.

Camp Holmes (New Hanover/Wake) NC

There appear to have been two camps of this name, one near Wilmington in March 1862 and another at Raleigh in May 1864. They were named in honor of General Theophilus H. Holmes (1804–1880), "an unpretentious North Carolina patriot and gentleman" who later commanded the North Carolina reserves.

Camp Holt *see* **Fort DeRussy**

Camp Holton *see* **Camp Reno**

Camp Hood (Washington) TX

This was established near Brenham in 1862 and named for General John B. Hood (1831–1879), who had served in Texas before the war and took command of the Texas Brigade that year.

Camp Houghtaling (Alexander) IL

Near Cairo, it was named for Captain Charles Houghtaling (d.1883) of the 1st Illinois Artillery and established in 1861.

Camp Howard (Hanover) VA

It was probably named for Union General Oliver O. Howard (1830–1909) when it was established near Hanover Junction.

Camp Hubbard (Smith) TX

This camp at Sulphur Springs was named for Colonel Richard B. Hubbard (1832–1901) of the 22nd Texas Infantry.

Camp Hudson (Val Verde) TX

On San Pedro Creek, it was established in 1857 near Del Rio and named for Lieutenant Walter W. Hudson, killed in an Indian fight in 1850. It was abandoned by its U.S. garrison in March 1861. The Texas troops who were subsequently here published their own newspaper, the *Camp Hudson Times.*

Camp Hunter (Cherokee) KS

Established in 1862 at Baxter Springs to deal with the problem of Confederate guerrillas and Indians, this was a short-lived Union camp named for General David Hunter (1802–1886).

Camp Ingalls DC

Was probably named for General Rufus Ingalls (1820–1893), chief quartermaster of the Army of the Potomac, 1862–1864. It was situated south of the Potomac.

Camp Jackson (Benton) AR

Near Maysville, it was no doubt named for General Thomas J. "Stonewall" Jackson (1824–1863).

Camp Jackson (Nassau) FL

It was north of Jacksonville, and although the town commemorates President Andrew Jackson, the camp was probably named for "Stonewall" Jackson whose death had sent shock waves through the South. This was in existence in 1864.

Camp Jackson (LaPorte) IN

A short-lived camp at LaPorte, in existence in 1861 and probably named for Andrew Jackson (1767–1845).

Camp Jackson (St. Louis) MO

Named for Claiborne F. Jackson (1807–1862), the secessionist governor of Missouri, 1860–1862, it was a drill camp at St. Louis for state militia, but after it was surrendered to U.S. troops in May 1861, became a drill ground for Federal soldiers.

Camp Jackson (Washington/Montgomery/Kleberg/Montague) TX

There were four camps called this in Texas. At least one of them may have been named for James W. Jackson (d.1861), the first Southern martyr. An Alexandria hotel keeper, he "was killed by Federal soldiers while defending his property," after shooting Colonel E. Elmer Ellsworth for removing a Confederate flag. Others perhaps commemorated President Andrew Jackson or General "Stonewall" Jackson.

Camp Jackson (Henrico) VA

Was a training camp at Richmond, named for "Stonewall" Jackson.

Camp Jefferson Davis (Red River) TX

Was one of the few camps named for President Davis.

Camp Jennison (Clay) MO

At Kansas City, it was named for the notorious Colonel Charles R. Jennison (1834–1884) of the 7th Kansas Volunteer Cavalry ("Jennison's Jayhawkers"), who were described as "no better than a band of robbers."

Camp Jerusalem *see* Camp Benjamin

Camp Joe Holt (Scott) IA

A training camp at Davenport, it was one of several named for Colonel Joseph Holt (1807–1894), who was judge advocate general, U.S. Army (1862), head of the Bureau of Military Justice (1864), and then served on the military commission which tried the Lincoln conspirators (1865).

Camp Joe Holt (Clark) IN

Near Jeffersonville, it was established in July 1861 as a recruiting center and also served as a hospital till Jeffersonville General Hospital opened in 1862.

Camp Jourdan *see* Roanoke Island

Camp Junaluska (Jefferson) TN

At Strawberry Plains, on the East Tennessee & Virginia Railroad, it became a base for the Cherokee troops of the Thomas Legion in 1862, commanded by Colonel William H. Thomas, CSA. It was named for Junaluska (d.1858), a Cherokee chief who had fought with General Andrew Jackson in the Creek War of 1813–1814.

Camp Kane (Kane) IL

The training camp of the 8th Illinois Cavalry took its name from Kane County, called after Elias Kane (1775?–1840), a senator and the first secretary of state of Illinois, rather than the better-known General Thomas L. Kane, a pre-war abolitionist. It was at St. Charles.

Camp Kenton (Mason) KY

Established at Maysville in 1861, it was probably named for Simon Kenton (1755–1836), a noted Indian fighter. It was a Union training camp.

Camp Keyes (Arlington) VA

Was probably named for Union General Erasmus D. Keyes (1810–1895).

Camp King (Campbell) KY

At Covington, it may have been named for Union Colonel William S. King (1818–1882) of the 4th Massachusetts Artillery, who served as provost marshal of Kentucky and was military commander of the Lexington District.

Camp Kinsman (Scott) IA

Originally called Camp Roberts, it was later renamed, possibly for Union Colonel William H. Kinsman (d.1863). It was at Davenport.

Camp Kirkwood (Pottawattamie/ Clinton) IA

Two training camps in Iowa were named for Governor Samuel J. Kirkwood (1813–1894), who was active in raising troops for the Union. One was established at Council Bluffs in 1861, the other at Clinton in 1862.

Camp Kyle (Harris) TX

On Buffalo Bayou, near Harrisburg, it was named for General W.J. Kyle of the Texas state troops.

Camp Lamb (New Hanover) NC

In existence near Wilmington in March 1862, it was named for Colonel William Lamb (1835–1909) of the 36th North Carolina Artillery, who also gave his name to Fort Lamb (q.v.) and became commandant of Fort Fisher (q.v.).

Camp Lander (Essex) MA

Was named for General Frederick W. Lander (1821–1862), a pre-war railroad surveyor. At Wenham, it was in use 1862–1865.

Camp Langford (Duval) FL

In April 1862, the ladies of Orange Lake Soldiers' Association presented a battle flag to the Marion Light Artillery, Florida Battery, here at Camp Langford. Near Jacksonville, it may have been named for Captain George R. Langford, 4th Florida Infantry. It was in existence in 1861–1862, then appears to have been abandoned before being re-established in 1864.

Camp Latty (Henry) OH

At Napoleon, it was established in 1861 for the 68th Ohio Volunteers by Judge Alexander Latty. It closed early in 1862.

Camp Lauman (Des Moines) IA

Established at Burlington in 1862, it was named for General Jacob G. Lauman (1813–1867), who began the war as colonel of the 7th Iowa.

Camp Lawton (Jenkins) GA

Alexander R. Lawton (1818–1896) was a prominent figure in antebellum Georgia, and Confederate quartermaster general when this short-lived military prison near Millen was established in October 1864 on the Central Railroad of Georgia, to relieve the overcrowding at Andersonville. While here, approximately 350 Union prisoners enlisted in the Confederate Army. Because of the threat from General William T. Sherman the prisoners were moved in November to Blackshear and Thomasville.

Camp Lay (Leon) FL

Near Tallahassee, it may have been named for Lieutenant Colonel George W. Lay, who was designated inspector-general of conscription in 1864. That year, slaves being held here were sent to St. Marks on the Gulf coast to pack salted fish into barrels for transportation into Georgia to supplement meager army rations.

Camp Lee (Henrico) VA

Established on the fair grounds at Richmond under the command of Colonel William Gilham, this important camp of instruction was named for General Robert E. Lee (1807–1870) and included a hospital. Cadets from the Virginia Military Institute came here to help with the training of recruits who were from all over the South. After the fall of Richmond, it was occupied initially by black cavalry, infantry and artillery regiments.

Camp Leon (Leon) FL

Leon County was named for Ponce de Leon (1460–1521), the Spanish explorer who discovered Florida in 1513. This was a Confederate camp near Tallahassee.

Camp Letterman (Adams) PA

At Gettysburg, it was named for Major Jonathan Letterman (1824–1872), medical director of the Army of the Potomac, 1862–1864, who reorganized field hospitals and introduced an efficient ambulance service.

Camp Leventhorpe (Northampton/New Hanover) NC

There were two camps named for Collett Leventhorpe (1815–1889), a former English army officer who was successively colonel of two North Carolina regiments, commanded the District of Wilmington, and then became brigadier general of state troops. One was at Garysburg, the other at Wilmington.

Camp Lewis (Vanderburgh) IN

Was established near Evansville in August 1862 and named for a Colonel Andrew Lewis.

Camp Lovell (St. Mary) LA

A camp for Louisiana volunteers, it was established at Berwick in 1861 and named for General Mansfield Lovell (1822–1884), who was later blamed for the loss of New Orleans.

Camp Lubbock (Harris) TX

Was named for Francis R. Lubbock (1815–1905), governor of Texas, 1861–1863, and subsequently a colonel in the Confederate Army. It was at Harrisburg.

Camp Lyon (Kane/Peoria) IL

There were two camps of this name in Illinois, at Geneva and Peoria. They almost certainly commemorated General Nathaniel Lyon (1818–1861), the North's first military hero, who was killed at Wilson's Creek.

Camp Lyon (Wayne) MI

A training camp established at Detroit in 1861, it was also named for General Lyon.

Camp Mansfield (Fairfax) VA
A Union camp at Alexandria, almost certainly named for General Joseph K.F. Mansfield (1803–1862), who was mortally wounded at Antietam.

Camp Marion VA
Was a Confederate camp, probably named for Marion Lumpkin Cobb, the wife of Colonel Thomas R.R. Cobb, founder of Cobb's Georgia Legion. Its location has not been established.

Camp Mary Davis (Leon) FL
A camp for Confederate cavalry near Tallahassee, almost certainly named for the wife of Colonel (later General) William G.M. Davis, a wealthy cotton speculator who raised and outfitted the 1st Florida Cavalry.

Camp Mason (Cumberland) ME
The 20th Maine were trained here at Portland by their colonel, Adelbert Ames, in the summer of 1862 before their baptism of fire at Fredericksburg. It may have been named for Edwin C. Mason (d.1898), colonel of the 7th Maine.

Camp Mather (Cook/Gallatin/Peoria) IL
There were three camps called this in Illinois, at Chicago, Shawneetown and Peoria. They were possibly named for Colonel Thomas S. Mather (d.1890) of the 2nd Illinois Artillery.

Camp Maury (Stafford) VA
At Brooke, it was probably named for Confederate General Dabney H. Maury (1822–1900) who after the war organized the Southern Historical Society.

Camp Maxcy Gregg (Kershaw) SC
A prison camp at Killian's Mill, 14 miles northeast of Columbia, on the Charlotte & South Carolina Railroad, for both officers and enlisted men, was planned but never completed. It would have been named for General Maxcy Gregg (1814–1862), who was mortally wounded at Fredericksburg.

Camp Maxey (Marion) TX
Near Saline, it was named for Samuel B. Maxey (1825–1895), colonel of the 9th Texas, who later commanded three brigades of Native Americans in the Indian Territory.

Camp McClellan (Scott) IA
At East Davenport on the Mississippi River, it trained Iowa and Illinois troops. It was named for General George B. McClellan (1826–1885), army commander and later unsuccessful presidential candidate. In August 1864 several "women of easy virtue" who had been pestering soldiers in the camp hospital were given a cold bath in the Mississippi to discourage them.

Camp McClernand (Alexander) IL
It was named for General John A. McClernand (1812–1900), who was in command here at Cairo, October 1861-February 1862.

Camp McCulloch (McLennan) TX
This was a camp at Waco, named for General Ben McCulloch (1811–1862), "one of the most popular figures in Texas" who was killed at Pea Ridge.

Camp McDonald (Cobb) GA
At Big Shanty (now Kennesaw), this was an important camp of instruction for state troops, and cadets from the Georgia Military Institute came here to train the officers and N.C.O.s of the 4th Brigade of Georgia Volunteers. Established in June 1861, it closed in the fall of that year, but was reopened in 1862 and 1863; it was destroyed by General William T. Sherman in 1864. It was named for Charles J. McDonald (1793–1860), governor of Georgia, 1839–1843.

Camp McIntosh (Franklin) AR
This was probably named for Confederate General James McIntosh (1828–1862) who served in the Indian Territory and was killed at Pea Ridge. It was near Ozark.

Camp McKean (Johnson) IA
At Mount Pleasant, Iowa City, it was called Camp Harlan when first established in 1861 before being renamed the following year, probably for General Thomas J. McKean (1810–1870).

Camp McLeod (Galveston) TX
Was named for Colonel Hugh McLeod (1814–1862) of the 1st Texas Infantry, who had been secretary of war for the Republic of Texas.

Camp McNeel *see* Camp Wharton

Camp Meigs (Suffolk) MA

Established in 1863 at Readville, then just outside Boston, it was the training camp of the 54th and 55th Massachusetts Colored Infantry and the 5th U.S. Colored Cavalry, three of the first African American regiments raised after the Emancipation Proclamation. The 54th Massachusetts, commanded by Colonel Robert G. Shaw, took part in the assault on Fort Wagner, South Carolina. Also sometimes known as Camp Readville, it was named for Montgomery C. Meigs (c.1816–1892), the quartermaster general of the U.S. Army. Massachusetts troops were mustered out here in 1865.

Camp Meigs (Tuscarawas) OH

Though this camp at Dover may also have been named for General Meigs, Return J. Meigs (1764–1824) who was governor of Ohio, 1810–1814, might have been the origin.

Camp Meigs (Philadelphia) PA

The camp of the 6th Cavalry (Rush Lancers), commanded by Colonel R.H. Rush, it was also named for General Meigs.

Camp Memminger (Mobile) AL

Near Mobile, it was named for German-born Christopher G. Memminger (1803–1888), Confederate secretary of the Treasury, 1861–1864.

Camp Miller (Bradford) FL

A Confederate cavalry camp near Hampton in 1864, almost certainly named for William Miller (1820–1909), colonel of the 1st Florida Infantry and later general commanding reserve forces in the state.

Camp Milner (Spalding) GA

At Griffin, it was named for local citizen Ben Milner who helped equip troops from Spalding County.

Camp Milton (Duval) FL

Named for Governor John Milton of Florida (1807–1865) who served throughout the war, it was the most strongly fortified camp in Civil War Florida. Near Jacksonville, it appears to have been projected as early as 1862, but was mostly built in March 1864 on the orders of General Pierre G.T. Beauregard after the battle of Olustee.

Camp Moore (Mobile) AL

Near Mobile, it was named for Thomas O. Moore (1803–1876), Confederate governor of Louisiana, 1860–1864.

Camp Moore (Hickman) KY

A Confederate camp near Columbus, possibly named for Kentucky Congressman James W. Moore.

Camp Moore (Tangipahoa) LA

A Confederate recruitment and training camp on the New Orleans, Jackson & Great Northern Railroad, near Tangipahoa, also named for Governor Moore. It was attacked by Union cavalry in April 1863 and again in October 1864, and burned the following month.

Camp Morris DC

The 15th New Jersey, commanded by Colonel S. Fowler, and the 138th New York (9th New York Heavy Artillery), commanded by Colonel J. Welling, were here in 1862. It may have been named after the versatile General William H. Morris (1827–1900), a pre-war journalist and inventor of a repeating carbine.

Camp Morris (Marion) IN

At Indianapolis, it was established in September 1861 and named for General Thomas A. Morris (1811–1904), a former railroad engineer, who commanded a brigade of Indiana volunteers.

Camp Morton (Marion) IN

Originally a training camp for Indiana troops at Indianapolis, it was named for Oliver P. Morton (1823–1877), governor of Indiana, 1861–1867, who personally supervised it during its first spell as a military prison, February-August 1862. Its barracks became a prison again early in 1863, this time under army administration. Its commandant, Colonel Richard D. Owen, was so well regarded by his Confederate prisoners that after the war some of them commissioned a memorial bust of him. Others took the oath of allegiance and in June 1863 joined the Union Army. Later, more were recruited for service on the frontier as galvanized Yankees.

Camp Nelson (Lonoke) AR

Colonel Allison Nelson (1822–1862) of the

10th Texas Infantry, for whom it was named, died of typhoid fever shortly after being promoted to brigadier general. Several hundred Confederate soldiers at this training camp near Austin also died when there was an outbreak of measles.

Camp Nelson (Jessamine) KY

It was named for Union General William Nelson (1824–1862), who was killed, not in battle but by a fellow officer at Louisville where he was organizing the defenses. Established in 1861 by General George H. Thomas for Kentucky troops, this supply depot and training camp south of Nicholasville, became an important mustering site for black Union troops from Kentucky, Tennessee and Ohio from 1863 onwards. It was also used as a contraband camp and for convalescent soldiers.

Camp Nevin (Hardin) KY

A Union training camp in 1861–1862, named for David Nevin who owned the land here. In December 1861 it was the headquarters of General Alexander M. McCook, one of the "Fighting McCooks" of Ohio.

Camp Nicholls (Bedford) VA

After twice being badly wounded, at First Winchester and Chancellorsville, Confederate General Francis R.T. Nicholls (1834–1912) was given command of Lynchburg, where this camp was located, before taking charge of the Bureau of Conscription in the Trans-Mississippi.

Camp Noble (Floyd) IN

At New Albany, it was named for Indiana's adjutant general, Laz Noble. It was also sometimes called Noble Barracks.

Camp N.P. Banks (Philadelphia) PA

Near Germantown, on the outskirts of Philadelphia, it was named for General Nathaniel Prentiss Banks (1816–1894) who led the Red River campaigns of 1863 and 1864. It was the camp of a regiment of zouaves commanded by Colonel Charles H.J. Collis in 1862.

Camp Oglethorpe (Jones) GA

A stockade was in use at this prison for Federal officers at Macon in 1861–1864. It was named for General James Oglethorpe (1696–1785), one of the founders of the state of Georgia.

Camp Olden (Mercer) NJ

Was a training camp at Trenton, named for Charles S. Olden (1799–1876), governor of New Jersey, 1859–1863.

Camp Palmer (Craven) NC

The camp of the 12th New York Cavalry, it was probably named for General Innis M. Palmer (1824–1900), who commanded the XVIII Corps and the defenses of New Bern.

Camp Parsons (Collin) TX

Near McKinney, it was named for lawyer and newspaper editor Colonel William H. Parsons (1826–1907) who commanded the 12th Texas Cavalry and later a brigade, though he never made general.

Camp Pender (Martin) NC

Was named for General William D. Pender (1834–1863) who commanded a North Carolina brigade during the Seven Days and died from wounds received at Gettysburg. It was at Hamilton.

Camp Pettus (Clarke) MS

This was established near Enterprise as early as January 1861, initially for state militia. It was named for John J. Pettus (1813–1867), governor of Mississippi, 1859–1863.

Camp Pickens (Prince William) VA

At Manassas Junction, it was probably named for Francis W. Pickens (1805–1869), governor of South Carolina at the time of the Fort Sumter crisis.

Camp Pickett (Bexar) TX

Was named for Confederate General George E. Pickett (1825–1875), who had served on the Texas frontier in 1849–1855 and will be forever remembered for "Pickett's Charge" on the third day at Gettysburg. It was on Salado Creek, near San Antonio.

Camp Pope (Nelson) KY

Near New Haven, it was named for Union General John Pope (1822–1892), a Kentuckian, who was relieved of command after his failure at Second Bull Run.

Camp Pratt (Iberia) LA

In May 1862, General John G. Pratt (1816–1866) of the Louisiana militia, established a training camp near New Iberia for Confederate army conscripts, on the orders of Governor Moore.

Camp Quantico (Prince William) VA

At Dumfries, it took its name from Quantico Creek, an Indian word of uncertain meaning. Texas troops were quartered here, a long way from home, in the winter of 1861–1862.

Camp Quarles (Obion) TN

General William A. Quarles (1825–1893), CSA, for whom it was named, had been a judge and railroad president before the war and was colonel of the 42nd Tennessee. It was at Union City.

Camp Raguet (Brazos) TX

Near Millican, it was named for Major Henry M. Raguet, 4th Texas Cavalry, who took part in the Confederate invasion of New Mexico Territory and was mortally wounded at Glorieta Pass in March 1862.

Camp Randall (Dane) WI

Was established in 1861 as a training camp for Wisconsin troops on land at Madison donated by the Wisconsin State Agricultural Society; it was named for Alexander W. Randall (1819–1872), governor of Wisconsin, 1857–1861. The barracks were used as a military prison in 1862.

Camp Randolph (Gordon) GA

An instruction camp for Georgia troops at Calhoun on the Western & Atlantic Railroad, probably named for George W. Randolph (1818–1867), who served as a Confederate general and was secretary of war when this was established in 1862.

Camp Randolph (Wayne) NC

At Goldsboro, it was also probably named for George Randolph.

Camp Rankin (Lee) IA

A short-lived camp established in the fall of 1861 for the 3rd Iowa Cavalry and named for Colonel J.W. Rankin of nearby Keokuk. It was abandoned in November of that year.

Camp Ransom (Lenoir) NC

Near Kinston, it was named for either Matthew W. Ransom (1826–1904) or Robert Ransom (1828–1892), brothers who both commanded North Carolina regiments and became Confederate generals.

Camp Readville see Camp Meigs

Camp Reeves (Grayson) TX

Was named for George R. Reeves (1826–1882), who became colonel of the 11th Texas Cavalry.

Camp Reno (Milwaukee) WI

At Milwaukee, it was originally called Camp Holton for abolitionist Edward D. Holton, but later renamed, first for General Franz Sigel, and then in 1864 for General Jesse L. Reno (1823–1862), who was killed at South Mountain.

Camp Reynolds (Spencer/Marion) IN

Two camps in this state were named for General Joseph J. Reynolds (1822–1899), a former artillery officer who began the war as colonel of the 10th Indiana. Both were established in 1862 for regiments of Indiana volunteers, one near Rockport, the other at Indianapolis.

Camp Reynolds see Camp Copeland

Camp Roberts (Smith) TX

Was a muster and rendezvous station established in 1861 and named for Oran M. Roberts (1815–1898), president of the Texas Secession Convention and colonel of the 11th Texas.

Camp Roberts see Camp Kinsman

Camp Robertson (Greene) NC

Near Snow Hill, this camp may have been named for General Beverly H. Robertson (1826–1910), who commanded Confederate cavalry in North Carolina in 1862–1863.

Camp Robertson (Grimes) TX

A prominent figure in pre-war Texas, General Jerome B. Robertson (1815–1891) succeeded

John B. Hood as commander of the Texas Brigade in 1862, but by the time this camp was established in 1865, he had been relegated to command of the reserve forces in the state.

Camp Robinson (Marion) IN
In existence at Indianapolis in September-October 1861, it was named for a Lieutenant Colonel W.J. Robinson.

Camp Rogers (Craven) NC
At New Bern, it was the camp of the 43rd Massachusetts Volunteer Infantry, commanded by Colonel Edward H. Rogers.

Camp Rose (St. Joseph) IN
Was a camp for Indiana volunteers, in existence August-October near South Bend, and named for a Colonel David G. Rose.

Camp Rugely (Matagorda) TX
Near Matagorda, it was named for Captain E.S. Rugely, a well-known local citizen. The Matagorda peninsula expedition set out from here in January 1864, 21 members of which froze to death.

Camp Rusk (Cherokee) TX
Near Rusk, it was named for Thomas J. Rusk (1803–1857), an important figure in the early history of Texas. He served as secretary of war and later as chief justice in the Republic, and worked towards its annexation by the United States.

Camp Salomon (La Crosse) WI
Was named for Edward S. Salomon, the Prussian-born governor of Wisconsin, 1861–1863, who also gave his name to the Salomon Guards (9th Wisconsin). It was at La Crosse.

Camp Saxton see Port Royal Island

Camp Schuyler see Camp Stanton

Camp Scott (Worcester) MA
A short-lived camp near Worcester, in existence June-August 1861, and named for General Winfield Scott (1786–1866), still at that time general-in-chief of the U.S. Army.

Camp Scott (Milwaukee) WI
Was established at Milwaukee in 1861 and also named for General Scott.

Camp Scott see Staten Island

Camp Scroggs (New York) NY
A training camp in New York City named for Gustavus A. Scroggs, a general in the state militia, which was the scene of a serious disturbance in September 1862 involving men of the 53rd New York Infantry (Vosburgh Chasseurs).

Camp Sellers (Robertson) TX
On the Brazos, near Stirling, it was named in 1863 for Captain John S. Sellers, assistant quartermaster to General William R. Scurry who commanded Confederate troops at Galveston.

Camp Semmes see Mustang Island

Camp Shaefer (Rutherford) TN
Was established at Murfreesboro in 1863 and named for Union Colonel Frederick Shaefer who was killed at Stones River.

Camp Sherman (Grayson) TX
Near Sherman, which was named for General Sidney Sherman (1805–1873) of the Republic of Texas Army, legislator and organizer of the first railroad in the state. It was an important rendezvous station in 1861.

Camp Shorter (Mobile/Lee) AL
Two camps were named for John G. Shorter (1818–1872), governor of Alabama, 1861–1863. One was near Mobile, the other at Loachapoka.

Camp Sibley (Bexar) TX
Was on Salado Creek, near San Antonio, and named for General Henry H. Sibley (1816–1886), who led Confederate operations in the Southwest in 1861–1862.

Camp Sidney Johnston (Chambers/Matagorda) TX
There were two camps named for General Albert Sidney Johnston (1803–1862), who had served in the Texas Army, been secretary of war for the Republic of Texas, later commanded the Department of Texas, and was killed at Shiloh.

One was near Baytown, in Trinity Bay, and the other was on Caney Creek.

Camp Sigel (Jefferson) KY
A Union camp named for German-born General Franz Sigel (1824–1902) who rallied his countrymen to the Northern cause; "I fights mit Sigel" was the cry.

Camp Sigel see Camp Reno

Camp Sill (Rutherford) TN
Was named for Union General Joshua W. Sill (1831–1862) who was killed at Stones River. It was at Murfreesboro.

Camp Slaughter (Brazoria) TX
On the Brazos River, near Columbia, it was named for General James E. Slaughter (1827–1901), who became General Magruder's chief of artillery in 1863, and later commanded Confederate troops in the last significant engagement of the war near Brownsville in May 1865.

Camp Smithers (New Castle) DE
Was a camp for the 1st Delaware Cavalry, in existence 1862–1863 near Wilmington. It was probably named for Nathaniel B. Smithers (1818–1896), a Delaware Republican.

Camp Sorghum (Richland) SC
This prison camp near Columbia, south of the Congaree River, got its name from the sorghum-molasses issued with the rations of cornmeal. The prison guards included cadets from the Hillsborough Military Academy in North Carolina. Because of the large number of escapes it was only in use September-December 1864, when the prisoners were moved to a more secure location at nearby Camp Asylum.

Camp Sprague DC
A camp for Rhode Island troops, it was named for William Sprague (1830–1915), governor of Rhode Island, 1859–1863, and colonel of the Rhode Island militia. He became the husband of Kate Chase, considered the leading beauty in wartime Washington.

Camp Stanton (Anne Arundel) MD
Near Annapolis, it was a training camp for General Burnside's colored division. It was named for Edwin M. Stanton (1814–1869), President Lincoln's secretary of war, 1862–1865.

Camp Stanton (Essex) MA
Originally called Camp Schuyler, perhaps for Philip J. Schuyler, a general in the Continental Army, it was renamed for Secretary Stanton in 1862. Infantry and artillery trained here, on the outskirts of Lynnfield.

Camp Stephens (Benton) AR
Established in July 1861 on Little Sugar and Brush Creeks, this was named for Alexander H. Stephens (1812–1883), vice-president of the Confederacy.

Camp Stillwell (Madison/Howard) IN
There were two camps of this name in Indiana. One near Anderson, was established in September 1861 for the 34th Indiana Volunteers, the other, near Kokomo, was in existence 1863–1864. One of them was called Camp Anderson, but they were both renamed for a Colonel T.N. Stillwell.

Camp Stoneman DC
Named for General George Stoneman (1822–1894), who carried out a number of raids in Virginia, Georgia and North Carolina, it was at Giesboro Point, a major cavalry depot.

Camp Streight (Marion) IN
Established in October 1861 for the 51st Indiana, it was one of many camps at Indianapolis. This was named for their colonel, Abel D. Streight (d.1892), who led a brigade of mounted infantry on a raid through Alabama in 1863.

Camp Sulakowski see Galveston Island

Camp Sullivan (Marion) IN
A conscript camp at Indianapolis, named for Colonel Jeremiah C. Sullivan (1830–1890) of the 3rd Indiana, who later achieved general's rank and divisional command.

Camp Sumter (Sumter) GA
Sumter County was named for Revolutionary War hero Thomas Sumter (1734–1832), though Camp Sumter may also have celebrated the capture of Fort Sumter. It was the original name of

the infamous prison camp better known as Andersonville (q.v.).

Camp Taylor (Sangamon) IL
At Springfield, it may have been named for Irish-born Colonel Ezra Taylor (d.1885) of the 1st Illinois Artillery.

Camp Thomas (Franklin) OH
Was a regular army training camp at Columbus, and named for Colonel Lorenzo Thomas (1805–1875), adjutant general, U.S. Army. It was in existence throughout the war.

Camp Tod (Cuyahoga) OH
Was established at Cleveland in 1861 for the 45th Ohio. It was named for David Tod (1805–1868), governor of Ohio, 1861–1863.

Camp Totten (Howard) MO
At Franklin, it was named for Union General James Totten (c.1818–1871), who served in the Department of the Missouri, 1861–1864.

Camp Trousdale (Trousdale) TN
Trousdale County took its name from William Trousdale (1790–1872), a veteran of the War of 1812, the Creek War, the Seminole War and the Mexican War, and governor of Tennessee, 1849–1851.

Camp Troy see Camp Hamilton

Camp Tupper (Hinds) MS
Was named for Tullius C. Tupper (1809–1866), who served as a major general in the Mississippi militia in 1862–1863.

Camp Tuttle (Mahaska) IA
At Oskaloosa, it was established in 1862 and probably named for General James M. Tuttle (1823–1892), a brigade and divisional commander at Shiloh while still a colonel.

Camp Upton (Arlington) VA
A Union camp on the Alexandria, Loudon & Hampshire Railroad, called after Upton's Hill, named for local resident Charles H. Upton (1812–1877), a newspaper editor.

Camp Van Dorn (Harris/Bexar) TX
Two Confederate camps were named for General Earl Van Dorn (1820–1863), commander of the Department of Texas. One was near Harrisburg; the other, a prison camp, established at San Antonio in 1861, was in use for only a few months. When it closed, many of the prisoners were transferred to Camp Verde.

Camp Vance (Buncombe/Burke) NC
A camp near Sulphur Springs was named for Robert B. Vance (1828–1899), who became colonel of the 29th North Carolina and later achieved general's rank. A number of other camps were also named for his brother, Zebulon B. Vance (1830–1894), who served in the Confederate Army as colonel of the 26th North Carolina before becoming state governor in 1862. One example was a camp of instruction for state troops between Morganton and Drexel.

Camp Verde (Kerr) TX
Established on Verde Creek in 1855, its Spanish name was *Val Verde*, "Green Valley." The following year it became the headquarters of the U.S. Army's Camel Corps and acquired the nickname "Little Egypt." Camels purchased in Egypt and Turkey were shipped to America for use in the Southwest, chiefly as pack animals. The scheme was backed by Secretary of War Jefferson Davis. When Camp Verde was taken over by Confederates in February 1861, a few camels were used to transport salt and cotton and deliver mail. It served briefly as a prison for Union soldiers in 1861, but they were subsequently transferred to San Antonio Springs and it remained in Confederate hands until 1865.

Camp Vest (Howard) MO
Was named for George G. Vest (1830–1904), a lawyer and Confederate congressman; it was near Boonville.

Camp Vredenburgh (Monmouth) NJ
Near Freehold, it was named for Major Peter Vredenburgh (1837–1864) who was killed at Third Winchester (Opequon Creek).

Camp Wade (Cuyahoga) OH
This camp near Cleveland was established in 1861 for the 2nd Ohio Cavalry by Republican Senator Benjamin F. Wade (1800–1878), for whom it was named.

Camp Walker (Benton) AR
This may have been named for Leroy P. Walker (1817–1884), who was the first Confederate secretary of war for nine months in 1861, before becoming a general, then presiding judge of a military court in Alabama. It was near Maysville.

Camp Wallace (Franklin) OH
At Columbus, it was probably named for Union General Lewis Wallace (1827–1905), later to become famous as the author of *Ben Hur*.

Camp Washburn (Milwaukee) WI
At Milwaukee, it was named for Colonel (later General) Cadwallader C. Washburn (1818–1882) who raised the 2nd Wisconsin Cavalry. It was in existence throughout the war.

Camp Watts (Macon) AL
Thomas H. Watts (1819–1892), who was attorney general in the Confederate Cabinet, 1862–1863, then governor of Alabama, 1863–1865, gave his name to this camp of instruction at Notasulga.

Camp Waul (Washington) TX
On the Brazos River, it was named for General Thomas N. Waul (1813–1903), who raised Waul's Texas Legion in 1862.

Camp Webb (Colorado) TX
Was on the outskirts of Alleyton and named for Colonel Henry L. Webb (1795–1876), inspector general of Texas state troops.

Camp Wharton (Brazoria/Goliad/Wharton) TX
There were four camps of this name in Texas. One, established on Jones Creek in 1863, was renamed Camp Dixie in 1864; another, about two miles away, was also called Camp McNeel, for plantation owner John G. McNeel; a third, near Goliad, was named for General John A. Wharton (1828–1865) who was killed in a private quarrel at the end of the war; and one near Wharton, was named for William H. Wharton (1802–1839), a Texas Republic patriot and minister to the United States. This was also known as Camp Buchel, named for Prussian-born soldier-of-fortune, Colonel August Buchel (1811–1864) of the 1st Texas Cavalry.

Camp Whiting (New Hanover/Brunswick) NC
Two camps were named for General William H.C. Whiting (1824–1865), known to his men as "Little Billy," who commanded the Military District of Wilmington, 1862–1864, and was mortally wounded in the defense of Fort Fisher. One, established in January 1863, was near Wilmington, the other, an artillery camp, established a year later, was at Lockwood Ferry Inlet.

Camp Whitwell (Augusta) VA
Was a very short-lived camp near Staunton of cadets from the Virginia Military Institute in May 1864, just prior to the battle of Newmarket. It was probably named for Captain A.C. Whitwell, the VMI's chief of subsistence.

Camp Wickliffe (Larue) KY
A Union camp south of Bardstown, named for Daniel C. Wickliffe (1810–1870), the Kentucky secretary of state.

Camp Wightman *see* Long Island

Camp William Penn (Montgomery) PA
Opened in 1863, this training camp at Cheltenham, near Philadelphia, was the first one to be established for African American recruits. Commanded by Colonel Louis Wagner, it was described as "the largest camp existing for the organization and disciplining of colored troops." Named for William Penn (1644–1718), the English-born Quaker who founded Philadelphia, it took in men from Delaware, New Jersey and Pennsylvania.

Camp Williams (Lenawee) MI
This was a training camp established at Adrian in 1861. It may have been named for Alpheus S. Williams (1810–1878), who was appointed a brigadier general of Michigan Volunteers at the start of the war, or Adolphus W. Williams (d.1879), colonel of the 20th Michigan.

Camp Winfield Scott (York) VA
Named for General Winfield Scott (1786–1866), a hero of the War of 1812 and the Mexican War, and the oldest and most senior general in

the U.S. Army, who put forward the Anaconda Plan for defeating the Confederacy. At Yorktown, it served as a base for the topographical engineers.

Camp Withers (Baldwin/Dallas) AL
There were two camps in Alabama named for General Jones M. Withers (1814–1890), who commanded reserve forces in the state in the second half of the war. One was in Baldwin County, the other near Selma.

Camp Wood (Fond du Lac) WI
At Fond du Lac, it was known successively as Camp Hamilton, for Colonel Charles S. Hamilton of the 3rd Wisconsin, then as Camp Wood, for Colonel David E. Wood.

Camp Wyatt (New Hanover) NC
Near Fort Fisher, this was named in honor of the first North Carolina soldier killed in action at Big Bethel in June 1861, one of the first land battles of the war.

Camp Yates (Sangamon) IL
Near Springfield, was named for Richard Yates (1818–1873), governor of Illinois, 1861–1865, who was active in raising troops throughout the war and suppressing Southern activists.

Campbell's Station (Loudon) TN
The first settlement here just south of Knoxville was a fort built in 1787 by Captain David Campbell (1753–1832). Federal troops fought a successful delaying action here, on the East Tennessee & Georgia Railroad, in November 1863 during the Knoxville campaign, though General William P. Sanders was mortally wounded in the course of it. (The name is no longer in use.)

Canton (Madison) MS
On the Big Black River, it was probably called after the Chinese seaport, at a time when exotic names were in vogue, or it may derive from a canton, a French administrative sub-division of land. It was the scene of skirmishing in July 1863, and again in February and March 1864.

Cape Fear River NC
Takes its name from Cape Fear at the southern tip of Smith Island, the site of several miles of treacherous sand bars known as Frying Pan Shoals. The river was the entrance to Wilmington, the Confederacy's last major port, captured in February 1865.

Cape Girardeau (Cape Girardeau) MO
Was named for Jean Baptiste de Girardot, a French soldier who built a temporary trading post here c.1733. The "Cape" was a rock promontory overlooking the Mississippi River and already known as Cape Girardot or Girardeau by 1765. A permanent trading post and settlement was established in 1793, laid out c.1806 and named in 1812. Occupied by Federal troops in July 1861, it became an important communications center. General Ulysses S. Grant assumed command here in south-eastern Missouri at the beginning of September. A Confederate attack in April 1863 was repulsed and there was more fighting near here in February and December 1864.

Carlisle (Cumberland) PA
First settled in 1720, it was laid out in 1751 and named after the English town of Carlisle. Before the war Carlisle was a station on the Underground Railroad and became a Union recruiting center. Carlisle Barracks, built in 1751, was burned with the rest of the town by General Stuart's Confederate cavalry in July 1863.

Carnifix Ferry (Nicholas) WV
Derives from a personal name. The engagement which took place here on the Gauley River in September 1861, involving General Rosecrans' Federals and General Floyd's Confederates, though inconclusive, nevertheless held western Virginia for the Union.

Carrollton (Carroll) AR
This and the following were named for Charles Carroll (1737–1832), a leader of the American Revolution and one of the signers of the Declaration of Independence. It was settled c.1840. There was skirmishing here in January 1863 and March 1864.

Carrollton (Carroll) MO
On the Missouri River, it was first settled in 1819 but not laid out till 1834. There was a skirmish here in August 1862. It surrendered to Confederate General Sterling Price in October 1864 during his raid into Missouri.

Cartersville (Bartow) GA

Was founded in 1832 as Birmingham, but renamed c.1850 for Colonel Farish Carter (1780–1861), a wealthy Milledgeville citizen who owned not only land, but gold mines, textile factories, grist mills, quarries and slaves. The Etowah Iron Works (named after the Etowah Mounds, the site of an ancient Indian village), owned by Mark Cooper, and possibly later by Quinby & Robinson of Memphis, were sold to the Confederate government in 1863. A leading supplier of iron, they were destroyed during the Atlanta campaign the following year. There was also a wool carding factory here which was state-run. Fighting took place at the depot on the Western & Atlantic Railroad in May 1864, there was further skirmishing around Cartersville in July and September, and in November the town was burned by General Sherman's troops.

Carthage (Jasper) MO

Laid out in 1842, it took its name from the ancient city in present-day Tunisia. An engagement here in July 1861 was claimed as a "victory" by pro-Confederate forces led by Governor Claiborne Jackson. It was the scene of further skirmishing in November 1862, January, May, June, September and October 1863 and September 1864, when it was burned by Confederate guerrillas.

Caruthersville (Pemiscot) MO

Was originally established as a French trading post on the Mississippi c.1794, though it was not laid out till 1857. It was named for the Hon. Samuel Caruthers (1820–1860), a lawyer and judge. There was a skirmish near here in December 1864.

Cassville (Bartow) GA

Was named for Lewis Cass (1782–1866), secretary of war under President Andrew Jackson, 1831–1836 and established in 1832 as a county seat. There was military activity here in May 1864 during the Confederate retreat to Atlanta, and the town was burned by Union troops in November in retaliation for attacks by Confederate guerrillas.

Castle Morgan (Dallas) AL

Was the nickname given to the Confederate prison camp at Cahaba, in honor of Confederate General John H. Morgan, whose successful escape from the Ohio Penitentiary was greatly admired.

Castle Pinckney see Shute's Folly Island

Castle Williams see Governors Island

Catoosa Station (Catoosa) GA

On the Western & Atlantic Railroad, this was the name of a Cherokee chief. It was the main detraining point for General Longstreet's corps when it was transported from Virginia in September 1863 to reinforce General Bragg's army, prior to the battle of Chickamauga. There was also skirmishing here in February 1864. (The name is no longer in use.)

Cedar Bluff (Cherokee) AL

The frequent occurrence of cedar trees makes this a common descriptive placename. This town was established in 1836. Samuel Noble's Cornwall Iron Furnace, established just before the war, produced pig iron for the Confederacy. Colonel Streight's raid through Alabama, an attempt to wreck the strategically important Western & Atlantic Railroad, ended in failure only 28 miles from his objective of Rome, Georgia, when after a skirmish he was tricked into surrendering to General Forrest's much smaller force in early May 1863, here on the Coosa River.

Cedar Creek (Frederick) VA

Union Generals Daniel D. Bidwell and Charles R. Lowell were mortally wounded in October 1864, at "the last great battle in the Shenandoah Valley," but General Sheridan's belated arrival from Winchester helped save the day for the Federals and inspired Thomas Buchanan Read's poem, "Sheridan's Ride." This Union victory is also known as Belle Grove (q.v.). Confederate General Stephen D. Ramseur, badly wounded during Sheridan's counterattack, died the next day. Cedar Creek is a branch of the Shenandoah River.

Cedar Key (Levy) FL

The western terminus of the Florida Railroad, it was attacked by the Union Navy in January

1862 when blockade runners and other vessels and some railroad flatcars were burned. A saltworks here was raided twice by U.S. marines in October 1862 and there was further skirmishing in February 1865.

Cedar Mountain (Culpeper) VA

Another example of a descriptive placename, deriving from the presence of cedar trees. Though the engagement here in August 1862, part of the Second Manassas campaign, was a Confederate victory, it was a close-run thing and diminished by the loss of General Charles S. Winder, who was mortally wounded.

Cedar Springs (Dallas) TX

A saltworks owned by a Mr. Lucas were located here, as were the Dallas Steam Mills, owned by W.A. Gould, which had several Confederate contracts and could supply 500 bushels of wheat or flour every 24 hours.

Celina (Clay) TN

Commemorates Celina Fisk (1814–1884), a daughter of Moses Fisk, a pioneer educator. Skirmishing occurred here in March 1865.

Centralia (Boone) MO

Was established in 1857 on the proposed route of the North Missouri Railroad (1859). It was given a pseudo-Latin name indicating its central position on the road, between St. Louis and Ottumwa, Iowa. Centralia was the scene of a massacre of Federal soldiers by Confederate guerrillas led by William ("Bloody Bill") Anderson in September 1864.

Centreville (Fairfax) VA

Was established in 1792 and so called because of its central location. President Jefferson Davis and Generals Joseph E. Johnston, Pierre G.T. Beauregard and Gustavus W. Smith discussed strategy here at the beginning of October 1861. John R. Thompson, Richmond correspondent of the *Memphis Appeal*, described it then as "a long straggling street, with dilapidated houses at considerable intervals, the roadway very much obstructed by rocks ... camps all around, horses hitched to every rail of the tumbledown fences." Johnston's troops withdrew from here in March 1862. Because of its location, Centreville featured in both battles of Bull Run, and there was further skirmishing near here in September and October 1863.

Chalk Bluff (Clay) AR

The self-evident name of a settlement which began in the early 1840s as a ferry crossing on the St. Francis River. There was skirmishing here in April 1863 and again in May, after General Marmaduke's return from his raid into Missouri, when he built rough fortifications on the bluff. In May 1865, General Meriwether ("Jeff") Thompson of the Missouri State Guard surrendered his command here to Union General Grenville M. Dodge. Chalk Bluff ceased to exist after its residents moved to St. Francis, a railroad town, in the early 1880s.

Chambersburg (Franklin) PA

Was laid out in 1764 by landowner, physician, judge and militia colonel Benjamin Chambers (1708–1788), for whom it was named. It was the target of a raid by General Stuart's cavalry in October 1862, when quantities of military equipment and clothing were seized or destroyed. In late July 1864 it received another visit from Confederates, this time under General John McCausland, and was burned when its inhabitants refused to pay a levy of $100,000 in gold or $500,000 in greenbacks, as compensation for damage done to property in Virginia. "They deliberately went from house to house & fired it. The whole heart of the town is burned. They gave us no time for people to get any thing out," wrote local diarist Rachel B. Cormany, and the destruction was still evident a year later when a Connecticut writer visited the town: "On every side were the skeletons of houses burned by the Rebels, and we looked across their roofless and broken walls at the red sunset."

Chancellorsville (Spotsylvania) VA

In 1816 George Chancellor announced that his "large and commodious" roadside inn called Chancellorsville, built the previous year, was now open for business. By 1863 it was the home of Mrs. Sanford Chancellor and her children, and General Joseph Hooker made it his headquarters. The battle of Chancellorsville at the beginning of May 1863 resulted in a Confederate victory, marred by the accidental and ultimately fatal shooting of General "Stonewall" Jackson by his own men; General Elisha F.

Paxton was also killed. In addition, Union General Hiram G. Berry was killed, and Generals Amiel W. Whipple and Edmund Kirby were mortally wounded. "Of Chancellorsville House, formerly a large brick tavern, only the half-fallen walls and chimney stacks remained," noted a visitor in September 1865.

Chantilly (Fairfax) VA

Was called after the Chantilly Plantation, named for a town in northern France. Two Union generals—Philip Kearny and Isaac I. Stevens—were killed in the battle here at the beginning of September 1862; it was a Confederate victory. There was further skirmishing near here in February, March and October 1863.

Chapel Hill (Orange) NC

The name derives from New Hope Chapel, built in 1752 at the junction of the New Bern and Petersburg roads. A community was founded in 1819 to serve the University of North Carolina which had been established here. Described by one resident as "the safest place in the Confederate States," it naturally attracted refugees during the war. There was a skirmish near here in April 1865.

Charles Town (Jefferson) WV

Was named for Colonel Charles Washington (1737–1799), George Washington's brother, and laid out in 1786. The scene of John Brown's trial and execution in 1859, it witnessed skirmishing in July 1861, May and November 1862, February and May 1863, March, May-August and November 1864, and February-April 1865. Generals Ulysses S. Grant and Philip H. Sheridan met here to confer in September 1864 about General Early's supply lines in the Shenandoah Valley.

Charleston (Coles) IL

Settled in 1826, it was named for Charles Morton, its first postmaster. Here Abraham Lincoln practiced and held his fourth debate with Stephen Douglas in 1858. An anti-war riot broke out in March 1864 when Federal soldiers on furlough were attacked here, leaving five men dead and more than 20 wounded.

Charleston (Mississippi) MO

It took its name from Charleston, South Carolina, when it was founded in 1837. There were skirmishes here in August and December 1861, a Confederate camp was broken up in October 1861 by Federals from Illinois, and further skirmishing occurred in January 1862, and February, April and November 1864.

Charleston (Charleston) SC

Founded in 1670, it was named in honor of King Charles II (1630–1685) and originally known as Charles Town, but renamed after 1783. The Citadel Academy, established that year, became part of the South Carolina Military Academy in 1861.

A naval station, opened in late 1861, constructed gunboats and ironclads in 1862–1864 and served as the base for the Charleston Squadron; there was also a naval hospital. The arsenal, seized by state troops in December 1861 and later handed over to the Confederate government, manufactured small-arms ammunition and shells. Cameron, Taylor & Johnson, also known as Cameron & McDurmit or the Phoenix Iron Works, made wrought iron cannon. The Palmetto Button Factory, established by Bernard Schurr, produced buttons for South Carolina troops, and the Soldiers' Relief Association and the Ladies' Clothing Association, both established in July 1861, made uniforms. Union prisoners were held at a number of places in Charleston, including Castle Pinckney, the City Jail, the Guard House, the Roper Hospital and the Race Course.

Martial law was imposed between May and August 1862, following the fall of Fort Donelson and then New Orleans. Unsuccessful attempts to capture Charleston—the "Cradle of Secession"—were made in April and July 1863, and in August the "Swamp Angel," an eight-inch parrott gun using 200 pound shells, caused great alarm but little damage. There were further bombardments in December that year, but it was not finally abandoned by the Confederates till February 1865. "The Rebel troops, departing, adhered to their usual custom of leaving ruin behind them. They fired the upper part of the city, burning an immense quantity of cotton with railroad buildings and military stores," observed a Northern writer who came here in early 1866.

Charleston (Bradley) TN

Was also named after Charleston, South Carolina. There was skirmishing here during a Union raid on the East Tennessee & Georgia Railroad in November 1863, with further fighting later that month and in December, and in August 1864.

Charleston (Kanawha) WV

Developed around Fort Lee, named for Governor Henry Lee of Virginia and erected in 1788 at the confluence of the Elk and Great Kanawha Rivers. The town was founded in 1794 by Colonel George Clendenin and named for his father, Charles Clendenin. Originally called Charles Town, its present name dates from 1818. It was occupied by Federal troops in July 1861, but evacuated by them in September 1862. Charleston became the state capital of West Virginia when it was made a separate state in June 1863. There was further fighting in October 1863. The jail here was used as a U.S. military prison in 1862–1863. It became a salt producing area with salt workings on the Great Kanawha River, but these were abandoned in November 1862.

Charlotte (Mecklenburg) NC

First settled in 1750 by British, German, Swiss and Huguenot immigrants, it was named for Princess Charlotte of Mecklenburg-Strelitz (1744–1818), who married King George III in 1761.

The North Carolina Military Institute, founded in 1859, closed when most of the instructors and cadets joined the 1st North Carolina Infantry. By the fall of 1861, refugees from the coast were already flocking here, and a year later a newspaper correspondent wrote, "Charlotte is filled up with refugees," attracted by the prospect of work in the government factories.

The Charlotte Navy Yard was established in May 1862, when the Confederate Navy leased the Mecklenburg Iron Works for the ordnance stores and equipment brought from the Norfolk Navy Yard when that was evacuated. Naval gun carriages and projectiles were made here, and there was an important naval storehouse and hospital. The pre-war Rock Island Manufacturing Co. established here by Messrs Young and Wriston, produced cloth for uniforms for both North and South Carolina troops.

Union prisoners transferred from Columbia were here for a few months in 1865. The last full meeting of the Confederate cabinet was held here in April 1865 when Jefferson Davis and his party stayed in the town for eight days and learned of Lincoln's assassination.

Charlottesville (♦) VA

First settled c.1737 on the Rivanna River, the town was established in 1762 and also named for Queen Charlotte, wife of King George III. General Carnot Posey, CSA, died here in November 1863 from a wound received the previous month at Bristoe Station. The Delevan Hospital was located here and Charlottesville was one of many places in Virginia which became a center for refugees. There were cavalry skirmishes in February and June 1864, and it was occupied, unopposed, by General Sheridan's troops in March 1865.

Chatham (Pittsylvania) VA

Established in 1777, it was named for William Pitt, Earl of Chatham (1708–1778), British prime minister, 1756–1757 and 1766–1767. The firm of Bilhartz, Hall & Co. began manufacturing carbines here in 1862.

Chattahoochee River GA

Derives from a Creek word meaning "painted stone" or "marked rocks" found in the river. In July 1864 Federal forces crossed the Chattahoochee as the Confederates fell back on Atlanta, with fighting at Peachtree Creek (q.v.).

Chattanooga (Hamilton) TN

Originally established in 1815 on the Tennessee River by John Ross as Ross's Landing, the city of Chattanooga was founded in 1838 and became important as a center of salt trading. The name derives from a Creek word meaning "rock rising to a point," what we know as Lookout Mountain. It was occupied by Confederates from March 1862 to September 1863. A number of Confederate hospitals—Academy, Bragg, Buckner, Foard, Gilmer and Newsom—were located here; Newsom was subsequently moved to Cleveland, Tennessee, and Academy, Foard and Gilmer to Marietta, Georgia.

Chattanooga was an important rail center—the meeting place of the East Tennessee & Georgia, the Nashville & Chattanooga and the Western & Atlantic Railroads—and its loss was a major blow to the Confederacy. A Federal army was besieged here from late September 1863 after its defeat at the battle of Chickamauga. The siege ended in November with a three day battle and a Union victory. Major machine shops and locomotive repair facilities for the U.S. Military Railroad were established here, as at Nashville. A Northern newspaper correspondent called it "a dirty, dusty garrison town," and another Northerner who came here in December 1865 referred to "its multitude of long, low, whitewashed wooden buildings, government storehouses, barracks, shops, rows of huts and corrals such as make haste always to spring up around an army's base of supplies."

Cheat Mountain (Randolph) WV

It takes its name from the Cheat River, of which there are several theories about the origin, the most likely being that it derives from the deceptive nature of its depth or the variableness of the volume of water. A key location in this part of western Virginia, an attempt by Confederates under General Robert E. Lee to take it during several days of fighting in incessant rain in September 1861, failed and brought him considerable criticism and the unenviable nickname of "Granny" Lee.

Cheraw (Chesterfield) SC

On the Pee Dee River, it was settled in 1752 and derives from an Indian tribal name. The Cheraw Tannery & Shoe Factory made shoes and infantry equipment for South Carolina troops, there was a Confederate supply depot here and towards the end of the war the town attracted so many refugees, they almost outnumbered the residents. After a skirmish nearby in late February 1865, Federal troops entered the town at the beginning of the following month.

Cherokee Station (Colbert) AL

The Cherokees were regarded as one of the Five Civilized Tribes because they had a written language and a formal constitution. On the Memphis & Charleston Railroad, this was the scene of fighting in April and October 1863.

Chester (Delaware) PA

Now a suburb of Philadelphia, Chester, on the Delaware River, is the second oldest settlement in Pennsylvania. First settled in 1644, it was in turn Swedish, Dutch, then English by 1664. It was named in 1682 by William Penn after Chester, England, the original home of many of the settlers who came here. It was the site of the Pennsylvania Military College, founded in 1821, and there was a military prison here in 1863, housed in a converted building.

Chesterfield (Chesterfield) SC

Was named for Philip Stanhope, Earl of Chesterfield (1694–1773), English statesman, wit and letter-writer. After a skirmish nearby, it was occupied by General Sherman's troops at the beginning of March 1865.

Chewalla (McNairy) TN

Comes from an Indian word, probably meaning "cedar." There was skirmishing near here in early October 1862 as Confederates under General Earl Van Dorn withdrew following the battle of Corinth.

Chicago (Cook) IL

Started life in 1803 as Fort Dearborn, named for secretary of war Henry Dearborn. The name Chicago comes from an Algonquin word meaning "place of garlic" or "wild onions" which originally grew here. The settlement began in 1830, and expanded with the completion of the Illinois & Michigan Canal in 1848 and the first railroad connection in 1853. By the time of the Civil War, newspapers were calling it "the great metropolis of the west" with "its bustling, struggling, eager commercial life."

The Northwestern Sanitary Fair, organized by Mary A.R. Livermore and Jane Hoge on behalf of the U.S. Sanitary Commission, the first of many across the North, was held in October-November 1863 and raised nearly $100,000 to provide aid and comforts to soldiers. The Democratic National Convention, meeting in August 1864 to choose a candidate for president, voted for General George B. McClellan.

In November 1864, Colonel Benjamin J. Sweet, the commandant of nearby Camp Douglas, imposed martial law across Chicago in the face of a supposed plot to free Confederate prisoners-of-war and take over the city. A number of people were arrested and went on trial at Cincinnati. The body of President Lincoln lay in state here at the beginning of May 1865 as thousands paid their respects, and it was a state rendezvous point for the mustering out of Illinois regiments.

Chickahominy River VA

Is from an Indian word meaning "land of much grain," so called because of its fertile surroundings. It featured in many of the Seven Days' battles, during the Peninsula campaign, May-June 1862, and was another name for Gaines' Mill or First Cold Harbor (q.v.). Beaver Dam Creek (q.v.), another of the engagements, is a branch of the Chickahominy.

Chickamauga Creek (Catoosa) GA

Chickamauga Creek is a branch of the mighty Tennessee. Confederate nurse Kate Cumming who visited it in September 1862, referred in her journal to the Indian legend from which it took its name: a desperate battle between two tribes, "with great slaughter on both sides," caused it to be known as Chickamauga. This was the American version of a Cherokee word which might mean "River of Death," though this is uncertain. A year later, in the two-day battle in September 1863, there was more "great slaughter," with more than 34,000 casualties. Among them were Confederate Generals James Deshler and Preston Smith who were killed, and Benjamin H. Helm and Colonel James A. McMurry, sometimes referred to as a general, mortally wounded; Union General William H. Lytle was also mortally wounded. Though a Confederate victory, it was not followed through, and General George H. Thomas gained the nickname the "Rock of Chickamauga" when he saved the battered Union Army from total defeat and rout.

Chickasaw Bluffs (Warren) MS

Comes from an Indian tribal name. An unsuccessful attempt was made to attack this Confederate stronghold north of Vicksburg, overlooking Chickasaw Bayou and the Yazoo River, in late December 1862, during the first Vicksburg campaign. Fighting lasted several days and there were heavy Union losses.

Chicopee (Hampden) MA

First settled in the 17th century at the confluence of the Chicopee and Connecticut Rivers, it was and still is part of Springfield. Its name, dating from 1848, derives from a Nipmuck word meaning "swift or violent water." It became one of the stations on the Underground Railroad for runaway slaves. The Ames Manufacturing Co. of James T. Ames produced smoothbore Napoleon cannon as well as cavalry sabers and swords for the Union Army.

Cincinnati (Hamilton) OH

Founded on the Ohio River in 1788, it had several rapid changes of name before becoming Cincinnati in 1790, in honor of General Arthur St. Clair, governor of the Northwest Territory, 1787–1802, and president of the Pennsylvania Society of the Cincinnati, named after the Roman general Cincinnatus. It developed with the opening of the Miami & Erie Canal in 1832.

In May 1862 the "Black Regiment," a short-lived labor battalion, helped build fortifications around the city. A Union Army quartermaster depot was located here. Miles, Greenwood & Co. manufactured smoothbore cannon for the Union Army at their Eagle Iron Works, and both they and McWhinney, Ridge & Co. made a small number of prototype machine guns for the inventor Dr. Richard Gatling. McLean Barracks were converted into a military prison in 1863–1864.

Though Cincinnati became a focus of Copperhead influence in the Northwest, it was also a Union army recruiting center for southern Ohio and parts of Indiana and Kentucky. The approach of General Morgan's Confederate raiders in September 1862 and again in July 1863 caused alarm, leading the authorities to declare martial law, and there was skirmishing nearby. In January 1865 the eight ringleaders of the plot to seize control of Camp Douglas and capture the city of Chicago the previous November went on trial here before a military commission and were given harsh prison sentences. It became a state rendezvous point for the demobilization of Ohio troops at the end of the war.

Citronelle (Mobile) AL

Was settled in 1811 and took its name from the citronella grass common in these parts. Confederate General Richard Taylor surrendered the troops of the Departments of Alabama, Mississippi and East Louisiana to General Edward R.S. Canby here in early May 1865. At the same time, arrangements were also made for the surrender of remaining Confederate naval forces to Rear Admiral Henry K. Thatcher.

City Point (Prince Edward) VA

One of Virginia's oldest settlements, it was founded in 1613 at the confluence of the James and Appomattox Rivers, but in spite of its name, was still only a small village at the time of the Civil War. Between June 1864 and April 1865, however, it became a major supply depot for Union troops besieging Petersburg and Richmond, and a busy port. New wharves and warehouses were built, and eventually seven hospitals, the largest being the Depot Field Hospital. It was also the terminus of the Petersburg & City Point Railroad, rebuilt by the U.S. Military Railroad as a supply line.

General Ulysses S. Grant, who made his headquarters here in 1864–1865, had a narrow escape when Confederate agents detonated ammunition on board a nearby Union transport in August 1864, killing 70 men and wounding 130 more. President Lincoln visited City Point twice, in June 1864 and March 1865, when he met with Generals Grant and Sherman and Rear Admiral Porter. (Now part of Hopewell.)

Clarksville (Montgomery) TN

Founded in 1784 and named for General George Rogers Clark (1752–1818), frontiersman, military leader, and brother of William Clark (of Lewis and Clark fame). The Clarksville Foundry & Machine Works made cannon and cannon balls for the Confederate Army. It was occupied by Federal troops in February 1862, but surrendered to Confederate forces without a fight in August, only to be retaken by the Federals the following month. There was further skirmishing here in October 1863. It was also the site of a camp for contrabands.

Clarksville (Mecklenburg) VA

Was named in 1818 for its founder, Clarke Royster, a property owner on the Roanoke River. It became a major tobacco market and manufacturing center. The harness shops here, transferred from Richmond in May 1862, made artillery and cavalry saddles, harness and cartridge boxes.

Clarkton (Dunklin) MO

When laid out in 1860 it was named for Henry E. Clark, one of the contractors for the Weaverville-Clarkton Plank Road (the "Devil's Washboard"). It was the site of a skirmish in October 1862.

Cleveland (Bradley) TN

First settled in 1820, it was established in 1836 and named for Colonel Benjamin Cleveland (1738–1806), a Revolutionary War commander. The Tennessee Rolling Works processed copper from local mines and the Newsom Hospital was moved here from Chattanooga. It saw skirmishing in September and October 1863, in November during a Union raid on the East Tennessee & Georgia Railroad, in December and in April 1864.

Clifton (Wayne) TN

On the Tennessee River, it was apparently so called because of the cliffs in the area. General Forrest's cavalry crossed the river here in December 1862 on their way to attack General Grant's lines of communications. There was skirmishing in January 1863, and again in July and August 1864.

Clinton (Jones) GA

A number of places were named for DeWitt Clinton (1769–1828), governor of New York, 1817–1823, and the main promoter of the Erie Canal. There was fighting at this small village in July and November 1864 and the iron foundry was destroyed by General Sherman's troops.

Clinton (Hinds) MS

Originally an Indian agency, it was named in 1828 for DeWitt Clinton who had died that year. A Military Aid Society organized here in June 1861 made clothing for Mississippi troops. There was skirmishing near here in July and October 1863, and February and April 1864. It was the northern terminus of the Clinton & Port Hudson Railroad.

Cloutierville (Natchitoches) LA

Was established in 1822 on the plantation of Alexis Cloutier, for whom it was named. On the Cane River, it was the scene of skirmishing in March and April 1864.

Cloyd's Mountain (Pulaski) VA

This was probably named for Joseph Cloyd

(1742–1833), a major in Colonel William Preston's regiment of Virginia militia in the Continental Army in 1781, or another member of his family. An attack by a numerically superior force of Federals under General George Crook on the important Virginia & Tennessee Railroad in May 1864 resulted in vicious fighting around Cloyd's Mountain, a Confederate defeat and the mortal wounding of General Albert G. Jenkins, CSA.

Cockspur Island GA

Designed by French military engineer Simon Bernard and built in 1829–1847 to protect the city of Savannah, **Fort Pulaski** here was named for General Casimir Pulaski (1747–1779), a Polish nobleman who served in the Continental Army. Seized by Georgia troops in January 1861, it fell in April 1862 following a heavy Federal bombardment. It was used as a military prison in 1864–1865. The island got its name from the shape of its reef which was thought to resemble the spurs worn in cock-fighting matches.

Coffeeville (Yalobusha) MS

It may have been named for General John Coffee (1772–1833), who fought in the War of 1812 and the Creek War, or derive from the fact that coffee was once traded here. There was an engagement here on the Mississippi Central Railroad in December 1862 when Union cavalry was repulsed.

Cokesbury (Greenwood) SC

Was an amalgamation of the names of Thomas Coke (1747–1814) and Francis Asbury (1745–1816), British-born bishops of the Methodist Episcopal Church. Jefferson Davis and his party reached here at the beginning of May 1865 on their flight south from Richmond.

Cold Harbor (Hanover) VA

Attacks on well-entrenched Confederate positions at Cold Harbor, near Mechanicsville, just east of the Chickahominy, at the beginning of June 1864 resulted in massive Union casualties, leading General Ulysses S. Grant to call off further assaults after the third day; he later regretted that the last one had ever been ordered. First Cold Harbor (June 1862) was another name for the battle of Gaines' Mill (q.v.) in the Peninsula campaign. Cold Harbor, the site of a crossroads tavern, was a common place or locality name in England; it originally implied a walled shelter on a road.

Cold Spring (Putnam) NY

Is a fairly self-evident placename. The West Point or Cold Spring Foundry, across the Hudson River from the United States Military Academy, was established in 1814. It was operated by Robert P. Parrott, inventor of the rifled, muzzle-loading Parrott gun, and produced not only field pieces and ordnance but also boilers and steam engines. It was visited by President Lincoln in June 1862.

Columbia (Boone) MO

Started as a trading post called Smithton, established near the Missouri River in 1819 by the Smithton Land Co. founded by General Thomas A. Smith. It was renamed Columbia, the feminine version of Columbus, after Columbia, Kentucky, when a new town was laid out in the early 1820s, and one of many so named. The University of Missouri, founded here in 1839, trained officers for the U.S. Army. There was skirmishing near here in October 1862, January 1863, June and August 1864 and February 1865.

Columbia (Richland) SC

First settled c.1700, Columbia was founded in 1786 at the confluence of the Broad and Saluda Rivers as the state capital of South Carolina. It was also the site of the Arsenal Academy, founded in 1833 and part of the South Carolina Military Academy from 1861. Treasury notes were engraved and printed here from April 1862, and the Treasury Note Bureau was moved here in April 1864.

William Glaze had converted his Palmetto Iron Works into the Palmetto Armory in 1850, and as well as muskets, rifles, pistols, swords and sabers manufactured pre-war, it also made shells, roundshot and bullets and several cannon during the Civil War. The Congaree Iron Works, owned by John Alexander, made howitzers from donated iron. The Confederate Naval Powder Works were moved here from Petersburg in 1862, and the Atlanta Rolling Mill in 1864. An arsenal was established at the end of 1863 and the Asheville Armory became part of it. The Ladies' Industrial Association made clothing for South Carolina soldiers.

On his way back to Richmond from a visit to Georgia, President Davis received an enthusiastic welcome here in October 1864. As they marched towards it in February 1865, General Sherman's troops sang, "Hail, Columbia, happy land, If I don't burn you, I'll be damned!"

The city, then full of refugees who tried to flee, was looted indiscriminately and much of it destroyed by fire on the night it was captured. A Northern writer who came here just after the war painted a depressing picture: "The entire heart of the city is a wilderness of crumbling walls, naked chimneys and trees killed by flames. The fountains of the desolated gardens are dry, the basins cracked; the pillars of the houses are dismantled or overthrown; the marble steps are broken."

Columbia (Maury) TN

On the Duck River, it was settled in 1807. Confederate General N. Bedford Forrest was seriously wounded here when he was shot by a disgruntled junior officer in June 1863. There was fighting near here in July and September 1862, October 1864, and a three-day battle in November 1864. It was occupied by General Hood's Army of Tennessee that month, but abandoned by them in December following the battles of Franklin and Nashville.

Columbiana (Shelby) AL

Is a manufactured name, from Columbia + na. The C.B. Churchill Co. which made shells for the Confederate Army, moved here from Corinth in 1862 after its capture; the plant was destroyed in April 1865 during General Wilson's Alabama raid. Columbiana was also the site of the Shelby Iron Co. which did work for the Confederate War and Navy Departments.

Columbus (Muscogee) GA

Founded in 1828 as a trading post on the Chattahoochee River, it was one of many towns named for Christopher Columbus (1451–1506), the Spanish explorer and discoverer of the New World.

The Columbus Iron Works, established in 1853, was taken over to become the Confederate States Naval Iron Works and produced steam engines, cannon and two gunboats for the C.S.N. The Confederate Navy Yard was opened in late 1862, building and repairing warships, including the gunboat *Chattahoochee* after her disastrous boiler explosion; an arsenal, opened in the same year, manufactured small-arms ammunition and artillery shells, as well as harness and knapsacks; and a quartermaster depot supplied uniforms, shoes, weapons and equipment. The Eagle Manufacturing Co. made cloth for both state and Confederate uniforms, and the Water Proof Cloth Co. made waterproof overcoats. Lee, Marshall and Walker Hospitals were also located here, as well as a parole camp.

Its many employment opportunities attracted refugees who came here in large numbers. Columbus was captured by General Wilson's Federal cavalry in April 1865 and all the town's military installations, locomotives and railroad cars and even an ironclad ram were wrecked.

Columbus (Hickman) KY

Situated on the Mississippi River, it was once proposed as the site for a new federal capital after the burning of Washington in 1814. Its Confederate fortifications caused it to be known as the "Gibraltar of the West." One of its huge guns exploded in November 1861, killing seven men and injuring General Leonidas Polk. Shelled by the Federals in January 1862, it was occupied by them at the beginning of March after it was evacuated by its defenders. Strategically placed as the terminus of the Mobile & Ohio Railroad, it subsequently became a major Federal supply depot and its jail was used as a military prison.

Columbus (Lowndes) MS

On the Tombigbee and Luxapalila Rivers, it was called Possum Town in 1817 when first settled, but received a more dignified name in 1821. It became a hospital center after the battle of Shiloh in April 1862. A Confederate arsenal, established here early in 1862, using ordnance stores moved from Tennessee, was transferred to Selma, Alabama, in 1863. It became the temporary state capital after the fall of Jackson in May 1863.

Thomas Leech and Charles Rigdon moved here from Memphis in 1862 and made revolvers for the Confederate Army until forced to move to Greensboro, Georgia, later that year. After their partnership was dissolved at the end of 1863, Rigdon moved to Augusta, Georgia, where he went into partnership with Jesse Ansley. The

Choctaw Factory near here made cloth for uniforms for Mississippi troops, while Sherman & Ramsay made shirts for the Confederate quartermaster depot here, and Hale & Sykes supplied hats and caps.

Columbus (Franklin) OH

When first settled in 1797 on the Scioto River it was called Franklinton, probably for Benjamin Franklin. It was laid out in 1812 as the new state capital and renamed in 1816. The coming of the Baltimore & Ohio Railroad in 1850 speeded its development. Columbus Barracks together with an arsenal were established in 1863, and the Ohio State Penitentiary was used as a military prison in 1863–1864. Confederate General John H. Morgan was imprisoned here in July 1863, but escaped in November. President Lincoln's body lay in state in Columbus at the end of April 1865. It was also a rendezvous point for the mustering out of Ohio troops.

Concord (Merrimack) NH

On the Merrimack River, it was first settled in 1727 and became Concord in 1765, apparently because many of the original inhabitants came from Concord, Massachusetts (named for a peaceful resolution of a boundary dispute between local Indians and settlers). It became the state capital in 1808. It was the scene of a disturbance in August 1861 when men of the 1st New Hampshire Volunteers attacked the office of the Concord *Democratic Standard* because of derogatory remarks it had made about them. In 1865 it was a state rendezvous point for the mustering out of New Hampshire troops.

Corinth (Alcorn) MS

Corinth was known as "the Crossroads of Ancient Greece" and Corinth, Mississippi, was called the "Crossroads of the Confederacy" because of its strategic importance, at the junction of the Memphis & Charleston and Mobile & Ohio Railroads. It was named in 1857.

Large numbers of Confederate troops were assembled here by rail in March 1862 prior to the battle of Shiloh and withdrew here afterwards. For most of April and May Corinth was full of badly wounded men. Volunteer nurse Kate Cumming was appalled by what she found on her arrival: "Nothing that I had ever heard or read had given me the faintest idea of the horrors witnessed here." The Tishomingo Hotel and Corona College were just two of the buildings used as hospitals. There was considerable skirmishing around Corinth during May and it was evacuated by the Confederates at the end of that month.

In July 1862 a soldier in the 15th Iowa noted in his diary that Corinth was now "full of 'fast womin' who have come in within a few days and are demoralizing many of the men." An attempt by the Confederates to retake the town in October of that year failed. In the course of a two day battle, Union General Pleasant A. Hackleman and Confederate Colonel John D. Martin, an acting brigadier general, were mortally wounded. A camp for contrabands was later set up here. The Federals themselves withdrew from Corinth in January 1864. John T. Trowbridge described it as "a bruised and battered village surrounded by forts, earthworks and graves" when he came here in December 1865.

Corpus Christi (Nueces) TX

Meaning "body of Christ," Corpus Christi Bay was first named by the Spanish in 1519 in commemoration of Corpus Christi day, the Thursday after Trinity Sunday. Founded at the mouth of the Nueces River in 1839 by Colonel Henry L. Kinney as Kinney's (Trading) Post, this was renamed after the bay c.1847. It was bombarded by Federal warships in August 1862 and in Union hands by October. Corpus Christi was reoccupied by Federal troops in November 1863, and there was further fighting in March 1864.

Corrick's Ford (Tucker) WV

On Shavers Fork River, its name derives from William Corrick (1800–1882), a local farmer. (It is also sometimes called Carrick's Ford.) General Richard S. Garnett, CSA, the first general officer to die in the Civil War, was mortally wounded near here on the Cheat River in July 1861. It was a Federal victory, only a week before the disaster at Bull Run and brought Union commander General George B. McClellan instant fame.

Corsicana (Navarro) TX

A Latinized form of "Corsica," it was named in 1848 for the wife of Jose Antonio Navarro, a Texas citizen of Mexican origin. J.T. Oakes made guns and pistols here for Texas troops. Locally raised units included the Corsicana Invincibles.

Corydon (Harrison) IN

Was founded c.1805 on land owned by William H. Harrison, governor of the Territory of Indiana, who named it after Corydon, a young shepherd in Greek and Latin pastoral poetry. Laid out in 1808, it was in turn the territorial capital of Indiana, 1813–1816, then the first state capital, 1816–1825. The town was raided by General John H. Morgan in July 1863, when the only battle on Indiana soil took place, involving home guards and militia.

Cotton Plant (Woodruff) AR

Was laid out in 1840 by local plantation owner William Lynch and has a descriptive name, referring to the growing of cotton here. There was skirmishing here in May and July 1862, and more fighting in April 1864.

Covington (Newton) GA

A number of towns were named for General Leonard W. Covington (1768–1813), a hero of the War of 1812. There were no fewer than six military hospitals in Covington, including the Hill, Hood and Lumpkin Hospitals, and the Southern Masonic Female College was also converted into one.

Covington (Campbell) KY

Now a suburb of Cincinnati, Covington, situated between the Ohio and Licking Rivers, was founded in 1815. There was a skirmish near here in September 1862. It was a rendezvous point for the demobilization of Kentucky troops in 1865.

Covington (♦) VA

Laid out in 1819, it was named for Peter Covington, the oldest inhabitant. It was the scene of fighting in November 1863 and June 1864.

Craney Island VA

At the time of the Civil War, when it was the site of Confederate batteries and later a camp for unemployed contrabands, Craney Island, in Hampton Roads, at the mouth of the Elizabeth River, really was an island. Its name derives from what were thought by early settlers to be cranes (they were actually herons). In May 1862, when Portsmouth and Norfolk were evacuated by the Confederates, the CSS *Virginia* was run ashore and set on fire here, her destruction ending with a vast explosion. It is now an extension of Portsmouth, and a military area under the control of the U.S. Army Corps of Engineers.

Crawford (Russell) AL

Founded in 1814 as Crockettsville, named for frontiersman Davy Crockett, it was renamed Crawford in 1843 for Joel Crawford (1783–1858), who had distinguished himself in the Creek War of 1813–1814. A skirmish took place here in April 1865.

Crittenden (Grant) KY

Was named for John J. Crittenden (1787–1863), governor of Kentucky, 1848–1850, who gave his name to the Crittenden Compromise (1860), an unsuccessful attempt at conciliation between North and South. There was fighting here in June 1864.

Cuba (Crawford) MO

Was established in 1857 on the proposed route of the St. Louis-San Francisco Railroad, and probably named for the island of Cuba. Fighting occurred here in May and September 1864.

Cubero (Cibola) NMT

Takes its name from Pedro Rodriguez Cubero (1645–1704), Spanish governor of New Mexico, 1699–1704. A Federal depot established here before the war for an anticipated campaign against the Navajo was captured by the Confederates in March 1862.

Culpeper Court House (Culpeper) VA

Was named for Sir Thomas Culpeper (1635–1689), governor of Virginia, 1680–1683, who obtained a land grant from King Charles II in 1673. It was a station on the Orange & Alexandria Railroad. Confederate General James Longstreet had his headquarters here from November 1862 to June 1863. Occupied by Federal troops in September 1863, there was skirmishing from then until December 1863. General Ulysses S. Grant made his headquarters here in March 1864.

Cumberland (Allegany) MD

Was founded as Fort Cumberland on the Potomac River in 1755, named for William Augustus, Duke of Cumberland (1721–1765), a son of King George II and a professional soldier. A settlement was laid out in 1785 and named Cumberland in 1787. It was a junction of the Baltimore & Ohio and the Cumberland & Pennsylvania Railroads, as well as the Chesapeake & Ohio Canal. Raided by Confederate cavalry in June 1862, it was again attacked in August 1864 by troops returning from their destructive raid on Chambersburg, and was also the target of an audacious night-time strike by partisan rangers in February 1865, when Union Generals Benjamin F. Kelley and George Crook were captured and sent to Libby Prison at Richmond.

Cumberland River KY/TN

Probably has the same name origin as the preceding entry. It witnessed the Confederate defeat at Logan's Crossroads (q.v.) in January 1862, the surrender of Fort Donelson (q.v.) in February, and there was further activity at the start of General Morgan's raid into Kentucky, Ohio and Indiana the following year. The Union Army of the Cumberland was in existence 1861–1864, its commanders including Generals William Rosecrans and George H. Thomas.

Cynthiana (Harrison) KY

It was established on the Licking River in 1793. Cynthia and Anna Harris were the daughters of Robert Harris, the first settler, and Cynthiana was an amalgamation of their names. It was twice attacked and captured by General Morgan's Confederate raiders, in July 1862 and June 1864.

Dallas (Paulding) GA

Was named for George M. Dallas (1792–1864), diplomat, politician and U.S. vice-president, 1845–1849. There was fighting here at the end of May 1864 during the early part of the Atlanta campaign.

Dallas (Dallas) TX

Was originally called Peters Colony, after William S. Peters of Louisville, Kentucky, and his associates formed the Texan Emigration Land Co. in 1841. Settlement here on the Trinity River began the following year and it was laid out in 1846. Dallas County was named for Vice-President George M. Dallas, and the city of Dallas is usually thought to have the same origin.

During the Civil War a Confederate quartermaster depot was located in the Dallas Hotel. The firm of Tucker, Sherrard & Co. was contracted to supply Texas troops with Colt revolvers in 1862, but was unable to do so fully and the contract was subsequently cancelled. Isiah W. Wells & Brother produced woolen and cotton clothing. The Eagle Ford Grist Mill Co., owned by Messrs. Horton and Newton, and Pleasant Run Mills, owned by T.C. Hawpe, both near here on the Trinity River, were operating in the fall of 1861, producing flour.

Dalton (Whitfield) GA

Founded in 1837; there are at least two explanations for the name. It may be from John Dalton, the engineer who laid out the town, or from the maiden name of the wife of Edward White, the leader of the syndicate that bought the site. A station on the Western & Atlantic Railroad, it was a suitable location for an ordnance depot, established in August 1862 for the Army of Tennessee. There was also a prison camp here in 1864.

Following his defeat at Chattanooga in November 1863, General Braxton Bragg, now at Dalton, resigned from command of the Army of Tennessee and was replaced by General Joseph E. Johnston who set up his headquarters in December. There was fighting around here in February 1864 and Johnston was forced to evacuate the town after several more days of fighting in May. The Union garrison was in turn forced to surrender to General Hood's army on its way north in October.

Dandridge (Jefferson) TN

Was named for Martha Dandridge Custis (1732–1802), George Washington's wife, and first settled in 1783. Fighting occurred here in January 1863, and January and May 1864.

Danville (Boyle) KY

First settled c.1775 and named for Walker Daniel, Kentucky's first district attorney, who bought the deed for the site, the town was founded in 1783–1784 and was the seat of government for the area, 1785–1792, till Kentucky became a state. There was skirmishing here in

October 1862, in March 1863, involving General Morgan's Confederate cavalry, and in January 1865.

Danville (Montgomery) MO

Established in 1834 on land belonging to Daniel M. Boone, the son of Daniel Boone, it was probably named for him. It was attacked by "Bloody Bill" Anderson's Confederate guerrillas in October 1864.

Danville (♦) VA

Founded in 1793, it took its name from the Dan River, which has a biblical origin: the city of Dan was in the north of the Holy Land (present-day Israel). Six tobacco warehouses were converted into military prisons to house prisoners transferred from Richmond in 1863 and 1864; an ordnance depot was in operation here in 1862–1865, as well as an arsenal; and the firm of Keen, Walker & Co. made breech-loading carbines. Danville was one of a number of places in Virginia popular with refugees. It was also the first stop on Jefferson Davis's flight from Richmond at the beginning of April 1865. He arrived by train and stayed for seven days, and it has become known as the "Last Capital of the Confederacy."

Dardanelle (Yell) AR

Was laid out in 1843 on the site of a Cherokee trading post. The name may derive from *Derdonnai* (Indian-French) or from Jean Baptiste Dardenne, a former landowner. Its situation on the Arkansas River may also have suggested a similarity with the Dardanelles, the straits in Turkey. It changed hands several times during the Civil War. Skirmishing in May and August 1864 was followed by an attack on a steamer by Confederate guerrillas in November.

Darien (McIntosh) GA

Established on the Altamaha River in 1736 by families from the Scottish Highlands, it was originally called New Inverness, but later renamed Darien, after the Isthmus of Darien in Panama, an example of exotic usage. It was attacked and burned by Federal troops in June 1863, and the salt works were destroyed in September.

Darkesville (Berkeley) WV

Named for General William Darke (1736–1801), an officer in the Revolutionary War, it was established in 1791. Skirmishing occurred here in December 1862, and July and September 1864.

Dauphin Island AL

At the entrance to Mobile Bay, this was called Dauphine Island in 1708 for the wife of Dauphin Louis, Duke of Burgundy. (Dauphin was the title of the heir to the French throne.) Federal troops landed here at the beginning of August 1864 with the intention of capturing **Fort Gaines**, one of several forts named for General Edmund P. Gaines (1777–1849), who served in the War of 1812, the Seminole Wars and the Mexican War. Built in 1853–1861, it had been taken over by Alabama militia in January 1861 and strengthened, but it surrendered after the Confederate naval defeat at the battle of Mobile Bay in August 1864.

David's Island NY

In Long Island Sound, it was named for Thaddeus David (1816–1894), an ink manufacturer. It was the site of **Fort Slocum**, named for General Henry W. Slocum (1827–1894), and De Camp General Hospital. A military prison, consisting of barracks and tents, was also here in 1863–1865.

Dayton (Rockingham) VA

May be named for Jonathan Dayton (1760–1824), a member of the Continental Congress and speaker of the House of Representatives, 1795–1799. Following the murder in October 1864 of staff officer Lieutenant John Meigs (son of Quartermaster General Montgomery Meigs), apparently by Confederate guerrillas, General Philip H. Sheridan ordered all houses within five miles of this village to be burned in retaliation. He subsequently revoked the order, replacing it with one seizing all able-bodied men in the area as prisoners-of-war.

Decatur (Morgan) AL

Established in 1820 as a ferry crossing on the Tennessee River, it was named in 1826 for Commodore Stephen Decatur (1779–1820), a hero of the War of 1812. It was occupied by Federal troops in April 1862 and a camp for contrabands was set up here. It was the scene of fighting between March and May 1864. General Hood's Army of Tennessee was here briefly in October 1864, after the fall of Atlanta, and there was further skirmishing near here in December.

Decatur (Dekalb) GA

Was settled by people from Virginia and the Carolinas and also named for Stephen Decatur. There was fighting here during General Sherman's advance on Atlanta in July 1864.

Decherd (Franklin) TN

Was named for Peter Decherd, who came here in 1831 and established a plantation. Wounded at Mill Springs in January 1862, General Robert L. McCook was subsequently murdered near here by Confederate guerrillas while traveling in an ambulance. His Ohio regiment hanged several of his assailants in revenge. Fighting also occurred near here in June 1863 during General Rosecrans' Tullahoma campaign.

Detroit (Wayne) MI

Was founded in 1701 as Fort Pontchartrain du Détroit (Fort Pontchartrain on the Straits, i.e. those between Lakes St. Clair and Erie), by French explorer Antoine de la Motte, and named in honor of his patron, the Comte de Pontchartrain, Louis XIV's minister of state. The settlement which grew up around it became known as Detroit and was turned over to the United States in 1796. It served as the capital of Michigan Territory, 1805–1837, and of the state, 1837–1847. A meeting held here in July 1862 to answer President Lincoln's call for troops was broken up by anti-war protesters and Confederate sympathizers from across the Canadian border, though a second meeting resulted in the raising of the 24th Michigan Infantry. In 1865 it was one of the assembly points for the demobilization of Michigan troops.

Dinwiddie Court House (Dinwiddie) VA

Took its name from Robert Dinwiddie (1693–1770), the Scottish-born lieutenant governor of Virginia, 1751–1758. There was fighting here at the end of March 1865.

Doaksville (Choctaw) IT

Was named for trader and storekeeper Josiah Doak and established between 1824 and 1831. It served as the capital of the Choctaw Nation, 1860–1863. Stand Watie, the only Indian to hold general's rank in the Confederate Army, surrendered his force of Cherokees, Creeks, Seminoles and Osages here in June 1865 to Lieutenant Colonel Asa C. Mathews. He was the last Confederate general to surrender.

Donaldsonville (Ascension) LA

Beginning as a trading post on the Mississippi c.1750, it was named in 1822 for William Donaldson, who developed land here from 1806 onwards. It served as the state capital in 1830–1831. Subjected to a Federal naval bombardment in August 1862, it was the scene of fighting in October, followed by its capture by the Federals when much of it was in ruins or burnt. It was attacked in turn by Confederates in June 1863, and there was more fighting in July and September of that year, and February, July and September 1864.

Doniphan (Ripley) MO

Was settled c.1847 and named for Colonel Alexander W. Doniphan (1808–1887), who commanded a force of Missouri volunteers in the Mexican War. Some skirmishing took place here in April 1862, June 1863 and September 1864, at the start of General Price's expedition to attempt to recover Missouri for the Confederacy.

Dover (Kent) DE

Originally founded in 1683 and named by William Penn after the famous English Channel port, it was laid out in 1717 and became the state capital of Delaware in 1777. In June 1861 a peace convention meeting here urged recognition of the Confederacy.

Dover (Strafford) NH

First settled in 1623, it was named in 1637 for Robert Dover (1575–1641), an English lawyer and soldier. The Union Powder Works here made gunpowder for the Union Navy.

Dover (Stewart) TN

Was laid out in 1806. The trade name of iron produced in the area apparently gave rise to this placename, though ultimately it also derives from Dover, England. Following the battle at Fort Donelson in February 1862, Confederate

Generals John B. Floyd, Gideon J. Pillow and Simon B. Buckner met here, on the Cumberland River, to discuss the fort's surrender, which took place the next day. Dover was subsequently burned by Union troops.

Dranesville (Fairfax) VA

Washington Drane (c.1790–c.1832) came here in 1810 from the District of Columbia, opened a tavern and also became its first postmaster. There was fighting in December 1861, and skirmishing in February 1863 and 1864, and March 1865.

Drewry's Bluff (Chesterfield) VA

Took its name from local landowner Major Augustus H. Drewry (1817–1899) of Westover Plantation. Seven miles south of Richmond, overlooking the James River, Drewry's Bluff was a key element in the defense of the Confederate capital, and fortifications, barracks and gun emplacements were constructed here early in 1862. It also became the site of the Confederate Naval Academy and the Marine Corps' Camp Beall. Two battles took place here, in May 1862 and again in May 1864. The first involved Federal ironclads and wooden warships, the second, an attempt by Federal troops to move on Richmond; both were repulsed.

Dublin (Pulaski) VA

Was named by the first settler, Irishman William Christian. A small ordnance establishment was set up here in 1861. A successful attempt by Union troops to cut the Virginia & Tennessee Railroad resulted in heavy fighting near here at Cloyd's Mountain in April 1864.

Ducktown (Polk) TN

The name, first recorded in 1799, is of uncertain origin. It may derive from a Cherokee chief called Duck; from a Cherokee village previously here known as *Kawana*, meaning "duck town;" or may refer to the large numbers of wild ducks in the area. Copper was discovered here in 1843 and mined from 1847 onwards, supplying most of the South's copper, with numerous companies operating in the 1850s. The mines were lost to the Confederacy in 1863, probably after the battle of Chattanooga.

Dumfries (Prince William) VA

Was established in the 1730s on Quantico Creek and named by early settler John Graham after his Scottish birthplace of Dumfries. It was the scene of a raid by Confederate General J.E.B. Stuart in December 1862 when he attacked the Union garrison here, stealing horses and supplies, and there was further fighting in March and May 1863.

Durham Station (Durham) NC

It was first settled c.1750 and originally called Prattsburg, for landowner William Pratt. When the North Carolina Railroad was being constructed in the early 1850s, the Pratt family refused to grant right-of-way or land for a station, which was subsequently named for Dr. Bartlett S. Durham (1822–1858), who donated four acres for this purpose, and the railroad bypassed Prattsburg. At James Bennett's farmhouse a few miles from here, in late April 1865, General Joseph E. Johnston surrendered the remaining Confederate troops under his command to General William T. Sherman.

Dyersburg (Dyer) TN

On the Forked Deer River, it was established in 1823 and named for Joel H. Dyer (1754–1825) who donated land for a new county seat. There was skirmishing here in August 1862.

Eagleville (Rutherford) TN

First settled c.1790, it was named Eagleville in 1836, supposedly because an unusually large eagle had been killed nearby. There was skirmishing here in March, April and December 1863.

Eatonton (Putnam) GA

Named for William Eaton (1764–1811), a Revolutionary War officer and naval agent to the Barbary States in North Africa. There was a skirmish here in November 1864.

Ebenezer Church (Chilton) AL

Derives from a Hebrew word meaning "stone of help" which became a popular 19th century name for churches and chapels. It was the scene of a cavalry engagement in April 1865 during General Wilson's raid to Selma, when the men of General Forrest's command were put to flight.

Edenton (Chowan) NC

First settled in 1658, it was already well established by 1710 and named in honor of Charles Eden (1673–1722), proprietary governor of North Carolina, 1714–1722. It served as the colonial capital, 1722–1766. Edenton was occupied by Federal forces from February 1862 until the end of the war, though there was skirmishing here in February 1863.

Edmonton (Metcalfe) KY

Edmund P. Rogers, a Virginian, who came here after the Revolutionary War, became a major landowner and is commemorated here, with variant spelling. He laid out the town which was established as a trading post in 1836. There was a skirmish here in June 1863.

Edwards' Depot (Hinds) MS

A short-lived settlement of the 1830s disappeared following an outbreak of cholera and the fact that it was bypassed, when the Southern Railroad of Mississippi arrived in 1839. This station, named for R.O. Edwards' nearby plantation, was the scene of considerable military activity in May 1863 during the second Vicksburg campaign, and skirmishing also occurred here in June and July. Edwards' Depot was burned and a new town was not established till after the war. (Now called Edwards.)

Egypt Station (Holmes) MS

Was established when the Mobile & Ohio Railroad arrived in 1858, and apparently so called because of the corn grown here — in the Bible, Egypt was the "land of corn" — though it may also be an example of the fashion for exotic names. There was a skirmish here in February 1864, and more fighting took place in December when General Samuel J. Gholson was severely wounded and along with 500 Confederates, about half of them former Union soldiers (galvanized Confederates), taken prisoner. (The name is no longer in use.)

Elizabeth (Wirt) WV

On the Little Kanawha River, it was originally called Beauchamp's Mills, 1796–1817, but was renamed for Elizabeth Beauchamp (d.1838), the wife of founder William Beauchamp. It was the site of a skirmish in October 1863.

Elizabeth City (Pasquotank) NC

Founded on the Pasquotank River in 1793, it was named Elizabeth Town for Elizabeth Tooley, the wife of landowner Adam Tooley; it became Elizabeth City in 1801. Some ship construction for the Confederate Navy was projected here. The remaining part of its "mosquito" fleet was destroyed by the Federals when they occupied the town in February 1862, and there was skirmishing in December.

Elizabethtown (Hardin) KY

Settled in 1780, it was laid out in 1793 by Colonel Andrew Hynes and named in 1797 for his wife. It was on the Louisville & Nashville Railroad. The Federal garrison here was captured by General Morgan's Confederate raiders in late December 1862.

Elkhorn Tavern (Benton) AR

Originally built c.1833, this crossroads tavern was sold in 1858 to Jesse Cox who named it Elkhorn Tavern, because an elk had been shot nearby and the horns given to him. During the battle of Pea Ridge (q.v.) in March 1862 it was used as a temporary hospital for Confederate wounded and was also briefly General Van Dorn's headquarters. The building was burned by bushwhackers in the following January but was subsequently rebuilt.

Ellis Island NY

It took its name from Samuel Ellis, who was the owner by 1785. In New York harbor, it was leased in 1794 by the state of New York, then acquired in 1808 by the Federal government who built Fort Gibson here. Named for an officer killed in the War of 1812, this was replaced in 1861 with a naval magazine and it was an ammunition supply depot during the Civil War. It was the site of the famous immigration station, 1892–1954.

Ellisville (Jones) MS

Was named for Powhatan Ellis (1790–1863), a member of the Supreme Court, U.S. senator and minister to Mexico, 1839–1842. In 1864 Confederate deserters and Unionists in Jones County, led by former shoemaker Newton Knight, resentful of being part of "a rich man's war and a poor man's fight," attempted to secede from the Confederacy. Declaring themselves the Free State of Jones (or Kingdom or Republic of Jones), they made Ellisville their capital and attacked both Confederate and Union supply depots.

Elmira (Chemung) NY

On the Chemung River, it was first settled c.1788 and named in 1808 for Phoebe Elmira Teall, the daughter of settler Nathan Teall. The Woolen Manufacturing Co. here made large amounts of cloth for army uniforms, and a former barracks was turned into a military prison for enlisted men, the first Confederates arriving in July 1864. Conditions at Elmira were little better than those at Andersonville, with half of the prisoners living in tents, even during the harsh Northern winters; food was scanty and the sickness rate very high. In 1865 Elmira was one of the state rendezvous points for the demobilization of New York troops.

Eltham's Landing (New Kent) VA

Took its name from the nearby Eltham Plantation on the Pamunkey River, which may have derived from Eltham in Kent, England, now in south-east London. The engagement here in May 1862 during the Seven Days' battles is also known as Barhamsville or West Point (q.v.).

Elyton (Jefferson) AL

Was established c.1819 by William Ely, surveyor-agent for a New England deaf and dumb asylum, who came to lay out land given it by the Federal government. Named Elyton, it was described by one modern historian as "a nondescript hamlet." Small furnaces and iron works were built here in 1863 to supplement those at Selma. There was skirmishing here in March 1865. Elyton later developed into the city of Birmingham.

Emmitsburg (Frederick) MD

The first settlers came here in the early 1780s and it was named in 1785 for local landowner William Emmit. There was a cavalry skirmish near here in July 1863 during the Gettysburg campaign, and the Daughters of Charity who were based here provided aid to the wounded from the battle. There was more fighting in July 1864.

Enon Church (Hanover) VA

A simplified form of *Aenon*, a biblical reference from the New Testament meaning "there was much water there." It is another name for the cavalry engagement in May 1864 known as Haw's Shop (q.v.).

Fairburn (Fulton) GA

Was named after a village in Yorkshire, England. There was fighting here in August 1864, and the Atlanta & West Point Railroad was earmarked for destruction by General Howard's Army of the Tennessee when it arrived later that month.

Fairfax Court House (Fairfax) VA

Thomas Fairfax, Lord Fairfax of Cameron (1692–1782), who settled in Virginia in 1747 and entrusted the young George Washington with the surveying and mapping of his estate in the Shenandoah Valley, is commemorated here. There was skirmishing in June, July and November 1861, September 1862, and January, June and August 1863. Colonel Mosby's Confederate raiders were active hereabouts, capturing General Edwin H. Stoughton in March 1863 and a wagon train in August.

Captain John Marr, killed here in June 1861, was the first Confederate officer to die in the war. General George B. McClellan met his newly appointed corps commanders here in March 1862. Union General Francis E. Patterson "was found dead in his tent ... killed by the accidental discharge of his own pistol," in a camp near here in November 1862.

Fairfax Station (Fairfax) VA

Lord Fairfax (1692–1782) is also remembered here. Volunteer nurse Clara Barton of Massachusetts arrived at Fairfax Station, on the Orange & Alexandria Railroad, in August 1862 during the second battle of Manassas, with two assistants and three railroad cars loaded with medical supplies, to give what help she could to the wounded. There was also skirmishing here in August and November 1864.

Fairmont (Marion) WV

A settlement on the Monongahela River (1793) became Middletown in 1819, then merged with nearby Palatine in 1843 to become Fairmont, a contraction of Fair Mountain. On the Baltimore & Ohio Railroad, it was a Federal supply center till captured in April 1863 during the Jones-Imboden West Virginia raid, when the B&O bridge over the river was also destroyed by the Confederates.

Falling Waters (Berkeley) WV
Established in 1815, its name refers to its position near the Potomac River. There was skirmishing here in July 1861, a Union success. Two years later, Confederate General James J. Pettigrew was mortally wounded here in an engagement during the retreat to the Potomac after the battle of Gettysburg, and there was further skirmishing in July 1864.

Falls Church (♦) VA
Took its name from the Great Falls on the Potomac River, and the Episcopalian church first built here in 1733. Abandoned in 1789, it was re-established in 1836 when Falls Church was beginning to develop. A balloon belonging to aeronaut Thaddeus S.C. Lowe was launched here in June 1861 to observe Confederate positions. There was fighting near here in November 1861, and further skirmishing in September 1862 and August 1863. The church was used as a hospital for Union wounded and later as a stable for cavalry horses.

Falmouth (Pendleton) KY
At the confluence of the Main and South Licking Rivers, it was established in 1799 and named after Falmouth, Virginia. Until the arrival of the Kentucky Central Railroad in 1854, it was a village of "mud roads, tin lanterns and tallow dips." It was the scene of a skirmish in September 1862.

Falmouth (Stafford) VA
Was first settled in 1727 and named after the seaport in Cornwall, England. General Ambrose E. Burnside set up his headquarters here in November 1862 and President Lincoln reviewed Union troops in April 1863 before they moved out later that month.

Farmington (St. Francois) MO
This and the following are descriptive names, indicative of good farmland. Farmington, Missouri, was laid out in 1823. There was skirmishing near here in July 1861, November 1863 and September 1864, and Confederate bushwhackers were pursued by Federal cavalry in April 1865.

Farmington (Marshall) TN
General Wheeler's cavalry, retreating from their middle Tennessee raid in early October 1863, was badly beaten in an encounter near here with Federal troops led by General George Crook.

Farmville (Prince Edward) VA
Settled in 1754 and also with a descriptive name, this tobacco town became popular with refugees and by May 1862 was already filled with them. It was the scene of fighting in the Appomattox campaign in April 1865, during which Union General Thomas A. Smyth was fatally wounded by a sniper.

Fayette (Howard) MO
The French Marquis de La Fayette (1757–1834) served in the Continental Army and was an associate of George Washington. His popularity in America is demonstrated by the number of towns named for him, as Fayette, Fayetteville or La Fayette. Skirmishing in July and August 1864 was followed by an attack on the town by General Price's Confederate troops, and there was further action in November.

Fayetteville (Washington) AR
First laid out in 1828, it was named in 1829, probably as a result of the Marquis de La Fayette's return visit to America in 1824–1825. There was fighting around Fayetteville in July, October and November 1862, culminating in the battle of Prairie Grove (q.v.) in December; Colonel Alexander E. Steen, who had been promised promotion to brigadier general, was among the Confederate dead. After an unsuccessful Confederate attack in April 1863, it remained in Union hands till the end of the war, though there was further skirmishing hereabouts in June, August and October 1863, May, June and August 1864 and January 1865.

Fayetteville (Cumberland) NC
On the Cape Fear River, it was founded in 1739 by Scottish settlers and originally called Campbelltown. They were joined in 1746–1747 by survivors from the battle of Culloden in the Jacobite Rebellion, who settled at Cross Creek. The two communities were united in 1783 and renamed Fayetteville the following year. It served as the state capital, 1789–1793.

The arsenal was seized by state militia in April 1861 and later turned over to the Confederate government, for whom it made and repaired pistols and rifles. It was destroyed, along with the relocated Atlanta Ordnance Works, when General Sherman's army arrived in March 1865.

Fayetteville (Franklin) PA
The iron works of Thaddeus Stevens, who was also a noted lawyer and politician and a vigorous opponent of slavery, were destroyed by General Early's Confederates in June 1863.

Fayetteville (Lincoln) TN
Was founded in 1809 and named after Fayetteville, North Carolina, where some of the settlers had previously lived. May 1862, and also October–December 1863 saw skirmishing here.

Fayetteville (Fayette) WV
First settled in 1818 and called Vandalia, for Abraham Vandal, it was laid out in 1836 and renamed for the Marquis de La Fayette the following year. Fighting broke out near here in November 1861, September 1862 and July 1863.

Fitchburg (Worcester) MA
On the Nashua River, it was first settled in 1730 and named for John Fitch (c.1707–1795), an early inhabitant and leading citizen. Its development was aided by the arrival of the Boston & Fitchburg and Vermont & Massachusetts Railroads. The Putnam Machine Co. made light rifled guns here in 1862.

Five Forks (Dinwiddie) VA
The meeting point of five roads, northwest of Dinwiddie Court House, it was the scene of an engagement during the Appomattox campaign at the beginning of April 1865, when Confederate forces under General George Pickett were overwhelmed and many were captured. It proved to be the turning point in the siege of Petersburg.

Florence (Lauderdale) AL
Was originally established as a trading post on the Tennessee River c.1779 and laid out in 1818. It was named by the Italian surveyor Ferdinand Sanona after his native city of Florence. During the Civil War the firm of Rice & Wright made howitzers here. Federal gunboats raided the town in February 1862, and there was skirmishing in April 1863, and April, May and October 1864. It was occupied by General Hood's Confederate troops at the end of that month, and there was further skirmishing in November.

Florence (Florence) SC
In the 1850s the Wilmington & Manchester Railroad built a depot at a place called the Wilds. This became the junction of the W. & M. and the Northeastern Railroad in 1853–1854, and the Cheraw & Darlington in 1859, and was renamed Florence for the baby daughter of William W. Harllee, a director of the W. & M., lieutenant governor of South Carolina and colonel of the Harllee Legion. Florence became important as a shipping center, a point of embarkation for Confederate troops, a hospital town and the site of a military prison. A stockade housed Union prisoners in 1864–1865, and some Irish and other foreign-born prisoners who were willing to enlist in the Confederate Army were concentrated here in October 1864. John H. Winder, commissary general of prisoners east of the Mississippi, died here in February 1865.

Forsyth (Monroe) GA
This was named for John Forsyth (1780–1841), governor of Georgia, 1827–1829, and secretary of state under Andrew Jackson and Martin Van Buren, 1834–1841. Hardee and Clayton Hospitals were located here.

Fort Abbott (Prince Edward) VA
A Union fort near City Point, possibly named for Major Henry L. Abbott of the 20th Massachusetts who was killed at the Wilderness in May 1864.

Fort Alexander see Fort Sumner

Fort Alexander Hays (Prince George) VA
At Petersburg, was named for Union General Alexander Hays (1819–1864), who was killed at the Wilderness; it was built in August–September 1864.

Fort Alexandria see Fort Ellsworth

Fort Amory (Craven) NC
Was a Union fort on the Trent River at James City, begun in 1862 and probably named for Thomas J.C. Amory (c.1830–1864). Colonel of the 17th Massachusetts, he died of yellow fever at New Bern. Camp Amory (q.v.) was also named for him.

Fort Anderson (McCracken) KY
At Paducah, on the Ohio River, it was probably named for General Robert H. Anderson (1805–1871), the "Hero of Fort Sumter," who commanded the Department of Kentucky, May–August 1861. It was attacked unsuccessfully by General Forrest's cavalry in March 1864.

Fort Anderson (Brunswick) NC
Overlooking the Cape Fear River, it was almost certainly named for Confederate General George B. Anderson (1831–1862), once colonel of the 4th North Carolina, who died from a wound received at Sharpsburg. It was bombarded by Federal warships and captured in February 1865.

Fort Anderson (Craven) NC
Probably also named for General Anderson, this was a Union fort on the Neuse River near New Bern.

Fort Arbuckle (Garvin) IT
Six miles west of Davis, on Wild Horse Creek, it was built in 1851 and named for Colonel Matthew Arbuckle (1776–1851), 7th U.S. Infantry. Evacuated by Federal troops in May 1861, it was taken over by Texas state troops.

Fort Archer see Fort Wheaton

Fort Armstrong see Rock Island

Fort Attaway (Floyd) GA
Built at Rome in 1863, it was named for Thomas Attaway, a Confederate soldier from there killed in the war.

Fort Baker DC
Part of the Washington defenses east of the Anacostia, it was named for Colonel Edward D. Baker (1811–1861) of the 71st Pennsylvania, who was killed at Ball's Bluff.

Fort "Baldy" Smith see Fort Marcy

Fort Bankhead (New Madrid) MO
A Confederate fort at New Madrid, built in 1862 and named for Colonel Smith P. Bankhead (1823–1867), who in that year was successively chief of artillery to Generals Leonidas Polk and John B. Magruder.

Fort Bankhead see Galveston Island

Fort Banks (Shenandoah) VA
At Strasburg, was probably named for Union General Nathaniel P. Banks (1816–1894), whose capture of Port Hudson in 1863 resulted in his being given the Thanks of Congress.

Fort Barker (Jackson) AL
Was constructed in 1862 by Colonel A.S. Barker to guard the approaches to Stevenson, a Union supply base.

Fort Barnard DC
South of the Potomac, it was built in 1861 and named for General John G. Barnard (1815–1882). As well as planning Washington's defenses, in 1861–1862 he also served with the Army of the Potomac, and was on General Grant's staff as "Chief Engineer of the Armies in the Field," 1864–1865.

Fort Barrancas (Escambia) FL
Originally a Spanish fort called San Carlos de Barrancas (*barranca* is Spanish for "bluff" or "ravine"), it was rebuilt in 1839–1843 to defend the Pensacola Navy Yard. Taken over by Florida troops in January 1861, it was bombarded by the guns of Fort Pickens and two Federal warships in November, but without much result. There was a further inconclusive bombardment at the beginning of January 1862, but the fort was abandoned by the Confederates in May 1863 at the same time as Fort McRee.

Fort Bartow (Chatham) GA
At Savannah, this was named for Colonel Francis S. Bartow (1816–1861) of the 8th Georgia, an early Confederate hero, killed at First Manassas.

Fort Bartow see Roanoke Island

Fort Baxter see **Fort Blair**

Fort Bayard DC
One of the forts north of the Potomac defending Washington, it was named for General George D. Bayard (1835–1862), a cavalry officer who was mortally wounded at Fredericksburg.

Fort Beauregard (Graves) KY
A number of Confederate forts were named for General Pierre G.T. Beauregard (1818–1893), who supervised the Confederate attack on Fort Sumter in April 1861. This one was at Mayfield.

Fort Beauregard (Catahoula) LA
At Harrisonburg on the Ouachita River, this fort, although shelled, succeeded in stopping Federal gunboats searching for the CSS *Webb* and *Queen of the West* in May 1863. It was abandoned in September of that year.

Fort Beauregard see **Fort Pettus**

Fort Beauregard see **St. Phillip's Island**

Fort Belknap (Young) TX
Established in 1851 on the Brazos River near Eliasville, it was named for General William G. Belknap (1794–1851). Colonel James B. ("Buck") Barry raised a volunteer company which was mustered into military service here in 1861 and he later took command of the fort.

Fort Bennett DC
South of the Potomac, this was one of the first forts to be built for the defense of Washington. It was named for Captain Michael P. Bennett of the 28th New York who supervised its construction in 1861.

Fort Berry DC
One of the forts south of the Potomac, it was built in 1863 as part of the Washington defenses and named for General Hiram G. Berry (1824–1863) who was killed at Chancellorsville.

Fort Bishop (Lawrence) KY
Was named for Captain William Bishop of the 100th Ohio who was killed at Dallas, Georgia, in May 1864.

Fort Bisland (St. Mary) LA
Between Pattersonville and Centerville, it was built in February 1863 near *Fairfax*, the plantation of Dr. Thomas Bisland, a sugar planter and physician. Originally a Confederate fort, it was occupied by Federal troops following an engagement in April 1863.

Fort Blair (Cherokee) KS
A short-lived fort, established in May 1863 at Baxter Springs and named for Colonel Charles W. Blair (d.1899) of the 2nd Kansas Cavalry; it was also known as Fort Baxter. The only Kansas fort to be attacked by Confederates, in October 1863, it was subsequently abandoned.

Fort Blaisdell (Prince George) VA
A Union fort at Petersburg, named for William Blaisdell, colonel of the 11th Massachusetts, who was killed in action here in June 1864.

Fort Blanchard see **Roanoke Island**

Fort Blenker see **Fort Reynolds**

Fort Bliss (El Paso) TX
Built in 1854 at El Paso, it was named for Lieutenant Colonel William W. S. Bliss (1815–1853), chief of staff to General Zachary Taylor in the Mexican War. Surrendered by the U.S. Army in March 1861, it became a focal point for Confederate troops in the Southwest.

Fort Blunt see **Fort Gibson**

Fort Boggs (Chatham) GA
One of the forts defending Savannah, it was named for General William R. Boggs (1829–1911), Georgia's chief engineer.

Fort Boreman (Wood) WV
Was built at Parkersburg in 1863 and named for Arthur I. Boreman (1823–1896), who was elected the first governor of West Virginia that year.

Fort Boykin (Isle of Wight) VA
Near Smithfield, on the James River, it was originally built during the War of 1812. Enlarged during the Civil War, it was named for Francis M. Boykin (1837–1906), a Virginia state senator, a militia general and owner of the site. He was also colonel of the 31st Virginia and a relative of diarist Mary Chesnut. Fort Boykin was cap-

tured in May 1863 by the Union Navy, along with Fort Huger.

Fort Boyle (Marion) KY

Was named for General Jeremiah T. Boyle (1818–1871), a brigade commander in the Army of the Ohio, who later helped organize the defense of Kentucky and was military governor, 1862–1864.

Fort Branch (Martin) NC

Near Hamilton, it was named for General Lawrence O. Branch (1820–1862) who was killed at Sharpsburg. There was an unsuccessful Federal attempt in July 1862 to destroy this Confederate fort built to protect the Roanoke River, and it remained in Confederate hands till April 1865.

Fort Breckinridge (Pincal) NMT

Established in 1860 and named for John C. Breckinridge (1821–1875), who was vice-president under James Buchanan, 1857–61, before serving the Confederacy as a general and then as secretary of war in 1865. It was abandoned by Federal troops in July 1861.

Fort Brooke (Hillsborough) FL

At the head of Tampa Bay, it was named for Colonel George M. Brooke (d.1851), who with Colonel James Gadsden established a military post here in 1823 to contain the Seminoles. It was attacked unsuccessfully by Federal gunboats in October and December 1863, but captured in May 1864.

Fort Bross (Prince George) VA

At Petersburg, it was named for Lieutenant Colonel John A. Bross (1826–1864) of the 29th U.S. Colored Troops who was killed leading an assault there.

Fort Brown (Chatham) GA

Part of the defenses of Savannah, it was named for Thomas Brown (1750–1825), who fought in the Revolutionary War.

Fort Brown (Cameron) TX

Built in 1846 on the banks of the Rio Grande, it was originally called Fort Taylor, for General Zachary Taylor, but renamed in honor of Major Jacob Brown (1788–1846), its commander, who was killed during a Mexican attack. Abandoned by Federal troops in March 1861, it was retaken, then again abandoned, and remained in Confederate hands till May 1865 when it finally surrendered.

Fort Bruce (Montgomery) TN

What was known as Fort Defiance at Clarksville was destroyed by retreating Confederates in February 1862. When retaken by them in August, the fort was rebuilt by Colonel Sanders D. Bruce (1825–1902) and named for him.

Fort Buchanan (Terrebonne) LA

Opposite the entrance to the Teche River, it was named for Captain Thomas M. Buchanan, USN, and in use in 1863–1864.

Fort Buhlow (Rapides) LA

A Confederate fort built in 1864 near Alexandria and named for Lieutenant A. Buhlow, an engineer officer on General Buckner's staff.

Fort Bull (Charleston) SC

Near the Ashley River, it was built in 1863 by slave labor and may have been named for Colonel William I. Bull (1813–1894), who was on the staff of General Pierre G.T. Beauregard.

Fort Burnham (Henrico) VA

Was built at Richmond in 1861. After fierce fighting during two days in September 1864 in the battle of Chaffin's Farm, what was known as Fort Harrison (named for Confederate engineer Lieutenant William Harrison), was renamed Fort Burnham in honor of Union General Hiram Burnham (1814?-1864) who was killed during its capture. General John Dunovant, CSA, was also killed here the following month.

Fort Butler (Lake) FL

This was a Union post at Astor. In existence from 1861, it was captured by Confederates in May 1864. Both this and the following were presumably named for General Benjamin F. Butler (1818–1893).

Fort Butler (Ascension) LA

A Confederate attempt to capture this Union fort at Donaldsonville in June 1863 during the Port Hudson campaign was unsuccessful.

Fort Byington (Knox) TN
A Union fort at Knoxville, named for Major Cornelius Byington of the 2nd Michigan who was mortally wounded in the fighting here in late-1863.

Fort Calhoun *see* Fort Wool

Fort Cameron (Hamilton) TN
Part of the defenses of Chattanooga at Cameron Hill, it was named for James Cameron, whose house was on the site.

Fort Campbell (New Hanover) NC
There were two Confederate forts of this name, one south of Wilmington on the Cape Fear River and previously known as Fort Means, the other near Smithville, on Oak Island. They may have been named for John A. Campbell (1811–1889), the Confederate assistant secretary of war.

Fort Carroll DC
Like Fort Greble it was intended to protect the cavalry depot at Giesboro Point, on the banks of the Anacostia River. Built in 1861, it was named for Colonel Samuel S. Carroll (1832–1893) of the 18th Ohio.

Fort Cass DC
One of the forts south of the Potomac defending Washington, it was originally called Fort Ramsey when built in 1861, for General George D. Ramsay (c.1802–1882) who commanded the Washington Arsenal, but renamed for Colonel Thomas Cass (1822–1862) of the 9th Massachusetts; he was mortally wounded at Malvern Hill during the Peninsula campaign.

Fort Caswell *see* Fort Spinola

Fort Caswell *see* Oak Island

Fort C.F. Smith DC
South of the Potomac, it was one of the many forts guarding Washington, It was built in 1863 and named for the highly-regarded General Charles Ferguson Smith (1807–1862), who died of a leg infection at Savannah, Tennessee, during the Shiloh campaign.

Fort C.F. Smith (Warren) KY
Originally a Confederate fort, it was renamed for General Smith when the Union Army occupied Bowling Green in 1862.

Fort Chadbourne (Coke) TX
Established on Oak Creek in 1852, it was abandoned by its U.S. garrison in March 1861. It was named for Lieutenant Theodore L. Chadbourne (1823?–1846), who was killed at Resaca de la Palma in the Mexican War.

Fort Chambers (Chambers) TX
It was named for Thomas J. Chambers (1802–1865), a Texas judge and militia general, and perennial candidate for governor. It was also called Fort Chambersia.

Fort Chaplin DC
One of the forts defending Washington east of the Anacostia River, it was never completed or garrisoned. It was named for Colonel Daniel Chaplin of the 1st Maine Heavy Artillery who was killed in August 1864 during the Petersburg campaign.

Fort Clark (Jefferson) KY
Named for Lieutenant Colonel Merwin Clark of the 183rd Ohio who was killed at Franklin in November 1864, it was one of the forts defending Louisville.

Fort Clark *see* Hatteras Island

Fort Clark (Kinney) TX
On Las Moras Creek, opposite Bracketville, it was established in 1852 and originally called Fort Riley, perhaps for Colonel Bennett C. Riley (commemorated by Fort Riley, Kansas, q.v.), but renamed for a Major J.B. Clark who was killed during the Mexican War. Abandoned by U.S. troops in March 1861, it was occupied by Confederates and became a major training center for Texas cavalrymen. There was fighting near here in August 1862.

Fort Cleburne *see* Fort Pillow

Fort Clifton (Prince George) VA
A Confederate fort built in 1862–1864 to protect Petersburg, near the confluence of the Appomattox River and Swift Creek, at Colonial Heights. It may have been named after a local mansion called Clifton House. A combined

army and navy attempt to capture it in May 1864 failed, and it was not taken till the fall of Petersburg in April 1865.

Fort Clinch see Amelia Island

Fort Cobb (Caddo) IT

Howell Cobb (1815–1868) was secretary of the treasury under President James Buchanan when this was established in 1859 by his friend Major W.H. Emory. The two men went on to become generals, though on opposite sides. Fort Cobb was occupied by Texas state troops in May 1861 after it was abandoned by its U.S. garrison.

Fort Coffee (Le Flore) IT

Was named for General John Coffee (1772–1833) and before the war housed the boys' academy for the Chickasaws. It was abandoned by the U.S. Army in 1861, then occupied by a regiment of Confederate Cherokees.

Fort Collier (Frederick) VA

Originally a Confederate fort built in July 1861 by engineer officer Lieutenant Collier and the Virginia militia, with help from Federal prisoners of war, on the orders of General Joseph E. Johnston, as part of the defenses of Winchester, it was evacuated in March 1862 and later occupied by Union troops.

Fort Columbus see Governor's Island

Fort Comstock (Knox) TN

One of the Union forts defending Knoxville, it was named for Lieutenant Colonel Lorin L. Comstock of the 17th Michigan who was killed here in late-1863.

Fort Conahey (Prince George) VA

At Petersburg, it was built in October 1864 on ground captured by the Federals in the battle of Peeble's Farm and named for 2nd Lieutenant John Conahey of the 118th Pennsylvania who was killed there.

Fort Corcoran DC

One of the first forts intended for the defense of Washington, it was named for Irish-born Colonel Michael Corcoran (1827–1863) of the 69th New York, whose men built it in 1861. He raised the Corcoran Legion, composed of four New York regiments, but was accidentally killed near Fairfax, Virginia, when his horse fell on him.

Fort Craig DC

Another of the forts south of the Potomac, it was built in 1861 as part of the defenses of Washington and named for Lieutenant Presley Craig, a Massachusetts officer killed at First Bull Run.

Fort Craig (Socorro) NMT

It was established in 1854 on the Rio Grande and named for a Lieutenant Colonel Louis T. Craig who was later killed by deserters in California. Its defenses were strengthened in 1861–1862 to guard against Confederate attacks, and a converted building was used as a military prison. There was skirmishing here in August 1861 and May 1862. It was near Socorro.

Fort Craig (Prince Edward) VA

A Union fort near City Point, possibly named for Colonel Henry K. Craig (d.1869), who was chief of the Ordnance Bureau, 1851–1861.

Fort Crawford (Crawford) WI

Like Crawford County, it was named for William H. Crawford (1772–1834), secretary of war under President James Madison, 1815–1816. It was built in 1829–1832 and though abandoned in 1856, was used as a recruiting center and hospital during the Civil War. It was at Prairie du Chien.

Fort Creighton see Fort Wood

Fort Cummings (Luna) NMT

Was established in 1863 near Cooke's Springs by General James H. Carleton's California Volunteers and named for a Major Joseph Cummings who was killed in an Indian ambush that year.

Fort Curtis (Phillips) AR

Named for Union General Samuel R. Curtis (1817–1866), it was built in 1862 at Helena, which was occupied by him after his victory at Pea Ridge.

Fort Dahlgren (Fairfax) VA

A small fort near Alexandria, it was unusual

in having a naval garrison in 1861—marines from the USS *Pawnee* and sailors from the USS *Perry*. It was named for Commander, later Rear Admiral, John A. Dahlgren (1809–1870), commandant of the Washington Navy Yard and inventor of the Dahlgren naval gun.

Fort Davidson (Iron) MO

Was erected at Ironton by the Federals in 1861 to protect Pilot Knob and the Iron Mountain mineral deposits, and probably named for General John W. Davidson (1823–1881), who commanded the Department of Missouri, 1862–1863. Attacked unsuccessfully in September 1864 by General Sterling Price, it was blown up when evacuated by its Federal garrison.

Fort Davis DC

East of the Anacostia River, this was built in 1861 as part of the defenses of Washington and named in honor of Colonel Benjamin F. Davis (1832–1863) of the 8th New York Cavalry who was killed at Brandy Station.

Fort Davis (Muskogee) IT

A Confederate fort built in 1861 as military headquarters for the Indian Territory and named for President Jefferson Davis (1808–1889). It was burned by the Federals in December 1862.

Fort Davis (New Hanover) NC

Previously called Fort Strong, this was on the Cape Fear River and was attacked by Union gunboats in February 1865. It was presumably also named for President Davis.

Fort Davis (Jeff Davis) TX

Established in 1854 near Limpia Creek and named for the then secretary of war, Jefferson Davis. It was abandoned by Federal troops in April 1861, and then by Confederate forces in December 1862, when it was recaptured by Union Indians and destroyed.

Fort Davis (Prince George) VA

This Union fort was one of the largest surrounding Petersburg. Previously called Fort Warren for General Gouverneur K. Warren, it was renamed for Colonel P. Stearns Davis of the 39th Massachusetts who was killed in July 1864 during the siege.

Fort Defiance *see* Fort Bruce

Fort DeKalb *see* Fort Strong

Fort Delaware *see* Pea Patch Island

Fort DeRussy DC

North of the Potomac, it was originally called Camp Holt, for Lieutenant Colonel William Holt of the 31st New Jersey. It was subsequently renamed, though it is unclear whether it was for Colonel René E. DeRussy (c.1790–1865), superintendent of West Point, 1838–1845, and commandant of the Corps of Engineers, 1858–1861, or his son General Gustavus A. DeRussy (1818–1891), an artillery officer who commanded the defenses south of the Potomac in 1863–1865.

Fort DeRussy (Avoyelles) LA

Built in 1862, it was named for Confederate Colonel Lewis G. DeRussy (1796–1864) of the 2nd Louisiana. The first fort here was destroyed in a Federal gunboat attack in May 1863, but subsequently rebuilt. It was captured at the start of the Red River campaign in March 1864.

Fort DeWolf (Bullitt) KY

South of Shepherdsville, it was built in 1862 and named for Lieutenant William DeWolf of the 3rd U.S. Artillery who was killed at Williamsburg in May of that year.

Fort Dickerson (Knox) TN

One of a number of Union forts built to protect Knoxville, it was named for Captain Jonathan C. Dickerson, 112th Illinois Mounted Infantry, who was killed in the fighting here in late-1863.

Fort Dix (Southampton) VA

Part of the Union defenses of Suffolk, it was named for General John A. Dix (1798–1879), who commanded the Department of Virginia 1862–1863, and was begun in September 1862.

Fort Donelson (Stewart) TN

Was named for General Daniel S. Donelson (1801–1863), CSA, who chose the site at Dover on the Cumberland River; construction began in May 1861. It was surrendered by its Confederate garrison in February 1862 after a short siege. Further skirmishing occurred near here in August 1862 and January 1863. An attempt by General N. Bedford Forrest to retake it in February 1863, failed. There was more skirmishing near here in July, September and October.

Fort Du Pont DC
Part of the Washington defenses east of the Anacostia, it was built in 1861–1862 and named for Rear Admiral Samuel F. Du Pont (1803–1865) who helped plan the war's naval operations and received the Thanks of Congress for his victory at Port Royal.

Fort Duffield (Hardin) KY
Was built at West Point in November 1861, and named for Colonel William W. Duffield (1823–1907) of the 9th Michigan.

Fort Duncan (Maverick) TX
Established in 1849 on the banks of the Rio Grande, opposite Piedras Negras, it was named for Colonel Thomas Duncan (1819–1887) who served on the frontier in the 1850s. Abandoned by its U.S. garrison in March 1861, it was occupied by Confederate troops and became a major C.S. cavalry post. Here, in July 1865, General Joseph O. Shelby and some of the Iron Brigade buried their battle flag in the Rio Grande before crossing into Mexico.

Fort Early (Bedford) VA
Was erected at Lynchburg in 1863 and named for Confederate General Jubal Early (1816–1894). It repelled a Federal attack in June 1864.

Fort Edward Johnson (Augusta) VA
A Confederate fort near Churchville, it was built in 1862 to protect the Shenandoah Valley and named for General Edward "Allegheny" Johnson (1816–1873) who was twice taken prisoner during the war.

Fort Ellis (Craven) NC
On the Neuse River below New Bern, was named for John W. Ellis (1820–1861), governor of North Carolina, 1858–1861, who had enlarged the state militia and seized Federal arsenals. It was captured in March 1862 in a combined army-navy operation.

Fort Ellsworth (Fairfax) VA
One of the forts defending Washington, it was built in 1861 just outside Alexandria. Originally called Fort Alexandria, it was renamed in honor of Colonel E. Elmer Ellsworth (1837–1861) of the 11th New York Zouaves, who was killed when removing a Confederate flag from the roof of the Marshall House tavern in Alexandria during the Federal occupation of the city. The first prominent Union casualty of the Civil War, he became an instant martyr; Camp Ellsworth, Iowa (q.v.) was also named for him.

Fort Elstner (Jefferson) KY
One of the forts built to defend Louisville in 1864, it was named for Lieutenant Colonel George R. Elstner of the 50th Ohio who was killed at Atlanta in August 1864.

Fort Emory (Prince George) VA
At Petersburg, it was probably named for Union General William H. Emory (1811–1887).

Fort Engle (Jefferson) KY
Captain Archibald H. Engle, 13th U.S. Infantry, who was killed in Georgia in May 1864, is remembered in this fort built to defend Louisville in 1864.

Fort Ethan Allen DC
Built in 1861 south of the Potomac as a companion to Fort Marcy as part of the Washington defenses, it commemorated Ethan Allen (1738–1789), commander of the Green Mountain Boys in the Revolutionary War. It housed the 4th New York Artillery.

Fort Evans (Loudoun) VA
Built to defend Leesburg, it may have been named for Confederate General Clement A. Evans (1833–1911), who afterwards became a Methodist preacher and Civil War historian.

Fort Ewell (La Salle) TX
Was built in 1852 on the Nueces River, and named for Captain Richard S. Ewell (1817–1872), 2nd U.S. Dragoons, who spent his prewar military career in the Southwest; he later became a Confederate general.

Fort Farnsworth (Fairfax) VA
Near Alexandria, it was built in 1862 as part of the Washington defenses and named for

General Elon J. Farnsworth (1837–1863) who was killed at Gettysburg.

Fort Fillmore (Dona Ana) NMT

Near Mesilla, it was established in 1851 and named for Millard Fillmore (1800–1874), 13th president of the United States, 1850–1853. After a half-hearted skirmish, it was abandoned by its Federal garrison in July 1861; its commander, Major Isaac Lynde, was subsequently dismissed from the service for deserting his post. It was taken over, then abandoned, by Confederates later the same year.

Fort Fisher (New Hanover) NC

Was built in 1861 to guard the Cape Fear River and the approaches to Wilmington, and named for Colonel Charles F. Fisher (1816–1861) of the 6th North Carolina, who was killed at First Manassas. It withstood a two-day bombardment in December 1864, but was finally captured in January 1865 following a combined army-navy attack commanded by General Alfred H. Terry and Rear Admiral David D. Porter. Several camps in North Carolina were also named for him.

Fort Foote (Prince George) MD

Was named in honor of Rear Admiral Andrew H. Foote (1806–1863) who received the Thanks of Congress for his services on western waters. The fort, on land belonging to Francis W. Rozier (Rozier's Bluff) overlooking the Potomac, was built in 1863–1865 to protect Washington.

Fort Franklin see Fort Sumner

Fort Frederick (Washington) MD

A pre–Revolutionary fort built at Big Pool by the Potomac in 1756 and named for Frederick Calvert, Baron Baltimore (1731–1771). It was the site of a skirmish in December 1861.

Fort Gadsden (Franklin) FL

James Gadsden (1788–1858) negotiated the sale of 29,000 square miles of Mexican territory in 1853–1854, now part of Arizona and New Mexico (the Gadsden Purchase). Originally built by the British on the Apalachicola River in 1814, it was rebuilt after 1818 as a supply base and later renamed. Occupied by Confederate troops in 1862–1863, they were driven out, not by the enemy but by malaria.

Fort Gaines DC

Was one of the forts north of the Potomac defending Washington and built in 1861. It was named for General Edmund P. Gaines (1777–1849), a hero of the War of 1812, the Seminole Wars and the Mexican War.

Fort Gaines see Dauphin Island

Fort Garrott (Warren) MS

Part of the defenses of Vicksburg, it was named for Colonel Isham W. Garrott (1816–1863) of the 20th Alabama. He was killed by a sharpshooter during the siege; his commission as brigadier general was only received after his death.

Fort Gaston (Craven) NC

Near New Bern, it was a Union fort built in 1862 and named for local landowner Judge William Gaston.

Fort Gates (Coryell) TX

Was built in 1849 on the Leon River, near Gatesville and named for Major G.R. Gates, 4th U.S. Infantry. Abandoned in 1852, it was reopened in 1861 as a Confederate training camp.

Fort Gibson (Muskogee) IT

Was built in 1824 near the confluence of the Arkansas and Neosho Rivers, and enlarged in 1831. It was named for Colonel George Gibson (1783–1861) of the Army Commissary Department. Abandoned by U.S. troops in May 1861, it was subsequently re-occupied, then again evacuated and retaken, and was the scene of various skirmishes during the war. From April 1863 it was in Union hands, and renamed Fort Blunt, for General James G. Blunt (1826–1881), who commanded the District of the Frontier. Several Indian home guard units were based here. An attack by Quantrill's guerrillas in December 1863, and a siege in September 1864 by a combined force of Confederate Cherokees and Texas cavalry failed to deter its defenders. The *J.R. Williams*, a steamboat carrying food and clothing up the Arkansas River from Fort Smith to Fort Gibson was captured, looted and burned by Confederate Cherokees in June 1864.

Fort Gillem (Davidson) TN
Part of the Union defenses of Nashville, it was built in 1862 and named for Colonel Alvan C. Gillem (1830–1875), who was provost marshal there.

Fort Gilmer (Henrico) VA
This fort, part of the Richmond defenses, was named for General Jeremy F. Gilmer (1818–1883), a leading Confederate engineer who was also second-in-command of the Department of South Carolina, Georgia and Florida. There was fighting here in September 1864 but it was abandoned in April 1865.

Fort Granger (Williamson) TN
A Union fort constructed in 1864 at Franklin near the Harpeth River, and named for General Gordon Granger (1822–1876), the garrison commander. It saw action in April 1863 during a raid by General Van Dorn's cavalry, and again in November, during the battle of Franklin, when it also served as General John M. Schofield's command post.

Fort Greble DC
Part of the Washington defenses east of the Anacostia and built in 1861, it was named for Lieutenant John T. Greble, 2nd U.S. Artillery who was killed at Big Bethel in June 1861.

Fort Gregg (Prince George) VA
At Petersburg, it was probably named for Confederate General John Gregg (1828–1864), who commanded Hood's Texas Brigade and was killed on the Darbytown road. There was fighting here at the beginning of April 1865 during the final assault on the Confederate defenses.

Fort Gregg (Prince George) VA
A Union fort at Petersburg, possibly named for General David M. Gregg (1833–1916).

Fort Gregg *see* **Morris Island**

Fort Griffin (Jefferson) TX
At Sabine Pass, it was established in 1824 and subsequently named for a Colonel William H. Griffin (1816?–1871). Also sometimes called Fort Sabine, it was the scene of an engagement in September 1863 when Union gunboats, moving up the Sabine River into Texas, were disabled by artillery fire or forced to withdraw. It was described as "the most extraordinary feat of the war" by General John B. Magruder, and the small Confederate garrison received the only medals ever issued by their government.

Fort Griswold (New London) CT
Was built at Groton on the east bank of the Thames River to defend the port of New London, in conjunction with Fort Trumbull (q.v.) and named for Matthew Griswold (1714–1799). Both were for former governors of Connecticut.

Fort Haggerty DC
One of the first forts built for the defense of Washington in 1861, it was named for Lieutenant Colonel James Haggerty of the 69th New York, who was mortally wounded at First Bull Run.

Fort Halleck (Southampton) VA
Named for Union General Henry W. Halleck (1815–1872), Lincoln's military adviser and general-in-chief before the appointment of General Ulysses S. Grant as supreme commander in 1864, it was part of the defenses of Suffolk.

Fort Hamilton (New York) NY
In New York harbor, at the western end of Long Island, it was completed in 1831. Alexander Hamilton (1755–1804) for whom it was named was the first secretary of the Treasury, 1789–1795. General Charles P. Stone was imprisoned here in April-August 1862 on unspecified charges connected with the Union debacle at Ball's Bluff in October 1861. Troops from here were sent to help suppress the New York draft riots in July 1863.

Fort Hardeman (Chatham) GA
May have been named for Colonel William P. Hardeman (1816–1898) of the 4th Texas Mounted Volunteers who achieved general's rank at the end of the war. It was part of the defenses of Savannah.

Fort Harker (Davidson) TN
Was erected at Nashville in 1862 and originally called Fort Negley, for General James S. Negley who commanded Union forces here. After he was relieved of his command after

failure at Chickamauga, it was renamed Fort Harker for General Charles G. Harker (1837–1864), who was killed during the Atlanta campaign.

Fort Harris (Shelby) TN

Isham G. Harris (1818–1897), for whom it was named, was the Confederate governor of Tennessee, 1861–1863. Near Memphis, it was built in April 1861 but evacuated by its garrison in June 1862.

Fort Harrison *see* **Fort Burnham**

Fort Haskell (Prince George) VA

A Union fort at Petersburg whose defenders were heavily engaged during the Confederate attack on Fort Stedman in March 1865. It was possibly named for Colonel Llewellyn F. Haskell of the 41st U.S. Colored Infantry.

Fort Hatteras *see* **Hatteras Island**

Fort Hébert *see* **Galveston Island**

Fort Heiman (Calloway) KY

Built in 1861 on the west bank of the Tennessee River, it was named for Prussian-born Adolphus Heiman (1809–1862), Mexican War veteran and colonel of the 10th Tennessee. Abandoned by the Confederates in February 1862, it was occupied by Federal troops for a while, then re-occupied by General Forrest's cavalry in October 1864, with a view to attacking Federal transports and gunboats going to and from the supply depot at Johnsonville.

Fort Henry (Stewart) TN

On the east bank of the Tennessee River, it was named for Tennessee senator Gustavus A. Henry (1804–1880); construction began in May 1861. It was shelled by Flag Officer Foote's gunboats in January 1862, and surrendered to the Federals the following month.

Fort Hill (Jefferson) KY

Built at Louisville in 1864, this Union fort was named for Captain George W. Hill of the 12th Kentucky Infantry, who was killed at Atlanta in August 1864.

Fort Hindman (Arkansas) AR

A Confederate fort built in 1862 on the Arkansas River, near Arkansas Post, it was probably named for General Thomas C. Hindman (1818–1868), CSA, who, though twice wounded survived the war, only to be assassinated by an unknown assailant at Helena, Arkansas. After a two-day battle, Fort Hindman fell to a combined Union Army and Navy attack led by General John A. McClernand and Rear Admiral David D. Porter in January 1863 and was subsequently destroyed.

Fort Hoke (Henrico) VA

At Richmond, it was built in 1861 and named for Confederate General Robert F. Hoke (1837–1912).

Fort Holt (Ballard) KY

Was on the Ohio River. Colonel Joseph Holt (1807–1894), a pre-war Kentucky lawyer, was appointed judge advocate general by President Lincoln in 1862. A number of camps were also named for him.

Fort Hood (Fulton) GA

Built to the north-west of Atlanta in 1864, it was named for General John B. Hood (1831–1879) who replaced General Joseph E. Johnston in July 1864 as commander of the Army of Tennessee during the Atlanta campaign.

Fort Horton (Jefferson) KY

Built to defend Louisville in 1864, it was named for Captain M.C. Horton of the 104th Ohio, who was killed in Georgia in May 1864.

Fort Howell *see* **Hilton Head Island**

Fort Huger (Mobile) AL

Several forts were named for General Benjamin Huger (1805–1877). This one was abandoned by its Confederate garrison in April 1865.

Fort Huger (Isle of Wight) VA

On the James River near Smithfield, this Confederate fort was captured in May 1863 by the Union Navy, along with Fort Boykin.

Fort Huger *see* **Roanoke Island**

Fort Inge (Uvalde) TX

Built in 1849 on the banks of the Leona River and originally called Camp Leona, it was renamed Fort Inge, for Lieutenant Zebulon M.P. Inge (1814–1846). It was abandoned by its U.S. garrison in March 1861 and occupied by Texas troops.

Fort Jackson DC

On the banks of the Potomac, it was one of the first forts built for the defense of Washington. It was on the site of a failed property speculation of the 1830s, optimistically named Jackson City for President Andrew Jackson (1767–1845).

Fort Jackson (Chatham) GA

At Savannah, it was probably also named for Andrew Jackson. It was seized by state troops in January 1861.

Fort Jackson (Iberville) LA

At Plaquemine Bend, on the west bank of the Mississippi, it was begun in 1822 and completed in 1832. Again named for Andrew Jackson, it was one of the forts guarding New Orleans. Taken over by state troops in January 1861 and refortified, it was subjected to an eleven-day Federal naval bombardment in April 1862, and surrendered following a mutiny by its garrison. There was a further mutiny here by black troops of the 4th Regiment of the Corps d'Afrique in December 1863, described by General Nathaniel P. Banks as "an unpleasant affair."

Fort Jackson *see* Galveston Island

Fort James Jackson (Chatham) GA

It was built in 1808–1812 to protect Savannah from attack by sea and named in honor of James Jackson (1757–1806), governor of Georgia, 1798–1801.

Fort Johnson (Sandusky) OH

Was probably named for L.B. Johnson, the owner of Johnson's Island, the site of a Union prison camp. It was in Sandusky Bay.

Fort Johnson (Henrico) VA

At Richmond, it was probably named for Confederate General Edward "Allegheny" Johnson (1816–1873), who was twice captured during the war. There was another Fort Johnson in the Shenandoah Valley, built by his troops in 1862.

Fort Johnston (Brunswick) NC

Completed in 1764 at Smithville, it was named for Gabriel Johnston (1699–1752), the Scottish-born governor of North Carolina, 1734–1752. Rebuilt c.1794 after a fire, it was seized by state troops in April 1861. It was evacuated in January 1865.

Fort Jones (Hardin) KY

Built near Colesburg to protect the Louisville & Nashville Railroad bridge over the Rolling Fork River, it was originally called Fort McAlester, for Captain M.D. McAlester of the Corps of Engineers, but was renamed for Captain Toland Jones of the 113th Ohio. It was attacked by Confederate raiders in February 1865.

Fort Karnasch (Jefferson) KY

A Union fort built at Louisville in 1864 and named for 2nd Lieutenant Julius E. Karnasch of the 35th Missouri, who was killed at Atlanta in August 1864.

Fort Kearny DC

Named for General Philip Kearny (1814–1862), who served in the Mexican War and was killed at Chantilly. North of the Potomac, it was one of the forts defending Washington.

Fort Knox (Hancock) ME

At Bucksport, it was intended for the defense of the Penobscot River and construction began in 1844. It was named for General Henry Knox (1750–1806), secretary of war, 1785–1794. Maine troops trained at this fort but its guns never saw action.

Fort Lafayette NY

Built in 1822 in New York harbor, it was originally called Fort Diamond, perhaps because of its shape, but renamed for the French soldier and statesman, Marquis de Lafayette (1757–1834), who had served in the War of Independence. It received its first prisoners in July 1861, mostly Confederate officers and disloyal citizens, and did not release the last ones till March 1866, the last Union military prison to do so.

Fort Lamar *see* James Island

Fort Lamb (Brunswick) NC

Guarding the approaches to Wilmington, it

was named for Colonel William Lamb (1835–1909) of the 36th North Carolina Artillery and subsequently commandant of Fort Fisher.

Fort Lane *see* **Fort Spinola**

Fort Larned (Pawnee) KS
Established in 1859 and named in honor of Benjamin F. Larned (1794–1862), the paymaster general of the U.S. Army. Some of the 2nd U.S. Volunteers, ex–Confederates who had taken the oath of allegiance and become galvanized Yankees, were based here in 1865.

Fort Leaton (Presidio) TX
On the Rio Grande, it was originally built in 1846 by Ben Leaton (d.1851) as a fortified Indian trading post on the site of an abandoned Spanish mission, before becoming a U.S. Army fort.

Fort Leavenworth (Leavenworth) KS
Established in 1827 as a frontier post by Colonel Henry H. Leavenworth (1783–1834), it was used to train Union volunteers during the Civil War. In 1865 it became an important staging post for galvanized Yankees, ex-Confederates who enlisted for frontier service against the Indians.

Fort Lee (Henrico/Prince George) VA
There were two forts in Virginia named for General Robert E. Lee (1807–1870). One was at Richmond, the other at Petersburg, part of the defenses and otherwise known as Battery 45.

Fort Lewis O. Morris (Prince George) VA
A Union fort at Petersburg, named for Lewis O. Morris (1824–1864) who in 1862 took part in the capture of Fort Macon and was later colonel of the 7th New York Heavy Artillery.

Fort Lincoln DC
Built in 1861, it was one of the forts north of the Potomac defending Washington. Both this and the following were named for President Abraham Lincoln (1809–1865).

Fort Lincoln (Bourbon) KS
A Union fort established in August 1861 on the Little Osage River by James H. Lane, it later became a prisoner-of-war camp. It was abandoned as a military post in the summer of 1863 and destroyed by General Price's retreating Confederates during their raid into Kansas in October 1864.

Fort Livingston *see* **Grande Terre Island**

Fort Loudon *see* **Fort Sanders**

Fort Lyon (Benton) MO
Near Windsor, this was built in late 1861 and named for General Nathaniel Lyon (1818–1861), the North's first military hero, who was killed at Wilson's Creek.

Fort Lyon (Fairfax) VA
Near Alexandria, Fort Lyon, one of the forts defending Washington, was built shortly after General Lyon's death at Wilson's Creek.

Fort Lytle (Warren) KY
A Confederate fort at Bowling Green begun in 1861 and subsequently occupied by Union forces. It was named in honor of General William H. Lytle (1826–1863), who was mortally wounded at Chickamauga.

Fort Mackinac *see* **Mackinac Island**

Fort Macomb (Orleans) LA
Built 1820–1828 at the entrance to Lake Pontchartrain, it had several names before becoming Fort Macomb, in honor of Alexander Macomb (1782–1841), the commanding general of the U.S. Army, 1828–1841. It was occupied by Louisiana troops in January 1861. Later taken over by Federals, it was abandoned after a fire.

Fort Macon *see* **Bogue Island**

Fort Magruder (James City) VA
Part of the Confederate defenses of Williamsburg—the Williamsburg Line—it was named for General John B. Magruder (1810–1871) and featured in the battle there in May 1862.

Fort Magruder *see* **Galveston Island**

Fort Mahan DC
One of the forts east of the Anacostia, it was named for Denis H. Mahan (1802–1871), who

taught military science and engineering at West Point for over 40 years and published a number of influential military textbooks. It was built in 1862.

Fort Mahone (Prince George) VA

Named for General William Mahone (1826–1895), CSA, popularly known as "Little Billy," an outstanding divisional commander in the latter part of the war. Begun in 1861, Fort Mahone, at Petersburg, was called "Fort Damnation" by the besieging Federals.

Fort Mansfield (Montgomery) MD

North of the Potomac, it was one of the forts defending the Federal capital and named for General Joseph K.F. Mansfield (1803–1862), who commanded the Department of Washington, 1861–1862, and was mortally wounded at Antietam.

Fort Marcy (Santa Fe) NMT

Was built in 1846 at Santa Fe and named for William L. Marcy (1786–1857), secretary of war, 1845–1849. It became the headquarters of the Union Department of New Mexico.

Fort Marcy (Nueces) TX

Near Corpus Christi, it was established during the Mexican War and also named for William Marcy. During the Civil War it was restored and strengthened by Confederate engineers.

Fort Marcy (Fairfax) VA

Was named for General Randolph B. Marcy (1812–1887), General McClellan's chief of staff and also his father-in-law. At McLean, it was built in 1861, along with Fort Ethan Allen (q.v.), as part of the Washington defenses. It was originally called Fort "Baldy" Smith, for General William F. Smith, whose men helped build it.

Fort Marion (St. Johns) FL

At St. Augustine, on the site of the Spanish Castillo de San Marcos, this became Fort Marion when it was rebuilt in 1825. It was named for General Francis Marion (1732?–1795), a commander in the War of Independence known as "the Swamp Fox." Fort Marion was taken over by Florida troops in January 1861 but abandoned and captured in March 1862.

Fort Martin Scott (Gillespie) TX

Was established in 1849 near Fredericksburg, on a branch of the Colorado River, to guard against marauding Comanches, and named for Major (later Lieutenant Colonel) Martin Scott (1788–1847), 5th U.S. Infantry, who was killed during the Mexican War. Abandoned in 1853, it passed into private hands but became a Confederate army post during the Civil War.

Fort Mason (Mason) TX

Mason County was named for Lieutenant George T. Mason who was killed in the Mexican War; Fort Mason, begun in 1851, may also have been named for him, or for General Richard B. Mason (1797–1850). It was Lieutenant Colonel Robert E. Lee's last command before the war. Abandoned by its U.S. garrison in March 1861, it was taken over by Confederate troops.

Fort Massachusetts *see* **Fort Stevens**

Fort Massachusetts *see* **Ship Island**

Fort McAlester *see* **Fort Jones**

Fort McAllister (Bryan) GA

This fort on the Ogeechee River, begun in 1861, was named for Captain Joseph McAllister of the Hardwicke Mounted Rifles, who owned the site. It withstood three fierce Federal bombardments, in July 1862, and January and March 1863. Defended not only by cannon but also by torpedoes or land mines around it, Fort McAllister was nevertheless captured in a short but determined Federal assault in December 1864, resulting in the evacuation of Savannah by its Confederate defenders.

Fort McCausland (Bedford) VA

Near Lynchburg, it was built in 1864 to protect the Virginia & Tennessee Railroad. It was named for General John McCausland (1836–1927), CSA.

Fort McClary (York) ME

Was built at Kittery in 1808 to protect the Piscataqua River, and named for Major Andrew McClary (d.1775) who was killed at Bunker Hill. It was repaired and garrisoned during the Civil War.

Fort McClellan (Southampton) VA
One of the forts defending Suffolk, it was named for General George B. McClellan (1826–1885), who succeeded General Winfield Scott as commander-in-chief of the Union armies.

Fort McCook (Marion) TN
At the confluence of the Tennessee River and Battle Creek, near South Pittsburg, what was originally Confederate Fort Rains (probably named for James E. Rains, colonel of the 11th Tennessee), was renamed for General Alexander M. McCook (1831–1903), one of the "Fighting McCooks" of Ohio. It was the scene of an engagement in August 1862.

Fort McCulloch (Bryan) IT
A Confederate fort on the Blue River near Kenefic, it was established by General Albert Pike in 1862 and named for General Ben McCulloch (1811–1862), who was killed at Pea Ridge.

Fort McGilvery (Prince George) VA
At Petersburg, it may have been named for Union Lieutenant Colonel Freeman McGilvery (1823–1864) of the 1st Maine Artillery.

Fort McHenry (Baltimore) MD
Irish-born Colonel James McHenry (1753–1816) had been aide to General Washington, and served as secretary of war, 1796–1800, under both him and John Adams. First built in 1800–1805 to defend Baltimore Harbor, it was rebuilt in 1823–1836. Fort McHenry housed Confederate prisoners during the Civil War.

Fort McIntosh (Webb) TX
Established at Laredo as Camp Crawford in 1848, it was renamed Fort McIntosh c.1850, possibly for Lachlan McIntosh (1725–1806), a general in the Revolutionary War. It was abandoned by the U.S. Army in March 1861, then occupied by Confederate troops for the rest of the war.

Fort McKavett (Menard) TX
Was established in 1852 near the source of the San Saba River and named for Captain Henry McKavett, 8th U.S. Infantry, who was killed in the Mexican War. It was abandoned in 1859 but re-occupied by Confederates during the Civil War.

Fort McMahon (Prince George) VA
At Petersburg, it was possibly named for Canadian-born Lieutenant Colonel Martin T. McMahon (1838–1906), who served as adjutant general and chief of staff for the Union VI Corps.

Fort McPherson DC
Work began on this fort south of the Potomac in 1864 but it was never completed. It was named for General James B. McPherson (1828–1864), who was killed near Atlanta while commanding the Army of the Tennessee.

Fort McRee (Escambia) FL
Built at Pensacola in 1834–1839 for the defense of Pensacola Bay, it was named for Colonel William McRee (1788–1833), an engineer officer and U.S. surveyor general. Occupied by Florida troops in January 1861, it was bombarded by Fort Pickens and two Federal warships in November. It was burned when the Confederates evacuated it in May 1863.

Fort Means see Fort Campbell

Fort Meigs DC
One of the forts defending Washington east of the Anacostia River, it was named for General Montgomery C. Meigs (c.1816–1892), the Union Army's quartermaster general.

Fort Meikle (Prince George) VA
At Petersburg, it was named for Lieutenant Colonel George W. Meikle of the 20th Indiana.

Fort Mercer (Chatham) GA
Was named for General Hugh W. Mercer (1808–1877), who was in command here at Savannah for most of the war.

Fort Mifflin see Mud Island

Fort Mihalotzy (Hamilton) TN
Part of the Chattanooga defenses, it was named for Colonel Geza Mihalotzy of the 24th Illinois who was killed at Dalton, Georgia, in February 1864.

Fort Mitchel (Kenton) KY
Near Covington, just south of the Ohio River, was begun in 1862 to protect Cincinnati, and

named for Union General Ormsby M. Mitchel (1810–1862), who was also commemorated by Mitchelville (q.v.), a community of freed slaves on Hilton Head Island. Fort Mitchel was the scene of a skirmish in September 1862.

Fort Monroe (York) VA

James Monroe (1758–1831) was secretary of war, 1814–1815, before serving two terms as fifth president of the United States, 1817–1825. Built 1819–1837 to protect the entrance to Hampton Roads, Fort Monroe was known as the "Gibraltar of Chesapeake Bay," the largest stone fortification in America. In spite of its location, at the tip of the Virginia Peninsula, it remained in Federal hands throughout the war, partly thanks to General John E. Wool, whose action in sending reinforcements saved it for the Union. It was a military prison throughout 1861–1865; ex-President Jefferson Davis was held here as a state prisoner from May 1865 to May 1867.

Fort Montgomery (Greenwood) KS

Was built at Eureka in 1861 to guard against attacks by Confederate guerrillas and named for Colonel James Montgomery (1814–1871), of the 3rd Kansas Infantry, a fanatical pre-war abolitionist.

Fort Moore *see* Galveston Island

Fort Morgan (Mobile) AL

Was built at Mobile, 1819–1834 and named for General Daniel Morgan (1736–1802), the victor of Cowpens (1781). Occupied by Alabama militia in January 1861, it was forced to surrender after the battle of Mobile Bay in August 1864.

Fort Morton DC

One of the forts defending Washington and situated south of the Potomac, both this and the following were probably named for General James St. Clair Morton (1829–1864), who was successively chief engineer, Army of the Ohio and Army of the Cumberland, and assistant to the chief engineer in Washington, as well as the author of books on fortifications.

Fort Morton (Prince George) VA

General Morton was killed leading an assault here at Petersburg in June 1864, and there was further skirmishing in October and November.

Fort Moultrie *see* Sullivan's Island

Fort Mouton (Mobile) AL

Was part of the defenses of Mobile. It was named for Confederate General J.J. Alfred A. Mouton (1829–1864), who had been a railroad engineer before the war; he was killed at the battle of Mansfield.

Fort Mulligan (Lafayette) MO

Colonel James A. Mulligan (1830–1864) of the 23rd Illinois ("Irish Brigade") was captured here at Lexington in September 1861 but exchanged in November. Fort Mulligan established that fall was named for him. The following year he became the first commandant of Camp Douglas (q.v.), the prison camp in Illinois.

Fort Mulligan (Grant) WV

At Petersburg, it was built in 1863 by Colonel Mulligan's "Irish Brigade," but evacuated in January 1864 because of an impending attack by General Jubal Early.

Fort Munson (Fairfax) VA

Part of the Washington defenses, it took its name from Daniel O. Munson, a Virginia Unionist who owned the land on which it was constructed. Near here, General McClellan's army held its famous "Grand Review" in November 1861, watched by President Abraham Lincoln and his cabinet.

Fort Murrah (La Salle) TX

On the Nueces River, it was named for Pendleton Murrah (1824–1866), who was governor of Texas, 1863–1865, and fled to Mexico after the war. It was near Fort Ewell (q.v.).

Fort Myer (Arlington) VA

Was established at Arlington in 1863 and named for Colonel Albert J. Myer (1827–1880), the Union Army's chief signal officer, who developed the "wigwag" signal system.

Fort Myers (Lee) FL

Was built in 1850 on the banks of the Caloosahatchee River and named for Colonel Abraham C. Myers (c.1811–1889), who had served in the Seminole Wars and was quartermaster general of the Confederate Army, 1861–1863. It was unoccupied when taken over by Union troops in December 1863. Though attacked unsuccessfully by Confederates in February 1865, it was abandoned by its Union garrison the following month.

Fort Negley see **Fort Harker**

Fort Nelson (Norfolk) VA
What had been a Revolutionary War fort at Portsmouth was rebuilt in 1799 and was probably named for Thomas Nelson (1738–1789), a member of the Continental Congress and governor of Virginia in 1781. It was strengthened by the Confederates in 1861, then occupied by Federal troops when the city was evacuated in May 1862 and became the site of the Portsmouth Naval Hospital.

Fort Norfolk (Norfolk) VA
Taking its name from Norfolk, England, this coastal fortification, originally built in 1794, was occupied by both Union and Confederate troops during the Civil War. There was an arsenal here and the fort was used as a Federal military prison in 1864.

Fort Norton (Floyd) GA
One of three forts built at Rome by the Confederate Army in 1863, it was named for Charles Norton, a local man killed in the war.

Fort Oglethorpe (Catoosa) GA
Was a Confederate fort named for General James Oglethorpe (1696–1785), the founder of Savannah.

Fort O'Rourke (Fairfax) VA
Near Alexandria, it was established in 1862 and named for Colonel Patrick H. O'Rourke (1837–1863) of the 140th New York, who was killed at Gettysburg.

Fort Patrick Kelly (Prince George) VA
At Petersburg, it was built in 1864 and named for Union Colonel Patrick Kelly who was killed that year.

Fort Pemberton (Leflore) MS
Was constructed near Greenwood, near the junction of the Yazoo and Tallahatchie Rivers, in early 1863 on the orders of General John C. Pemberton (1814–1881), commander of the Department of Mississippi, to obstruct Federal gunboats trying to move on Vicksburg. It successfully repelled a number of attacks and the Federals were forced to withdraw.

Fort Pemberton see **James Island**

Fort Pennsylvania see **Fort Reno**

Fort Pettus (Warren) MS
Originally called the Railroad Redoubt or Fort Beauregard when established in 1862, it became known as Fort Pettus after Colonel Edmund W. Pettus (1821–1907) of the 20th Alabama succeeded in recapturing it in May 1863. Part of the defenses of Vicksburg, it controlled the tracks of the Southern Railroad of Mississippi. It was abandoned later in 1863.

Fort Philpot (Jefferson) KY
Captain J.D. Philpot of the 103rd Ohio who was killed at Resaca in May 1864 was remembered in this fort built at Louisville in 1864.

Fort Pickens (Lewis) WV
This was a Union fort named for James Pickens, Sr., who owned the land on which it was built. It was burned by Confederate guerrillas in December 1864.

Fort Pickens see **Santa Rosa Island**

Fort Pickering (Shelby) TN
The original Fort Pickering at Memphis was named for Timothy Pickering (1745–1829), adjutant general and quartermaster general in the Continental Army, and secretary of state, 1795–1800. A Confederate fort was built on the same site in 1861, and two ironclads were begun here in the fall of that year. After the capture of Memphis by the Federals in June 1862, the fort was enlarged. In January 1863, the arrival at the smallpox hospital of Mary Ann Bickerdyke, the "cyclone in calico," caused a considerable stir.

Fort Pike see **Petites Coquilles Island**

Fort Pillow (Lauderdale) TN
On the east bank of the Mississippi, 40 miles

below Memphis, it started life in June 1861 as Fort Cleburne, named for Confederate Colonel (later General) Patrick R. Cleburne, but was enlarged later that year and renamed for General Gideon J. Pillow (1806–1878). It was evacuated in June 1862 after the loss of Island No. 10 and Corinth, but after being occupied by Federal troops, was recaptured by General Forrest's Confederate cavalry in April 1864; the killing of wounded Federal soldiers, many of them black, who had surrendered, caused an outcry across the North.

Fort Popham (Sagadahoc) ME

At the mouth of the Kennebec River at Phippsburg, it was begun in 1862 but never completed. It was named for George Popham (1550–1608), leader of the short-lived Popham Colony, an early attempt at settlement.

Fort Porter (Prince Edward) VA

Was a Union fort near City Point, named for Rear Admiral David D. Porter (1813–1891).

Fort Powhatan (Prince George) VA

Powhatan (1550?-1618) was an American Indian chief, the father of Pocahontas. At Little Brandon, it was originally built in 1776. It was captured by Federal troops in July 1863 and was the scene of a skirmish in May 1864.

Fort Preble (Cumberland) ME

Construction of Fort Preble, for the defense of Portland Harbor, began in 1845 but was never completed. It was named for Captain Edward Preble (1761–1807), USN, who was born in Portland and served in the war with Tripoli. In June 1863 some of its garrison saw action during a Confederate attempt to steal a revenue cutter from Portland.

Fort Prentiss (Pulaski) IL

Established at Cairo in May 1861, it was originally called Camp Defiance, but renamed for Colonel Benjamin M. Prentiss (1819–1901) of the 10th Illinois.

Fort Prescott (Prince George) VA

Named for George L. Prescott, colonel of the 32nd Massachusetts, who was wounded leading his regiment at Petersburg in June 1864 and died the next day. The fort was built on ground gained by the assault.

Fort Pulaski see Cockspur Island

Fort Quitman (Orleans) LA

Several forts were named for General John A. Quitman (1798–1858), a hero of the Mexican War. One of the forts protecting New Orleans, it surrendered to Union forces in April 1862.

Fort Quitman (Hudspeth) TX

Established on the Rio Grande in 1858, it was abandoned by U.S. troops in April 1861. Confederate troops camped here periodically during the Civil War.

Fort Rains see Fort McCook

Fort Ramsay (Arlington) VA

Originally called Fort Upton, from Upton's Hill, named after local resident Charles H. Upton, it was renamed Fort Ramsay, probably for General George D. Ramsay (1802–1882), who commanded the Washington Arsenal.

Fort Ramsay see Fort Cass

Fort Randolph (Rapides) LA

Was built in 1864 near Alexandria and named for Captain Christopher M. Randolph, an engineer on General Buckner's staff.

Fort Randolph see Fort Wright

Fort Reno DC

Originally called Fort Pennsylvania by men from that state who built it north of the Potomac, as part of the Washington defenses, it was renamed Fort Reno in honor of General Jesse L. Reno (1823–1862), who was killed at South Mountain.

Fort Reynolds DC

One of the forts defending Washington south of the Potomac, it was originally called Fort Blenker for German-born General Louis Blenker whose men built it in 1861. He died, not in battle but from injuries received in falling from his horse. It was renamed for General John F. Reynolds (1820–1863), who commanded a brigade in the defenses of Washington, 1861–1862, and was killed at Gettysburg.

Fort Rice (Prince George) VA
At Petersburg, was named for Union General James C. Rice (1829–1864) who was killed near Spotsylvania Court House.

Fort Richardson DC
At Arlington Heights, was named for General Israel B. Richardson (1815–1862), who was mortally wounded at Antietam. One of the forts defending Washington, it was built in 1861.

Fort Ricketts DC
Part of the Washington defenses east of the Anacostia River, the origin of its name is uncertain: it was probably in honor of Captain (later General) James B. Ricketts (1817–1887), 4th U.S. Artillery, who served throughout the war and was wounded six times, though another contender is Major Robert B. Ricketts, 1st Pennsylvania Light Artillery, who became chief of artillery for the IX Corps.

Fort Riley (Riley) KS
Was established near the Republican River in 1853 and named in memory of Colonel Bennett C. Riley (1787–1853), a long-serving, regular army officer who was military governor of California, 1849–1850, before it became a state. It became an important cavalry post and there was a Federal military prison here in 1862. William Darnell, a civilian teamster with the army, recalled that some of the 2nd U.S. Volunteers, ex-Confederates who had taken the oath of allegiance to become galvanized Yankees assigned to frontier duty, were here in March 1865. He described them disparagingly as "a miserable looking, decrepit lot, run down physically, and unable to make a long march."

Fort Riley see Fort Clark

Fort Ringgold (Starr) TX
Established by the Rio Grande in 1848 near present-day Rio Grande City, it was named for Captain Samuel Ringgold who was killed in 1846 in the Mexican War. An important U.S. cavalry post, also known as Ringgold Barracks, it was abandoned by its garrison in March 1861 and taken over by Confederate troops.

Fort Ripley (Charleston) SC
In Charleston Harbor, it was named for General Roswell S. Ripley (1823–1887), "an excellent field officer," but forever at odds with both superiors and subordinates.

Fort Ripley see Fort Sumner

Fort Rodman (Bristol) MA
Was built from 1857 onwards for the defense of New Bedford but never completed. Local people called it Fort Taber, in honor of their mayor Isaac C. Taber, but its official military name was Fort Rodman, for Lieutenant Colonel Logan Rodman of the 38th Massachusetts, who was killed at Port Hudson in 1863.

Fort Rosecrans (Rutherford) TN
Was a large Union defensive system and supply base, built in 1863 near Murfreesboro and more correctly known as Fortress Rosecrans. It was named for General William S. Rosecrans (1819–1898), who had commanded the Army of the Cumberland at Stones River.

Fort Runyon DC
One of the first forts protecting Washington, it was built in 1861 and named for General Theodore Runyon (1822–1896), whose men of the New Jersey Brigade worked on its construction.

Fort Sabine see Fort Griffin

Fort St. Clair Morton (Jefferson) KY
Built at Louisville in 1864, it was named for Union General James St. Clair Morton (1829–1864), who had been chief engineer of the Armies of the Ohio and the Cumberland and was killed at Petersburg.

Fort St. Philip (Plaquemines) LA
On the east bank of the Mississippi, it was originally built in 1793 on the site of the Spanish Fort San Felipe (1746), and rebuilt from 1819 onwards to guard the approaches to New Orleans. It was captured after a Federal naval bombardment in April 1862 when the garrison mutinied.

Fort Sanders (Knox) TN
Originally called Fort Loudon, it was re-

named Fort Sanders in September 1863 after the Union occupation of Knoxville, in honor of General William P. Sanders (1833–1863). He was mortally wounded near here when Confederates launched an attack in a desperate attempt to recapture Knoxville in November.

Fort Sands (Hardin) KY

First built in 1862 to protect the Louisville & Nashville Railroad, it had to be rebuilt in 1863 after it was burned by General John H. Morgan during his raid into Kentucky in December 1862. It was named for Alexander C. Sands, the U.S. marshal for the Southern District of Ohio.

Fort Saratoga DC

Another of the forts guarding Washington, it was probably built and named by troops from New York, after the place where the British surrendered in 1777, the turning point in the Revolutionary War. North of the Potomac, it was constructed in 1861–1862.

Fort Saunders (Jefferson) KY

Built at Louisville in 1864, it was named for Union Lieutenant E.D. Saunders, assistant adjutant general of volunteers who was killed in Georgia in June 1864.

Fort Scammon (Fayette/Kanawha) WV

Two Union forts in West Virginia named for General Eliakim P. Scammon (1816–1894) were built in 1863. One was at Fayetteville, the other at Charleston.

Fort Schuyler (Westchester) NY

Philip J. Schuyler (1733–1804) was a general in the Continental Army and one of the first two U.S. senators from New York. It was built as part of the New York Harbor defenses in 1833–1856 and used as a military prison in 1864–1865. McDougall Hospital, named for Major Charles McDougall who was medical director in New York, was also located here.

Fort Scott DC

One of the forts defending Washington, it was built in 1861 and was one of several named in honor of the venerable General Winfield Scott (1786–1866), a hero of the War of 1812 and the Mexican War, who commanded the Union Army till November 1861.

Fort Scott (Bourbon) KS

Established in 1842 and also named for General Scott, this was only in use 1843–1855, though it was reinstated in 1862 and a general U.S. Army hospital was established here. There was skirmishing in September 1861, and June and September 1863.

Fort Scurry see **Galveston Island**

Fort Sedgwick (Prince George) VA

Was built at Petersburg in July and August 1864 and named for John Sedgwick (1813–1864), a highly competent and much-loved Union general, known to his men as "Uncle John," who was killed by a Confederate sharpshooter at Spotsylvania. There was skirmishing here in October 1864 and it was nicknamed "Fort Hell" because it attracted so much Confederate mortar and sniper fire. It was the site of a major Union attack at the beginning of April 1865 in which Colonel George Gowan of the 48th Pennsylvania was killed.

Fort Seward (Southampton) VA

At Suffolk, this was probably named for William H. Seward (1801–1872), Lincoln's secretary of state, rather than his son and namesake who was lieutenant colonel of the 9th New York.

Fort Seward see **St. Phillip's Island**

Fort Shaw see **Morris Island**

Fort Sheridan (Hamilton) TN

Part of the defenses of Chattanooga, named for General Philip H. Sheridan (1831–1888).

Fort Sherman (Hamilton) TN

One of the forts defending Chattanooga, it was named for General William T. Sherman (1820–1891).

Fort Sherman see **Hilton Head Island**

Fort Sidney Sherman see **Galveston Island**

Fort Simmons (Montgomery) MD

Was named for Colonel Seneca G Simmons (1809?–1862), 5th Pennsylvania Reserves, who was killed at the battle of Glendale during the Peninsula campaign. It was one of the forts defending Washington north of the Potomac.

Fort Slemmer DC

Another of the forts north of the Potomac guarding Washington, it was named for Lieutenant Adam J. Slemmer (1828–1868), 1st U.S. Artillery, who successfully defended Fort Pickens, Florida, in early 1861; he subsequently achieved general's rank.

Fort Slocum DC

Was named for Colonel John S. Slocum (1824–1861) of the 2nd Rhode Island, who built it in 1861; he was killed at First Bull Run. It was one of the forts defending Washington north of the Potomac.

Fort Slocum *see* David's Island

Fort Smith (Sebastian) AR

Established in 1817 on the Arkansas River as a frontier post, it was named for General Thomas A. Smith (1781–1844), the departmental commander who ordered its construction. It developed into a town and was seized by Arkansas troops in April 1861. There were skirmishes here in March and May 1863 and it was abandoned by its Confederate garrison in August. It remained in Federal hands for the rest of the war, though it was the scene of skirmishing between July and December 1864.

Fort Snyder DC

East of the Anacostia, it was part of the Washington defenses. It was probably named for 1st Lieutenant George W. Snyder of the Corps of Engineers who died from exposure in November 1861.

Fort Southworth (Jefferson) KY

One of the forts built at Louisville in 1864, it was named for a Captain A.J. Southworth who was killed at Atlanta in August 1864.

Fort Spinola (Craven) NC

Previously called Fort Caswell, perhaps for former governor Richard Caswell (1729–1789), it was renamed Fort Lane, probably for General James H. Lane (1833–1907), who had commanded the 28th North Carolina at Second Manassas. Captured in March 1862 in a joint army-navy operation, it was renamed Fort Spinola for Union General Francis B. Spinola (1821–1891). It was on the Neuse River below New Bern.

Fort Stanton DC

It was named for Edwin M. Stanton (1814–1869), President Lincoln's secretary of war, 1862–1865, when it was built east of the Anacostia River to defend Washington.

Fort Stanton (Lincoln) NMT

Was built in 1855 by its own garrison and named for a Captain Stanton who had been killed that year. It was abandoned in August 1861 following the surrender by Union Major Isaac Lynde at San Augustine Springs. Briefly occupied by Confederates and then again abandoned, it was re-occupied by Federal troops in April 1863.

Fort Stedman (Prince George) VA

Named for Colonel Griffin A. Stedman (1838–1864) of the 11th Connecticut who was mortally wounded in the mine explosion here at Petersburg, its capture by Confederate troops in March 1865 was a minor, and ultimately costly, victory.

Fort Steele (Duval) FL

A Confederate fort at Mayport established in 1861, it was abandoned in March of the following year, but rebuilt by the Federals in 1864. It is unclear whether it was named for Confederate General William Steele (1819–1885) who had served in the Seminole War, or Union General Frederick Steele (1819–1868), who was in command of the District of West Florida in 1865.

Fort Stevens DC

Built in 1861 as Fort Massachusetts, it was expanded and renamed in 1863 in memory of General Isaac I. Stevens (1818–1862), who was killed at the battle of Chantilly. One of the forts built north of the Potomac to defend Washington, it was the scene of fighting in July 1864, some of it witnessed by President Lincoln, who came under enemy fire when General Early's raid on the capital was repulsed. During it, 59 Union soldiers were killed and 145 wounded, in

Washington's only Civil War battle, as well as 17 Confederates.

Fort Stevenson (Craven) NC

A Union fort near New Bern, on the Neuse River, probably named for General Thomas G. Stevenson (1836–1864), who served in North Carolina in 1862–1863 and was later killed at Spotsylvania Court House.

Fort Stockton (Pecos) TX

Established as Camp Stockton near Comanche Springs on the Pecos River in 1859, it became Fort Stockton in 1860. It was named for Commodore Robert F. Stockton (1795–1866), USN, who as commander of both land and naval forces conquered California in 1846, proclaiming it a U.S. territory. The fort was abandoned by Federal troops in April 1861 and taken over by Confederates.

Fort Stovall (Floyd) GA

Built at Rome in 1863, it was named for George Stovall, a Confederate soldier from there killed in the war.

Fort Strong DC

Was one of the forts defending Washington south of the Potomac. Originally called Fort De Kalb, for the German soldier Baron DeKalb who served in the Continental Army, it was renamed for General George C. Strong (1833–1863), who was wounded in the attack on Fort Wagner, South Carolina, and subsequently died of lockjaw in New York.

Fort Strong see Fort Davis

Fort Sumner MD

Several redoubts built north of the Potomac in 1861 to protect Washington's water supply and called Forts Alexander, Franklin and Ripley, were renamed Fort Sumner for General Edwin V. Sumner (1797–1863), a Mexican War and frontier veteran who died from wounds received at Antietam.

Fort Sumter (Charleston) SC

Was named for Thomas Sumter (1734–1832), the "Carolina Gamecock," who fought against the British in South Carolina during the Revolutionary War. Its construction in Charleston Harbour started in 1828, but it was still unfinished when the Civil War began in April 1861, with a bombardment and the surrender of its Federal garrison. It was subjected to an unsuccessful attack by Federal warships in April 1863, but successive bombardments by naval guns from August 1863 through September 1864 reduced it to rubble. Its southern face, wrote one newspaper reporter early on in this attack, was already "one vast ruin. A pile of rubbish—brick, mortar, stone, timber and guns—rises from the water and forms an inclined plane to the original parapet, some fifty feet in height." In spite of this, it was not abandoned by the Confederates till February 1865 and was re-occupied by Federal troops the next day.

Fort Taber see Fort Rodman

Fort Tattnall (Chatham) GA

One of the forts defending Savannah, it was named for Commodore Josiah Tattnall (1795–1871), who had served in the U.S. Navy before joining the Georgia State Navy and then the Confederate Navy, and commanded the naval defenses of Georgia.

Fort Taylor (Fairfax) VA

Was built in 1861 by New York troops on land belonging to tavern owner L. William Taylor.

Fort Taylor see Fort Brown

Fort Thayer DC

Was named in honor of Colonel Sylvanus Thayer (1785–1872), an engineer officer who was superintendent of West Point, 1817–1833, and known as the "Father of the Military Academy." North of the Potomac, it was part of the Washington defenses.

Fort Thompson (New Madrid) MO

Constructed in 1861 at New Madrid, it was named for General Meriwether ("Jeff") Thompson (1826–1876) of the Missouri State Guard.

Fort Thorn (Dona Ana) NMT

Established on the Rio Grande in 1853 and named for a Captain Herman Thorn (d.1849), it was abandoned by its U.S. garrison following Major Isaac Lynde's surrender at San Augustine

Springs in July 1861. There was skirmishing near here in September 1861.

Fort Tillinghast DC
One of the forts defending Washington, it was situated south of the Potomac and named for Captain Ottis H. Tillinghast. General McDowell's chief quartermaster, he was mortally wounded at First Bull Run in July 1861.

Fort Tompkins see Staten Island

Fort Totten DC
Constructed between 1861 and 1863, it was one of several forts named for General Joseph G. Totten (1788–1864), who commanded the U.S. Corps of Engineers; this one was north of the Potomac, part of the Washington defenses.

Fort Totten (New York) NY
Was one of the forts defending New York Harbor. At Willet's Point, Queens, it was begun in 1863 though it was apparently not called Fort Totten till after the war.

Fort Towson (Choctaw) IT
Near Doaksville, it was established in 1824 on the Red River and named for Nathaniel Towson (1784–1854), the U.S. Army's paymaster-general. Originally called Cantonment Towson, it became Fort Towson in 1831. Abandoned in 1854, it was used as the Choctaw Agency till the outbreak of the Civil War when it was occupied by Confederate troops, and served as military headquarters in 1864–1865.

Fort Tracy (Baldwin) AL
Near the mouth of the Tensas River, it was probably named for General Edward D. Tracy (1833–1863), CSA, who commanded an Alabama brigade and was killed at Port Gibson. One of the forts defending Mobile, it was finally abandoned in April 1865.

Fort Tracy (Prince George) VA
A Union fort at Petersburg, possibly named for Colonel Benjamin F. Tracy (1830–1915), who became commandant of the prison camp at Elmira in 1864.

Fort Trenholm see John's Island

Fort Trumbull (New London) CT
Originally constructed at New London 1775–1777 for the defense of the Thames River and rebuilt 1839–1852, it was named for Jonathan Trumbull (1710–1785) who served as state governor, 1769–1784. During the Civil War it was a recruitment and training center for the Union Army.

Fort Twiggs see Ship Island

Fort Tyler (Troup) GA
General Robert C. Tyler (1833?-1865), CSA, was killed here defending this fort on the east bank of the Chattahoochee River protecting West Point, a desperate attempt by a few wounded and convalescent Confederate soldiers to resist General Wilson's cavalry as it swept through Alabama in April 1865.

Fort Union (Mora) NMT
Erected in 1851 by Colonel Edwin V. Sumner, this was then the largest fort west of the Mississippi. A second, somewhat stronger fort was built nearby in 1861 and included an arsenal. There was a short-lived mutiny here in early 1862 among volunteer Union militia, aggrieved at the government's failure to pay and clothe them.

Fort Upton see Fort Ramsay

Fort Urmston (Prince George) VA
Built at Petersburg in October 1864 and named for a Captain Thomas D. Urmston, a Union officer killed at the battle of Peeble's Farm.

Fort Wade (Claiborne) MS
Near Port Gibson on the Mississippi, was named for Captain William Wade of the 1st Missouri Light Artillery, who was killed when it was attacked by Rear Admiral Porter's ironclads in April 1863.

Fort Wadsworth (Prince George) VA
Built at Petersburg in 1864, it was named for General James S. Wadsworth (1807–1864) who died at the Wilderness.

Fort Wadsworth see Staten Island

Fort Wagner DC
One of the forts defending Washington east of the Anacostia, its derivation is uncertain: it may have been named for 1st Lieutenant Orlando O. Wagner of the U.S. Corps of Topographical Engineers who died of his wounds near Yorktown in 1862, or Colonel Gustav Wagner of the 2nd New York Heavy Artillery. It was constructed in 1861–1862.

Fort Wagner see **Morris Island**

Fort Walker (Fulton) GA
Was built in 1864 south-east of Atlanta and named for Confederate General William H.T. Walker (1816–1864), who was killed in the battle for the city.

Fort Walker see **Hilton Head Island**

Fort Ward (Wakulla) FL
At the confluence of the Wakulla and St. Marks Rivers, this was an 18th century Spanish fort called San Marcos de Apalache. Occupied by Confederate troops in 1861, it was renamed Fort Ward for Colonel George T. Ward (1810–1862) of the 2nd Florida Infantry, a local plantation owner who was killed at the battle of Williamsburg.

Fort Ward (Fairfax) VA
It was built near Alexandria in 1861 as part of the Washington defenses and named for Commander James H. Ward (1806–1861), USN. He was the first Union naval officer to be killed in the war, in an engagement at Mathias Point on the Potomac.

Fort Warren see **George's Island**

Fort Warren see **Fort Davis**

Fort Washington (Fairfax) VA
The capital's only pre-war fortress, built in 1814–1846 on the site of Fort Warburton on the Potomac at Alexandria. Though abandoned in 1853, it was re-garrisoned during the Civil War.

Fort Washita (Bryan) IT
Established in 1843, it took its name from the Washita River. Abandoned by its Federal garrison in May 1861, it was taken over by Texas militia the following month. This became a major base for Confederate Indian units, including Cherokees, Creeks, Seminoles, Choctaws and Chickasaws. Near Durant, it was destroyed by fire in 1865.

Fort Wayne (Adair) IT
Named for General "Mad Anthony" Wayne (1745–1796), this fort near the Arkansas border was the scene of a skirmish in October 1862 when Indian troops under Colonel (later General) Douglas H. Cooper were attacked and forced to retreat, losing their artillery in the process.

Fort Wead (Chesterfield) VA
A Federal fort constructed at Chester in May 1864 during the Bermuda Hundred campaign and named for Colonel Frederick Wead who was killed at Cold Harbor the following month.

Fort Weed (Fairfax) VA
Near Alexandria, it was established in 1862 and named for Union General Stephen H. Weed (1834–1863) who was killed at Gettysburg.

Fort Welch (Prince George) VA
A Union fort at Petersburg built in October 1864 and named for Colonel Norval E. Welch of the 16th Michigan who had been killed at Peeble's Farm the previous month.

Fort Welles see **Hilton Head Island**

Fort Wheaton (Prince George) VA
At Petersburg, it was originally called Fort Archer, for Confederate General James J. Archer (1817–1864), but renamed for Union General Frank Wheaton (1833–1903).

Fort Whipple DC
South of the Potomac, it was one of the many forts guarding Washington. It was named for General Amiel W. Whipple (1816–1863), who died in Washington from wounds received at Chancellorsville.

Fort Whitworth (Prince George) VA
This Confederate fort at Petersburg was named for the Whitworth family of Mayfield on whose land it was built. There was intense fight-

ing here at the beginning of April 1865 before the final collapse of the Petersburg defenses.

Fort Willard (Fairfax) VA

Established near Alexandria in 1862 and named for Colonel George L. Willard of the 125th New York, who was killed at Gettysburg the following year.

Fort Williams (East Baton Rouge) LA

At Baton Rouge, it was built in 1862 and named for Union General Thomas Williams (1815–1862), killed during the fighting here in August 1862.

Fort Williams (Fairfax) VA

Constructed near Alexandria in 1863 as part of the Washington defenses, it was also named in honor of General Williams, killed the previous year at Baton Rouge.

Fort Wingate (McKinley) NMT

Commemorated Union Captain Benjamin Wingate, who was killed at the battle of Valverde in 1862. The original fort, established in 1850 at Seboyta, was relocated in 1862 at El Gallo by General James H. Carleton.

Fort Wood (Orleans) LA

Named for Lieutenant Colonel Eleazar Wood (1783–1814), a hero of the War of 1812, it was one of the forts protecting New Orleans and surrendered to Union forces in April 1862.

Fort Wood (Hamilton) TN

One of the Union forts defending Chattanooga, it was originally called Fort Creighton, for Colonel William R. Creighton of the 7th Ohio who was killed in November 1863; it was subsequently renamed, possibly for General Thomas J. Wood (1823–1906) who commanded a division at Chickamauga.

Fort Wood see Bedloe's Island

Fort Woodbury DC

South of the Potomac, it was one of the forts defending Washington and was named for General Daniel P. Woodbury (1812–1864), an engineer officer who helped build the Washington defenses. He died of yellow fever at Key West, Florida.

Fort Wool (York) VA

Like Fort Monroe it was built to protect the entrance to Hampton Roads. It was begun in 1819 and originally called Fort Calhoun for John C. Calhoun, secretary of war under James Monroe, 1817–1825. It was renamed in 1862 for General John E. Wool (1784–1869), for many years inspector general of the U.S. Army, who was instrumental in saving Fort Monroe for the Union.

Fort Worth (Fairfax) VA

Was established near Alexandria in 1861 as part of the Washington defenses and named for General William J. Worth (1794–1849), who served in the Mexican War.

Fort Wright (Tipton) TN

At Randolph on the Mississippi, it was built in April 1861 as Fort Randolph, the first military training camp in Tennessee. It was subsequently renamed for Lieutenant Colonel Marcus J. Wright (1831–1922) of the 154th Senior Tennessee, who is remembered now for his postwar work on Confederate records. Confederate guerrillas attacked the steamer *Belle Saint Louis* near here in October 1864.

Fort Wyman (Phelps) MO

Was built at Rolla in 1861 and named for Union Colonel John B. Wyman (1817–1862).

Fort Zachary Taylor (Monroe) FL

President Zachary Taylor (1784–1850), "Old Rough and Ready," served in Florida in the Seminole War; his brief administration, 1849–1850, lasted only sixteen months. Built in 1846–1854, the fort at Key West was occupied by Union troops during the Civil War.

Fort Zarah (Barton) KS

Was established in 1864 by General Samuel R. Curtis and named in memory of his son, Major H. Zarah Curtis, who was killed by Quantrill's guerrillas in the massacre at Baxter Springs in October 1863.

Frankfort (Franklin) KY

First settled in 1779, it was originally called Frank's Ford, for Stephen Frank, a frontiersman killed by Indians at a ford on the Kentucky River in 1780; in due course, Frank's Ford became

Frankfort. Founded in 1786, it has been the state capital since 1792. It was occupied by Confederate troops in September 1862 and Richard Hawes was installed as governor of Kentucky the following month.

Franklin (Howard) MO

Is one of many towns named for Benjamin Franklin (1706–1790), statesman, scientist and philosopher. Fighting broke out here in October and December 1864.

Franklin (Williamson) TN

Was settled by the Harpeth River in 1799. Federal troops first appeared here in March 1862, there was skirmishing in December, and it was occupied by the Federals in February 1863; further skirmishing occurred in March, April, June and July 1863, and General John H. Kelly, CSA, was killed near here in August 1864.

The battle of Franklin in November 1864, a Union victory, was described by Lieutenant Colonel Isaac R. Sherwood of the 111th Ohio as "the most destructive of human life, in proportion to the number engaged, of any battle in the four years war." Franklin resident Fanny Courtney counted "forty-four hospitals in town — three for Federal wounded, and the rest for the Confederates." The Confederate Army of Tennessee was devastated; among the many casualties were Generals Patrick R. Cleburne, Hiram B. Granbury, States Rights Gist, John Adams and Otho F. Strahl, killed, and John C. Carter, mortally wounded, and many regimental commanders were also lost.

Franklin (Southampton) VA

By the Blackwater River, it began to develop in the 1830s. It was the scene of skirmishing in August, and October-December 1862, and March 1863.

Franklin (Pendleton) WV

First settled in 1769 and established in 1794, it was originally called Frankford for Francis (Frank) Evick, a surveyor who had mapped the area, but later changed to Franklin because there was already one Frankford in the state. There was military activity here in May 1862 and August 1864. The saltpeter works near here were destroyed by Federal troops in February 1864.

Frederick (Frederick) MD

Was settled in 1733 close to the Monocacy River, laid out in 1744 and named Frederick Town for Frederick Calvert, Baron Baltimore (1731–1771). It changed hands in rapid succession in September 1862, going from Federal control to Confederate occupation, then back again to the control of the Army of the Potomac, and was the scene of further military activity during General Early's raid on Washington in July 1864, when he exacted a $200,000 ransom from the town. It was also the scene of Barbara Frietchie's almost certainly apocryphal encounter with passing Confederates in 1862, immortalized by poet John Greenleaf Whittier. At the end of the war, it was a rendezvous point for the mustering out of Maryland troops.

Fredericksburg (♦) VA

On the Rappahannock River, it was first settled in 1671 and laid out in 1727. It was named for Prince Frederick Louis (1707–1751), son of King George II and father of King George III. In a strategic location, between Washington and Richmond, it changed hands several times during the war. In December 1862, it was the scene of a destructive bombardment by the Union Army commanded by General Ambrose E. Burnside, followed by fierce fighting in which it sustained very heavy losses and was forced to withdraw. Union Generals George D. Bayard and Conrad F. Jackson were killed; so too were Confederate Generals Maxcy Gregg and Thomas R.R. Cobb. During the fighting, volunteer nurse Clara Barton converted a house into a hospital and worked tirelessly for the wounded. "It was not a battle; it was a butchery," remarked Governor Curtin of Pennsylvania to President Lincoln afterwards.

What is sometimes called Second Fredericksburg in May 1863 was really part of the battle of Chancellorsville (q.v.). Following the fighting in the Wilderness in May 1864, large numbers of wounded men were brought here; it had become "a great charnel house," wrote a soldier in the 10th New York. In September 1865 a Connecticut writer observed that "Fredericksburg had not yet begun to recover from the effects of Burnside's shells. Scarcely a house in the burned portions had been rebuilt. Many houses were destroyed and only the solitary chimney stacks remained."

Fredericktown (Madison) MO
Established on Saline Creek c.1819, it was named for Major George Frederick Bollinger (1770–1842), an early settler and former member of the state legislature. General Thompson's Confederate irregulars were defeated here in October 1861 by General Joseph B. Plummer. Further skirmishing involving Confederate General John S. Marmaduke took place in April 1863.

Free State of Jones *see* Ellisville

Front Royal (Warren) VA
Originally called LeHewtown, after Peter LeHewe, a French Huguenot who bought land here in 1754, it had become Front Royal by 1788 after being purchased by a group of real estate speculators. The name may derive from *"le front royal,"* a French reference to the land grant made by King Charles II and meaning the British frontier; or from a legendary incident in colonial days, when an exasperated sergeant drilling raw militia in the town square, ordered "front the Royal Oak," this being the royal tree of England.

There was a battle here in May 1862, when it was captured by General Jackson's Confederates, with another skirmish later that month. More skirmishing occurred between February and November 1864, and there was another engagement near here in August, this time a Union victory. The town also witnessed the hanging of seven of Colonel Mosby's rangers in September 1864, in retaliation for raids in the Shenandoah Valley.

Fulton (Callaway) MO
Founded in 1825 as Volney, named for Comte Constantin de Volney, the French scholar and politician, it was renamed for Robert Fulton (1765–1815), the steamboat pioneer. There was skirmishing here in July 1861 and 1862.

Funkstown (Washington) MD
Was named in 1840 for Henry Funk (c.1729–1793), who was granted land here in 1754 by Frederick Calvert, Baron Baltimore. Funkstown was the scene of skirmishing in July 1863.

Gadsden (Etowah) AL
On the Coosa River, it was first settled in the 1830s. Founded in 1840, it was named in 1845 in honor of James Gadsden (1788–1858), who had visited the area when the town was being planned, and commented favorably on it. In 1854, as United States minister to Mexico, he negotiated the Gadsden Purchase, 29,000 square miles of Mexican territory, now part of New Mexico and Arizona. General Hood's Army of Tennessee was here in October 1864.

Gaines' Mill (Hanover) VA
It was named Gaines' Mill after its purchase by Dr William F. Gaines, c.1857. One of the battles of the Seven Days, in the Peninsula campaign in June 1862, also known as First Cold Harbor (q.v.), took place here. One of the Confederate casualties was John F. Marshall, colonel of the 4th Texas. In a letter home, one of his men, A.N. Erskine, described it as "one of the hardest fought battles ever known.... I assure you I am heartily sick of soldiering."

Gainesville (Sumter) AL
Established in 1832 and named for Indian agent George S. Gaines (1784–1873), the brother of Edmund P. Gaines, it was a thriving cotton port on the Tombigbee River before the Civil War. The Buckner Hospital, where Fanny Beers was matron, cared for wounded Confederate soldiers after the battle of Shiloh in 1862. General N. Bedford Forrest and his cavalry were paroled here by General Edward R.S. Canby in May 1865.

Gainesville (Alachua) FL
Originally established in 1830 as a trading post, it was laid out and named in 1853 for General Edmund P. Gaines (1777–1849), whose service included the War of 1812, the Seminole Wars and the Mexican War. The site of a Confederate quartermaster depot, it was described by the *New York Tribune* as "a place of some importance as a depot for Confederate government stores, and the residence of many wealthy rebels" after Federal troops captured it in February 1864.

Gainesville (Cooke) TX
Founded in 1850 on the California Trail, the route of the 49'ers, it was also named for General Gaines. It was the site of the "Great Gainesville Hanging" in 1862: following the discovery of a

supposed plot to return Texas to the Union, martial law was declared, a "citizens' court" set up, and there were mass arrests of suspected Unionists, 42 of whom were subsequently hanged in October of that year.

Gainesville (Prince William) VA

Was named in 1852, probably also for General Gaines, when the Manassas Gap Railroad arrived. There was skirmishing here in August 1862, and June and October 1863. The cavalry engagement later that month at Buckland Mills became known as the "Buckland Races."

Gallatin (Sumner) TN

Was established in 1802 and named for Albert Gallatin (1761–1849), a Swiss-born politician, who served as secretary of the Treasury under Thomas Jefferson, 1801–1809, and James Madison, 1809–1814. During the Civil War the firm of Knight & Mills made knapsacks here. The Federal garrison at this town on the Louisville & Nashville Railroad was captured by General Morgan's cavalry in August 1862, though they were driven out the next day. There was more fighting here in November. A camp for contrabands was also set up here.

Galveston Island TX

Was named for Don Bernardo de Galvez (1746–1786), a former governor of what was then the Spanish territory of Louisiana. There were a number of forts here defending the port of Galveston. **Fort Bankhead** was named for Colonel Smith P. Bankhead (1823–1867), who became chief of artillery for the District of Texas. **Fort Hébert** was established in 1861 and named for General Paul O. Hébert (1818–1880) who commanded the District of Texas and the defenses of Galveston. **Fort Jackson**, also built in 1861, commemorated President Andrew Jackson (1767–1845). **Fort Magruder** was named for General John B. Magruder (1810–1871) who succeeded General Hébert in command here. **Fort Moore** recalls Captain John C. Moore (1824–1910), who became colonel of the 2nd Texas Infantry and subsequently a Confederate general. **Fort Scurry** was named for General William R. Scurry (1821–1864), who commanded the Confederate troops who recaptured the port in January 1863. **Fort Sidney Sherman** was named in honor of General Sidney Sherman (1805–1873), an important figure in the early history of Texas, who commanded here early in the war. **Camp Sulakowski** was named for Polish-born Colonel Valery Sulakowski (d.1873), General Magruder's chief engineer, who designed several of the forts.

Galveston itself was laid out in 1839. During the Civil War, Kolbe & Wixforth made lances, Robert Kuhnel produced cartridge boxes, belts and bayonet scabbards, E.B. Nichols made cannon and the Southern Hat Manufactory, owned by A. Pickert & Co. made military hats and caps. Converted buildings served as a Confederate military prison in 1863. Blockaded and shelled by the Federal Navy in August 1861, it was captured and occupied in October 1862, but retaken by Confederate forces in January 1863. Though bombarded again by Federal warships that month, one of which, the USS *Hatteras*, was sunk by the CSS *Alabama*, it remained in Confederate hands till the beginning of June 1865.

Gatlinburg (Sevier) TN

Established c.1830, named in 1860 for Radford Gatlin (c.1798–1880), who had opened a store here in 1855. There was a skirmish near here in December 1863 in which the Confederate Cherokees of the Thomas Legion were soundly beaten.

George's Island MA

Situated in Boston harbor, it was the site of **Fort Warren**, built in 1834–1845 as a coastal fortification and named for Joseph Warren (1741–1775), a hero of the Revolutionary War killed at Bunker Hill. A training camp for state volunteers at the start of the Civil War, it was used to house Confederate prisoners from August 1861 onwards. Conditions here were remarkably good, with ample space and food, and the death rate was very low. Confederate commissioners James M. Mason and John Slidell were imprisoned here in November-December 1861, following their seizure in the *Trent* Incident. George's Island was probably named for King George, though it is not clear which one.

Germanna Ford (Culpeper) VA

Took its name from the German miners who were brought here in 1714 to mine iron ore. There was skirmishing in April, October and November 1863, and the Army of the Potomac crossed the Rapidan here in May 1864 at the start of the Petersburg campaign.

Germantown (Shelby) TN

Was so called because it was settled by German immigrants. There was fighting near here in January and July 1863, and more skirmishing in March and April 1865.

Gettysburg (Adams) PA

Samuel Gettys (d.1790), a Scotch-Irish pioneer settler, opened a tavern here at the Shippensburg-Baltimore and Philadelphia-Pittsburgh crossroads in 1774–1775. His son, James Gettys (1759–1815), "a man of brains, force of character and resources," a general in the state militia, a town clerk and state legislator, laid out a town in 1786. Originally called Marsh Creek Settlement, then Gettystown, it was renamed Gettysburg in 1800 when it became the seat of Adams County.

At the time of the 1860 census, the town's population consisted of 2,202 whites and 188 free blacks. Since the 1830s it had been the home of the Lutheran Theological Seminary and Pennsylvania College, and students from there formed part of the 26th Pennsylvania Emergency Infantry during General Lee's second and final attempt to invade the North, which ended in the great three-day battle at the beginning of July 1863.

Confederate General Richard B. Garnett was killed, and Lewis A. Armistead, William Barksdale, W. Dorsey Pender and Paul J. Semmes were mortally wounded. Union casualties included Generals John F. Reynolds and Stephen H. Weed killed, and Elon J. Farnsworth, Strong Vincent and Samuel K. Zook mortally wounded. "It's all my fault. I thought my men were invincible," confessed Robert E. Lee to James Longstreet the day after the battle, but his subsequent offer to resign was rejected by President Davis.

In a letter written two weeks after the battle, Confederate Captain James Pleasants described it as "the worst failure that the South has ever made ... no blow since the fall of New Orleans has been so telling against us." Cornelia Hancock, a Quakeress from Salem, New Jersey, was a volunteer nurse who came here and stayed till September, helping to tend the wounded in various makeshift hospitals. The Gettysburg & Hanover Railroad had reached the town in 1859, and President Lincoln was able to come here by special train in November 1863 to deliver his Gettysburg address.

Ghent (Carroll) KY

Founded in 1809, its name derives from the Belgian town where the Treaty of Ghent, ending the War of 1812, was signed in 1814; one of the American delegates was Henry Clay of Kentucky. There was a skirmish here in August 1864.

Giesboro Point DC

An unusual placename which may be a phonetic version of Guisborough, a town in Yorkshire, England. A huge Union cavalry depot covering 625 acres was established here in June–August 1863 on the banks of the Potomac. It included a remount depot capable of handling thousands of horses, stabling, a horse-shoeing shop and barracks, and though it helped transform cavalry operations for the rest of the war, was expensive to operate and troubled with equine diseases. The men were trained at Camp Stoneman (q.v.) and it was defended by Forts Carroll and Greble (q.v.). It closed in 1866.

Gilmer (Upshur) TX

Was named for Thomas W. Gilmer (1802–1844), who had been President Tyler's secretary of the Navy for only 13 days when he was killed on board the USS *Princeton* by the bursting of a gun. The CSA Leather Factory and the CSA Hat Factory were both located here.

Girard (Russell) AL

Stephen Girard (1750–1831), the Philadelphia financier and philanthropist, who owned land here is commemorated by this town on the west bank of the Chattahoochee River. It started as a trading post and was named in 1832. There was skirmishing here in April 1865 during General Wilson's raid to Selma. (Now part of Phenix City.)

Glasgow (Barren) KY

Was settled in 1799 and called after Glasgow, Virginia, named for the city in Scotland. It was occupied by Confederates in September 1862, there was fighting here later that month, and it was occupied by General Morgan's Confederate raiders in December. There was further fighting in October 1863 and March 1865.

Glasgow (Howard) MO

On the Missouri River, it was named for Edward James Glasgow (1820–1908), a St. Louis merchant and laid out in 1836. Federal troops surrendered to Generals John B. Clark and Joseph O. Shelby here when it was captured after a bombardment in October 1864, during General Price's raid in Missouri.

Glendale (Alcorn) MS

Is a descriptive name. There was skirmishing here in May 1862 and September 1863; the latter engagement is also known as the battle of Jacinto (q.v.).

Glenville (Gilmer) WV

At the bend of the Kanawha River, it acquired its present name in 1856; it implies a sheltered place or glen. There was skirmishing here in July 1861, September 1862 and August 1863.

Glorieta Pass (Santa Fe) NMT

In Spanish, *glorieta* means "a small town square." There was a three-day engagement here, south-east of Santa Fe, in March 1862. Though the Federals were initially defeated, a raid on the Confederates' wagon train and destruction of their supplies forced them to withdraw to Santa Fe, halting their invasion of New Mexico Territory.

Gloucester Court House (Gloucester) VA

This and the following were probably named for Henry, Duke of Gloucester (1639–1660), the third son of King Charles I, rather than the English city of Gloucester. There was a cavalry skirmish here in January 1864.

Gloucester Point (Gloucester) VA

Confederate shore batteries mounted here in 1861 helped prevent General George B. McClellan from using the York River during the Peninsula campaign and there was skirmishing here in November. It was occupied by Union troops in 1862.

Goldsboro (Wayne) NC

On the Neuse River, it was first settled in 1838 and originally named Goldsborough, for Major Matthew T. Goldsborough, an engineer with the Wilmington & Weldon Railroad; the town was founded soon after that was completed in 1840. During the Civil War it became a center for refugees. Converted buildings here were turned into a prison camp in 1864–1865. There was skirmishing nearby in March and April 1865 during General Sherman's advance through the Carolinas.

Goochland Court House (Goochland) VA

Was named in 1727 for Sir William Gooch (1681–1751), governor of Virginia, 1727–1749, who supported the cause of the colonists. Union cavalry, part of General Kilpatrick's intended raid on Richmond, was here in February 1864. It also witnessed skirmishing in March 1865.

Gordon (Wilkinson) GA

William W. Gordon (1796–1842) gave his name to this town in 1835 when he became the first president of the Central Railroad of Georgia. There was a skirmish here in November 1864 during General Sherman's march.

Gordonsville (Orange) VA

Named for Nathaniel Gordon (1763–1820), who purchased 1,300 acres of land here in 1787, the town was established in 1813. The Exchange Hotel, built in 1860 to serve passengers on the Virginia Central and Orange & Alexandria Railroads, was turned into the Gordonsville Receiving Hospital in March 1862 and treated wounded from both sides. Swords were manufactured in the town by the firm of Fishback & Moyers. Gordonsville was captured by General John Pope in July 1862, and was the target of another Federal raid in December 1864.

Governors' Island NY

In New York harbor, it became known as Governors' Island when it was dedicated to the "benefit and accommodation of His Majesty's governors" by the New York Assembly in 1698. In 1860 it had a population of 696. **Castle Williams**, built in 1807–1811 and named for its architect, Lieutenant Colonel Jonathan Williams (1750–1815), housed Confederate prisoners (enlisted men). **Fort Columbus**, built in 1794 as Fort Jay and named for John Jay, governor of New York, 1795–1801, was used as a prison for Confederate officers throughout the war. Among those imprisoned here was General

William H.C. Whiting, former commander of the Military District of Wilmington, North Carolina, who died in March 1865 from wounds received in the defense of Fort Fisher.

Grafton (Taylor) WV

First settled in 1811, the town was established in 1852 by construction crews of the Baltimore & Ohio Railroad and apparently named for John Grafton, a B&O civil engineer, though Augustus Fitzroy, Duke of Grafton (1735–1811), who opposed the tea duty and favored reconciliation with the American colonists has also been suggested as the origin of the name. After a brief occupation by Federal troops in May-June 1861, there was skirmishing nearby in August. As a railroad depot it was a target during the Jones-Imboden raid into West Virginia in April 1863.

Granby (Newton) MO

Was named after Granby, Massachusetts, which commemorates John Manners, Marquis of Granby (1721–1770), a distinguished British soldier. There was fighting here in September and October 1862, and it was attacked by Confederate guerrillas in March 1863.

Grand Coteau (St. Landry) LA

Was originally called St. Charles Town, after the Jesuit college of St. Charles established here in 1837. There was skirmishing in October and November 1863. In French, *grand coteau* means "great hill."

Grand Gulf (Claiborne) MS

Took its name from the whirlpools and eddies formed in the Mississippi River by the current from the Big Black. Laid out in 1828, it "had before the war a thousand inhabitants, three churches and several steam mills.... The Yankees burned every vestige of the village," admitted a Northern visitor. Much of it was destroyed by fire from Federal gunboats in 1862. Evacuated by the Confederates in May 1863, it was used as a Federal supply base for the second Vicksburg campaign.

Grand Junction (Hardeman) TN

Was so called because it was at the junction of the Memphis & Charleston and Mississippi Central Railroads. Two wings of General Grant's Army of the Tennessee rendezvoused here in November 1862 during the first Vicksburg campaign. A camp for contrabands was established at this time, but moved to Camp Fiske near Memphis early in 1863.

Grande Terre Island LA

Otherwise known as Grand Isle and situated between Barataria Bay and the Gulf of Mexico, it was the site of **Fort Livingston**, one of the forts protecting New Orleans. Built in 1835–1861, this was named for Edward Livingston (1764–1836), the secretary of state, 1831–1833. It surrendered to Federal troops in April 1862.

Graniteville (Aiken) SC

Was so called because William Gregg's cotton mill, the Graniteville Manufacturing Co., and the houses, stores, church and school, established in 1845, were mostly built of blue granite. It was an early example of a company town, less common in the South than in the North. Gregg, who preferred to employ poor whites rather than slaves, made quantities of brown cloth for the Confederate quartermaster department. The Confederate Navy also had a shoe factory here which was taken over by the Army.

Greencastle (Franklin) PA

Was laid out in 1782 and named by Colonel John Allison after Greencastle, his native place in County Donegal, Ireland. It was the scene of skirmishing in June and July 1863 during the Gettysburg campaign. One soldier in General Lee's army called it "a very pretty little town," but inhabited by "the sorriest set of Yankees ... and the largest collection of ugly, dirty looking women I ever saw."

Greeneville (Greene) TN

Was one of a number of towns named for General Nathanael Greene (1742–1786), a hero of the Revolutionary War who defeated the British in a series of battles in the South in 1781. Settled in 1780 by Scots-Irish Covenanters (Presbyterians), it was the capital of the short-lived state of Franklin, 1784–1788. Greeneville witnessed skirmishing in October 1863 and April and May 1864, but is remembered now as the place where General John H. Morgan was surprised and killed by Union cavalry in September of that year. It was also the home of

Andrew Johnson, Abraham Lincoln's second vice-president and successor.

Greensboro (Guilford) NC

Founded in 1772, it was also named for General Greene. There was a Confederate supply depot in 1862–1863, as well as an ordnance depot, and the Tarpley carbine was also manufactured here. Early on it became a center for refugees from the North Carolina and Virginia coasts. Union prisoners, transferred from Salisbury in February 1865, were then repatriated. Jefferson Davis on his flight south rested here for three days in April 1865, met with Generals Joseph E. Johnston and Pierre G.T. Beauregard and held a cabinet meeting in a railroad car.

Greenville (Washington) MS

This port on the Mississippi was also named for General Greene and established c.1827. It was the scene of skirmishing in August 1862, gunboat action and skirmishing in May 1863, and further skirmishing in May 1864. Burned by Federal troops, it was rebuilt on a different site after the war.

Greenville (Pitt) NC

First established on the Tar River in 1774, it was refounded in 1786 and also named for General Greene. Skirmishing took place in November and December 1863.

Greenville (Greenville) SC

Laid out in 1797, it was developed by Vardry McBee, the "Father of Greenville," initially as a summer resort. It was named for Isaac Green (1762–1831), an early settler who operated a water mill around which the town grew. The State Military Works here made breech-loading, single-shot carbines for South Carolina troops. The firm of Leech & Rigdon, who moved here from Columbus, Mississippi, produced revolvers and George Morse made single-shot carbines for the Confederate Army. Greenville was a popular center for Confederate refugees.

Greenwood (Leflore) MS

Was established in 1834 as a landing on the Yazoo River. It was named in 1844 for Greenwood Leflore (1800–1865), a Choctaw chief and cotton planter, who also built the town of Leflore for his cotton business. Confederates launched attacks on Federal gunboats near here in May 1863.

Gretna (New Orleans) LA

On the Mississippi and originally called Mechanicsham when founded in 1836, it was the site of the Phoenix Iron Works which in May 1861 cast one of the first guns for the Confederate Navy. It was later renamed Gretna, after the celebrated Scottish village of Gretna Green, because it was also possible to be married here without a license. (Now part of New Orleans.)

Griffin (Spalding) GA

Was named for Colonel Lewis Griffin (1794–1867), a banker and railroad president, who began development here in 1840. Hospitals included the Catoosa, the Quintard, converted from a young ladies' college, and the S.P. Moore, named for Surgeon General Samuel P. Moore. This was destroyed by fire in February 1864. Confederate Colonel Samuel Benton of the 37th Mississippi died in hospital here in that July, of wounds received in the battle of Atlanta, just before he received his commission as a brigadier general.

Griswoldville (Jones) GA

In 1849 Samuel Griswold (1790–1867) moved his iron foundry and cotton gin factory to a new location here on the Georgia Central Railroad, where he built a substantial residence for himself and cottages for his workers. In 1862, in partnership with A.W. Gunnison, he set up the pistol-making factory of Griswold & Gunnison in his former cotton gin plant, producing copies of the Colt Navy revolver for the Confederate Ordnance Department; they became the South's largest producers of handguns.

In November 1864 the factory and the rest of the village were destroyed by General Sherman's troops, who also defeated three small brigades of raw, poorly trained, badly equipped Georgia militia commanded by General Pleasant J. Phillips, in the tragic battle of Griswoldville. Afterwards, hardened Yankee veterans were appalled when they found that "Old grey-haired and weakly looking men and little boys, not over 15 years old, lay dead or writhing in pain." Speaking for many of his comrades, one Illinois soldier said: "I hope we never have to shoot at such men again."

Guiney's Station (Caroline) VA
The first stop south of Fredericksburg, on the Richmond, Fredericksburg & Potomac Railroad, this small town, named for the Guiney or Guinea family, was the site of a Confederate supply depot. General Thomas J. ("Stonewall") Jackson, brought here in May 1863 following his accidental wounding at Chancellorsville, died from pneumonia in the office of *Fairfield*, Thomas C. Chandler's plantation. (Now called Guinea.)

Guntersville (Marshall) AL
Was founded c.1785 by the Tennessee River, on the site of a Cherokee village, by Scotsman John Gunter (1765–1835) and named for him in 1848; it was previously called Marshall. General Hood's Army of Tennessee was here in October 1864.

Guntown (Lee) MS
Was named for Virginia loyalist James Gunn who fled here during the Revolution. The engagement here in June 1864 is better known as Brice's Crossroads (q.v.).

Hagerstown (Washington) MD
Laid out in 1762 and called Elizabeth Town for the wife of Jonathan Hager (1714–1775), a German who settled here in 1737, it became Hagers Town in 1814, then Hagerstown. It was occupied by Confederate troops in September 1862. There was fighting here as General Lee's army retreated from Gettysburg in July 1863. In July 1864, after General Early's troops had captured the town, General John McCausland demanded a levy of $20,000 and 20,000 sets of clothing as compensation for General Hunter's depredations in the Shenandoah Valley; there was further skirmishing in early August.

Halltown (Jefferson) WV
It took its name from a family called Hall who were local landowners. There was skirmishing here near the Potomac in November and December 1862, July 1863 and May 1864. General Philip H. Sheridan was entrenched here in August 1864, too strongly for any Confederate attacks to succeed.

Hamilton (Martin) NC
Alexander Hamilton (1755–1804) was the first secretary of the Treasury, 1789–1795. The Confederate ram *Albemarle* was built near here at Edwards' Ferry on the Roanoke River in 1863 and sent to assist in the successful recapture of Plymouth in April 1864.

Hamilton (Butler) OH
On the Great Miami River, it was first established in 1795 and named for Alexander Hamilton when settled c.1803. Edward Gwyn and Abner C. Campbell of the Cosmopolitan Arms Co. manufactured their breech-loading carbines here. Confederate raiders led by General John H. Morgan were reported to be in the area in July 1863, though this proved to be a false alarm.

Hamlin (Lincoln) WV
Was established in 1852–1853 as Hamline, named for its founder, Bishop Leonidas L. Hamline (1797–1865), of the Methodist Episcopal Church; the "e" was later dropped by the local postmaster. There was a skirmish here in May 1864.

Hampton (♦) VA
First settled in 1610, it was laid out in 1680 and took its name from Hampton Creek, previously called Southampton River. This was named for Henry Wriothesley, Earl of Southampton (1573–1624), whose title derived from the English port of Southampton, from where the Pilgrim Fathers sailed in 1620. The town was set on fire by General Magruder's troops in August 1861, in an attempt to stop its occupation and use for runaway slaves by the Federals. It was the site of the Chesapeake Hospital, converted from a former female college, and the Hampton Military Academy which was also burned during the war.

Hancock (Washington) MD
Commemorates pioneer Edward Joseph Hancock who settled here in 1749 and was killed by Indians. It was laid out c.1789 and named c.1810. Its development was aided by the construction of the Chesapeake & Ohio Canal, completed to here in 1839. There was skirmishing in July and August 1864.

Hanover (York) PA
First settled in 1733, it was laid out in 1763 as McAllisters-town by Richard McAllister, a local

tavern owner. It was renamed Hanover on account of the large number of German settlers here, rather than for the House of Hanover whose head had succeeded to the British throne in 1714. An indecisive engagement here at the end of June 1863, when General Stuart's cavalry clashed with that of Generals H. Judson Kilpatrick and George A. Custer, was the first battle in the Civil War north of the Mason-Dixon Line.

Hanover Court House (Hanover) VA

Was founded in 1720 and named in honor of the German House of Hanover. There was fighting here in May 1862 and in June it witnessed Stuart's ride around McClellan and the Army of the Potomac. Federal troops fell back to here during the fighting at Cold Harbor in June 1864, and there was further skirmishing in March 1865.

Hanovertown (Hanover) VA

Laid out on the Pamunkey River as Hanover in 1762, it was also named for the House of Hanover. General Grant's army crossed the Pamunkey in May 1864, in an attempt to advance on Richmond, and there were a number of skirmishes around here and along Totopotomoy Creek.

Hard Times Landing (Tensas) LA

Although it is tempting to think that Charles Dickens' novel *Hard Times* (1854) might have been the origin of this placename, it probably derived from the nearby Hard Times Plantation which was used as a staging area by the Union Army during the Vicksburg campaign. Rear Admiral Porter's flotilla gathered here, on the west bank of the Mississippi in April 1863, after successfully running past the Confederate batteries at Vicksburg.

Harpers Ferry (Jefferson) WV

Robert Harper (d.1782) established a ferry here at the confluence of the Shenandoah and the Potomac in 1734 and a settlement grew up c.1747. The town was established in 1763 and became the site of an important U.S. arsenal in 1796, and Hall's Rifle Works. The coming of the Chesapeake & Ohio Canal and the Baltimore & Ohio Railroad helped its development.

Already famous, or infamous, because of John Brown's raid in 1859, it witnessed much military activity and changed hands several times during the Civil War. The arsenal, the target of that raid, was abandoned in April 1861 and taken over by Virginia troops. Reoccupied by Federal troops in February 1862, Harpers Ferry was the scene of fighting over several days in September when some 12,000 Federals surrendered to Confederate forces, but was again reoccupied by them later that month. President Lincoln first visited it in October 1862, conferring with General George B. McClellan. There was more skirmishing near here in July and October 1863, and it was threatened by General Jubal Early in July and August 1864. It was also the target of a raid by Colonel Mosby's partisan rangers in October 1864, when a train on the nearby Baltimore & Ohio Railroad was derailed and robbed.

Harrisburg (Dauphin) PA

A trading post and ferry crossing on the Susquehanna River, it was founded in 1718 by John Harris and settled in 1726. Called Harris's Ferry for many years, when it was laid out as a town by John Harris, Jr. it was renamed for his father. It became the state capital of Pennsylvania in 1812. President-elect Lincoln stopped here on his way to Washington in February 1861 and spoke about preserving peace if possible. General Lee's invasion of Pennsylvania in 1863 caused panic in the town, and there was skirmishing near here at the end of June. Camp Curtin (q.v.), an important training camp for Union troops near Harrisburg, served as a rendezvous point for the demobilization of Pennsylvania soldiers at the end of the war.

Harrison (Hamilton) OH

Named for William Henry Harrison (1773–1841), who represented Ohio in the House, 1816–1819, it was founded in 1810 and laid out in 1813. The ninth president of the United States, he died after only one month in office. Confederate General John H. Morgan passed through Harrison during his ultimately disastrous Ohio raid in July 1863.

Harrisonburg (♦) VA

First settled c.1739, the town was founded in 1780 and named for Thomas Harrison, an early settler and landowner. There was skirmishing here in May and June 1862, and General Turner Ashby, the celebrated Confederate cavalry leader, was killed near here in a rear-guard action that month. Further fighting occurred in June 1864.

Harrison's Landing (Charles City) VA

A wharf on the James River, it belonged to the Berkeley plantation, built by Benjamin Harrison, whose descendant, William Henry Harrison, was briefly ninth president of the United States in 1840. Following the Peninsula campaign, General McClellan's army withdrew to here at the beginning of July 1862, and remained until Second Bull Run. It was visited by President Lincoln who reviewed the troops. "Taps," the bugle call played at the end of a soldier's day, was composed while the army was camped here.

Harrisonville (Cass) MO

Founded in 1837, it was named for Congressman Albert G. Harrison (1800–1839) who represented Missouri. There was skirmishing here in July 1861, November 1862 and October 1863.

Harrodsburg (Mercer) KY

The first settlement in Kentucky, it was founded in 1774 as Harrodstown, then Harrodsburg, for James Harrod (1742–1792), a frontiersman who led the original band of settlers here. It became an antebellum resort, was the scene of fighting in October 1862, and there was further skirmishing in October 1864 and January 1865.

Hartford (Hartford) CT

On the Connecticut River, it was originally established in 1633 and named in 1637 for Hertford, England, the birthplace of Samuel Stone, one of its founders. With New Haven, it was the joint state capital, 1701–1875. Several leading manufacturers of small arms were located here. "I found that Hartford was all alive with trade, and that wages were high, because there are two factories for the manufacture of arms. Colt's pistols come from Hartford, as do also Sharps rifles," noted English novelist Anthony Trollope on his visit to the town in the fall of 1861. Samuel Colt's Patent Firearms Manufacturing Co., founded at Paterson, New Jersey, in 1836, moved here in 1848 and produced revolvers for the Union Army and Navy and also repeating rifles, though the output was reduced when the factory caught fire in 1864. The Sharps Rifle Manufacturing Co. and the Spencer Repeating Rifle Co. were also located here.

Hart's Island NY

The origin of the name is uncertain. It may derive from its heart-like shape or from a hart, a male deer, once common here. In Long Island Sound, this was one of the assembly places for black regiments in New York and also a state rendezvous point for the demobilization of New York troops at the end of the war. There was also a prison for enlisted men here for a few months in 1865.

Hartsville (Trousdale) TN

Was named for James Hart, an early settler. The Federal garrison here was captured by General John H. Morgan in December 1862, during his raid into Kentucky and Tennessee.

Hartville (Wright) MO

Isaac Hart, another early settler, gave his name to this place. After the Federal garrison here surrendered to General Marmaduke's Confederates in January 1863, there was fighting two days later as they retreated. There was more skirmishing in May 1863 and in August 1864.

Hatchie River TN

Its name derives from an Indian word meaning "small river." There was skirmishing here in September and October 1862 and February 1863.

Hatteras Island NC

Took its name from an Algonquin tribe. Two Confederate forts, **Clark** and **Hatteras**, were constructed in 1861 to protect Hatteras Inlet. Fort Clark was probably named for Henry T. Clark (1808–1874), governor of North Carolina, 1861–1862. They were attacked in August 1861 by a naval squadron under Commodore Silas Stringham and troops led by General Benjamin F. Butler. Fort Clark was occupied after its garrison abandoned it, Fort Hatteras after a determined bombardment by Federal warships. **Camp Wool**, named for General John E. Wool (1784–1869), inspector general of the U.S. Army, was subsequently established here as the camp of "Hawkins' Zouaves," the 9th New York Infantry.

Haw's Shop (Hanover) VA

Took its name from John Haw (1804–1872) who manufactured farming and milling machinery at his sawmill, foundry and machine shop. There was a fierce cavalry engagement here towards the end of May 1864, also known as Enon Church (q.v.).

Haymarket (Prince William) VA

It was laid out in 1799 on land owned by William Skinner. The name may derive from the Haymarket, a famous street in London, England, or merely be a reflection of its rural economy. Skirmishing took place in August 1862, it was burned by the Federals in November, and there was further skirmishing in June and October 1863.

Hazardville (Hartford) CT

On the Scantic River, it was named for Colonel Augustus G. Hazard (1802–1868), who took over the gunpowder manufacturing firm of Loomis, Denslow & Co. in 1837. This became Loomis, Hazard & Co. and was renamed the Hazard Powder Co. in 1843. In June 1861 gunpowder from there was seized by the Federal authorities. The firm, which also had premises in New York City, became one of the chief sources of gunpowder for both the Union Army and Navy.

Hazlehurst (Copiah) MS

A settlement here was named in 1857 for George H. Hazlehurst, chief engineer of the New Orleans, Jackson & Great Northern Railroad, who surveyed the site. Colonel Grierson's cavalry destroyed telegraph lines and track in the vicinity in April 1863 during their raid through Mississippi.

Hearne (Robertson) TX

Was named for either C.C. Hearne, who gave land for the town site, or Horatio R. Hearne, an early settler. The Brazos Manufacturing Co. located near here produced woolen and cotton fabrics for Texas troops.

Helena (Phillips) AR

On the Mississippi River, it was originally settled in 1797 and called Helena when it was established in 1820, for the daughter of Sylvanus Phillips (1766–1830), one of its founders. It became a Federal supply depot after it was captured in July 1862. A Confederate attempt to retake it in July 1863 was a failure.

Hempstead (Waller) TX

When established in 1856 it was named by Dr. R.R. Peebles for his brother-in-law and fellow physician G.S.B. Hempstead, of Portsmouth, Ohio. It was at the junction of the Houston & Texas Central and Washington County Railroads. There was a Confederate garrison here and a quartermaster depot which had a steam-powered foundry making skillets and kettles for Texas troops. The Hempstead Manufacturing Co., owned by H.S. Hubby, A. Verse and W.W. Williams, was making a wide range of goods here, including blankets, cotton cloth, spinning wheels and looms, and firearms in December 1863.

Henderson (Henderson) KY

First settled in 1784 and laid out in 1797, it was named for Richard Henderson (1735–1785), who formed the Transylvania Co. in 1775 to buy land in Kentucky from the Cherokees, following the treaty of Sycamore Shoals. Skirmishing took place here in June and September 1862 and again in September 1864.

Henderson's Station (Chester) TN

On the Mobile & Ohio Railroad, was named for either Colonel James Henderson, who served with Andrew Jackson in the War of 1812, or Colonel Richard Henderson of Kentucky. It was burned by General Wheeler's Confederate cavalry in November 1862. (Now called Henderson.)

Henrico (Henrico) VA

Was founded in 1634 and named for Henry, Prince of Wales (1594–1612), eldest son of King James I. The battle here, the first in the Peninsula campaign in June 1862, is also known as Oak Grove (q.v.).

Hermann (Montgomery) MO

Situated on the Missouri River, it was established in 1837 by members of the German Settlement Society of Philadelphia and named for a first century German tribal leader. There was a skirmish here in October 1864.

Hernando (DeSoto) MS

Hernando de Soto (c.1500–1542) was a Spaniard who explored parts of present-day Florida, Alabama, Tennessee, Mississippi, Arkansas, Oklahoma and Louisiana, and discovered the Mississippi River. Hernando became a town in 1837. Skirmishing took place here in March and June 1863 and October 1864.

Herndon Station (Fairfax) VA

Commemorates Captain William Herndon (1813–1857), USN, who was drowned when the mail ship *Central America* which he commanded was lost in a storm. There was skirmishing here in March 1863, on the Alexandria, Loudoun & Hampshire Railroad.

Hertford (Perquimans) NC

It was named in 1758 for Francis Conway, Marquis of Hertford (1719–1794). A skirmish took place here in December 1863.

Hickman (Fulton) KY

On the Mississippi River, it was first settled in 1819 and named in 1834 for Captain Paschal Hickman (d.1813) a Tennessee man who bought much of the land here. There was an engagement between Federal gunboats and Confederate shore batteries in September 1861 and it was occupied by Federal troops in July 1863.

Hillsborough (Orange) NC

Laid out in 1754, it was named in 1766 for Wills Hill, Viscount Hillsborough (1718–1793), secretary of state for the colonies. It was the summer capital of the state in the second half of the 18th century. The Hillsborough Military Academy, built in 1859, trained Confederate recruits. During the war the town became crowded with refugees living in every available building, including the schoolhouse, the bank and the masonic hall. General Joseph E. Johnston rejoined the Army of Tennessee here after meeting with President Jefferson Davis and General Pierre G.T. Beauregard at Greensborough in April 1865.

Hilton Head Island SC

Off the South Carolina coast, it was named by or for Englishman William Hilton (1617–1675) who made a voyage of exploration here in 1663. It was the scene of a remarkably successful joint Federal army-navy attack — the Port Royal Expedition — in November 1861, led by General Thomas W. Sherman and Flag Officer Samuel F. Du Pont, for which the latter received the Thanks of Congress. After its capture, **Fort Walker**, probably named for Confederate Secretary of War Leroy P. Walker, was renamed **Fort Welles**, in honor of Gideon Welles (1802–1878), the secretary of the Navy. It was joined in 1864 by **Fort Howell**, named for Joshua B. Howell (1899–1864), a Union brigade commander killed at Petersburg, and **Fort Sherman**, named for General William T. Sherman (1820–1891). **Mitchelville**, a purpose-built town for freed slaves, was established in late 1862 and named for General Ormsby M. Mitchel (1810–1862), commander of the Department of the South, who died of yellow fever about the time it was being laid out. Its occupants mostly worked for the Union Army, and it included a church and schools, staffed by the American Missionary Association.

Hockingport (Athens) OH

As the name suggests, this was a port on the Hocking River, which derives from a Delaware word meaning "high up there is land or soil." There was a skirmish in July 1863 at this town, where the Hocking meets the Ohio, during General Morgan's Indiana and Ohio raid.

Hodgenville (Larue) KY

Was settled in 1789 by Robert Hodgen (d.1810) who had a mill, a farm and a famous tavern here. A skirmish occurred here in October 1861.

Holden (Johnson) MO

Was named for Major N.B. Holden, a member of the state legislature. There were operations by the Federals near here in August 1864.

Holly Springs (Marshall) MS

Founded in 1835 by William Randolph of Virginia on the site of a spring surrounded by holly trees, it became an important rail center on the Illinois Central Railroad. The arms factory of Jones, McElwaine & Co., founded as the Marshall Manufacturing Co. in 1859, was bought by the Confederate government in 1862 and became the Holly Springs Armory.

There was fighting here in July 1862, and the town was captured by Federal troops in November. The huge supply depot they established for the advance on Vicksburg was attacked by General Earl Van Dorn in December, and a vast quantity of military supplies captured or destroyed and warehouses set on fire. The town was evacuated by the Federals in January 1863. There was further skirmishing in June, September and November 1863, and February, April, May and August 1864.

Homosassa Springs (Citrus) FL

Comes from a Seminole word of uncertain meaning — perhaps "river of fishes." A sugar plantation established here in 1851 by David L. Yulee, a former United States senator and president of the Florida Railroad, covered more than 5,000 acres and employed 1,000 slaves. Until destroyed by Federal troops in 1864, it supplied sugar products to Confederate soldiers.

Honey Springs (McIntosh) IT

Was probably so called because it was a place where wild honey was found. It was the site of a Confederate supply depot, and Federal troops under General James G. Blunt, which included Union Indians and the 1st Kansas Volunteer Colored Infantry, won a victory here in July 1863 over a larger, mixed force of Texans and Confederate Indians commanded by General Douglas H. Cooper. It was the largest engagement in the Indian Territory and gave the Union control of that region. "The 1st Kansas (Colored) ... fought like veterans," noted General Blunt approvingly.

Hookerton (Greene) NC

Was laid out in 1817 on land owned by William Hooker and originally called Hookertown. A skirmish took place here at the end of March 1865 during General Sherman's progress through the Carolinas.

Hopefield (Crittenden) AR

On the Mississippi, just across the river from Memphis, it was founded c.1797 as Fort Esperanza (Spanish for "hope"), became Hope Encampment, then Hopefield. Confederate partisan rangers captured the steamer *Jacob Musselman* here in January 1863, then the U.S. boat *Hercules* in February. Hopefield was burned that month by the Federals in retaliation for giving aid to the rebels, and there was more skirmishing here in March 1864. It was never rebuilt.

Hopewell (♦) VA

Captain Francis Eppes, who sailed to Virginia in the ship *Hopewell* in 1635, named part of his land grant Hopewell Farms. John Randolph Hospital, which probably commemorates politician John Randolph of Roanoke, was one of seven hospitals here caring for Union soldiers.

Hopkinsville (Christian) KY

Originally settled in 1796, it was named for General Samuel Hopkins (1756?-1819), a hero of the War of 1812. There was skirmishing here in September 1861, and it was the target of a Confederate raid in December 1864.

Hornersville (Dunklin) MO

Founded in 1840, it was named for William H. Horner. It was the scene of skirmishes in September 1862 and 1864.

Houston (Chickasaw) MS

One of several towns named for General Sam Houston (1793–1863), the first president of the Republic of Texas, 1836–1838. He was a friend of Joel Pinson who gave the land for its site when it was founded in 1838. There was skirmishing here in February 1864.

Houston (Texas) MO

Was laid out in 1846. There was fighting near here in September and November 1863 and it was twice largely destroyed during the war.

Houston (Harris) TX

The original settlement on the Buffalo Bayou was founded in 1823 as a trading post by John R. Harris and called Harrisburg. The present city was established in 1836 by New York speculators Augustus C. and John K. Allen as the "great interior commercial emporium of Texas." It was named for Sam Houston and served as the capital of the Texas Republic in 1837–1839 and 1842–1845.

Though slow in developing, by the time of the Civil War it was regarded as the "railroad center of Texas," the meeting place of four lines — the Houston & Texas Central, the Galveston, Houston & Henderson, the Texas & New Orleans and the Houston Tap & Brazoria. This was probably a reason for its choice as the site of the principal Texas quartermaster depot which produced uniforms, shoes, tents, tin goods and equipment for wagons. In addition, Charles Posner's Clothing & Shirt Manufactory made military clothing and the Houston City Mills Manufacturing Co., cotton and woolen goods. There was also an arsenal and a percussion cap factory here, as well as J.W. Wilson's Texas Sword Factory. The Texas Printing House, owned by E.W. Cave, supplied stationary and quartermaster forms for the Trans-Mississippi Department. Converted buildings in Houston were used as a military prison in 1863. By that time it had become a major center for refugees, crowded with people from Galveston, and much further afield — Louisiana, Mississippi, Arkansas and even Tennessee and Virginia.

Humansville (Polk) MO

Was named for James G. Human (1798–1875) who found the Big Spring in 1834 and declared: "Right here is where I'm going to live." It is a unique American placename. Fighting occurred here in March 1862 and October 1863 during raids into Arkansas and Missouri by General Shelby's Confederate cavalry.

Humboldt (Gibson) TN

Named for the remarkable German scientist, traveler and statesman, Alexander von Humboldt (1769–1859), who visited South America, Cuba and Mexico, though apparently not the United States. A junction on the Memphis & Ohio and Mobile & Ohio Railroads, it was the scene of a number of skirmishes between July and December 1862.

Hungary Station (Hanover) VA

The Hungary Branch Railroad was a spur leading from the Richmond, Fredericksburg & Potomac to coal mines. The name may derive from an Algonquin word meaning "goose." In April 1862 the Confederate Navy, desperate for armor plate, requisitioned the rails and fastenings, leading to loud complaints from Peter V. Daniel, president of the RF&P (The name is no longer in use.)

Hunnewell (Shelby) MO

Was named for Horatio H. Hunnewell (1810–1902), a Boston banker. There was fighting here in August 1861, January 1862 and April 1864.

Huntington (Huntington) IN

Built on the site of an Indian campground, it was named in 1831 for Samuel Huntington (1731–1796), a member of the first Continental Congress, 1776–1784. A group of Copperheads or Southern sympathizers seized arms and ammunition at the depot here in July 1863.

Huntsville (Madison) AL

When founded it was called Twickenham by Leroy Pope, after the English village in Middlesex which was the home of his 18th century ancestor, poet Alexander Pope. It was renamed in 1811 for John Hunt (fl. 1775–1805), a Virginian veteran of the Revolutionary War who had settled here in 1805, and served as the state capital, 1819–1847. The first cotton mill was established on the Flint River in 1818. Huntsville attracted many refugees who fled when it was occupied by Union troops in April 1862. The Memphis & Charleston Railroad depot became a prison for Confederate soldiers and a camp for contrabands was also established here. There was further skirmishing in June and July and attacks on trains by Confederate guerrillas in August. It subsequently returned to Confederate control. Yet more skirmishing occurred in October 1864.

Huntsville (Madison) AR

Was also named for Revolutionary War soldier, merchant and county coroner John Hunt. General Van Dorn's Confederates, retreating after the battle of Pea Ridge, passed through here in March 1862. There was skirmishing here in October 1862 and January 1865.

Huntsville (Randolph) MO

Laid out in 1831 and named for Daniel Hunt of Kentucky, one of the first settlers and the donor of the town site. It was the scene of skirmishing in November 1862, July, August and September 1864.

Huntsville (Walker) TX

Was founded in 1830 as a trading post by Pleasant Gray and named after his hometown of Huntsville, Alabama. The Lone Star Mill, set up in the Texas State Penitentiary in 1853, made cloth for uniforms for Texas troops; it was also used as a military prison for six months in 1863.

Huttonsville (Randolph) WV

Took its name from pioneer Jonathan Hutton (b.1769) who settled here in 1795. Skirmishing occurred in August 1862, July 1863 and August 1864.

Ilion (Herkimer) NY

On the Mohawk River, it was first settled in 1725 by Germans and named c.1800. Ilion was a variant of Ilium, another name for the ancient city of Troy in Asia Minor. Eliphalet Remington & Sons, established here in 1828, made rifles and revolvers for the Union Army and Navy.

Independence (Jackson) MO

Now part of Kansas City, Independence was first settled in 1825 and named following the celebration in 1826 of the 50th anniversary of the Declaration of Independence. Famous as the starting point for wagon trains heading west, it saw considerable military activity during the Civil War. There was skirmishing in November 1861, and February and May 1862, and it was captured by a mixed force of Confederate volunteers and guerrillas in August 1862, when Colonel John T. Hughes, popularly known as "General," was killed; the Confederates were driven out in October. Further skirmishing took place in February–April and August 1863, February, April and August 1864. It was evacuated by the Federals in October 1864 during the first phase of the battle of Westport.

Indianapolis (Marion) IN

Established on the West Fork of the White River, Indianapolis was an invented name: Indiana + *polis*, Greek for "city." It was laid out as the new state capital in 1821. Gilbert C. Van Camp produced tinned food here, in particular pork and beans, for the Union Army, and it was also the site of a large ammunition factory. General Ulysses S. Grant met Secretary of State Edwin M. Stanton here in October 1863 and received his orders as the new commander of the Military Division of the Mississippi. In 1865 it was the state rendezvous for the demobilization of Indiana troops.

Indianola (Calhoun) TX

Many German immigrants came here in the 1840s, a settlement was founded in 1846 and it was named in 1849, with another made-up name — Indian + *ola*, Spanish for "wave." It became a seaport on Matagorda Bay, and camels destined for Camp Verde (q.v.) arrived here in the mid–1850s. Before the Civil War this was also the main military depot for the U.S. Army in western Texas, and after its troops surrendered in April 1861, the warehouses were used as a Confederate quartermaster depot till it was recaptured by Federal gunboats in October 1862. It was occupied again in November 1863 and there was more skirmishing near here in February 1864.

Irondale (Jefferson) AL

So called from the Cahaba Iron Works and furnaces established here. Additional ones were built in 1863 to supplement the output from Selma, making artillery shot and shells and rifles. (Now part of Birmingham.)

Ironton (Iron) MO

Founded in 1857, its name derives from the local iron ore deposits. Ulysses S. Grant received his commission as a brigadier general here in August 1861. Fighting involving General Meriwether ("Jeff") Thompson and his Confederate irregulars took place hereabouts in October and November 1861.

Irvine (Estill) KY

Established in 1812, it was named for Colonel William Irvine (1741–1804), an Irishman who served in the Revolutionary War. There was a skirmish here in July 1863.

Irwinville (Irwin) GA

Named for Jared Irwin (1750–1818) governor of Georgia, 1796–1798, 1806–1809. Jefferson Davis was captured near here in May 1865.

Island No. 10 MO

Was so called because this was the tenth island south of where the Mississippi joins the Ohio; other islands in this stretch of the Mississippi were similarly numbered. The Confederate garrison from New Madrid was evacuated to Island No. 10, in the bend of the river, in

March 1862, but surrendered to Flag Officer Foote's flotilla the following month.

Iuka (Tishomingo) MS

The site of a Chickasaw village, it was named for an early 19th century chief of that tribe. It came into being when the Memphis & Charleston Railroad was completed in 1857 and the town of East Port was moved here. Occupied by General Price's Confederate troops in September 1862, they were forced to withdraw after a battle in which General Lewis H. Little was killed. There was further skirmishing here in July 1863.

Jacinto (Alcorn) MS

Although *jacinto* is Spanish for "hyacinth," this placename probably commemorates the victorious battle of San Jacinto (1836) in the Texan War of Independence. It is an alternate name for the engagement at Glendale (q.v.) in September 1863.

Jacksboro (Campbell) TN

Was named for John F. Jack (1766–1829), an early Tennessee legislator and judge. Skirmishing occurred here in March 1862 and August 1863.

Jackson (East Feliciana) LA

A large number of towns were named for General Andrew Jackson (1767–1845), "Old Hickory," hero of the War of 1812 and seventh president of the United States, 1829–1837. It was previously called Buncombe, after Buncombe County, North Carolina, before being renamed after the battle of New Orleans (1814). There was skirmishing here in August 1863, March and October 1864.

Jackson (Hinds) MS

Originally a trading post called LeFleur's Bluff, established on the Pearl River in 1792 by a French-Canadian called Louis LeFleur, it was laid out as the new state capital of Mississippi in 1821 and renamed in honor of Andrew Jackson.

Workshops in the Mississippi State Penitentiary, established in 1849, produced military clothing for state troops. J.M. McAlleny's "clothing manufactory" at Armory Hall also made uniforms for Mississippi soldiers, and the Ladies' Soldier Sewing Society made clothing for those Mississippi troops serving in Virginia. A naval station was established here after the fall of New Orleans in 1862. There was a Confederate arsenal here and an ordnance establishment, which suffered an explosion in the laboratory connected with it in November 1862. The following month Jefferson Davis made a speech to the Mississippi Congress in which he stated confidently that "our condition is in every respect greatly improved over what it was last year" and that "the articles necessary for the support of our troops, and our people ... are being produced in the Confederacy."

Converted buildings were used as a military prison for a while in 1863, and until its evacuation by General Joseph E. Johnston in May 1863, Jackson was the main refugee center in Mississippi. When they captured it, Federal troops burned much of it, causing it to be nicknamed "Chimneyville." Evacuated a second time by Confederates after a week's siege by General William T. Sherman in July 1863, there was more fighting here in February and July 1864.

Jackson (Madison) TN

A port on the Forked Deer River, many of the men who settled here in 1819 were veterans who had served under General Andrew Jackson, and in 1822 named their new home for him. It was attacked unsuccessfully by General Forrest's cavalry in December 1862.

Jacksonport (Jackson) AR

At the confluence of the White and Black Rivers, it was settled in 1822 and also named for Andrew Jackson. Fighting broke out near here in June 1862, November and December 1863, and there was a Confederate attack on it in April 1864.

Jacksonville (Duval) FL

The original settlement (1740) on the St. Johns River was named for Andrew Jackson after a new town was laid out in 1822. As the eastern terminus of the Florida, Atlantic & Gulf Central Railroad, it was an early base for blockade runners until occupied by Union troops, first briefly in March 1862 and March 1863, then in February 1864, prior to the battle of Olustee, and was devastated as a result.

Jacksonville (Onslow) NC

Was a ferry crossing on the New River c.1757 which was also renamed in honor of Andrew Jackson. Lieutenant William B. Cushing, USN, came up the river in the steamer *Ellis* and captured two schooners here in November 1862.

James Island SC

First known as James Island in 1671, probably for the future King James II, it became Boone Island for Governor Thomas Boone, then reverted to its original name in the early 18th century. Because of its strategic position opposite Charleston, it was the scene of numerous skirmishes and engagements between June 1862 and February 1865, including the unsuccessful Federal attack on Secessionville, and was twice abandoned by them. It remained in Confederate hands till the fall of Charleston in February 1865. **Fort Pemberton**, named for General John C. Pemberton (1814–1881), who commanded the Department of South Carolina, 1861–1862, and **Fort Lamar**, probably named for a member of the Lamar family of Georgia — either Mirabeau B. Lamar (1798–1859), second president of the Texas Republic, or Lucius Q.C. Lamar (1825–1893), colonel of the 18th Mississippi — were located here.

James River VA

Was named for King James I (1566–1625) who chartered the first English colony in the New World. Because of its location, it featured throughout the Civil War. In June 1864 Federal engineers built a huge temporary pontoon bridge across the 2,100 ft. of the river, allowing General Grant's army to cross to the south side with the aim of capturing Petersburg.

The James River Squadron, formed in July 1861 for the defense of Virginia and North Carolina, retreated up the James River towards Richmond after the battle of Hampton Roads; its last commander was Rear Admiral Raphael Semmes. The Union Army of the James, in existence 1864–1865, was commanded by Generals Benjamin F. Butler and Edward O. Ord.

Jamestown (Russell) KY

This was originally called Jacksonville for Andrew Jackson, but was renamed in 1826 for James Wooldridge (c.1762–1845) who gave 110 acres for a town site. There was a skirmish here in June 1863.

Jamestown (Guilford) NC

Was named c.1816 for James Mendenhall (1718–c.1782), a Quaker who had come here from Pennsylvania in the 1760s. The firm of H.C. Lamb & Co. made rifles here for North Carolina troops, 1862–1865.

Jarratt's Station (Brunswick) VA

The Jarratt family settled in this area as early as 1652. A skirmish took place here, on the Norfolk & Petersburg Railroad, in May 1864, and the town was afterwards burned by Union cavalry. (Now called Jarratt.)

Jasper (Marion) TN

Sergeant William Jasper (1750–1779), a hero of the Revolutionary War who served in South Carolina and Georgia, is commemorated here. There was skirmishing here in June 1862 and nearby in October 1863.

Jeanerette (Iberia) LA

Was named for Jean W. Jeanerette of South Carolina who came here in the 1820s and became its first postmaster. Skirmishing took place here in April 1863.

Jefferson (Frederick) MD

On the Catoctin River, this was one of many communities named for Thomas Jefferson (1743–1826), third president of the United States, 1801–1809. The first settlers arrived in the 1770s and it had various names before becoming Jefferson in 1831. It was the scene of a skirmish in September 1862.

Jefferson (Marion) TX

Was established in 1836 on a branch of the Red River, and became the main river port in Texas. There was a Confederate quartermaster depot here, established in November 1862, which produced shoes for the Confederate Army and the Jefferson Tannery near here, owned by D. Lucas & Co., made sole leather.

Jefferson City (Cole) MO

On the banks of the Missouri River, it was laid out as the state capital in 1821 by Daniel Boone's son, though it developed slowly. The state was divided during the Civil War, but Jefferson City stayed loyal to the Union after it was evacuated by Missouri troops in June 1861. There was fighting near here in September and October 1864. The Missouri Penitentiary, built 1836, was used as a U.S. military prison in 1864.

Jeffersonville (Clark) IN

Was first laid out in 1802 on a plan suggested by Thomas Jefferson on the site of Fort Steuben. On the Ohio, it became an important steamboat-building center. Jefferson General Hospital, established here in February 1864 and built on a radial pattern, was second only in size to Satterlee General Hospital at Philadelphia.

Jenkins' Ferry (Grant) AR

At Leola, on the Saline River, this takes its name from Thomas Jenkins (1788–1847) who established a ferry here in 1815. His sons William and John DeKalb operated it at the time of the Civil War when it was in Saline County. The engagement here in April 1864 was largely indecisive, though strategically it was a Confederate victory. During the fighting Confederate General William R. Scurry was killed and Horace Randal mortally wounded; Union General Samuel A. Rice was also mortally wounded.

Jenny Lind (Sebastian) AR

Was named for Jenny Lind (1820–1887), the international soprano known as the "Swedish Nightingale." Her visit to America in 1850–1852, organized by showman Phineas T. Barnum, was an enormous success. There was a skirmish here in September 1863.

Jericho Mill (Hanover) VA

Comes from the biblical city of that name, in the Second Book of Samuel and First Book of Chronicles. In May 1864 Federal troops crossing the North Anna River here successfully repulsed an attack by General A.P. Hill's Confederates.

Jetersville (Amelia) VA

Was named for its first postmaster, Thomas E. Jeter. On the Richmond & Danville Railroad, it was the scene of an engagement, also known as Amelia Springs (q.v.), during General Lee's retreat to Appomattox Court House in early April 1865.

John's Island SC

Its name origin is uncertain, but it may derive from the St. John family, once prominent here. Confederate shore batteries on this island at the mouth of the Stono River near Charleston fought a duel with the USS *Pawnee* in late December 1863. Federal troops who attempted to land in February 1864 were forced to withdraw and there was more fighting here in July. **Fort Trenholm** here was named for Confederate secretary of the Treasury George A. Trenholm (1806–1876) who was born in South Carolina.

Johnson's Island OH

In Lake Erie, it was originally called Bull's Island for owner E.W. Bull, then became Johnson's Island when sold to L.B. Johnson of Sandusky in 1852. In 1861 the U.S. government leased 40 acres of it and established the first prison camp for Confederates. Construction of barracks began in November 1861 and the first prisoners, mostly Confederate officers, arrived in February 1862. Colonel Charles W. Hill who took over as commandant in June 1864 was well regarded by the prisoners for his attempts to improve conditions. There were several plots to rescue them, none of them successful.

Johnsonville (Humphreys) TN

Was named for Andrew Johnson (1808–1875) who came to live in Tennessee and served as governor, 1853–1857, and military governor, 1862–1865. This Union supply base on the Tennessee River was the target of a raid by General Forrest's cavalry in November 1864, causing extensive damage and disrupting river traffic. "That devil Forrest ... was making havoc among the gunboats and transports," reported General William T. Sherman angrily. (Now replaced by New Johnsonville because of flooding.)

Jonesboro (Clayton) GA

A town first established here in 1823 was named for Captain Samuel G. Jones (1815–1886), one of the line engineers of the Central Railroad of Georgia, who had revived the bankrupt Macon & Western and become chief engineer of the Alabama & Florida Railroads. There was fighting here during the closing stages of the Atlanta campaign in August-September 1864.

Jonesborough (Washington) TN

Laid out in 1779 and named for William Jones (c.1741–1801), a North Carolina Revolutionary War leader and politician. There was a camp here for paroled and exchanged prisoners, and there was fighting in September 1863 and 1864.

Jonesville (Lee) VA

Was named for pioneer Frederick Jones who gave the land for the town site when it was established in 1794. It witnessed fighting in January, November and December 1863, and January 1864.

Kabletown (Jefferson) WV

Was named for David Kable who bought land here in 1814. There was skirmishing here in March, June, July and November 1864, the last one involving Colonel Mosby's partisan rangers and Captain Blazer's scouts.

Kearneysville (Jefferson) WV

Uriah and James Kearney, early settlers here, gave their name to this community. In February 1864 Major Gilmor's partisan rangers derailed a train on the Baltimore & Ohio Railroad near here, robbing the crew and passengers. There was some skirmishing in August, then in October Colonel Mosby's rangers also derailed a train on the B&O, seizing approximately $170,000, mostly from two army paymasters in what became known as the "Greenback Raid," and burned the train.

Keedysville (Washington) MD

Was established by 1770 and originally called Centerville. The name was changed in the 1860s when several well-known families called Keedy were living in the area. Skirmishing took place in September 1862, and July and August 1864.

Kelly's Ford (Culpeper) VA

This battle on the Rappahannock is also sometimes known as Kellysville, named for 18th century resident John P. Kelly, whose descendant Granville Kelly was the postmaster at the time of the Civil War. Skirmishing occurred here in August and December 1862, and the cavalry engagement in March 1863 was a Confederate victory, though in the course of it, Major John Pelham — "The Gallant Pelham"— was killed. Further skirmishing took place in July, October and November of that year.

Kenansville (Duplin) NC

Was named for Colonel James Kenan (1740–1810), who led a demonstration against the hated Stamp Act (1765) and was a member of the provincial congress. The firm of Louis Froelich manufactured swords here and there was a skirmish in July 1863.

Kennesaw Mountain (Cobb) GA

The name was that of an Indian chief who signed a treaty with the whites in 1791. The battle fought here in June 1864 during the Atlanta campaign resulted in heavy Union casualties, among them General Charles G. Harker, killed, and Daniel McCook, mortally wounded.

Keokuk (Lee) IA

On the Mississippi, was settled in 1836 and named in honor of Keokuk (1788–1848?), a Sauk chief and orator who aided the Americans in the Black Hawk War (1832). The Estes House Hotel became a Civil War hospital, organized by volunteer nurse Annie T. Wittenmyer. She set up a local soldiers' aid society, and worked for both the U.S. Sanitary Commission and the U.S. Christian Commission, providing relief and aid to soldiers at the front, paying particular attention to diet.

Kernstown (Frederick) VA

Was probably named for the Kerns family, long established residents of Frederick County; there were six different families of this name prior to the Revolutionary War. Two battles took place here, in March 1862, marking the opening of General "Stonewall" Jackson's Shenandoah Valley campaign, and in July 1864, involving General Early's Confederates.

Keytesville (Chariton) MO

Was founded in 1817 on the banks of the Chariton and Missouri Rivers but relocated in 1833 because of flooding. It was named for the Rev. James Keyte, a Methodist minister who gave 50 acres for a seat for Chariton County. It surrendered to General Price's Confederates in September 1864.

King and Queen Court House (King and Queen) VA

Established in 1691, it was named for King William III (1650–1702) and Queen Mary II (1662–1694). Union Colonel Ulrich Dahlgren was mortally wounded in a skirmish here in March 1864 during a failed raid on Richmond.

Kingsport (Sullivan) TN

Settled in 1761 on the Holston River, it had become King's Port by 1774, named for Colonel James King of Virginia who brought his salt here for shipment down river, and built an iron works and nail factory. Skirmishing occurred here in September 1863 and October 1864.

Kingston (Bartow) GA

Was named for John P. King (1799–1888), president of the Central Railroad of Georgia, 1841–1878. One of the first Confederate military hospitals was established here at the Wayside Home. There was fighting near here during the Atlanta campaign in May, June and July 1864. Here, in November, General William T. Sherman issued the orders for his march to the sea, stating ominously that "the army will forage liberally on the country" and that any resistance would result in "a devastation more or less relentless." The town was subsequently burned. The last Confederate troops in Georgia surrendered here the following May; Colonel Richard G. Earle was among the final casualties.

Kingston (Roane) TN

Established in 1799 and named for Major Robert King, a Revolutionary War soldier, trader and tavern keeper. It witnessed skirmishing in November and December 1863 and October 1864.

Kinston (Lenoir) NC

First settled in 1740, it was called King's Town in 1762 for King George III who had come to the British throne two years previously. It became Kingston, which after the Revolution was changed to Kinston in 1784, though the old name was still being used in the 1860 census. It was captured but not held by Federal troops in December 1862. Confederates from here under General George Pickett made an unsuccessful attempt to retake New Bern in February 1864. The three-day battle of Kinston in March 1865 was a desperate attempt to delay the relentless Federal advance through the Carolinas, and the town was re-occupied by Union troops under General Jacob D. Cox.

Kirksville (Adair) MO

Founded in 1841, it was named in honor of Jesse Kirk (1793–1846), its first postmaster. Fighting nearby in August 1862 resulted in a Federal victory.

Knobnoster (Johnson) MO

Founded in 1856, it is a pseudo-Latin name, inspired by two nearby knoblike hills. Knobnoster was the scene of a skirmish in January 1862.

Knoxville (Knox) TN

First established in 1786 on the Tennessee River as White's Fort, named for Captain James White, it was renamed in 1791 in honor of General Henry Knox (1750–1806), the first U.S. secretary of war, 1789–1794. It served as the state capital in 1796–1812 and 1817–1819. Conflict between pro- and anti-secessionists surfaced in rioting in May 1861. A small ordnance shop was set up here and the city jail was used as a military prison in 1861 and possibly also in 1862. It remained under Confederate control till September 1863. There was an unsuccessful attempt to retake it in November-December 1863, when it was besieged and attacked by General Longstreet's troops.

Kossuth (Alcorn) MS

It was named in 1852 for the celebrated Hungarian revolutionary Louis Kossuth (1802–1894), who visited America in 1851 and received an enthusiastic welcome. There was a skirmish here in August 1862.

La Fayette (Walker) GA

One of a number of towns named for the French Marquis de La Fayette (1757–1834), who served in the Continental Army in 1777–1782, and revisited America in 1824–1825. There was skirmishing near here in September and December 1863, and June and October 1864.

La Grange (Troup) GA

Several places were also named after the Marquis de La Fayette's country residence in France.

He came here as a guest of the governor of Georgia during his return visit to the United States in 1825 and this was named in 1828. Wartime hospitals here included Cannon, Law, Oliver and St. Mary's. The town was unique in having its own female home guard, the Nancy Harts, named for a Revolutionary War heroine. It became a center for refugees, particularly ones from Louisiana. Confederate Secretary of the Navy Stephen R. Mallory was captured here in May 1865.

La Grange (Fayette) TN

Was intended as the terminus of the La Grange & Memphis Railroad (1836), but this project was abandoned. It was occupied by General Grant's troops in November 1862, there was skirmishing here in March 1863 and further skirmishing in January 1865. Colonel Benjamin H. Grierson and three regiments of Union cavalry set out from here in April 1863 on their diversionary raid through Mississippi, to Newton Station and Baton Rouge, Louisiana. It also became the site of a contraband camp.

La Grange (Fayette) TX

On the Colorado River, it was founded in 1828 by Colonel John H. Moore. It was the location of the Alexander Hat Manufacturing Co. which produced large numbers of military hats—as many as 18,000 monthly in 1864—as well as powder, shoes, leather and rope for the Confederate government.

Lake Erie OH

It takes its name from the Native American Erie tribe, and despite its location near the Canadian border, Lake Erie, ringed by four states, was not immune from the Civil War. Johnson's Island in Sandusky Bay housed Confederate prisoners-of-war, 1862–1865. A plot to free them by capturing two steamers, then boarding the guard ship USS *Michigan* in September 1864, failed.

Lake Pontchartrain LA

This was named for the Comte de Pontchartrain (1643–1727), a French statesman and explorer. Two experimental Confederate submarines, built in nearby New Orleans, were tested in the lake. The first, in the fall of 1861, was not very successful but the second one, in February 1862, proved to be more satisfactory. She was given the appropriate name of *Pioneer* but before she could enter service as a privateer, was scuttled to keep her from falling into enemy hands when New Orleans was captured in April 1862.

Lamar (Benton) MS

Was named for Lucius Q.C. Lamar (1825–1893), who served as representative from Mississippi, 1857–1860, was colonel of the 18th Mississippi, then went to Europe as a Confederate commissioner in 1863. A skirmish took place here in August 1864.

Lamar (Barton) MO

Founded in 1856, it was named for Mirabeau B. Lamar (1798–1859), president of the Texas Republic, 1838–1841, and uncle of L.Q.C. Lamar. There was skirmishing nearby at Coon Creek in August 1862 and further military action in November. More fighting occurred in May 1864, and the town was sacked by Confederates later that month.

Lancaster (Garrard) KY

Was named in 1798 by settlers from Lancaster, Pennsylvania, who had come from Lancaster, England. There was skirmishing here in October 1862 and July 1863.

Lancaster (Dallas) TX

Now a suburb of Dallas, Lancaster was founded in 1852 and named by "Honest A." Bledsoe after Lancaster, Kentucky. The firm of Tucker, Sherrard & Co. (later, Sherrard, Taylor & Co.) made pistols here for the Confederate Army.

Laredo (Webb) TX

Was established as a ferry crossing on the Rio Grande in 1755 and named after Laredo on the northern coast of Spain. It was the capital of the short-lived Republic of the Rio Grande in 1839–1841. There was a Federal attack on Laredo in March 1864.

Lavaca (Calhoun) TX

The 17th century French explorer Robert La Salle thought that buffaloes resembled cows. "The cow" in French is *la vache*, and in Spanish, *la vaca*, which was the name chosen when this place was founded by Spaniards in 1815. Edgar C. Singer, a gunsmith and relative of sewing machine inventor Isaac Singer, and J.R. Fretwell developed and made torpedoes here. There was also a Confederate arsenal and a small arms manufactory. It was bombarded by Federal forces at the end of October and beginning of November 1862. (Now called Port Lavaca.)

Lawrence (Douglas) KS

This town on the Kansas River was founded in 1854 by the New England Emigrant Aid Society and named for Boston textile manufacturer Amos A. Lawrence (1814–1886), a prominent member and anti-slavery supporter. Two years later it was attacked and looted by pro-slavery Missourians, but was the scene of an even more savage attack by Quantrill's Confederate guerrillas in August 1863, partly in revenge for the burning of Osceola, Missouri, and nearly 200 men and boys were killed. "The town is a complete ruin. The whole of the business part, and all good private residences are burned down…. I cannot describe the horrors," reported one eyewitness. At the end of the war, it served as a rendezvous point for the mustering out of Kansas troops.

Lawrenceburg (Anderson) KY

This and the following were named in honor of Captain James Lawrence (1781–1813) of the USS *Chesapeake*, who was fatally wounded in the engagement with HMS *Shannon* during the War of 1812, and whose dying words were "Don't give up the ship!" It became a town in 1820. There was skirmishing here in October 1862 involving General Kirby Smith's cavalry during the Perryville campaign, followed by its capture by Union troops later that month.

Lawrenceburg (Lawrence) TN

Was founded in 1815. There was skirmishing here in November 1863, and more fighting in November 1864 during General Hood's advance towards Nashville.

Lebanon (Marion) KY

Several towns took their names from Mount Lebanon in the Bible. Skirmishing near here in July 1862 was followed by its capture by General John H. Morgan during his first Kentucky raid. Almost exactly a year later it was captured by them again.

Lebanon (Laclede) MO

Was founded c.1849 and named after Lebanon, Tennessee. Between Springfield and St. Louis, it was occupied by Federal troops in January 1862 and there was skirmishing near here in November 1864.

Lebanon (Wilson) TN

Established in 1802 and so called because of the profusion of cedar trees for which the biblical Lebanon was famous. The Lebanon Soldiers' Aid Society made uniforms for Tennessee troops in the early part of the war. Fighting broke out here in May and November 1862, and there was further skirmishing in September 1863.

Leighton (Colbert) AL

Was named for William Leigh, its first postmaster. There was skirmishing here in April 1863 and December 1864.

Lenoir's Station (Loudon) TN

May be named for William Lenoir (1751–1839), a hero of the American Revolution, or William B. Lenoir who owned one of the first cotton mills in the South. There was fighting here, on the East Tennessee & Georgia Railroad, in June and November 1863. (Now called Lenoir City.)

Lewisburg (Greenbriar) WV

It commemorates its builder, Irish-born General Andrew Lewis (1720–1781) who defeated the Shawnees at Point Pleasant in 1774. Fighting took place here in May 1862, 1863 and 1864. It was also the target of a Federal cavalry raid in December 1863.

Lexington (Fayette) KY

One of a number of places named directly or indirectly after Lexington, Massachusetts, which derived from the English village of Lexington (now Laxton), Nottinghamshire, the birthplace of some of the original settlers. The battles of Lexington and Concord (1775) were the first engagements of the Revolutionary War. Lexington, Kentucky, was founded in 1779. Wool manufacturer Richard Loud and "jeans and linsey manufacturer" Richard Morgan both made cloth for Confederate uniforms. The jail here was used as a U.S. military prison in 1862–1863 and possibly also in 1864. The Federal garrison was captured by General Morgan's cavalry in October 1862 during his first Kentucky raid, and the town was visited by them again in June 1864, when they burned the Federal depot and stables and requisitioned 7,000 horses. The following year it became a rendezvous point for the mustering out of Kentucky troops.

Lexington (Lafayette) MO

On the Missouri River, it was laid out in 1822 and named after Lexington, Kentucky, from where many of the settlers came. It was captured by Confederates after a siege in September 1861 involving the Missouri State Guard, then by Federal troops in October. There was further military activity near here in October 1862, July and November 1863, June, September and October 1864, and January and May 1865.

Lexington (Henderson) TN

General Forrest's Confederate cavalry defeated Federal troops here in December 1862, and there was further fighting near here in June 1863.

Lexington (♦) VA

Established in 1777 and named after the battle of Lexington (1775). Federal troops under General David Hunter bombarded the town in June 1864 and looted and burned the Virginia Military Institute, America's oldest, state-supported military college, founded in 1839 and known as the "West Point of the South." A book stolen from its library by one of the soldiers was returned in April 2009, 145 years later, by a friend of one of his descendants. Many of the students from Washington College (now Washington & Lee University), also located here, joined the Rockbridge Artillery, an elite unit organized in April 1861 which included private Robert E. Lee, Jr.

Liberty (Clay) MO

Extolling the concept of liberty, this was a common placename. Liberty, Missouri, was laid out in 1822. The U.S. arsenal here was seized by pro-secessionists and Missouri state troops in April 1861. There was skirmishing here in October 1862 and July 1864.

Little Rock (Pulaski) AR

The smaller of two rocky formations on the banks of the Arkansas River, called *La Petite Roche* by French explorer Bernard de la Harpe in 1722, gave its name to what became Little Rock. Founded in 1820 by two rival land companies, it became the territorial capital in 1821 and the state capital in 1836. An attempt to rename it Arkopolis, an invented name, was unsuccessful.

There was an arsenal here in 1861, and a naval station where the steamer *Pontchartrain* was repaired in 1862–1863. The Soldiers' Aid Society made uniforms for Arkansas troops. These, together with shoes, tents and drums were also made by convict labor in the state penitentiary. Both the Rock Hotel and St. John's College (a military academy) were used as Confederate hospitals in 1862–1863. Little Rock was a refugee center until captured by Federal troops in September 1863. Four days before that, General Lucius M. Walker had been mortally wounded in a duel with General John S. Marmaduke. A converted building was turned into a Federal military prison in 1864–1865.

Livingston (Overton) TN

Was established as a county seat in 1835 and named in honor of Edward Livingston (1764–1836), secretary of state under Andrew Jackson, 1831–1833. General Morgan's command arrived here in July 1862 after their Kentucky raid, and skirmishing occurred in December 1863 and March 1865.

Logan's Crossroads (Wayne) KY

May be named for General Benjamin Logan (c.1743–1802), a Virginia soldier and Indian fighter associated with Kentucky. In an engagement here, also known as Mill Springs (q.v.), in January 1862, in which General Felix K. Zollicoffer was killed, the Confederates were repulsed, causing them to retreat across the Cumberland River.

London (Laurel) KY

The name was chosen as a way of resolving an argument between Scottish and Irish settlers who wanted to call it either Edinburgh or Dublin. It was captured in October 1862 by General Wheeler's Confederate cavalry and there was further skirmishing in July 1863.

Lone Jack (Jackson) MO

Founded in 1841 and so called because of a prairie landmark, a blackjack tree near a spring. There was fighting near here in August 1862, when Federal troops were defeated, and again in March 1865.

Long Island MA

In Boston harbor and called this on account of its shape, it was the site of **Camp Wightman**, established in May 1861 and named for Joseph M. Wightman (1812–1885), mayor of Boston, 1861–1863. Several Massachusetts regiments — the 3rd, 4th and 9th — were here at various times.

Longwood (Pettis) MO

Was possibly named after the Emperor Napoleon I's house on St. Helena and his place of death. It was the scene of skirmishing in September 1862 and May 1865.

Lookout Mountain (Hamilton) TN

A common descriptive name for a place noted for the views from its summit, in this case the Tennessee River and the city of Chattanooga. The engagement here, in November 1863, which came to be known as the "Battle above the Clouds" on account of the heavy fog which covered parts of the mountain, ended the siege of Chattanooga and from here the Confederates withdrew to Missionary Ridge (q.v.).

Loudon (Loudon) TN

John Campbell, Earl of Loudoun (1705–1782) was the British commander-in-chief in America in 1756–1758. It was the scene of skirmishing between October and December 1863.

Louisa (Lawrence) KY

Was named c.1750 for Princess Louisa (1724–1751), a daughter of King George II, who in 1744 became Queen of Denmark through her marriage to King Frederick V. There was skirmishing here in March 1863.

Louisa Court House (Louisa) VA

Dating from c.1741, it was probably also named for Princess Louisa. It was on the Virginia Central Railroad and in May 1863 was the scene of skirmishing during General Stoneman's central Virginia raid when the depot was wrecked and track ripped up.

Louisville (Jefferson) GA

Laid out in 1786, it was Georgia's state capital, 1796–1804, till replaced by Milledgeville. There was skirmishing here in November 1864 during General Sherman's march through Georgia and much of the town was burned. Like Louisville, Kentucky, it was named for King Louis XVI (1754–1793) of France, in recognition of the help given to the American colonies in the War of Independence.

Louisville (Jefferson) KY

Founded in 1778 by French settlers, it was named two years later for King Louis XVI. From 1820 onwards it was a major river port on the Ohio.

Gordon, Castlen & Gordon made Navy pistols, Myer & Linz made cavalry swords, and both R.E. Miles and John Stokes & Son made knapsacks and other items of military equipment. The Louisville Woolen Mills, owned by L. Richardson, manufactured "white and colored jeans and linsey," Alexander Craig made military caps and Wolf & Durringer produced state buttons. David Faulds was a manufacturer of "drums and fifes of every description."

It became the headquarters of the Union Department of Ohio in November 1861. Rumors of General Morgan's raiders in September 1862 caused alarm, and while organizing the city's defenses, General William Nelson was shot and killed by General Jefferson C. Davis in a dispute in a Louisville hotel. There was a temporary ordnance depot here during the war and the Louisville Jail was used as a U.S. military prison in 1863–1865.

Dr. Mary Walker, the first woman assistant surgeon in the Union Army, was appointed superintendent of the Female Military Prison here in the fall of 1864. Confederate guerrilla leader William C. Quantrill, a self-appointed colonel, died here in June 1865 of wounds received the previous month. Louisville was a mustering-out place for Kentucky troops.

Lovejoy's Station (Clayton) GA

This may derive from a personal name, or be

a euphonious one. There was fighting in August 1864 when General Kilpatrick's cavalry was repulsed in its raid on the Macon & Western Railroad. Confederate forces, retreating after the fall of Atlanta, succeeded in repelling pursuing Federals at the beginning of September, and the remainder of General Hood's army was able to consolidate here. Inhabitants expelled from Atlanta were brought here by wagon and ambulance from Rough and Ready Station for trains to take them south. (Now called Lovejoy.)

Lovettsville (Loudoun) VA

Was established in 1820 on land owned by David Lovett. There was skirmishing here in August 1861 and January 1865.

Lowndesboro (Lowndes) AL

Was founded after 1815 by settlers from the Carolinas and named for William J. Lowndes (1782–1822), a South Carolina legislator and U.S. representative who died at sea. It was the scene of a minor cavalry skirmish in April 1865 between troops under Generals N. Bedford Forrest and James H. Wilson.

Lumpkin's Station (Stewart) GA

On the Augusta & Savannah Railroad, it was named for Wilson Lumpkin (1783–1870), who was governor of Georgia, 1831–1835. There was skirmishing near here in December 1864. (Now called Lumpkin.)

Lynchburg (Moore) TN

May be named for local resident Tom Lynch, a "frail little man ... who was always chosen to wield the lash on men sentenced to be whipped," or after a "famous beech tree" used for lynching early offenders. There was a skirmish here in September 1864.

Lynchburg (♦) VA

John Lynch (1740–1820) was an Irish Quaker who established a ferry on the James River in 1757 and built a tobacco warehouse. A small arsenal was established here in 1861; an ordnance depot that made cartridges and minié balls was later transferred to Danville. F.B. Deane, Jr. & Son made shot, shells and light artillery pieces, probably howitzers. A Soldiers' Aid Society made uniforms for a number of Virginia units. The Pratt Hospital and the Ladies' Aid Hospital were located here, and the city jail and the fairground housed Union prisoners in 1862–1863 and possibly also in 1864.

Lynchburg, at the junction of the Orange & Alexandria, the South Side and the Virginia & Tennessee Railroads, was an important Confederate supply depot. It became a center for refugees from 1862 onwards and was the only significant place in Virginia not captured by Federal troops. For a few days in early April 1865, between the fall of Richmond and General Lee's surrender, it served as the temporary state capital.

It was the scene of General Early's victory over General David Hunter in a two-day battle in June 1864. General James Dearing, CSA, who died here in April 1865 after being wounded in the Appomattox campaign, was the last Civil War general to die from his wounds.

Lynnville (Giles) TN

The name derives from Lynn, Massachusetts, called after the English town of King's Lynn, Norfolk. It was the scene of skirmishing in November and December 1864.

Mackinac Island MI

In Lake Huron, it was the site of **Fort Mackinac**, built in 1780, which was used to house Confederate prisoners during the Civil War. The name comes from an Ojibwe word for "island of the large turtle." The French version of this was shortened by the British to *mackinac*.

Macon (Bibb) GA

On the Ocmulgee River, it began to grow in 1818–1819, was laid out in 1823 and named for General Nathaniel Macon (1758–1837), a North Carolina senator and Revolutionary War hero, and an early defender of states' rights.

Starting in 1862, Macon became a major armaments center for the Confederacy, with a newly-built armory which repaired muskets, rifles and carbines; an arsenal created from the arms factory of D.C. Hodgkins & Son and the Findlay Iron Works; and the huge, purpose-built Confederate States Ordnance Laboratories, for testing and developing new munitions and weapons. Swords were also made here, by the firms of E.J. Johnston & Co. and W.J. McElroy. The Central Railroad of Georgia established workshops here in 1863 to replace those at

Savannah which had been converted into arsenals.

The Confederate Treasury Department had a depository here and there was also a supply depot. The hospitals established here — Floyd House, Ocmulgee, Polk and Stout — seem to have been highly regarded. In 1864 it became a magnet for refugees, particularly from Atlanta. Converted buildings and the fairground housed Union prisoners in 1861–1864.

Union troops were repulsed in July 1864, when General George Stoneman, on his way to liberate prisoners at Andersonville, was cut off and captured, and a further Federal attack was beaten off in November. In April 1865, however, General Howell Cobb surrendered the town to General James H. Wilson. Jefferson Davis, who had paid an unexpected visit to the town in September 1864, telling a meeting, "Our cause is not lost.... Let no one despond," was brought here after his capture near Irwinville in May 1865.

Macon (Macon) MO

This was also named for Nathaniel Macon and developed with the coming of the Hannibal & St. Joseph Railroad in 1858. Skirmishing occurred here in February 1864 and 1865.

Madison (St. Francis) AR

A large number of towns were named for James Madison (1751–1836), who served two terms as fourth president of the United States, 1809–1817. There was skirmishing here in March and June 1863.

Madison (Morgan) GA

It became a Confederate hospital center, with Asylum, Blackie, May and Stout Hospitals all located here. Later it became known as the "town Sherman refused to burn," apparently for personal reasons, though the Georgia Railroad depot and a slave pen were destroyed.

Madison (Dane) WI

On the isthmus between Lakes Mendota and Monona, it was founded and laid out as the territorial capital in 1836. It was the location of the Harvey Soldiers' Hospital, opened in 1863 and named in memory of Louis P. Harvey, governor of Wisconsin, who was drowned in the Tennessee River in April 1862 while visiting Shiloh with supplies for wounded Wisconsin soldiers, and authorized by President Lincoln following urgent appeals by Cordelia Harvey, his widow. She had also nursed in field hospitals and worked with war orphans. At the end of the war, Wisconsin troops came here to be mustered out.

Madisonville (St. Tammany) LA

Founded in 1800, it was named in 1810. Skirmishing occurred here in July 1862 and near here in February 1864.

Magnolia Springs (Clay) FL

A number of places were called after the magnolia tree, named for the French physician and botanist Dr. Pierre Magnol (1638–1715). There was skirmishing here in September and October 1864.

Magnolia Station (Harford) MD

During General Early's move on Washington in July 1864, partisan rangers led by Major Harry Gilmor destroyed two trains and damaged a trestle bridge here, on the Baltimore & Ohio Railroad, and captured Union General William B. Franklin, though he escaped the next night.

Malvern Hill (Henrico) VA

Was named after the Malvern Hills, on the borders of Herefordshire and Worcestershire, England. The last of the Seven Days' battles in the Peninsula campaign, fought at the beginning of July 1862, it resulted in heavy Confederate losses. It "was not war — it was murder," wrote General Daniel H. Hill afterwards. There was more fighting here in August of that year, and further military activity in June and July 1864.

Manassas (♦) VA

Probably deriving from an Indian word, though of uncertain meaning, it gave its name to two major battles of the Civil War. The first, in which General Thomas J. Jackson and his brigade earned the sobriquet of "Stonewall," took place in July 1861 and resulted in a humiliating Federal defeat, though Confederate General Barnard E. Bee was mortally wounded and Colonel Francis S. Bartow killed. The second, in late-August 1862, in which Union General George W. Taylor was mortally wounded, also resulted in a victory for the South. The battles are also known as First and Second Bull Run (q.v.).

Manassas Junction (Prince William) VA

Was established in 1853 and originally called Manassas Gap Junction when the Manassas Gap and Orange & Alexandria Railroads were joined. It played an important part in the first battle of Manassas or Bull Run in July 1861, and was also the scene of skirmishes in August and October 1862 and October 1863.

Manchester (Clay) KY

A number of towns were named after Manchester, England, the center of cotton manufacturing in the 19th century and often known as Cottonopolis. The salt works at Goose Creek near here, which supplied Virginia and Tennessee as well as Kentucky, were destroyed by the Federals in October 1862.

Manchester (Hillsborough) NH

On the Merrimack River, it was settled in 1722. The first cotton mill was built in 1805 and it was named Manchester in 1810 at the suggestion of local merchant Samuel Blodget, who had visited Manchester, England, and been impressed by the canal system there. He subsequently built a canal around the Amoskeag Falls. During the Civil War the Amoskeag Manufacturing Co. made rifle muskets for the Union Army. New Hampshire troops came here to be mustered out in 1865.

Mansfield (Tolland) CT

Named for Major Moses Mansfield (1709–1754), an important landowner and mayor of New Haven, it was in existence by the early 1700s. The Eagle Manufacturing Co. made rifle muskets here.

Mansfield (DeSoto) LA

Was apparently named for a prominent local planter, though Jared Mansfield (1759–1830), surveyor general of the United States, has also been suggested as the origin. The Mansfield Female College, founded in 1855, the first women's college west of the Mississippi, was used as a hospital following the battle of Mansfield in April 1864, during General Banks' Red River campaign. This is better known as Sabine Crossroads (q.v.).

Mansura (Avoyelles) LA

Probably named after the Egyptian city of Mansura, another example of the adoption of exotic placenames. An engagement took place here in May 1864 during the Red River campaign.

Maplesville (Chilton) AL

Was founded prior to 1850 and named for store owner Stephen W. ("Billy") Maples (d.1835). There was a skirmish here in April 1865.

Marais des Cygnes River KS

This is French for "swans' marsh," dating from the time when the area was part of the Louisiana Purchase. There was some skirmishing here, near the Kansas-Missouri border, in August 1863, but in October 1864 General Price's Confederates, retreating from their raid into Missouri, were overtaken by Federal cavalry under General Alfred Pleasanton and badly beaten in a rearguard action which cost them numerous prisoners, including Generals John S. Marmaduke and William L. Cabell, and most of their artillery and they were forced to burn many of their wagons to escape. It also included a major cavalry engagement at Mine Creek. One of the participants was Lieutenant Colonel Frederick Benteen, whose military career was to end in ignominy 12 years later at the Little Big Horn in Montana.

Marianna (Lee) AR

Established in 1848, it was named in 1852 for Mary and Anna, the daughters of the woman who owned the town site. There was fighting here in November 1862.

Marianna (Jackson) FL

On the Chipola River, it was founded in 1829 and took its name from Mary and Anna, the daughters of pioneer merchant Robert Beveridge. It was the scene of a skirmish in October 1864.

Marietta (Cobb) GA

Settled by 1824, it was established in 1832, laid out the following year and named c.1837 for Mary Cobb, the wife of Judge Thomas W. Cobb. It developed with the arrival of the Western & Atlantic Railroad. "From 1850 to 1861 Marietta was the gayest, most fashionable, most flourishing, most entertaining and fastest town in Georgia," recalled one old resident, and volunteer nurse Kate Cumming, who came here in October 1863, described it as "quite an aristocratic place." President Davis visited Marietta shortly afterwards and praised Georgia's war effort. The Academy, Foard, Gilmer and Polk Hospitals were located here.

There was skirmishing near here in June 1864, culminating in the battle of Kennesaw Mountain. The Western & Atlantic depot where the Andrews Raiders boarded the train in what became known as the Great Locomotive Chase (1862), was burned by General Sherman's troops in July 1864, and the Sweetwater factory, which had made cloth for the Confederate Quartermaster Department, was destroyed and the women who worked there expelled from the area. The Georgia Military Institute, founded in 1851 and used as a hospital by both sides, was burned in November at the start of Sherman's march, along with other buildings of military use.

Marietta (Prentiss) MS

Was named after Marietta, Ohio, which commemorated the unfortunate French Queen Marie Antoinette (1755–1793). There was a skirmish here in August 1862.

Marion (Smyth) VA

General Francis Marion (1732?-1795), a hero of the Revolutionary War and known as the "Swamp Fox," is commemorated here. It was the location of Breckinridge Hospital and there was fighting during two days in December 1864.

Marion Station (Lauderdale) MS

Was also named for General Marion. On the Mobile & Ohio Railroad, it was the scene of a skirmish in February 1864.

Mars Bluff (Florence) SC

Established on the Pee Dee River in the 1730s, Mars is apparently a corruption of Maers, the name of an early settler. The Confederate gunboat *Pee Dee* was built at the navy yard here and commissioned in 1864. Both the yard and the steamer were destroyed in March 1865.

Marshall (Saline) MO

A number of towns were named for John Marshall (1755–1835), the chief justice of the United States Supreme Court, 1801–1835. This was settled in 1839. Skirmishing occurred near here in March 1862, and also in July and October 1863.

Marshall (Harrison) TX

Founded in 1841 on land given by Peter Whetstone, Marshall had a unique role during the Civil War, serving as the temporary state capital of Missouri following the death of Claiborne F. Jackson in December 1862, when Thomas C. Reynolds moved here as the new Confederate governor. The Trans-Mississippi Post Office Department headquarters was also here, along with an ordnance depot, a commissary department and a quartermaster depot, which had a steam-powered foundry, like the one at Hempstead making similar utensils.

The Ladies' Sewing Society outfitted several local units. The Clothing Manufacturers Co., owned by S. Jacobs, made army coats and pantaloons; the Southern Hattery, owned by H.L. Berry produced hats for Texas troops; and the J. Marshall Tanning Yard made shoes. The Rebel Tannery, owned by G.G. Gregg & Co., and Ward's Tannery, both a few miles outside of town, accepted government contracts to make harness and shoe leather. The Confederate [Steam] Mills produced flour and corn meal, as well as lumber and gin cotton. The Marshall Powder Mill was also located here.

It became a center for refugees, particularly from Missouri, Arkansas and Louisiana. The Confederate governors of those states, and a representative of Texas met here with General E. Kirby Smith, commander of the Trans-Mississippi Department, in May 1865 to decide whether to continue the war.

Marshfield (Webster) MO

Was named after *Marshfield*, Massachusetts, the home of lawyer and statesman Daniel Webster, and settled in the 1830s. There was skirmishing here in February and October 1862.

Martinsburg (Audrain) MO

Was founded in 1857 by William R. Martin. There was a skirmish here in July 1861.

Martinsburg (Berkeley) WV

Founded in 1778 on land belonging to the Fairfax estate, it was originally called Martin's Town or Martinsville, for Colonel Thomas B. Martin, a nephew of Lord Fairfax. The Baltimore & Ohio Railroad reached here in 1842 and it developed as a railroad center; its workshops were attacked as early as June 1861 by "Stonewall" Jackson's troops and Stuart's cavalry. Confederate spy Belle Boyd was arrested at Martinsburg in June 1863 and General Paul J. Semmes, CSA, died here in July after being wounded at the battle of Gettysburg. There was more fighting here in September 1864.

Maryville (Blount) TN

Founded as Fort Craig in 1785 and established in 1795, it was named for Mary Grainger Blount (c.1753–1802), the wife of Governor William Blount, after whom Blountville (q.v.) was named. There was skirmishing in November 1863 and February 1864, and more fighting in August when it was attacked by General Wheeler's cavalry.

Matagorda (Matagorda) TX

Was settled in 1825. Its name derives from two Spanish words, *mata*, meaning "bush" and *gorda*, meaning "coarse" or "thick." This coastal town was the scene of fighting in November 1862.

Mayfield (Graves) KY

Was settled in 1820 and named in 1823 from a local creek into which a George Mayfield had supposedly fallen, mortally wounded by robbers. Evacuated by the Confederates in September 1861, it was the target of Confederate raids in February and March 1864, and there was skirmishing here in May.

Maynardville (Union) TN

First established in the early 1800s, it was named in 1856 for Horace Maynard (1814–1882), a Union-supporting congressman. It was the scene of a skirmish in December 1863.

Maysville (Mason) KY

Established on the Ohio River in 1787, at the site of a tavern run by Daniel Boone, it became an important river port. It was laid out by Simon Kenton and John May of Virginia, for whom it was renamed. General Kirby Smith's Confederate troops occupied it in September 1862 and there was skirmishing in June 1863.

McDowell (Highland) VA

Was probably named for James McDowell (1796–1851), governor of Virginia, 1842–1846. Fighting here in May 1862 resulted in a Confederate victory.

McMinnville (Warren) TN

First settled c.1800, it was named in 1810 for General Joseph McMinn (1758–1824), governor of Tennessee, 1817–1821. A Federal supply base, it was captured by General Wheeler's Confederate cavalry during his middle Tennessee raid in early October 1863, after the garrison had surrendered "without making any resistance," then looted, and quartermaster and commissary stores were destroyed. There was further skirmishing near here in December and February 1865.

Meade's Station (Prince George) VA

A temporary station on the United States Military Railroad, the Army of the Potomac's supply route from City Point to the siege works around Petersburg, it was named for General George G. Meade (1815–1872), its commander, 1863–1865.

Mechanicsville (Hanover) VA

Implies the presence of factories and factory workers. The second of the Seven Days' battles in the Peninsula campaign took place near here in June 1862 and resulted in defeat and heavy casualties for General Lee's Confederates. The engagement is also known as Beaver Dam Creek (q.v.).

Memphis (Shelby) TN

Takes its name from the similarity of its location on the Mississippi to that of the ancient city of Memphis on the Nile, the first capital of Egypt. On the site of a Chickasaw village and a French, Spanish then U.S. fort, it was laid out and settled in 1819 by a group sent out by Andrew Jackson, John Overton and James Winchester.

Quinby & Robinson, who apparently also owned the Etowah Iron Works in Georgia, manufactured brass cannon here; Schneider &

Glassick were pistol makers; and Leech & Rigdon's Memphis Novelty Works produced swords, cavalry sabers and knives. There were a number of military hat makers in Memphis, including J.D. Blumenthal's Southern Cap Manufactory, and M.H. Miller and Richard Dunn's Memphis Hat Manufactory. E.A. Benson's Southern Military Drum Manufactory catered for army musicians. The South Memphis Patriotic Ladies' Association was one of several volunteer aid societies formed to make clothing for Tennessee troops.

A navy yard, originally established in 1844, was reinstated in 1861 and the ironclad CSS *Arkansas* was built here in 1861–1862, but the yard was lost to the Confederacy when the city surrendered to Union forces in June 1862 after a battle on the Mississippi, and it remained under their control.

The Overton Hospital was located here, and converted buildings were used as a Confederate military prison in 1861–1862, and as a Federal one in 1864–1865. A camp for contrabands was also set up here.

Mercersburg (Franklin) PA

First settled c.1729, it was laid out in 1803 and named c.1831 for General Hugh Mercer (c.1721–1777), who was killed at the battle of Princeton. It was the site of the Mercersburg Academy which trained officers for the United States Army. There was skirmishing nearby in July 1863 and 1864.

Meridian (Lauderdale) MS

First established in 1831 as a plantation, it was founded in 1854 as the junction of the Southern Railroad of Mississippi and the Mobile & Ohio. It was really a misnomer, so called because "meridian" was thought to mean "junction." Yandell and St. Mary's Hospitals were located here. It became the Confederate state capital in 1863. Federal troops occupied it for a few destructive days in February 1864, after which General William T. Sherman was able to boast: "Meridian, with its depots, store-houses, arsenals, hospitals, offices, hotels ... no longer exists." It was subsequently rebuilt.

Miami (Saline) MO

First laid out on the Missouri River in 1838, it was named for an Algonquin tribe, the Miami, in 1843. There was a skirmish near here in late April 1865.

Middleburg (Loudoun) VA

Established in 1787 on land previously owned by Joseph Chinn and called Chinn's Crossroads, it was renamed to reflect its position as the middle "burg" or town on the stage road between Alexandria and Winchester. There was skirmishing here in January and June 1863 and May 1864.

Middletown (Middlesex) CT

On the Connecticut River, it was settled in 1650 on the site of an Indian village and named in 1653 because it was midway between Saybrook and Windsor. During the Civil War, the Savage Revolving Firearms Co. made revolvers for the Union Army and Navy here.

Middletown (Frederick) MD

Was founded in 1767 by people of English and German extraction and named after a house called *Middletown*. Less well known than Barbara Frietchie, local resident Nancy Crouse defied a group of Confederate cavalrymen with an American flag in September 1862 during the Antietam campaign, and inspired a ballad celebrating "Nancy Crouse, the Valley Maid." Skirmishing also occurred here in June 1863 and July 1864.

Middletown (Frederick) VA

Founded in 1796, it was named for its location between Winchester and Woodstock. Skirmishing occurred here in March, May and July 1862, June 1863, and April, September and November 1864. Union General Charles R. Lowell died here in October 1864 from wounds received at the battle of Cedar Creek.

Mifflin (Chester) TN

Was possibly named for Thomas Mifflin (1744–1800), a general in the Revolutionary War and governor of Pennsylvania, 1790–1799. A skirmish occurred here in February 1864.

Mill Springs (Wayne) KY

A grist mill was built here c.1817 by the Metcalf family, near Lake Cumberland and the site of a number of springs, and a post office called Mill Springs was established in 1825. The battle of Mill Springs, a two-day engagement in January 1862, also known as Logan's Crossroads (q.v.), was a Confederate defeat, in which General Felix K. Zollicoffer was killed.

Milledgeville (Baldwin) GA

Was laid out in 1803 on the banks of the Oconee River and named for John Milledge (1757–1818), a Revolutionary War soldier and governor of Georgia, 1802–1806. Though it was the state capital of Georgia, 1804–1868, it was described as "a mere village" by one visitor, and a Wisconsin soldier called it "a sort of one-horse town." The Milledgeville Manufacturing Co. made cloth for uniforms for Georgia troops, and what became known as the Georgia Armory was established in the state penitentiary in 1861–1862, with convict labor used to make and repair rifles. There were two military hospitals here, Brown, relocated from Atlanta, and Midway. As early as 1862 it was already crowded with refugees from Maryland, Kentucky, Tennessee and Louisiana. It was occupied and sacked in November 1864 by General Sherman's troops who burned the penitentiary.

Millican (Brazos) TX

Robert H. Millican was the first white settler here in the 1820s. What became known as Millican Crossroads was renamed Millican for his son, Dr. Elliott M. Millican, who sold land for development in 1859. It was the northern terminus of the Houston & Texas Central Railroad, 1860–1867, and also the site of a large Confederate training camp.

Milton (Santa Rosa) FL

Founded as a trading post on the Blackwater River in 1825, it may have been named for Milton Amos, an early settler, though John Milton (1807–1865), the wartime governor of Florida, has also been suggested as the possible origin. There were skirmishes here in August and October 1864.

Missionary Ridge (Hamilton) TN

Takes its name from the Brainerd Mission (called after David Brainerd, an 18th century Indian missionary), a school established here for the Cherokees in 1817 by the Rev. Cyrus Kingsbury on behalf of the American Board of Commissioners for Foreign Missions. The Ridge witnessed heavy fighting in the Chattanooga campaign in November 1863 following the Confederate withdrawal from Lookout Mountain, and the defeat of General Bragg's army which retreated into Georgia.

Mississippi River

The second longest river in America derives its name from Algonquin words meaning "great water" or "great river." Control of its lower reaches, from Cairo to the Gulf, was a major Union objective, part of General Winfield Scott's Anaconda Plan, finally achieved in July 1863 with the capture of Vicksburg and Port Hudson, splitting the Confederacy in two. It witnessed military activity for much of the war and in April 1865 was the scene of the *Sultana* disaster when a steamer carrying former Union prisoners of war sank with great loss of life. The Mississippi Marine Brigade was a volunteer amphibious force intended to operate against Confederate partisans along this and other rivers; it was in existence, March 1863–August 1864.

Mitchelville *see* Hilton Head Island

Mobile (Mobile) AL

It may derive from *Maubila*, the name of an Indian village, or *Mauvila*, the French version of this, but it is uncertain. Founded in 1711, it was in French, British and Spanish hands between then and 1813, when it was seized for the United States. A naval station established in 1862 built, fitted out or repaired a number of vessels and floating batteries and there was also a naval storehouse here. Skates & Co. made marine engines for the Confederate Navy, and two gunboats were built and commissioned here; Skates also produced field guns. Two submarines, the *Pioneer II* and the *H.L. Hunley*, were constructed at the Park & Lyons machine shop. There were also five military hospitals—Cantey, Nott, Garner, Ross and Levert (for officers)—as well as a naval hospital. It became a center for refugees, the largest group of whom came from New Orleans in 1862–1863.

The battle of Mobile Bay in August 1864 resulted in the loss of the CSS *Tennessee*, the pride of the Confederate Navy, but Mobile itself remained in Southern hands until its evacuation in April 1865. The following month, captured

Confederate powder exploded in a warehouse, setting off other explosions, destroying many buildings and killing several hundred people.

Monroe Station (Monroe) MO
Named for President James Monroe (1758–1831), fifth president of the U.S.A., 1817–1825, it was the scene of a skirmish in July 1861. It was on the Hannibal & St. Joseph Railroad. (Now called Monroe City.)

Monterey (Putnam) TN
The capture of Monterrey by General Zachary Taylor in the Mexican War in 1846 no doubt explains the popularity of this placename, with slightly altered spelling. There were a number of skirmishes here, during April 1862 and in January 1863.

Montevallo (Shelby) AL
Settled in 1815, its name is pseudo-Italian, meaning "mountain-valley." There was a cavalry skirmish here in March 1865 during General Wilson's raid to Selma.

Montgomery (Montgomery) AL
On the Alabama River, it started life as two separate settlements, New Philadelphia and East Alabama, which were merged in 1819 and renamed Montgomery, probably for General Richard Montgomery (1736–1775), an Irish-born, Revolutionary War officer, though Major Lemuel P. Montgomery (d.1814), killed during the Creek War, has also been suggested as the origin. The state capital of Alabama since 1847, it was the meeting place of the Alabama & Florida and Montgomery & West Point Railroads.

In February 1861 Jefferson Davis described it as "a gay and handsome town of some 8000 inhabitants," and from then until May it served as the first capital of the Confederate States, until it was moved to Richmond, Virginia. There was an arsenal operating here by the end of 1861, repairing small arms and making leather accoutrements, and also a shipyard where an ironclad, the CSS *Nashville*, was built in 1863–1864. The textile firm of Phillips, Fariss & Co. manufactured cloth for uniforms for both state and Confederate troops, and Ethelbert Halfmann made uniforms, gold lace and buttons. There were also six hospitals in Montgomery, including Madison House, St. Mary's, Stonewall and Watts.

By 1863 it had a large number of refugees living here, many of them from Mobile. Though the target of a Federal raid in July 1864, Montgomery, "the Cradle of the Confederacy," was not finally occupied till April 1865 when General Wilson's cavalry entered the town. Before leaving, they destroyed factories, warehouses and steamboats on the Coosa River.

Monticello (Drew) AR
A number of towns were called after *Monticello*, Thomas Jefferson's celebrated home in Virginia, begun in 1769. (It is Italian for "little mountain.") Established as a county seat in 1851, Monticello, Arkansas, was the scene of skirmishing in March 1864.

Monticello (Jefferson) FL
Was settled in the early 1800s by planters from Georgia and the Carolinas. Founded in 1853, the Bailey Cotton Mill near here, owned by William M. Bailey, one of "the most wealthy and patriotic ... gentlemen in the Confederate States," worked at full capacity during the war, turning out cloth. An attempt by the Confederate Commissary Department to take control of the mill in 1864 was defeated, largely due to the objections of Governor John Milton.

Moorefield (Hardy) WV
When established in 1777, it was named for Conrad Moore (d.1800), the original landowner. There was a Confederate raid nearby in January 1863, and numerous skirmishes throughout 1862–1864.

Moreauville (Avoyelles) LA
French General Jean-Victor-Marie Moreau (1763–1813), who lived in exile in America, 1805–1813, after his involvement in a conspiracy against Napoleon, may have given his name to this place. There was fighting here in May 1864.

Morehead City (Carteret) NC
Was named for John M. Morehead (1796–1866), governor of North Carolina, 1841–1845, and president of the North Carolina Railroad. Salt works were established at this coastal place by the state of North Carolina, which appointed its own salt commissioner, Dr. John M. Worth,

and later his nephew, Daniel G. Worth. The works were burned by Federal troops in April 1862 after the capture of New Bern.

Morganfield (Union) KY

General Daniel Morgan (1736–1802), a hero of the Revolution, received the land here in reward for his military service. There was skirmishing here in August 1862 and May and June 1864.

Morganton (Burke) NC

This was also named for General Morgan, and originally called Morganborough, then Morgantown. It was full of refugees in the winter of 1864–1865. General Stoneman's troops burned county courthouse records here in February 1865 and there was fighting at the Catawba River in April.

Morgantown (Monongalia) WV

Colonel Zackquill Morgan (1735–1795) founded a settlement here on the Monongahela River in 1767 after a previous one was wiped out in an Indian attack. The town established here in 1785 was named for him. It was the target of a raid by General "Grumble" Jones' Confederate cavalry in April 1863.

Morganza (Pointe Coupee) LA

Was named for early 19th century local planter and landowner, Colonel Charles Morgan. It was the scene of skirmishing in September 1863, May and October–December 1864.

Morris Island SC

Was originally called Morrison's Island, for an early resident, later shortened to Morris Island. Near the entrance to Charleston harbor, Forts Gregg, Wagner and Shaw were located here. **Fort Gregg**, named for General Maxcy Gregg (1814–1862) who was killed at Fredericksburg, was bombarded in August 1863. **Fort Wagner**, built in 1862, was named for Lieutenant Colonel Thomas M. Wagner (d.1862), who was killed in an accident during its construction. It was the scene of two costly and unsuccessful Federal assaults in July 1863, one of which involved the 54th Massachusetts Colored Infantry commanded by Colonel Robert G. Shaw, who was among those killed; General George C. Strong was also fatally wounded. Both forts were evacuated by the Confederates in early September, Fort Wagner after 60 days of almost constant Union bombardment. **Fort Shaw** was named in memory of Colonel Shaw (1837–1863), who was buried in a common grave with his black soldiers, a calculated insult.

Federal batteries set up here included a Parrott rifle called the "Swamp Angel" which fired incendiary shells at Charleston. A short-lived prison stockade established in September 1864 housed the "Immortal Six Hundred," Confederate prisoners placed within firing range of their own guns on Forts Sumter and Moultrie, in retaliation for alleged cruelties meted out to Union soldiers. The experiment did not work and in October they were moved to Fort Pulaski, Georgia.

Morrisania (Westchester) NY

Takes its name from the Morris brothers who bought the land here in 1670. Later members of the family included Lewis Morris (1726–1798), a signer of the Declaration of Independence, and Gouverneur Morris who developed the site in 1840–1855. During the war the Starr Arms Co. manufactured revolvers here for the Union Army and Navy. (Now part of New York City.)

Morristown (Hamblen) TN

Was named for Gideon, David and Absalom Morris who settled here in 1783. There was skirmishing in December 1861, December 1863 and October 1864.

Morrisville (Wake) NC

Settled in 1840, it was named for Jerry Morris, the owner of the land. It witnessed skirmishing in April 1865 during General Sherman's drive through the Carolinas.

Morton (Scott) MS

Colonel Caleb W. Taylor named this place for his wife, Elizabeth Morton. There was skirmishing here on several days in February 1864, during General Sherman's Meridian campaign.

Moscow (Fayette) TN

The fashion for foreign placenames is demonstrated here. Fighting occurred near here in February, March, September, November and December 1863, and June 1864.

Moulton (Lawrence) AL

Was established in 1818 and named for Indian fighter Lieutenant Michael Moulton (d.1814), who was killed at Horseshoe Bend in the Creek War. There was fighting here in March and May 1864.

Mound City (Pulaski) IL

Is on the Ohio River. In 1857 Mound City, founded by Moses M. Rawlings, and Emporium City, created by the Emporium Real Estate & Manufacturing Co., were merged. The name refers to Indian burial mounds at General Rawlings' hotel. The Union naval station from nearby Cairo was moved here in 1862, repairing and servicing vessels on the Mississippi and building gunboats, and the Marine Hospital was also located here.

Mount Ida (Montgomery) AR

Settlement here began in 1836 and it was given its present name in 1850: this derives from a ridge of mountains in present-day Crete. Skirmishing occurred here in November 1863.

Mount Jackson (Shenandoah) VA

This was named for General Andrew Jackson (1767–1845). A Confederate hospital complex was established here. There was skirmishing in March and June 1862, and it was occupied by the Federals later that month. There was more skirmishing here in September and October 1864.

Mount Olive Station (Wayne) NC

On the Wilmington & Raleigh Railroad, it opened in 1840. There was fighting here in December 1862 during Union General Foster's thrust towards Goldsboro, and Confederate troops were camped near here in March 1865, just before the battle of Bentonville. The name derives from the Mount of Olives, a range of hills east of Jerusalem, referred to in the Book of Luke in the New Testament.

Mount Pleasant (Marshall) MS

This is a descriptive or promotional name. Skirmishing occurred here in August and December 1863 and January and May 1864.

Mount Sterling (Montgomery) KY

Was laid out in 1793 and named Mount Stirling by local resident Hugh Forbes in memory of the Scottish town of Stirling; the spelling was later altered to Sterling. The Federal garrison here was captured by General Morgan's cavalry in March 1863, and there was more fighting in December. In June 1864 Morgan returned, again captured the garrison, and robbed a local bank of $18,000. His success was short-lived: the following day he was driven out by the Federals.

Mount Vernon (Mobile) AL

A number of towns were named after Mount Vernon, George Washington's home in Virginia, which commemorated English Admiral Edward Vernon (1684–1757). The arsenal, established in 1829, was seized by state troops in January 1861 and later taken over by the Confederate government. It repaired small arms and made ammunition, but was transferred to Selma in 1862.

Mud Island PA

Near Philadelphia, in the Delaware River, Mud Island was the name given it by Zachariah Connell who bought a piece of land here in 1787. **Fort Mifflin**, first built as a coastal fortification in 1771 and rebuilt in 1798, was named for General Thomas Mifflin (1744–1800), Washington's aide-de-camp and governor of Pennsylvania, 1790–1799. A naval ammunition depot was established here in 1855, and a military prison in 1863–1864, housing a mixture of Confederates and Federal soldiers awaiting trial for various misdemeanors.

Munfordville (Hart) KY

On the Green River, it was named for Richard J. Munford, who gave the land for development in 1816. In September 1862 General Braxton Bragg besieged the town and forced its garrison to surrender, but then failed to hold it, and the Federals reoccupied it a few days later.

Murfreesboro (Rutherford) TN

Was established in 1811 on land belonging to Colonel William Lytle, a Revolutionary War soldier, and originally called Cannonsburg, for Newton Cannon, a future governor of Tennessee, but later renamed for Colonel Hardy Murfree (1752–1809). It was the state capital of Tennessee, 1819–1825.

The town saw considerable military activity

in June and July 1862, culminating in the battle also known as Stones River (q.v.) at the end of that year. Here, Union General William S. Rosecrans won a strategic victory over General Braxton Bragg. Confederate General James E. Rains was killed and Roger W. Hanson mortally wounded; Union General Joshua W. Sill was also killed and Edward Kirk, severely wounded, died the following July. Federal troops occupied Murfreesboro in January 1863. A raid by General Forrest's cavalry in early December 1864 during the Franklin and Nashville campaign was unsuccessful, though the Confederates attacked and succeeded in capturing trains on the Nashville & Chattanooga Railroad later that month.

Mustang Island TX

Opposite Corpus Christi, it was originally called Wild Horse Island, then Mustang Island because of the wild horses brought here by the Spaniards. A small fort was built here during the Mexican War, and **Camp Semmes** was established in 1863, named for Captain Raphael Semmes (1809–1877), whose ship, the CSS *Alabama*, had sunk the USS *Hatteras* off Galveston in January of that year.

Mystic (New London) CT

First settled in 1654, it takes its name from the Mystic River, which derives from an Algonquin word meaning "great tidal river." An experimental torpedo boat was built in 1864 at the Pook Iron Works here and originally called the USS *Stromboli*, but renamed the *Spuyten Duyvil*.

Nanna Hubba Bluff (Mobile) AL

Derives from an Indian tribal name. As previously agreed with Rear Admiral H.K. Thatcher, USN, at Citronelle, Commodore Ebenezer Farrand, CSN, surrendered the four vessels and the officers and men of the Mobile Squadron to Captain Edward Simpson, USN, here on the Tombigbee River in May 1865.

Napoleon (Desha) AR

On the Mississippi and Arkansas Rivers, it was founded in the 1820s by Frederick Notrebe, a former French general, and named for the Emperor Napoleon I (1769–1821). U.S. ordnance stores here were seized by Arkansas state troops in February 1861.

Napoleonville (Assumption) LA

It was named for the Emperor Napoleon I, whose chief gunner at Waterloo settled here after 1815. Napoleonville was raided by Confederate troops in May 1864 and there was skirmishing here in July. Further skirmishing occurred nearby at Kittredge's Sugar House in February 1865.

Nashville (Davidson) TN

Founded in 1779 as Fort Nashborough on the Cumberland River, named for Francis Nash (1742–1777), a general in the Continental Army who was mortally wounded at Germantown. It was renamed in 1784 and became the state capital in 1843.

T.M. Brennan manufactured cannon, James Hamilton's Shoe Factory produced army boots and shoes and James McClure made drums for military bands. There were a number of firms producing leatherwork, including Robert Crenshaw and John Morrow & Son, and convicts at the Tennessee State Penitentiary also made various types of military equipment. Ladies in the Soldier's Friend Society made clothing for Tennessee troops.

It was the site of Nashville University's Western Military Institute and a temporary ordnance depot which was destroyed by fire in December 1861. The arsenal was transferred to Atlanta, Georgia, before the city was evacuated by the Confederates in February 1862; ship construction here also ended. From then on, the city remained under Federal control.

Major machine shops, car and locomotive works and repair facilities for the U.S. Military Railroad were established at Nashville. The Maxwell House Hotel was used as a military prison in 1863–1865, and the Gordon Hospital was located here, as was a camp for contrabands. Prostitution was a major problem for the military authorities, and an attempt by General William S. Rosecrans in July 1863 to solve it by shipping prostitutes north to Louisville and Cincinnati failed when they were sent back again.

Generals William T. Sherman and Ulysses S. Grant met here in March 1864 to discuss future strategy against the Armies of Virginia and of Tennessee. There had been considerable military activity around Nashville during 1862–1864, but the two-day battle in December 1864, which resulted in a decisive Federal victory, ended Confederate resistance in Tennessee for the rest of the war.

Natchez (Adams) MS

The oldest permanent settlement on the Mississippi River, it was founded by the French in 1716 and named following an attack by the Natchez in 1729. It was owned successively by the British and the Spanish until the United States took possession in 1798, and was the capital of Mississippi Territory, 1798–1802.

A Ladies' Military Aid Society and a Confederate Sewing Society were both formed in June 1861 to make clothing for Mississippi soldiers. Federal troops occupied Natchez in May 1862 and July 1863, following bombardment by a gunboat, and remained in control till the end of the war, though there was further military activity nearby in November and December 1863, and January and April 1864.

Natchitoches (Natchitoches) LA

On the Cane River, it is the oldest town in the Louisiana Purchase. It began life in 1715 and a town was founded in 1721, named for the Natchitoches whose name meant "chestnut eaters" or "pawpaw eaters." There was skirmishing here in March, April and May 1864.

Natural Bridge (Wakulla) FL

The St. Marks River disappears underground for a few yards here, 12 miles south of Tallahassee, thus making a "natural bridge." In March 1865 a Union attempt to capture the state capital was defeated by a scratch force of convalescents, old men, cadets from the West Florida Seminary and the 5th C.S. Cavalry during two days of fighting.

Naugatuck (New Haven) CT

Stands on the Naugatuck River, a name derived from an Algonquin word meaning a "single tree," i.e. a landmark. It was first settled in 1702. The J.P. Lindsay Manufacturing Co., the "sole manufacturers of Lindsay's patent firearms," made pistols here. They also had a factory at New Haven.

Neal Dow Station (Cobb) GA

It was so named by 1863. Neal Dow (1804–1897) gained a nationwide reputation pre-war for his work as a temperance advocate. During the Civil War, in which he attained general's rank, he was captured and sent to Libby Prison, Richmond, but later exchanged for General William H.F. "Rooney" Lee. During the Atlanta campaign there was a skirmish here, on the Western & Atlantic Railroad, in July 1864. (Renamed Smyrna in 1872.)

Neosho (Newton) MO

Was laid out in 1839. The name comes from an Osage word meaning "clear water." The secession members of the state legislature met here in October 1861 to declare Missouri's ties with the United States dissolved. Skirmishing occurred between April and December 1862, in March, October and November 1863, and June and November 1864.

Nevada (Vernon) MO

Means "snow cloud" or "snowy land" in Spanish. Settled by families from Kentucky and Tennessee, it was laid out in 1855 and named after Nevada City, California, by Colonel DeWitt C. Hunter, the first settler. The headquarters of Confederate guerrillas, it was known as the "Bushwhackers' capital" and burned to the ground by Union troops in May 1863.

New Albany (Union) MS

Large numbers of places named after ones elsewhere were given the prefix "New." This one was named after Albany, Georgia. There was skirmishing near here in April 1863, with the arrival of Colonel Grierson's Federal raiders, and again in October when General James R. Chalmers appeared with his Confederate cavalry.

New Baltimore (Fauquier) VA

Was founded in the 1820s. There was a skirmish in October 1863, followed later that month by an attack by Confederates on a wagon train near here.

New Bern (Craven) NC

On the Neuse River, it was originally settled in 1710 by German and Swiss immigrants and named after Bern, Switzerland. It was refounded after Indian depredations, serving as the colonial and state capital, 1746–1792. Captured by the Union Army in March 1862, it remained under its control, despite attempts by the Confederates to retake it, in March 1863, and February and May 1864. There was a contraband camp here, and after the capture of Wilmington in February 1865, it became a Federal supply base the following month.

New Haven (New Haven) CT

Settled in 1638, it was named in 1640. It was a "new harbor" or "haven," but possibly also called after the English seaport of Newhaven, Sussex. With Hartford, it served as the joint state capital, 1701–1875.

The Henry repeating rifle, known to the Confederates as "that damn Yankee rifle that can be loaded on Sunday and fired all week," was invented and patented in 1860 by Tyler Henry, the plant superintendent of Oliver F. Winchester's New Haven Arms Co., and manufactured here for the Union Army. John P. Lindsay, of the J.P. Lindsay Manufacturing Co. of Naugatuck, had a factory making rifle muskets. They were also made near here by the firm founded by Eli Whitney. The State Hospital, which became the Knight U.S. Army General Hospital, was located at New Haven and there was a training camp for black Connecticut troops here.

New Haven (Nelson) KY

Founded on the Rolling Fork River in 1820 as Pottinger's Landing, named for Colonel Sam Pottinger, it was renamed by him after his favorite town of New Haven, Connecticut. There was a skirmish here in December 1862.

New Hope Church (Paulding) GA

Numerous villages and small towns in 19th century America were given the optimistic name of "Hope" or "New Hope." This was the scene of heavy fighting in late May and early June 1864, as Federal troops attempted unsuccessfully to break through Confederate lines, during the early stages of the Atlanta campaign. (Now called New Hope.)

New Madrid (New Madrid) MO

It began as an Indian trading post on the Mississippi River c.1783, and was laid out as a town in 1789 by Revolutionary War veteran Colonel George Morgan, who had received a land grant from Spain, hence the name. Occupied by Confederate troops in July 1861, along with Island No. 10, it was captured by Union General John Pope in March 1862 following a siege and bombardment. Island No. 10 surrendered the following month. New Madrid was evacuated by the Federals in December but was reoccupied by them the following January. There was further skirmishing nearby in August 1863 and December 1864.

New Market (Shenandoah) VA

Was first settled in 1761 and laid out in 1784. It was named in 1796 after the English town of Newmarket, Suffolk. Skirmishing occurred here in December 1861 and June 1862. A battle which included cadets from the Virginia Military Institute (the katydids), took place here in May 1864 and resulted in a Federal retreat.

New Orleans (Orleans) LA

Was founded in 1718 and originally called Nouvelle Orléans after the French city, but also in honor of the Duc d'Orléans (1674–1723), who was regent of France at that time. The capital of France's vast colonial region of Louisiana, it passed to the United States in 1803 as part of the Louisiana Purchase, when it assumed its present name.

It was an important manufacturing and shipbuilding center. There were several firms making ordnance, among them Bennett & Surges, Leeds & Co. and S. Wolfe & Co. The Leeds and Clarke Foundries both made marine engines. The New Orleans Naval Station, established in 1861, converted steamers into naval vessels and manufactured cannon. There were also powder mills here, two of which exploded in March 1862, killing five people.

The New Orleans Rifle Factory, established in 1861 by Ferdinand W.C. and Francis L. Cook (Cook & Brother) made rifles and carbines, including copies of the British Enfield; after the fall of New Orleans they moved to Athens, Georgia. Thomas, Griswold & Co. and Agruider H. Dufilho made swords, and the arsenal produced small-arms ammunition.

The Southern Military Cap Manufactory, established in 1860 by T.W. Hutchinson, Jules Fiquet & Jean Bouvet and Elie Pousson & Co. all made military kepis; Casimir Rouyer made belt plates, buckles and military buttons; James Cosgrove manufactured cartridge boxes, belts and bayonet sheaths; William Boyd made knapsacks; and Guilbaux & Giefers produced military saddles and harness. Several firms made drums, among them Werlein & Halsey and Louis Grunewald. The Ladies' Volunteer Aid Association and the Ladies' Society of the Confederate Army also made clothing for Louisiana soldiers.

With New Orleans threatened by Federal naval forces, martial law was declared in March 1862. The largest city in the Confederacy, with many refugees, its capture the following month caused consternation across the South: "New Orleans gone — and with it the Confederacy," lamented diarist Mary Chesnut. After its capture, an ordnance depot was established here to serve the West Gulf Blockading Squadron, and Parish Prison housed Confederate prisoners of war, 1863–1865.

New Smyrna (Volusia) FL

The site of an Indian village and then a Spanish mission, it was colonized in 1767 by a mixture of Greeks, Minorcans and Italians. Their leader, Andrew Turnbull, named it after his wife's Turkish birthplace (present-day Izmir). Abandoned in 1777, it was re-established in 1803. It was shelled by Federal naval vessels in July 1863, following by troops landing and burning buildings. (Now called New Smyrna Beach.)

New York City (New York) NY

New York was founded as New Amsterdam by Dutch settlers in 1626. Seized by the British in 1664, it was renamed in honor of the Duke of York and Albany (1633–1701), later King James II. It was briefly the Federal capital, 1788–1790.

During the Civil War Norman Wiard manufactured rifles and other artillery and ammunition, possibly at O'Donnell's Foundry. A number of firms made small arms, among them William Brooks whose production of breech-loading carbines ended when the factory was destroyed in the riots of 1863; W.W. Marston, who made Gibbs carbines in 1861–1862; Sarson & Roberts, who made Springfield rifles; and William Muir & Co. Fitch & Waldo made military buttons and Richard Nichols manufactured boarding pikes for the Union Navy.

The state arsenal was in Central Park, and the city also housed the armory of the 69th New York Infantry (the "Fighting 69th") and an army quartermaster depot. The Tombs Prison housed Confederate prisoners-of-war in 1861–1862.

"Fort Lafayette looked black in the centre of the channel, and we knew that it was crowded with the victims of secession [Confederate prisoners]. Fort Tompkins [on Staten Island] was being built to guard the pass.... Fort Hamilton, on Long Island opposite, was frowning at us; and immediately around us a regiment of volunteers was receiving regimental stocks and boots from the hands of its officers," wrote English novelist Anthony Trollope who visited New York in November 1861.

Though there had already been a demonstration of "half-starved ... wives, mothers and relatives of volunteers" demanding "bread, bread, bread" in July 1861 and a similar outbreak in May 1862, the correspondent of the London *Times* observed complacently in February 1863 that "New York exhibits no outward signs of the war and desolation that afflicts the land." Five months later he found himself writing an account of the worst rioting the city had ever experienced. The draft riots of July 1863, caused initially by opposition to the Federal Conscription Act, were only brought under control when troops from Forts Hamilton and Wadsworth, and 20,000 more from the Gettysburg battlefield, were brought in to restore order; perhaps as many as 1,000 people were killed or wounded during the four days of rioting.

The Sanitary Fair held in April 1864, which included items for sale made by Confederate prisoners at Point Lookout, raised nearly $1,200,000 for the U.S. Sanitary Commission. In November, an attempt by Confederate agents to burn New York by starting fires in a number of hotels and Barnum's Museum was a failure.

Newark (Essex) NJ

On the Passaic River, it was founded by Puritans from Connecticut in 1666 and now thought to have been named after the biblical "New Ark" rather than the English town of Newark, Nottinghamshire. The Manhattan Firearms Co. made pistols for the Union Army and the firm of Sauerbier manufactured cavalry sabers. A submarine was built here by Cornelius S. Bushnell and Augustus Price's American Submarine Co. but completed too late to see service in the Civil War.

Newburgh (Warrick) IN

A river port on the Ohio, it was first settled in 1803 and originally called Sprinklesburg, for John Sprinkle. It was renamed in 1837, possibly after Newburgh, New York, which derived its name from the Scottish town of Newburgh, Fifeshire. It was raided by Confederate troops in July 1862.

Newnan (Coweta) GA

Founded in 1827, it was named for General Daniel Newnan (c.1780–1851), who fought in the War of 1812 and was later in the Georgia state assembly. The Bragg, Buckner, College, Foard and Gamble Hospitals were all located here, and convalescents from Bragg and Buckner fought Federal troops in September 1864. On the Atlanta & West Point Railroad, it became a center for refugees.

Newport News (♦) VA

First settled by Irish colonists in 1621, it was named for Christopher Newport, captain of the first ship to reach Jamestown, and Sir William Newce who chose the site at the mouth of the James River; over time, "Newce" became "News." It was occupied by Federal troops in May 1861, and though there was some skirmishing in July and December 1861, remained under their control throughout the war. Federal gunners stationed here participated in the duel between the CSS *Virginia* and the USS *Monitor* in Hampton Roads in March 1862, though to little effect, and there was further naval action when the USS *Minnesota* was damaged by the Confederate torpedo boat *Squib* in April 1864.

Newton Station (Newton) MS

Was named for Sir Isaac Newton (1642–1727), the English physicist and mathematician. Colonel Grierson's cavalry caused considerable damage here in April 1863, on the Southern Railroad of Mississippi, during their famous raid, capturing trains, and destroying bridges and track.

Newtonia (Newton) MO

Was apparently named for Sergeant John Newton who captured ten British soldiers during the siege of Savannah in the War of Independence. There was skirmishing here in August and September 1862, and an engagement later that month, when Confederate troops, including Choctaws, Chickasaws and Cherokees defeated Federal forces. More skirmishing occurred in October 1862 and September 1863. Another engagement near here in October 1864 as General Sterling Price retreated from his Missouri raid was claimed by both sides as a victory.

Newtown (King and Queen) VA

This was a common name for a new settlement. There was considerable military activity here, with skirmishing in November 1862, June and August 1863, and May, July, October and November 1864.

Norfolk (Litchfield) CT

Was first settled in 1746 and named after the English county of Norfolk. William W. Welch manufactured rifle muskets here during the Civil War.

Norfolk (♦) VA

Laid out in 1682 on the Elizabeth River, it was also named after Norfolk, England, from where early settlers had come. Abandoned by Federal troops in April 1861, it was recaptured in May 1862 and remained in Federal hands for the rest of the war.

North Anna River VA

Like the Rapidan (q.v.), it was also named for Queen Anne (1665–1714). After the fighting at Spotsylvania Court House in May 1864, there was a four-day battle here ending in a stalemate. It included fighting at Jericho Mill (q.v.).

Northport (Tuscaloosa) AL

Was so called because of its location on the Black Warrior River, where it was established in 1816. Skirmishing broke out here in early April 1865, involving cavalry from General Forrest's and General Wilson's commands. (Now part of Tuscaloosa.)

Norwich (New London) CT

At the confluence of the Yantic and Shetucket Rivers, it was established in 1658 and named after the English city of Norwich, Norfolk. In the 18th and 19th centuries it became an important center of firearms manufacture, and J.D. Mowry contracted to supply 30,000 Springfield rifles for the Union Army in 1862. The tanneries here had more orders for knapsacks, boots, belts, and cartridge boxes than they could fulfill.

Oak Grove (Westmoreland) VA

A descriptive name, it was the site of the first of the Seven Days' battles in the Peninsula campaign in June 1862, which is also known as Henrico (q.v.).

Oak Island NC

Was the site of **Fort Caswell**, built at the mouth of the Cape Fear River in 1827–1838 and named for Colonel Richard Caswell (1729–1798), governor of North Carolina, 1776–1780 and 1785–1787. Occupied by North Carolina troops in April 1861, it was the scene of an engagement in February 1863, but was blown up and abandoned in January 1865. Oak Island was presumably named for the oak trees growing there.

Occoquan (Prince William) VA

Industrial buildings grew up here along the Occoquan River, which comes from an Algonquin word meaning "hooked-inlet." Laid out in 1804, it was well established by the 1830s. The Confederates withdrew from here in March 1862, but there was further skirmishing in December and March 1863.

Ohio River OH

The name comes from an Iroquois word meaning "beautiful river." General John H. Morgan crossed the Ohio in July 1863 at the start of his Indiana and Ohio raid, ending in the battle of Buffington Island (q.v.). The Army of the Ohio was in existence 1862–1865, its commanders including Generals Ambrose E. Burnside, John M. Schofield and George Stoneman.

Okolona (Chickasaw) MS

Originally a stagecoach stop, it was moved in 1848 to the proposed route of the Mobile & Ohio Railroad and named Okolona, from a Choctaw word meaning "much bent." The railroad, however, did not arrive till 1859. The town was visited by Colonel Hatch's cavalry during the Grierson raid and quantities of cotton were burned. There was also skirmishing here in December 1863, February 1864, when Colonel Jeffrey E. Forrest (General N. Bedford Forrest's younger brother) was mortally wounded in an engagement with Federal cavalry, and June and December 1864.

Old Hen and Chickens Islands TN

The name probably derives from their shapes. The steamer *Sultana*, grossly overloaded with Union prisoners who had survived battles and prison camps and were now on their way home, exploded near here, north of Memphis on the Mississippi, and sank in late April 1865. Of some two thousand persons on board, more than two-thirds were killed or drowned. The official explanation was a faulty boiler, though sabotage by embittered Confederates was also widely believed at the time; it remains a mystery.

Olustee (Baker) FL

This is from a Seminole-Creek word meaning "water-black." Olustee was on the Savannah & Gulf Railroad, and the battle fought in February 1864 resulted in a Confederate victory, the Federals being forced to retreat with heavy losses.

Oostanaula River, GA

Its name comes from a Cherokee word meaning "a rock ledge across a stream." There was fighting here in May 1864 during the battle of Resaca (q.v.), in the early stages of the Atlanta campaign.

Opelousas (St. Landry) LA

Was founded in 1720 as a French garrison and trading post, and under Spanish control in 1765. The name derives from the Opelousas tribe. It served briefly as the Confederate state capital of Louisiana after the fall of New Orleans in 1862, but was under Federal occupation between April and November 1863.

Opequon Creek (Frederick) VA

Comes from an Algonquin word meaning "froth-white" or "rain-worn." It is an alternate name for the third battle of Winchester (q.v.) in September 1864, during General Sheridan's Shenandoah Valley campaign, and was a Union victory.

Orange Court House (Orange) VA

Dating from 1734, it was apparently named for William, Prince of Orange (1711–1751), who in that year married Princess Anne, daughter of King George II, and became stadholder (lieutenant governor) of the Dutch Republic. Skirmishing occurred in August 1862 and September 1863. Chaplains of the Army of Northern Virginia met here in December 1863 and reported a "high state of religious feeling throughout the army."

Orangeburg (Orangeburg) SC

Was established in 1735 by German, Swiss and Dutch settlers and like Orange Court House, also named for William, Prince of Orange. It became a center for refugees and there was a skirmish near here in February 1865 during General Sherman's march through the Carolinas.

Osceola (St. Clair) MO

Laid out c.1836 on the Osage River and named for Osceola (c.1804–1838), a celebrated chief who led his tribe in the Second Seminole War and died in prison at Fort Moultrie, South Carolina. It was burned by Kansas jayhawkers in September 1861 and there was a further skirmish here in May 1862.

Owensboro (Davies) KY

Founded c.1799 and originally known as Yellow Banks, from the color of the clay along the Ohio River. When it was laid out in 1816 it was called Rossborough, for David Ross, a local property owner, but renamed for Colonel Abraham Owen, a veteran of early Kentucky Indian wars, who was killed fighting the Shawnees in 1811. There was skirmishing here in September 1862 and August 1864, and Confederate guerrillas attacked and partly burned it down in September 1864.

Oxford (Lafayette) MS

Originally a trading post, it was named after the city and university in England. The University of Mississippi ("Ole Miss"), opened in 1848, was used as a hospital from December 1862 to August 1864. There was skirmishing here in December 1862 and August 1864, when it was looted and burned by Union troops.

Ozark (Christian) MO

Comes from the French *Aux Arks*, meaning "at the Arks," a shortening of the Indian tribal name *Arkansea* or *Arkansa*. It was laid out in 1843. Skirmishing occurred here in August 1862, and it was captured by Confederates under General John S. Marmaduke in February 1863.

Paducah (McCracken) KY

At the confluence of the Ohio and Tennessee Rivers, it was named by General George Rogers Clark for Chief Paduke of the Chickasaws and laid out in 1827 by his brother William Clark (of the Lewis & Clark Expedition). Occupied by Federal troops in September 1861, an attempt by General Forrest's cavalry to recapture it in March 1864 was only partly successful, and there was more skirmishing in April. A converted building held Confederate prisoners in 1862 and possibly also in 1863.

Paint Rock (Concho) TX

On the Concho River, it was so called because it was near a ledge of rock decorated with Indian paintings or pictographs. Chisum & Co. Meat Contractors, owned by John Chisum and located here were the largest suppliers of beef to Confederate troops.

Paintsville (Johnson) KY

Took its name from Paint Creek, so called because of trees embellished with Indian drawings, a form of Native American graffiti. Originally known as Paint Lick Station, a name in use as early as 1780, it was laid out in 1826 and established in 1834. It was the site of skirmishing in January 1862 and April 1864.

Palestine (Anderson) TX

Dating from c.1849 and named after Palestine, Illinois, this is another example of the prevailing fashion for exotic placenames. The Palestine Saltworks, owned by J.L. McMeans, provided salt to the Confederate Army as well as the civilian population. A few miles north of here, at Mound Prairie, a major Confederate quartermaster depot, described as "the finest C.S. depot in the South," was established. It included a sawmill, flour mill, cotton spinning mill, blacksmith shop, foundry, harness shop, shoe shop, tanyard and warehouses. There was also a small arms manufactory, operated by J. Llewellyn.

Palmetto (Fulton) GA

Derives from the name of a small palm tree.

General John B. Hood came here in September 1864, planning to cut Federal lines of communication. President Davis, who visited him, assured Hood's troops that they would make Sherman's retreat "more disastrous than was that of Napoleon from Moscow."

Palmyra (Marion) MO
Was laid out in 1819 and named after the ancient Syrian "City of Palms." There was fighting here in August and November 1861. The "Palmyra Massacre" took place in September 1862 when ten Confederates were shot for the non-return of a captured Union spy.

Palmyra (Montgomery) TN
Like its ancient namesake it was destroyed, in this case by Federal sailors, in early April 1863 in retaliation for an attack on a Union convoy, and described a few days later by one of Colonel Streight's aides as "only a heap of black and charred ruins." Further skirmishing occurred in November.

Paola (Miami) KS
Originally called Peoria Village, for Baptiste Peoria, an Indian leader and interpreter, it was renamed by an Italian missionary after the town of Paola on the coast of southern Italy and laid out in 1855. A skirmish took place here in August 1863.

Papinsville (Bates) MO
Was named for Pierre M. Papin, a St. Louis Indian trader, and laid out in 1847. There was skirmishing here in September 1861 and June 1863.

Paris (Bourbon) KY
One of a number of towns named in recognition of French help during the Revolutionary War, it was settled c.1775, and had several names before becoming Paris. Skirmishing took place here in July 1862, March, April and July 1863.

Parkville (Platte) MO
On the Missouri River, it was named for its founder, George S. Park (1811–1890), joint-editor of an abolitionist newspaper called the *Industrial Luminary*, and developed after 1838. It was attacked by Confederate guerrillas in July 1864. (Now part of Kansas City.)

Paterson (Passaic) NJ
Was founded in 1791 on the Passaic River as an industrial settlement by Alexander Hamilton's Society for Establishing Useful Manufactures. It was named for William Paterson (1745–1806), the Irish-born attorney general of New Jersey, 1776–1783, and governor, 1790–1793. Paterson became a center of locomotive manufacturing, and the New Jersey Locomotive Works, Rogers & Co. and Danforth & Cook all built railroad engines here for the Union war effort.

Pattersonville (St. Mary) LA
Was named for Captain John Patterson of Indiana who settled here in 1832. There was fighting here in March and April 1863. (Now called Patterson.)

Pea Patch Island DE
Delaware takes its name from Lord De La Warre (1577–1618), who landed in Delaware Bay in 1610. **Fort Delaware**, on Pea Patch Island in the Delaware River, was built in 1848–1859 after the previous fort was destroyed by fire. "A marvel of military architecture," it became one of the largest military prisons in the North, receiving its first Confederate prisoners in July 1861. Its commandant, Hungarian-born General Albin F. Schoepf, became known as "General Terror" and its high death rate earned it the nickname of the "Andersonville of the North." The name of the island supposedly derives from an occasion when a ship carrying a cargo of peas ran aground here, resulting in the proliferation of wild pea plants.

Pea Ridge (Benton) AR
This was established in 1850 as Pearidge, so called because it was on the ridge of the Ozark Mountains and peanuts or turkey peas were grown here, by local Indians and early settlers. It had become Pea Ridge by the time a two-day battle was fought in March 1862. The Confederates, numerically superior and including Indian troops, were nevertheless forced to retreat, and two of their generals, Ben McCulloch and James M. McIntosh, were killed and William Y. Slack mortally wounded. The battle is also known as Elkhorn Tavern (q.v.).

Peachtree Creek (Fulton) GA
Georgia is famous for its peaches. A branch

of the Chattahoochee River, this was the scene of an engagement in the Atlanta campaign in July 1864. Determined assaults by General Hood's Confederates resulted only in heavy casualties and they were forced to withdraw; during them, General Clement H. ("Rock") Stevens was mortally wounded leading the Georgia brigade. (Now part of Atlanta.)

Pekin (Washington) IN

Is another example of the popularity in the early 19th century of exotic names, in this case the Chinese city of Pekin(g), now Beijing. On the Illinois River, it was first settled in 1824 and laid out in 1831. There was a skirmish here in July 1863 during General Morgan's raid into Kentucky, Ohio and Indiana. (Now called New Pekin.)

Pelham (Grundy) TN

Was perhaps named for Henry Pelham (1696–1754), an English statesman who held various political offices, including that of prime minister, 1743–1754. There was a skirmish here in July 1863.

Pensacola (Escambia) FL

First settled in 1559–1561, it was at various times Spanish, French and British before finally coming under American control in 1821. Its name derives from a Choctaw word meaning "long-haired people." The Warrington Navy Yard, established in 1825, and Forts Barrancas and McRee were taken over by Florida troops in January 1861. Ship construction ended when the navy yard was lost to the Confederacy with the evacuation of the city in May 1862. It was in turn evacuated by the Federals in March 1863.

Peralta (Valencia) NMT

Was named for Don Pedro de Peralta (1585?-1666), the governor of the province of New Mexico, 1609; he was also the founder of Santa Fe. There was skirmishing here in April 1862.

Perryville (Boyle) KY

Along the Chaplin River, it was named in honor of Commodore Oliver H. Perry (1785–1819), the victor of Lake Erie in the War of 1812. The battle of Perryville in October 1862, where Union Generals James S. Jackson and William R. Terrill were killed, was indecisive, but nevertheless it caused General Bragg's invasion of Kentucky to be halted and then abandoned.

Petersburg (♦) VA

Originally a fort built in 1645 on the banks of the Appomattox River, it was called successively Peter's Point and Peter's Town, possibly for Major Peter Jones, who was in command here in 1675. It was given its present name in 1733 by William Byrd, a colonial official also responsible for the naming of Richmond.

Like Atlanta, Richmond and Chattanooga, it was an important Confederate rail center, the meeting place of the Richmond & Petersburg, the South Side, the Weldon & Petersburg, the Norfolk & Petersburg and the Petersburg & City Point Railroads.

A naval powder works located here was moved to Columbia in August 1862. A naval ropewalk began production in January 1863, supplying not only the Confederate Navy, but the Army, coal mines and railroad companies. The Petersburg Iron Works produced shot and shell, and the firm of Tappey & Lumsden made revolving cannon, one of which blew up, killing the crew. Among hospitals located here were the Poplar Lawn, the Confederate States, the West End Park and the Central Pavilion. As at Richmond and elsewhere, converted tobacco warehouses were used to house Union prisoners.

The city's defenses, constructed in 1862–1863 under the supervision of Colonel Charles H. Dimmock, were known as the Dimmock Line. When the siege of Petersburg began in June 1864, many of the refugees who had previously crowded into it, fled. Union forces constructed a ring of forts around it, 31 in all. Several determined attempts were made to capture it: Union General James S.C. Morton was killed leading an assault in June; Confederate General Archibald Gracie was killed in December, and Ambrose P. Hill during the final Union assault at the beginning of April 1865, when it was evacuated. Its fall sealed the fate of Richmond, and ultimately of the Confederacy.

Five months later a visiting Northern writer noted: "All the lower part of the town showed the ruinous effect of the shelling it had received. Tenantless and uninhabitable houses, with broken walls, roofless, or with roofs smashed and torn by missiles...."

Four Confederate soldiers from the 52nd

Georgia and the 43rd Louisiana, cut off from their units during the evacuation, hid in a cave along the Appomattox River and only reappeared in August 1866 when they were assured by a local man that the Confederacy no longer existed.

Petersburg (Grant) WV

May have been named for John Jacob Peterson (1706–1785), a German colonist who opened the first store here c.1745. There was skirmishing here in September 1861, September 1863, January, March and October 1864.

Petites Coquilles Island LA

Guarding the entrance to Lake Pontchartrain, Fort Pike, built in 1819–1826, was named for General Zebulon M. Pike (1779–1813), who explored the Mississippi, Arkansas and Red Rivers. It was taken over by Louisiana militia in 1861 but surrendered to Federal forces in April 1862. *Petites Coquilles* is French for "little shells."

Peytona (Boone) WV

Was named for Colonel William Madison Peyton, the owner of the Canneltown Coal Co. There was a skirmish here in September 1861.

Philadelphia (Philadelphia) PA

Founded in 1682 by the English Quaker William Penn, it took its name from the Greek word *philadelphos*, meaning "brotherly love," though it was also the name of two cities in the ancient world, in present-day Jordan and Turkey. It served as the capital of Pennsylvania, 1683–1799, and as the Federal capital, 1790–1800.

In the Philadelphia Navy Yard, William Cramp & Sons built transports and monitors for the Union Army and Navy, the Penn Works of J.G. Neafie and J.P. Levy constructed gunboats, and the Pennsylvania Iron Works of Thomas Reany, Son & Archbold also turned out monitors and gunboats. At least one submarine, the USS *Alligator*, designed by French inventor Brutus de Villeroi, was built here in 1862 though she never saw service.

The Frankford Arsenal was located here. In addition, a number of firms made small arms, among them Philip S. Justice who manufactured rifle muskets, Richardson & Overman who made Gallager breech-loading carbines, John Pondir who produced light minié rifles, and Alfred Jenks and John Rice, who both manufactured Springfield rifled muskets. Horstmann Bros. & Co. made swords and Wilson, Childs & Co. manufactured army wagons. Matthias W. Baldwin also built locomotives for Northern railroads at the Baldwin Locomotive Co., as did Norris & Son.

A Sanitary Fair was held in June 1864 to raise money for the U.S. Sanitary Commission. There were two major hospitals here — the Satterlee General, originally the West Philadelphia General, renamed in honor of army surgeon and chief medical purveyor, Lieutenant Colonel Richard S. Satterlee, and Mower, named for army surgeon Major Thomas Mower. A U.S. Army Laboratory was opened here in 1863 by Surgeon General William A. Hammond, testing and manufacturing drugs, and also making sheets, pillow cases and hospital clothing. It was a large establishment, employing some 350 women workers as well as trained chemists, and one of two (the other was at Astoria, New York).

When African American regiments began to be raised for the Union Army, a shortage of suitably qualified white officers led to the establishment of a training school for prospective commanders of colored troops in 1863. Philadelphia was also the site of an Army quartermaster depot. At the end of the war, some Pennsylvania troops were mustered out here.

Philadelphia (Loudon) TN

Named after Philadelphia, Pennsylvania, it was founded in the early 1820s by William Knox and Jacob Pearson. It witnessed skirmishing in September 1863, in October when a Union brigade was routed by a force of Confederate cavalry, and in December, and in March 1865.

Philippi (Barbour) WV

On the Tygart Valley River, it was first called Anglin's Ford, for William Anglin, then Booth's Ferry, for Daniel Booth. When established in 1844, it was renamed Philippi for Philip P. Barbour (1783–1841), an associate justice of the U.S. Supreme Court, 1836–1841, though there was also a town of this name in ancient Greece. The "Philippi Races" was the nickname given by Northern newspapers to a skirmish in June 1861, when Confederate troops were taken by surprise and fled. It has been described as the "first land battle between North and South."

Philomont (Loudoun) VA

Established by Quakers, this is a hybrid name, from the Greek *Philo*, "beloved" and the French *mont*, "mountain." It was the scene of skirmishing in November 1862 and July 1864.

Phoenixville (Chester) PA

It was first settled in 1732 on the Schuykill River. Iron works begun c.1785 were restarted in 1813 and named the Phoenix Iron Works, hence Phoenixville. Dating from 1855 in their modern form, they manufactured lightweight, rifled cannon for the Union Army during the Civil War.

Piedmont (Augusta) VA

Was named after the region of Piedmont in north-west Italy. Confederate General William E. "Grumble" Jones was killed in an engagement here in June 1864 while trying to rally his fleeing troops, over a thousand of whom were captured.

Piedmont (Mineral) WV

Laid out by the New Creek Company in 1855, the name comes from the French *piedmont*, meaning "at the foot of mountains" (the Baltimore & Ohio Railroad, which arrived in 1851, began a 17 mile climb here). Confederate partisan rangers led by Captain John H. McNeill carried out a destructive raid on the B&O depot and workshops here in May 1864.

Pikesville (Baltimore) MD

Now a suburb of Baltimore, Pikesville was settled before the Revolution but not named till after the War of 1812, for the explorer General Zebulon M. Pike (1779–1813), who was killed in the war. The U.S. arsenal here was seized by Maryland militia in April 1861.

Pikeville (Wayne) NC

Nathan Pike (1749–1791), who became the owner of the town site land in 1785, is remembered here. There was fighting in April 1865 during General Sherman's advance through the Carolinas.

Pine Bluff (Jefferson) AR

On the Arkansas River, it was founded as a trading post c.1820 and named in 1832 for its location and tree cover. United States Army stores here were seized by secessionists in April 1861. It was attacked by General Marmaduke's Confederates in October 1863 after it had refused to surrender, but he withdrew after only partial occupation. The following year it saw considerable military activity, with numerous skirmishes between May and August and in October. The USS *Miller* was also captured near here in August 1864. The 1st Kansas Colored Infantry (later redesignated the 79th U.S. Colored Troops), one of the first black regiments, was mustered out here in October 1865.

Pine Mountain (Harris) GA

So called because of the abundance of pine trees. There was fighting around here in June 1864 during the early stages of the Atlanta campaign. Watching Sherman's advancing troops from the top of Pine Mountain, General Leonidas Polk, the "Bishop-Militant," was killed by a Federal artillery shell.

Pittsburg Landing (Hardin) TN

A hamlet on the west bank of the Tennessee River, it was named for "Pitts" Tucker who had a tavern there. Before the war it consisted of "two log huts, a dwelling and a grocery.... There was not so much as a wharf there, but steamers made their landing against the natural bank." When John T. Trowbridge went there in December 1865, even these few buildings had vanished. It was an alternate name for the two-day battle of Shiloh (q.v.) in April 1862.

Pittsburgh (Allegheny) PA

The French Fort Duquesne, where the Allegheny and the Monongahela Rivers join to form the Ohio, was captured by the British in 1758 and renamed Fort Pitt, for prime minister William Pitt the Elder (1708–1778). The settlement around it, laid out from 1764 onwards, became known as Pittsburgh.

Singer-Nimich & Co. made rifled cannon, and the Fort Pitt Foundry of Knapp, Rudd & Co. manufactured navy cannon and one colossal 20-inch smooth-bore which was mounted at Fort Hamilton, New York. The American Iron Works, which was founded in 1851 and became Jones & Laughlin, produced ammunition, ordnance and equipment for the Union Army. The

Allegheny Arsenal, built in 1813–1815, was the scene of an explosion in September 1862 when a number of workers were killed.

The Western or Allegheny Penitentiary housed Confederate prisoners in 1863–1864. Pittsburgh served as a rendezvous point for the demobilization of Pennsylvania troops at the end of the war.

Pittsylvania Court House (Pittsylvania) VA

Like Pittsburgh, it was named (1769) for William Pitt. The suffix "sylvania" means "woods." Bilharz, Hall & Co. made both breech-loading and muzzle-loading, single-shot carbines here for the Confederate Army.

Plaquemine (Iberville) LA

On the west bank of the Mississippi, it takes its name from the Bayou Plaquemine, which is Louisianan French, but comes originally from an Indian word for the persimmon tree, the fruit of which was used to make bread. It was settled as early as 1775. There was skirmishing here in December 1862, June 1863 and August 1864.

Plattsburg (Clinton) MO

Established in 1834, it was named in 1835 for Zephaniah Platt (1796–1871), a landowner and fur trader. It was attacked by Confederates in July 1864.

Plattsburgh (Clinton) NY

On Lake Champlain, was settled c.1785 and named for its founder, Judge Zephaniah Platt (1735–1807). It was a rendezvous point for the demobilization of New York troops in 1865.

Plentitude (Anderson) TX

According to the *Oxford English Dictionary*, this is an erroneous form of "plenitude," meaning "completeness, abundance, fully supplied with everything." The firm of Billings & Hassel made rifles here for Texas troops.

Plymouth (Washington) NC

On the Roanoke River, it was named c.1780 after Plymouth, Massachusetts. (This took its name from the English port of Plymouth, Devon, from where the Pilgrim Fathers set sail.) It changed hands several times during the war. Occupied in 1862 by Federal troops, it was recaptured by Confederates in December 1862, then retaken by Federal forces the following year. There was another successful Confederate attack in April 1864 involving the ironclad ram CSS *Albemarle*, but it was finally recaptured by a joint Union Army-Navy force in October of that year.

Pocahontas (Randolph) AR

This and the following were named for the Indian Princess Pocahontas (c.1595–1617), daughter of Powhatan, who married English colonist John Rolfe and died of smallpox during a visit to England. Skirmishing occurred here on the Black River in April 1862 and February 1864.

Pocahontas (Hardeman) TN

There was fighting here in October 1862 as General Van Dorn's Confederate troops, retreating from their defeat at Corinth, were crossing the Hatchie River.

Pocotaligo (Jasper) SC

Takes its name from the Pocotaligo River which is probably a Yemassee word. The engagement here in October 1862, when a Union attack over two days was repulsed, is also known as Yemassee (q.v.). There had been a previous skirmish in May 1862 and there was another in January 1865.

Point Lookout (St. Marys) MD

This Union military prison was known as such from its location at the place where the Potomac River enters Chesapeake Bay. Established in July 1863, it housed enlisted men in tents surrounded by a high fence, guarded by African American troops, and became the largest prison camp in the North. Its official name was Camp Hoffman (q.v.). Within its boundaries was Hammond General Hospital, a large complex named for Surgeon General William A. Hammond who did much to reform the army medical service, but was dismissed in 1864 for "irregularities." In December 1863 Point Lookout was visited by President Abraham Lincoln and Secretary of War Edwin M. Stanton. The 1st U.S. Volunteers, a regiment of ex-Confederates, was raised from among the prisoners early in 1864 to become galvanized Yankees and later that year were authorized for frontier service.

Point of Rocks (Frederick) MD

The name describes its location on the Potomac River. It was laid out in 1835, but five years previously had been the site of a famous legal battle between the Baltimore & Ohio Railroad and the Chesapeake & Ohio Canal over right of way. Real battles began in earnest in June 1861 when a Confederate attempt to obstruct the B. & O. with a huge boulder was foiled by Union Army engineers. There was skirmishing in August and September, a Confederate camp near here was broken up in November, and further skirmishes occurred in December, September 1862 and June 1863. While General Joseph Hooker was here he received telegraphed orders at the end of that month to hand over command of the Army of the Potomac to General George G. Meade, only a few days before the battle of Gettysburg.

Poison Springs (Ouachita) AR

Was so called because of the presence of water impregnated with alkali and poisonous to cattle. A Union forage wagon train, whose escort included troops of the 1st Kansas Colored Volunteer Infantry, was attacked by a much larger Confederate force under General John S. Marmaduke in April 1864 and forced to abandon it. Afterwards, racial animosity resulted in a number of black soldiers being killed as they tried to surrender.

Pollocksville (Jones) NC

Founded on the Trent River in the 1770s, it was named for Colonel Thomas Pollock (1654–1722), a Scottish-born landowner and governor of North Carolina, 1712–1714 and 1722. There was skirmishing here in April, May and July 1862.

Pomeroy (Meigs) OH

Was named in 1840 for Samuel W. Pomeroy, a Boston merchant who had bought land here in 1804. It became an important producer of both coal and salt. General John H. Morgan passed through here during his Indiana and Ohio raid in July 1863.

Pontotoc (Pontotoc) MS

Established in 1832, it was named for a Chickasaw chief whose name meant "cat-tail prairie" or "cat's-tail grass." Skirmishing took place here in April 1863 during Colonel Grierson's Mississippi raid, and also in February and July 1864.

Poolesville (Montgomery) MD

Was named in 1793 for John and Joseph Poole, the first settlers. There was skirmishing here in September 1862 and again in July 1864 during General Early's retreat from his Washington raid.

Poplar Bluff (Butler) MO

On the Black River, was founded in 1849 and so called because of the presence of poplar trees. There was fighting here in February 1864 and it was largely depopulated as a result of guerrilla warfare.

Port Gibson (Claiborne) MS

On a tributary of the Mississippi, it was founded by and named for Samuel Gibson, a plantation owner, in 1788. General Edward D. Tracy, CSA, was killed in the fighting here at the beginning of May 1863. General Ulysses S. Grant, whose victorious troops passed through on their way to Vicksburg, called it "too beautiful to burn."

Port Hudson (East Baton Rouge) LA

Like the Hudson River in New York it may have been named for the English explorer and navigator Henry Hudson (d.1611). On the Mississippi, it was the southern terminus of the Clinton & Port Hudson Railroad. Union General Edward P. Chapin was killed during an attack on Confederate defenses in May 1863. Taking part were the 1st and 3rd Louisiana Native Guards who, wrote General Nathaniel P. Banks, "answered every expectation; no troops could be more determined or daring." This was the first major assault in the Civil War by African American troops, though the attack failed. The siege which followed finally ended in July 1863 with a Confederate surrender, a few days after the fall of Vicksburg, finally opening up the Mississippi to Union control.

Port Royal Island SC

Founded in 1562 by French Huguenots, then in Spanish hands, 1566–1650, and English ones from the 1670s onwards, **Port Royal** was named for its good harbor. Following a naval battle fought off here in November 1861, it was subsequently used by the Union Navy as a coaling station, supply and ordnance depot. The 54th Massachusetts Colored Infantry arrived here in June 1863, prior to their deployment for the attack on Fort Wagner the following month. **Beaufort**, laid out in 1710, was named for Henry Somerset, Duke of Beaufort (1684–1714). After its capture by Federal troops, it became a haven for runaway slaves. Union General Ormsby M. Mitchel died here from yellow fever in October 1862. **Camp Saxton** was a camp for freedmen, named for General Rufus K. Saxton (1824–1908), military governor of the Sea Islands. He successfully turned the 1st South Carolina Colored Volunteers, begun by General David Hunter, into the first black regiment in the Union Army.

Port Walthall Junction (Chesterfield) VA

Took its name from the Walthall family who were among the first people to settle between the Appomattox and James Rivers. There was a two-day engagement here, at this junction of the Richmond & Petersburg and Richmond & York River Railroads, when Union troops succeeded in breaking the line between Richmond and Petersburg and seizing control of the station in May 1864. (The name is no longer in use.)

Portland (Cumberland) ME

Founded in 1632 as Falmouth, named after the English seaport in Cornwall, it was twice destroyed by Indians, then by the French and later by a British fleet. Renamed after the Isle of Portland in Dorset, England, in 1786, it served as the state capital, 1820–1831. The Portland Co., operated by J. Sparrow, made cannon for both the Union Army and Navy. The Confederate schooner *Archer* took part in an unsuccessful attempt to seize a Federal revenue cutter in Portland harbor in June 1863. At the end of the war it served as a demobilization point for Maine regiments.

Portsmouth (Rockingham) NH

What began as a fishing settlement in 1624 acquired its present name in 1653. It was called after Portsmouth, in Hampshire, England, though it was by then also a port at the mouth of the Piscataqua River. It served as the state capital, 1679–1775. Like the city after which it was named, it became an important naval base, with a navy yard established in the 1790s. In July 1863 it witnessed a draft riot, though on nothing like the scale seen in New York.

Portsmouth (♦) VA

On the Elizabeth River opposite Norfolk, it was founded in 1752 and also named after the English city of Portsmouth. Abandoned by the U.S. Navy in April 1861, the Gosport Navy Yard (later renamed the Norfolk Navy Yard), established in 1801, was for a year the most important shipbuilding center in the Confederacy. The USS *Merrimack* was converted into the CSS *Virginia* here, and work begun on the construction of the ironclad *Richmond*. Portsmouth was evacuated by the Confederates in May 1862 and remained in Federal hands for the rest of the war. The Portsmouth Naval Hospital was used by both sides during the war.

Potomac River WV/VA/MD

Derives its name from an Iroquois word meaning "where goods are brought in." In 1863 it became the subject of a popular wartime song, James H. Hewitt's "All Quiet Along the Potomac Tonight." The Union Army of the Potomac was in existence virtually throughout the war, its commanders including Generals George B. McClellan, Ambrose E. Burnside, Joseph Hooker and George G. Meade. There was also a Confederate Army of the Potomac, from June 1861 to June 1862, when it became part of the Army of Northern Virginia.

Powhatan (Powhatan) VA

Powhatan (c.1550–1618) was an Algonquin chief in Virginia and the father of Pocahontas. There was a skirmish here in January 1865.

Prairie Grove (Washington) AR

Is a descriptive place name. The two-day battle here in December 1862 is also known as Fayetteville (q.v.).

Prattville (Autauga) AL

Was first settled in 1816 and named in 1838 for Daniel Pratt (1799–1873) who built a cotton gin mill here in 1833, the first one in Alabama. He later added other factories, making Prattville the industrial center of the state, and also pioneered the development of coal and iron mines in the South. During the Civil War he raised the Prattville Dragoons, and his Prattville Manufacturing Co. made cloth for uniforms for Alabama troops.

Prentiss (Jefferson Davis) MS

Was named for Sergeant Smith Prentiss (1808–1850), a Mississippi legislator. There was a skirmish here in September 1862.

Prestonsburg (Floyd) KY

Situated on the Big Sandy River, it was founded in 1797 on land belonging to Colonel John Preston, a surveyor from Virginia. It was occupied by Federal troops under General William Nelson in November 1861. An engagement at nearby Middle Creek in January 1862, for which both sides claimed victory, nevertheless drove the Confederates into south-east Virginia; the Union troops were commanded by Colonel James A. Garfield, a future president of the United States. In December of that year Confederates captured supply boats containing arms, ammunition and uniforms.

Prince George Court House (Prince George) VA

Was named for Prince George of Denmark (1653–1708), the husband of Queen Anne. It was the scene of a skirmish in November 1864.

Princess Anne Court House (Princess Anne) VA

Princess Anne (1665–1714), a daughter of King James II, became Queen Anne in 1702. There were military operations around here lasting several days in September 1863.

Princeton (Mercer) WV

First settled in 1826, it was laid out in 1837 and named after the battle of Princeton (1777) in the Revolutionary War. Skirmishing occurred here in September 1861, in May 1862 when it was burned by retreating Confederates, and again in May 1864 during an attack by Federal cavalry on the Virginia & Tennessee Railroad.

Providence (Providence) RI

The state capital of Rhode Island on the Providence River, founded in 1636 as a refuge for religious dissenters from Massachusetts, was named in recognition of "God's merciful providence." During the Civil War Zachariah Chaffee made naval cannon and ammunition at the Builder's Foundry, Caspar D. Schubarth & Co. made Springfield rifles and the Providence Tool Co. produced rifle muskets. The Burnside Works made small arms, and the Spencer carbine and Peabody rifle were also manufactured here. Providence was a mustering out point for Rhode Island troops in 1865.

Pryor's Creek (Mayes) IT

Nathaniel Pryor (c.1785–1831), for whom this was named, was a trader, scout for the Lewis and Clark Expedition, 1804–1806, Osage agent and veteran of the War of 1812. Fighting occurred here in September 1864 during General Price's invasion of Missouri.

Pulaski (Giles) TN

Was named for Casimir Pulaski (1747–1779), a Polish nobleman who served in the Continental Army. There was considerable military activity here, with skirmishing in May and August 1862, July and December 1863, and May and September 1864. General Grenville M. Dodge made his headquarters here in November 1863, when young Confederate scout Sam Davis was hanged as a spy. "He was game to the last [,] never flinched," wrote a soldier in the 66th Illinois. A year later it was headquarters for Union General John M. Schofield.

Purcellville (Loudoun) VA

Valentine V. Purcell opened the first store and post office here in 1832. It was named for him in 1853. A Confederate wagon train was captured here in July 1864.

Quincy (Hickory) MO

Was founded and probably named in 1848, in honor of John Quincy Adams (1767–1848), sixth president of the United States, 1825–1829. Fighting took place here in September 1863.

Quitman (Cleburne) AR

General John A. Quitman (1798–1858), a hero of the Mexican War and a former governor of Mississippi, is remembered here. There was skirmishing near here in March and September 1864.

Raccoon Ford (Orange) VA

One of a number of fords on the Rapidan,

this was the scene of skirmishing in August 1862, April, and September–December 1863. The name of the nocturnal, greyish-brown, North American raccoon comes from an Algonquin word, in use from the early 17th century.

Raleigh (Wake) NC

Laid out in 1792 as the state capital, it was named for Sir Walter Raleigh (1554–1618), the English navigator who sent an expedition which explored the coast from present-day Florida to North Carolina in 1584. There was a pre-war state arsenal, and Waterhouse & Bowes set up a powder mill near here in 1861. Government locomotive workshops were also established in 1862. North Carolina was the only Southern state to have its own clothing factory, which operated at Raleigh in 1861–1862, producing jackets, trousers, overcoats and blankets, hats and caps. C.W.D. Hutchings also made accoutrements for infantry, cavalry and artillery units.

Raleigh soon became a center for refugees; one temporary resident in 1862, at the time of the Peninsula campaign, was Mrs. Jefferson Davis. The offices of a pro–Union newspaper, the *Standard*, were attacked by Confederate soldiers in September 1863. Pettigrew Hospital, the largest of three here, was named in honor of General James J. Pettigrew, fatally wounded during the Confederate retreat from Gettysburg. Purpose-built, it opened in 1864. Converted buildings and barracks housed Federal prisoners in 1861–1863 and possibly till 1865. General Sherman's army entered Raleigh on its drive north in April 1865, four days after General Lee's surrender.

Randolph (Bibb) AL

Was named for the charismatic Virginia politician John Randolph of Roanoke (1773–1833), a vigorous supporter of states' rights. It was the scene of a skirmish in April 1865 during General Wilson's raid to Selma.

Rapidan River VA

Was a combination of "rapids" + (Queen) "Anne" (1665–1714) and originally called the Rapid Ann(e) River. It was the scene of fighting during the second Manassas campaign (July–August 1862), the Chancellorsville campaign (April–May 1863), in October–November 1863, and the Wilderness (May 1864).

Rapidan Station (Culpeper) VA

Was the northern terminus of the Orange & Alexandria Railroad, which crossed the Rapidan at this point. There were a number of skirmishes here, in May 1862, in July, when the railroad bridge across the river was destroyed by Union troops, and again in August. Yet more skirmishing occurred in September 1863.

Rappahannock River VA

Comes from an Indian word meaning "stream with an ebb and flow" or "river of quick-rising water." Because of its location, it featured in many actions and campaigns throughout the Civil War, from as early as June 1861 to March 1865, including Second Manassas (July–August 1862), Fredericksburg (December 1862) and Chancellorsville (April–May 1863).

Rappahannock Station (Fauquier) VA

This station on the Orange & Alexandria Railroad, at the crossing of the Rappahannock, witnessed fighting in August 1862, skirmishing in February and October 1863, and more serious fighting in November of that year when Confederate defenders were overwhelmed. (Now called Remington.)

Ravenswood (Jackson) WV

On the Ohio River, it was first settled in 1810 and laid out in 1835. It was apparently named for the English Ravensworth family, which was misspelled on early maps and never corrected. It was the scene of skirmishing in May and September 1862, and May and October 1863.

Raymond (Hinds) MS

Was established in 1830 and named for Raymond Robinson who gave land for the town site. An engagement took place here in May 1863 during the second Vicksburg campaign, when outnumbered Confederates were forced to retreat.

Raytown (Jackson) MO

Once an assembly point for wagon trains on the Santa Fe Trail, it is now a suburb of Kansas City. It was named for either William Ray, an Ohio man who established a blacksmith's shop here, or John Ray, a legislator. The settlement which grew up c.1848 was called Ray's Town, then became Raytown in 1854. There was a skirmish here in June 1862.

Reading (Berks) PA

On the Schuylkill River, it was laid out in 1748 on land owned by two of the sons of William Penn and named after the English town of Reading, Berkshire. Iron and steel making developed here, helped by the opening of the Schuylkill and Union Canals. The Scott Foundry, operated by Seyfert, McManus & Co., made cannon for both the Union Army and Navy.

Red River LA

A tributary of the Mississippi, so called because of the red clay forming its banks. A joint Union army-navy expedition in March-May 1864, commanded by General Nathaniel P. Banks and Rear Admiral David D. Porter and aimed at capturing Shreveport, capital of Confederate Louisiana, turned out to be a disaster. The tiny Red River Squadron of the Confederate Navy surrendered at Alexandria in June 1865.

Resaca (Gordon) GA

Was originally called Dublin by Irish laborers building the Western & Atlantic Railroad, but renamed after the American victory at Resaca de la Palma in 1846, during the Mexican War. Both sides suffered heavy losses at the two-day battle of Resaca in May 1864, during the Atlanta campaign, at the end of which General Johnston's troops were forced to retreat.

Rich Mountain (Randolph) WV

This is of uncertain origin, but may derive from a personal name. There was fighting in this pro–Union part of Virginia in the early part of the war, and in July 1861 Confederate troops holding strategically important Rich Mountain were overwhelmed when a Federal brigade under General William S. Rosecrans struggled up it in pouring rain. Their victory secured western Virginia for the Union and brought overall commander General George B. McClellan instant fame.

Richmond (Madison) KY

Settled in 1784, it was one of several Southern towns named after Richmond, Virginia. The two-day battle near here at the end of August 1862, during General Kirby Smith's invasion of Kentucky, resulted in the first Confederate victory in that state.

Richmond (Ray) MO

Was laid out in 1827 and also named after Richmond, Virginia. There was fighting near here in July 1864, and the notorious Confederate guerrilla William ("Bloody Bill") Anderson was killed in an ambush in October.

Richmond (♦) VA

Started life as a trading post in 1637, then became Fort Charles, built in 1644. It was given its present name in 1733 by William Byrd, a colonial official, apparently because of a perceived resemblance between his English home town of Richmond-on-Thames, Surrey, and Richmond on the James. Laid out in 1737 by Major William Mayo, it became the state capital of Virginia in 1780. Served by the Virginia Central, the Richmond & Petersburg, the Richmond & Danville, the Richmond, Fredericksburg & Potomac and the Richmond & York River Railroads, it became the capital of the Confederacy in May 1861.

The former Virginia State Armory was remodeled to become the Richmond Armory in June 1861; machinery from the Harpers Ferry Arsenal was installed, and the S.C. Robinson Arms Manufactory became part of it in 1863. The Tredegar Iron Works, founded in 1839 and owned by Joseph R. Anderson, operated night and day, producing artillery pieces, siege guns and armor plating for warships. The Shockoe Foundry was leased by the Confederate Navy to make marine engines; the Richmond Naval Ordnance Works, established in 1861, supplied the James River Squadron with ordnance and gun carriages; and the Rocketts Navy Yard, opened in 1862, built several ironclads. William J. Hubbard, near Richmond, also made brass cannon in conjunction with Thomas Sampson and James Pae.

Boyle, Gamble & Co. and Mitchell & Tyler made swords, knives and bayonets; the Crenshaw Woolen Co., converted from a flour mill by Lewis Crenshaw in 1860, produced cloth for uniforms for Virginia troops; and military caps were made by John Dooley's Southern Hat Manufactory and Conrad Saser.

The Henrico County Jail, the Virginia State Penitentiary and Castle Godwin (named for

General Archibald Godwin, assistant provost marshal of Richmond) housed political prisoners, deserters and Union prisoners of war. The warehouse of Luther Libby & Son, ship chandlers and grocers, was turned into a prison for Union officers in September 1862, and tobacco factories were also converted into temporary military prisons. Two of these were nicknamed Castle Thunder and Castle Lightning.

With its population swollen to several times its pre-war level by soldiers, large numbers of refugees and transient civilians, Richmond was plagued by drunken violence and crime, and martial law was imposed in March 1862, remaining in force till the fall of the Confederacy, with the provost guard — the military police — struggling to maintain control. In April 1863 a riot, which began as an attack on bread shops, spread to clothing and jewelry stores and was only quelled when troops were brought in. Like Washington, it was also infested with prostitutes, openly soliciting on the main thoroughfares and even in the grounds of the Capitol.

There were eventually 34 hospitals in Richmond, of which the largest was Chimborazo, named after a volcano in Ecuador, one of whose matrons was Phoebe Pember; others included Winder, named for General John H. Winder, provost marshal and commander of prisons in Richmond; Howard's Grove, named for the Howard family; and Jackson and Stuart, both named in honor of departed Confederate heroes; there was also a naval hospital. Among the many established in private houses was the Robertson Hospital, supervised by Sally L. Tompkins, the only woman to be granted a commission in the Confederate Army.

Richmond was under siege from June 1864 till evacuated by the Confederates at the beginning of April 1865 amid scenes of destruction, disorder and chaos. Visiting it five months later, a Northern writer painted a depressing picture: "All up and down, as far as the eye could reach, the business portion of the city ... lay in ruins. Beds of cinders, cellars half filled with bricks and rubbish, broken and blackened walls, impassable streets deluged with debris, here a granite front still standing and there the iron fragments of crushed machinery...."

Rienzi (Alcorn) MS

Was established in 1830 and probably named for Nicola Gabrina Rienzi (c.1313–1354), an Italian patriot who attempted to restore the glory of ancient Rome, and also the hero of a popular novel by Edward Bulwer-Lytton, *Rienzi, the Last of the Roman Tribunes* (1835). There was fighting here in June, August and September 1862. While stationed near here in spring 1862, General Philip H. Sheridan named his new horse after this place, though it was later renamed "Winchester" after his famous ride from there to Cedar Creek in October 1864.

Riker's Island NY

This small island in the East River, New York, took its name from Abraham Rycken (d.1669), a German immigrant who came here in 1638; his family name later became Riker. During the Civil War it was used as an assembly point for black regiments, and barracks to hold Confederate prisoners were built in 1864 and quickly filled. **Camp Astor** here was named for John Jacob Astor III (1822–1890) who served as a volunteer aide-de-camp to General George B. McClellan in 1861–1862 in the rank of colonel. It was sold to the city in 1884 and is now the site of a jail complex.

Ringgold (Catoosa) GA

Captain Samuel Ringgold (1800–1846) was the first American officer to die in the Mexican War and this town was named for him. The Bragg and Foard Hospitals were located here. The battle of Ringgold Gap in November 1863 was a successful Confederate attempt to stop the advance of General Joseph Hooker. There was also skirmishing here in September and December 1863, February 1864 and March 1865.

Ripley (Tippah) MS

Was named for General Eleazer W. Ripley (1782–1839), a hero of the War of 1812. There was considerable military activity around Ripley, with skirmishing in October 1862, in December during General Van Dorn's Holly Springs raid, in April 1863 during the Grierson raid, then in July, August and December 1863, and June and July 1864.

Roanoke Island NC

The name derives from a Native American word meaning a "place where white shells are found" or "shells used for money." Off the

North Carolina coast, it was the site of **Fort Bartow**, which commemorated Colonel Francis S. Bartow (1816–1861) of the 8th Georgia, killed at First Manassas; **Fort Blanchard**, probably named for General Albert G. Blanchard (1810–1891), who commanded in North Carolina in the latter part of the war; and **Fort Huger**, named for General Benjamin Huger (1805–1877). It was captured in February 1862 in a major Union army-navy operation, involving 13 regiments and 24 gunboats; more than 2,500 Confederates were taken prisoner. After its occupation General Ambrose E. Burnside admitted to General Lorenzo Thomas, "A few irregularities occurred in the way of destruction of property … but in no case has personal violence or indignities been offered." **Camp Jourdan**, established that month, was named for Irish-born Lieutenant Colonel James Jourdan of the 56th New York. A contraband camp was also opened here. Carrie Cutter, a volunteer nurse from New Hampshire, died from typhoid fever here after caring for Union wounded.

Roanoke Station (Randolph) VA

Took its name from the Roanoke River. There was fighting near here in June 1864, when an attack by Union cavalry on the bridge carrying the Richmond & Danville Railroad across the Staunton River was successfully repulsed. (Now called Randolph.)

Rocheport (Boone) MO

Was laid out in 1825. *Roche* is French for "rock," and it takes its name from rock formations near this port on the Missouri River. Skirmishing occurred near here in June 1863, August and September 1864 and May 1865.

Rock Island IL

In the Mississippi, it got its name from a foundation of limestone rock. It had belonged to the U.S. government since 1804 and housed **Fort Armstrong**, established in 1816 and named for former Secretary of War John Armstrong (1758–1843). Converted into a prison camp in 1863, barracks were constructed to house Confederate prisoners "in the roughest and cheapest manner." It was notable for the large number of prisoners who took the oath of allegiance to the Union in 1864, presumably to escape the appalling conditions and become galvanized Yankees, for service on the frontier. Rock Island was also the site of a Union arsenal, built in 1862.

Rockingham (Richmond) NC

Established in 1785, it was named for Charles Watson-Wentworth, Marquis of Rockingham (1730–1782), who had supported proposals to grant independence to the American colonies. There was a skirmish here in March 1865 during General Sherman's march through the Carolinas.

Rockport (Hot Springs) AR

Has the same origin as Rocheport (q.v.). After the fall of Little Rock in September 1863, General Price's Confederates withdrew to here, on the Ouachita River, and to Arkadelphia. There was also skirmishing here in March 1864.

Rockville (Montgomery) MD

Now a Washington suburb, it was first settled in the 1770s and named Rockville in 1803, after nearby Rock Creek. It was a frequent target of Confederate raids in search of horses, and in late June 1863 General Stuart's cavalry captured a large Federal supply train laden with foodstuffs. It proved to be a short-lived triumph: the wagons and mule teams were pronounced "an impediment" by General Robert E. Lee on Stuart's belated arrival at Gettysburg on day two of the battle. More skirmishing occurred here in September 1863 and in July 1864.

Rogersville (Hawkins) TN

Established in 1786, it was named for Irishman Joseph P. Rogers (1764–1833), who bought land from Davy Crockett's family and became its first postmaster. There was fighting near here in November 1863 and October 1864.

Rolla (Phelps) MO

The name was probably a phonetic rendering of Raleigh, North Carolina, by local resident George Coppedge who came from there. It began to develop c.1855, and by the time of the Civil War was the terminus of what was then called the South West Pacific Railroad (intended as the St. Louis-San Francisco Railroad).

A large fortified military encampment was established here and when English novelist Anthony Trollope visited Rolla early in 1862, just before the Pea Ridge campaign, it was the headquarters of Union General Samuel R. Curtis, commanding the Southwest District of Missouri. While here, Trollope met Generals Franz Sigel and Alexander S. Asboth; the latter, a Hungarian, was particularly hospitable. There was skirmishing near Rolla in August and November 1864, and March 1865.

Rome (Floyd) GA

Was founded in 1835 at the confluence of the Etowah and Oostanaula Rivers. "Like the renowned city, the name of which it bears, it is built on several hills," wrote Confederate nurse Kate Cumming, who visited it in July 1863. Polk and Quintard Hospitals were both located here. Dickson, Nelson & Co. made rifles and bayonets for Alabama troops, while Noble Bros. & Co., who came here from Pennsylvania in 1855, made marine engines for the Confederate Navy and cannon for the Army at their foundry. This was destroyed in November 1864 when General William T. Sherman ordered that the town be evacuated and "all bridges, foundries, shops ... barracks, warehouses and buildings especially adapted to military use," burned.

Romney (Hampshire) WV

Founded in 1762, it was named after the English town of New Romney, Kent. Because of its strategic location, near the Baltimore & Ohio Railroad, it changed hands several times during the Civil War—there was fighting, for instance, in September 1861, and a battle here in January 1862. Partisan leader Major Harry Gilmor was arrested near here by Federal cavalry in February 1865.

Roseville (Logan) AR

Situated on the Arkansas River, it probably took its name from nearby Roseville Creek, indicating the presence of wild roses. There was skirmishing here in November 1863 and March and April 1864.

Rossville (Catoosa) GA

Now largely a suburb of Chattanooga, Rossville was named for John Ross (1790–1866), a man of mixed Scottish and Indian ancestry who was head of the Cherokee Nation. He and his people lived here till forcibly removed to the Indian Territory in 1838–1839, in what became known as the "Trail of Tears." It was the scene of a skirmish in September 1863.

Roswell (Fulton) GA

Was named for Roswell King (1765–1844), a Connecticut Yankee who moved here from Darien c.1837. His Ivy Woolen Mill, established in 1839 and run by his grandsons by the time of the Civil War, produced a dark, bluish-gray cloth called "Roswell gray" which was supplied in large quantities to the Confederate War Department. After fighting here in June 1864, the factory was destroyed by Federal troops the following month, when General William T. Sherman ordered the arrest and deportation north of its women workers and their children. There was further skirmishing in September 1864.

Rough and Ready Station (Clayton) GA

Commemorated Zachary Taylor (1784–1850), 12th president of the United States, 1849–1850, whose nickname was "Old Rough and Ready." There was fighting here, on the Macon & Western Railroad, at the end of August 1864, after which the line between Jonesboro and Atlanta was cut by the Federals. In September it became an exchange point for citizens expelled from Atlanta who were being passed through the lines and heading south. They were brought in Federal wagons and ambulances, before transferring to Confederate transport, en route for Lovejoy's Station. Rough and Ready, said one Union officer, "as completely answers to the first part of its name as one could imagine," consisting of "two miserable shanties." It was also the site of a limited exchange of prisoners, including Union General George Stoneman and Confederate General Daniel C. Govan. (The name is no longer in use.)

Rowlesburg (Preston) WV

It was named in 1852 for an engineer on the Baltimore & Ohio Railroad called James Rowles. A Confederate attempt during the Jones-Imboden raid into West Virginia in April 1863 to capture this town and destroy the Cheat River railroad viaduct was a failure.

Rumsey (McLean) KY

Named for congressman and lawyer Edward Rumsey (1796–1868), a prominent local resident, it was the scene of a skirmish in November 1861.

Rusk (Cherokee) TX
Established in 1846, it was named for Thomas J. Rusk (1803–1857), an important figure in the history of the Texas Republic. Whitescarver, Campbell & Co. made rifles near here for the Texas Military Board.

Russellville (Franklin) AL
Was established c.1815 and named for its founder, Major William Russell (d.1870), who had been a scout for Andrew Jackson. During Colonel Streight's raid through Alabama in April 1863, it was described by one Ohio soldier in his command as "a small, mean-looking Secesh hole." There had been skirmishing here in July 1862, and there was more fighting in December 1864.

Russellville (Logan) KY
Was founded in 1790 and named for Colonel William Russell (1758–1825) of the Revolutionary War. A separate Confederate state government for Kentucky was created at a convention here in November 1861, with George W. Johnson as the first governor, 1861–1862, followed by Richard Hawes, 1862–1865. There was skirmishing in July and September 1862 and June 1863.

Russellville (Hamblen) TN
The second wife of Colonel James Roddey, the original landowner, was a Miss Russell. Fighting occurred here in December 1863, and October and November 1864.

Rutland (Rutland) VT
It started life as a military outpost in 1759 and was named for John Manners, Duke of Rutland (1696–1779). He had no connection with Vermont but his name was chosen to promote land sales to developers. The first settlers arrived in 1770, and it served as the territorial and state capital, 1784–1804. Rutland was the scene of a draft riot in July 1863, one of several in the North at that time.

Rutledge (Grainger) TN
General George Rutledge, brigadier general of the state militia, is commemorated here. It was established in 1798. There was skirmishing in December 1863.

Sabine Crossroads (DeSoto) LA
This and the following take their names from *sabinas*, the Spanish word for the cypress trees growing along the banks of the Sabine River. Confederate General J.J. Alfred A. Mouton was killed and German-born Colonel August Buchel fatally wounded in the battle fought here in April 1864 during General Banks' Red River campaign. It is also known as the battle of Mansfield (q.v.).

Sabine Pass (Jefferson) TX
At the entrance to the Sabine Lake and River, it was first laid out c.1836 as Sabine City. It was the scene of fighting in September and October 1862, and an encounter in January 1863 when Confederate cotton-clad steamers attacked and briefly captured Federal blockaders. There was further military activity in April and September, when a force of Federal gunboats tried unsuccessfully to capture the pass. Jefferson Davis called it the "Thermopylae of the Civil War." It was finally evacuated by the Confederates in May 1865. (Now part of Port Arthur.)

Saffold (Early) GA
Took its name from the Saffold family who came here from Virginia. A wooden gunboat was built in 1862 by David S. Johnston, an attorney and planter turned boatbuilder, at a steamboat landing on the Chattahoochee River described as a C.S. Navy Yard, and called appropriately the CSS *Chattahoochee*. Before it could see action, however, the boilers exploded in May 1863, killing or wounding a number of the crew.

Sailor's Creek (Prince Edward/ Amelia/Nottaway) VA
A tributary of the Appomattox River, this was known as Sailor's Creek both before and during the Civil War, though by 1879 it was called Sayler's Creek, the present-day spelling. This name may derive from a Marten Saylor, connected with an Appomattox River improvement scheme (1795), or a J.D. Sayler, mentioned in a legal document (1842). Exhausted, starving Confederate forces, including a naval brigade, retreating westward from Petersburg, fought a

desperate battle here in April 1865, when a quarter of General Lee's remaining troops were killed or captured, among them six generals, causing him to exclaim to General William Mahone, "My God! Has the army dissolved?"

St. Albans (Franklin) VT

Was settled from the 1760s onwards and named after St. Albans, a town in Hertfordshire, England. It was a station on the Underground Railroad, and the scene of an unsuccessful Confederate raid in October 1864, carried out by escaped prisoners of war from across the Canadian border.

St. Andrews Bay (Washington) FL

Saint Andrew, one of the twelve apostles, was a fisherman, and St. Andrews Bay, so called by 1845, became a center of fishing on the Gulf Coast. During the Civil War saltworks were established here, and numerous attempts were made by the Federal Navy to destroy them, particularly in December 1863, over a period of ten days, and in April 1864, and there was a final attack in February 1865.

St. Augustine (St. John's) FL

A fort established by the Spanish in 1565 was named *San Agostino* for Saint Augustine of Hippo, because the site was discovered on his feast day, August 28. The oldest, continuously occupied settlement in the United States, it remained under Spanish control, except for 1763–1783, when the British were here, until it became part of the United States in 1821. It surrendered to U.S. naval forces in March 1861. There was also skirmishing here in March and December 1863.

St. Francisville (Clark) MO

Took its name from the St. Francis River, named for Saint Francis of Sales (1567–1622), a French bishop and theologian. Skirmishing took place here in February 1862 and nearby, at Alexander's Creek, in October 1864.

St. James (Phelps) MO

Was laid out in 1859 in anticipation of the arrival of the St. Louis-San Francisco Railroad and named in 1860, apparently for Thomas James, its founder. He was owner of the Maramec Iron Works, the first commercially viable one west of the Mississippi, which made iron for cannon balls and Union gunboats. There was fighting near here in June 1864.

St. Louis (♦) MO

Founded as a French fur-trading post on the Mississippi in 1764, it was named for King Louis IX of France (1214–1270), who was canonized in 1297 as Saint Louis. In May 1861 there was serious rioting involving Federal soldiers and Southern sympathizers, in which a number of people were killed. St. Louis was made the Union state capital in July 1861.

It was the site of an arsenal. Gratiot Street Prison, converted from a medical college, and the smaller Myrtle Street Prison housed Confederate prisoners throughout 1861–1865; Schofield Barracks was also used for the same purpose in the early part of the war. Jefferson Barracks, established in 1826, was taken over by the U.S. Army Medical Department in 1862, to become one of the largest Union hospitals. In 1865 Missouri troops came here to be mustered out.

Benton Barracks, erected by General John C. Frémont, was visited by English novelist Anthony Trollope during his stay in St. Louis in the early part of 1862. He was not impressed. "Here ... two long rows of wooden sheds have been built opposite to each other, and behind them are other sheds used for stabling and cooking-places.... I went into one or two ... but found it inexpedient to stay there long. The stench of those places was foul beyond description. Never in my life before had I been in a place so horrid to the eyes and nose as Benton Barracks." Later, black recruits from Iowa, Minnesota and Missouri were trained for the Union Army here.

St. Marks (Wakulla) FL

Is an Anglicized form of the Spanish *San Marcos de Apalachee*. A fort originally built here on Apalachee Bay in the 1600s was abandoned in 1824. It was reoccupied by the Confederates and attacked unsuccessfully in June 1862. There was also a naval station here in 1862–1864. An important saltworks near here was operated by Daniel C. Barrow, a Georgia planter. The Goose Creek saltworks, nearby, were destroyed by the Federal Navy in February 1864.

St. Martinville (St. Martin) LA

Established in 1760 as *Poste des Attakapas* [Indians], the original occupants of the land. After the French Revolution of 1789 it attracted many royalist refugees and became popularly known as "*Le Petit Paris.*" It was renamed c.1812 for the French bishop, Saint Martin of Tours (c.316–397). There was fighting here in December 1863.

St. Phillip's Island SC

Near Port Royal, it was apparently named for Saint Philip, one of the Twelve Apostles. It was the site of **Fort Beauregard**, named for General Pierre G.T. Beauregard (1818–1893), which was captured by a Federal naval squadron in November 1861 during the Port Royal expedition, and then renamed **Fort Seward**, for Secretary of State William H. Seward (1801–1872).

Salado (Bell) TX

The name is Spanish for "salty," perhaps a reference to the waters of Salado Creek. It was established c.1859 by Sterling C. Robertson, who had a plantation near here and donated much of his personal fortune to the Southern war effort. Alexander's Medicinal Distillery which was located near here produced medicines for troops in the Trans-Mississippi Department.

Salem (Dent) MO

A biblical name from Genesis, Salem comes from the Hebrew word for peace, via its Anglicized version, "*shalom,*" and became a common American placename. Salem, Missouri, founded in 1851, was named after Salem, North Carolina. There was fighting here in December 1861, July and August 1862 and September 1863.

Salem (Forsyth) NC

Founded in 1766, this was one of a number of Moravian communities in North Carolina, part of an area known as Wachovia. During the Civil War the Francis & Henry Fries Woolen Mill made cloth for Confederate uniforms. In April 1865 General Stoneman's cavalry passed through the town, and though "violations of mild and gentlemanly conduct were very few indeed," the machinery in the Fries woolen factory was nevertheless destroyed. (Now part of Winston-Salem.)

Salineville (Carroll) OH

Salt was produced here from salt wells from 1809 onwards. It was laid out in 1839 and the arrival of the Cleveland & Pittsburgh Railroad in 1852 also encouraged the development of coal mines. General John H. Morgan and his remaining, exhausted raiders surrendered near here in late July 1863 to General James M. Shackleford, and were imprisoned in the Ohio State Penitentiary at Columbus.

Salisbury (Rowan) NC

Was founded in 1753 and called after Salisbury, Maryland, in turn named after the English cathedral city of Salisbury, Wiltshire. The Salisbury Arsenal, composed of a laboratory, foundry and blacksmith shops, operated in 1863–1864, making horseshoes and shells for Parrott guns.

A former cotton factory became a prison camp in November 1861 and existed for most of the war, becoming one of the largest in the Confederacy. Conditions, initially good, deteriorated drastically when large numbers of prisoners were transferred from Belle Isle and Andersonville in October 1864; nearly 12,000 died from exposure, malnutrition and disease. An attempted breakout in November 1864 was quelled when 16 prisoners were killed and 60 wounded.

In April 1865 Union cavalry under General George Stoneman defeated Confederate defenders and briefly occupied Salisbury, burning military stores, factories, railroad installations and public buildings; they also burned the prison camp. A few days later Jefferson Davis and his party halted here on their way south.

Saltville (Smyth) VA

Was named for the vital substance it produced. Salt wells were known to exist here as early as 1773 and became one of the main sources of supply for the entire Confederacy. Alongside the Virginia & Tennessee Railroad, it was the scene of a massacre in October 1864, when an unsuccessful attempt by Federal troops to capture the village was followed by the shooting, the next day, of wounded black cavalrymen by Confederate irregulars. Having previously destroyed the lead mines at Wytheville, General Stoneman's cavalry finally captured and destroyed the salt works in December.

Saluda (Saluda) SC

It takes its name from the Little Saluda River which derives from an Indian word meaning "river of corn," because it was grown here. Cotton factories were burned by General Sherman's troops in February 1865, which left the "female operatives weeping and wringing their hands in agony as they saw ... their only means of support in flames."

Salyersville (Magoffin) KY

On the Licking River, it was originally called Adamsville for Billy Adams, a town founder, when first settled in 1800, but renamed in 1860 for Samuel Salyers (1812–1890), a member of the state legislature. There was skirmishing here between October and December 1863 and in April 1864.

San Antonio (Bexar) TX

It stands on the San Antonio River, so called because it was discovered on Saint Anthony's day, May 19, 1691. The Spanish mission of *San Antonio de Valero* was founded in 1718. That, together with a presidio and a settlement were consolidated c.1793 to form what became San Antonio.

The arsenal, established in 1855, was seized by Texas troops in February 1861, and a company of U.S. infantry stationed here was captured by a citizens' militia in April. The headquarters of the Texas Ordnance Department was located here, making cartridges, Bowie knives and some small arms. There was also a Confederate quartermaster depot, producing leather goods and camp equipment. The barracks of the Alamo were used as a Confederate military prison for a short while in 1861, and there was also briefly a prison camp nearby at San Antonio Springs, to which prisoners were moved from Camp Verde in 1862. A large powder mill here exploded in July 1863. San Antonio attracted refugees throughout the war, one Virginian living here reporting that "all hotels and boarding-houses are filled" and there "isn't a vacant house to be found."

San Marcos (Hays) TX

Is on the San Marcos River, probably so called because Spanish missionaries first saw it on Saint Mark's day, April 25, 1709. An earlier settlement, abandoned in 1812, was re-established in 1846 and laid out in 1851 on land purchased by William Lindsey and Edward Burleson. The San Marcos Cotton and Woolen Manufacturing Co. was founded in 1864, though it is not clear if it actually began production. The San Marcos Meat Packing Plant was also located near here.

Sandersville (Washington) GA

Was established in 1796 and originally called Saunders Cross Roads, then Saundersville, for local storekeeper M. Saunders; over time, this became Sandersville. Union cavalrymen captured here in November 1864, during General Sherman's march to the sea, were murdered by local vigilantes, resulting in a retaliatory attack on the town and the burning of public buildings.

Santa Fe (Santa Fe) NMT

The present state capital of New Mexico was founded by Don Pedro de Peralta, the Spanish provincial governor, in 1610. Spanish missionaries called it *Villa Real de la Santa Fé de San Francisco de Asis* (the Royal Town of the Holy Faith of Saint Francis of Assisi), shortened in due course to Santa Fe. The first European settlement west of the Mississippi, it became the territorial capital and the western terminus of the Santa Fe Trail. Though occupied by Confederate troops in March 1862, during the attempted conquest of New Mexico, they withdrew in August.

Santa Rosa Island FL

Takes its name from Santa Rosa de Viterbo (Saint Rose of Viterbo), an Italian saint canonized in 1457. Built in 1838–1844 for the defense of Pensacola Bay in the Gulf of Mexico, **Fort Pickens** may have been named for Andrew Pickens (1739–1817), a general in the Revolutionary War. It was reinforced and remained in Federal hands throughout the war, in spite of an attempted Confederate landing on the island in October 1861 to try and capture Fort Pickens, and their occupation of Pensacola in 1861–1862. It was used as a military prison in 1862–1865.

Saratoga (Lyon) KY

Was called after Saratoga, New York, an Indian name and the scene of a British surrender in 1777. It was attacked successfully by troops brought up the Cumberland River in the gunboat USS *Conestoga* in October 1861.

Satartia (Yazoo) MS

Situated on the Yazoo River and founded in

the mid–1800s, *Satartia* is a Choctaw word meaning "pumpkins are here" or "pumpkin place." The Satartia Rifles from here became part of the 12th Mississippi. Skirmishing occurred here in October 1863 and February 1864.

Savannah (Chatham) GA

Founded in 1733 by James Oglethorpe, who had obtained a charter for the new colony of Georgia, it took its name from the Savannah River, so called from a Spanish word for a grassy plain with scattered trees.

There was an ordnance depot and arsenal and the workshops of the Central Railroad of Georgia were also converted into an arsenal. A naval station was established in 1861 to cater for the needs of the Savannah Squadron and Henry F. Willink, Jr., Krenson & Hawkes and Asa and Nelson Tift built or converted ironclads in their shipyards; they included the CSS *Atlanta* (1861–1862) and the CSS *Georgia* (1862–1863). There was also a naval hospital here. In addition, the firm of Henry Lathrop & Co. made uniforms for Georgia troops.

Federal prisoners began arriving in Savannah in July 1864, but a shortage of guards caused them to be moved to Charleston, South Carolina, then Millen and Blackshear, Georgia, shortly afterwards. Following the arrival of General Sherman's army in December 1864, General William J. Hardee and the city's Confederate garrison withdrew across the Savannah River. After Sherman had entered, he sent a message to President Lincoln: "I beg to present you, as a Christmas gift, the city of Savannah."

Savannah (Hardin) TN

It developed in the 19th century and was named after Savannah, Georgia. There was a large build-up of Federal forces here on the Tennessee River in March 1862, together with troop transports and gunboats, and General Ulysses S. Grant made it his headquarters. Two Union generals died here in April 1862, William H.L. Wallace from wounds received at Shiloh and Charles F. Smith from a foot infection caused by an injury got jumping into a rowing boat.

Schaghticoke (Rensselaer) NY

Near the confluence of the Hoosic and Hudson Rivers, the name comes from an Algonquin word meaning a "place where a river branches." Settlers first came here c.1668 and a town was established in 1788. The Schaghticoke Powder Co. manufactured powder here for the Union Navy.

Scottsville (Allen) KY

Was named for General Charles Scott (1739–1813), who was governor of Kentucky, 1808–1812. There was skirmishing here in June 1863 and it was raided by guerrillas in December of that year.

Searcy (White) AR

Originally called White Sulphur Springs because of its medicinal waters, it was renamed in 1838 for Judge Richard Searcy (1796–1832). There was fighting at Searcy Landing in May 1862 and at Searcy in May, June and September 1864.

Secessionville (Charleston) SC

Its name has nothing to do with South Carolina's withdrawal from the Union; it was so called before the war, when it was a popular summer resort on James Island for Charleston residents escaping or "seceding" from the heat and hustle of the city. In June 1862 Union General Henry W. Benham launched an unauthorized, and unsuccessful, attack on Confederate positions here, as a result of which he was relieved of his command.

Sedalia (Pettis) MO

Founded in 1857 as a new town on the Missouri-Pacific Railroad by General George Smith. Originally called Sedville for Sarah Elvira Smith, his daughter, whose pet name was "Sed," it was changed to its present form in 1860. It was a Union military post in 1861–1864. There was skirmishing here in June 1862, April 1863 and October 1864.

Selma (Dallas) AL

It was first settled in 1815 on the Alabama River. William R. King and Dr. George Phillips formed the Selma Land Company in 1817 and named it in 1820 after "The Song of Selma" by Ossian, a legendary Gaelic poet, whose work was mostly invented by 18th century Scottish writer James MacPherson. In 1848 the construction of the Alabama & Tennessee Railroad, plus the arrival of 300 skilled German ironworkers, made it into an important manufacturing center.

In the Civil War this also became a major Confederate supply depot. It also included a former ordnance works which was remodeled and equipped as an arsenal, and purchased jointly by the Navy and War Departments in early 1863. Then taken over entirely by the Navy Department as the Selma Naval Gun Foundry and Ordnance Works later that year, it manufactured rifled cannon and ammunition for the Charleston, Mobile and North Carolina Squadrons. As in other places, these were a magnet for refugees looking for jobs. A naval station was established on the Alabama River in 1862 for the construction of ironclads by local shipbuilder Henry D. Bassett. The CSS *Tennessee II* was built here in 1862–1864. The Bragg Hospital was located here, and converted buildings were used as a military prison in 1864 and possibly also in 1865.

Though well defended, Selma was captured at the beginning of April 1865 by General Wilson's cavalry, along with many prisoners and vast quantities of supplies, and factories, warehouses and all military installations were burned. It was, a Northern writer admitted when he visited it in January 1866, "A scene of 'Yankee vandalism' and ruin. The Confederate arsenal, foundries and rolling mills ... together with extensive warehouses containing ammunition and military stores, were burned when Wilson captured the place."

Sevierville (Sevier) TN

Was founded in 1795 and named for John Sevier (1745–1815), twice governor of Tennessee, 1796–1801 and 1803–1809. Fighting occurred here in January and February 1864.

Seymour (New Haven) CT

On the Naugatuck River, it was first settled in 1680. An earlier name was Humphreyville, for General David Humphrey who established paper and woolen mills here and built a model village, but it was renamed in 1850 for Thomas H. Seymour (1807–1868), governor of Connecticut, 1850–1853. The Humphreyville Manufacturing Co. made bayonets here for the Union Army.

Sharpsburg (Washington) MD

Founded by Joseph Chapline and laid out in 1763, it was named for Horatio Sharpe (1718–1790), the English-born governor of Maryland, 1753–1769. General Robert E. Lee made his headquarters just outside the town during his first invasion of the North in September 1862. That ended at Antietam Creek (q.v.), in the bloodiest single day of the war, with a total of 26,000 casualties, and the Confederates were forced to retreat across the Potomac into Virginia, with skirmishing along the river.

Shelbina (Shelby) MO

Was laid out in 1857 on the Hannibal & St. Joseph Railroad. This and the following were named for Colonel Isaac Shelby (1750–1826), a Revolutionary War commander, and twice governor of Kentucky, 1792–1796 and 1812–1816. There was a skirmish here in September 1861, and it was attacked by Confederate troops in July 1864.

Shelbyville (Bedford) TN

On the Duck River, it was laid out in 1810. The firm of S.A. & J.H. Bevins, saddle and harness makers, supplied the Confederate Ordnance Department with sets of leather infantry accoutrements. Fighting occurred here in June and October 1863 and November 1864. There was also skirmishing on the Shelbyville pike in January, February, April and June 1863.

Shelton Laurel (Madison) NC

In the 1790s David and Martin Shelton came to live on "Lorrel" [Laurel] Creek and the valley here became known as Shelton Laurel. Thirteen Unionists who had allegedly been involved in a raid on the village of Marshall, were massacred in January 1863 by men of the 64th North Carolina, following orders from General Henry Heth to clear the area of guerrillas. This caused an uproar, and a demand by North Carolina Governor Zebulon B. Vance and Secretary of War James Seddon for an inquiry, but it was never carried out.

Shepherdstown (Jefferson) WV

First settled in 1732 and laid out by Captain Thomas Shepherd (1705–1776) in 1762 as New Mecklenburg, probably in honor of Princess Charlotte of Mecklenburg-Strelitz (1744–1818), the new German wife of King George III. Considered as a site for the new Federal capital in 1790, it was renamed when enlarged in 1798. It was the scene of military activity in September

1861, September and October 1862, and July and August 1864. Confederate wounded from Sharpsburg were brought here for initial treatment, on their way to hospital.

Shepherdsville (Bullitt) KY

Was named for pioneer Adam Shepherd who built a mill here in 1793. A Federal outpost here surrendered in September 1862, and there was skirmishing in October and July 1863.

Shiloh (Hardin) TN

Shiloh, meaning "place of rest" in Hebrew, was called after the ancient village in Jordan. This gave its name to a stream which was a branch of Owl Creek, and to Shiloh Church, which as a Connecticut writer noted when he visited the site in December 1865, was "formerly a mere log cabin in the woods.... There Beauregard had his headquarters after Sunday's battle. It was afterwards torn down for its timbers, and now nothing remained but half-burned logs and rubbish."

The two-day battle fought here in early April 1862 resulted in a hard-won Union victory. Confederate casualties included Generals Albert S. Johnston, regarded by some as "the greatest soldier, the ablest man, civil or military ... then living," and Adley H. Gladden, who were mortally wounded, and George W. Johnson, the first provisional governor of Kentucky, who had fought as a private and died on a Federal hospital boat from his wounds. Union General William H.L. Wallace was also mortally wounded. Shiloh is otherwise known as the battle of Pittsburg Landing (q.v.).

Ship Island MS

With an excellent harbor, Ship Island in the Gulf of Mexico was taken over by the U.S. government in 1847 for military use. **Fort Massachusetts**, built 1858–1860, was partly destroyed by its departing Federal garrison in May 1861, then occupied by Confederate troops, July-September, who named it **Fort Twiggs** for General David E. Twiggs (1790–1862). In turn evacuated by them, it was then re-occupied by General Butler's forces in December, for whose home state it was renamed, and partly rebuilt. It was used as a military prison in 1864–1865. Some of the prisoners here were cadets from a military school in Alabama, a number of whom died.

Shohola (Pike) PA

Took its name from Shohola Creek, which comes from an Algonquin word possibly meaning "weak" or "faint." Established in 1851, it was the scene of a major accident in July 1864 when a crowded train on the Erie Railroad taking Confederate prisoners to the recently opened prison camp at Elmira, New York, collided with a coal train near Shohola, along the Delaware River; 48 prisoners and 17 guards were killed, 93 prisoners and 16 guards injured and 5 prisoners escaped in the ensuing confusion.

Shreveport (Caddo) LA

Was named for steamboat captain and builder Henry M. Shreve (1785–1851), who cleared the Red River of a vast blockage of natural debris and opened it up to navigation. A work-camp he founded here in 1834 became Shreveport in 1839. A Confederate naval station was established in 1862 for the construction of gunboats for the Red River Squadron, and the firm of Moore & Smoker contracted to build two ironclads. One of those built here was the CSS *Missouri* (1862–1863). Converted buildings were in use as a military prison in 1863. It was the headquarters of the Trans-Mississippi Department, 1862–1865, what came to be known as "Kirby-Smithdom" after its commander, General E. Kirby Smith, as well as the temporary Confederate state capital of Louisiana, 1863–1865, and also became a refugee center.

Shute's Folly Island SC

Built in 1812 in Charleston harbor to replace an earlier fort, **Castle Pinckney** was named for Charleston-born diplomat Charles Pinckney (1746–1825). It had been virtually abandoned by the Civil War, but was brought back into use and in September 1861 became a military prison for Union captives, though only for a few weeks as it was found to be too small. The island took its name from Joseph Shute, a Quaker merchant from Charleston, who owned it, 1746–1763. "Folly," meaning a cluster of shrubbery or dense foliage, was a term applied to some of the Carolina sea islands by the early colonists.

Sibley (Jackson) MO

Was named for Major George C. Sibley (1782–1863), an Indian agent, explorer and surveyor of the Santa Fe Trail. There was fighting here in

June and October 1862, and it was destroyed in June 1863.

Sikeston (Scott) MO

John Sikes who laid it out in 1860 is commemorated here. It was the scene of fighting in March 1862, June and September 1864.

Simpsonville (Shelby) KY

Takes its name from Captain John Simpson (d.1813), a Kentucky congressman. It was founded in 1816. There was a skirmish here in January 1865.

Smithfield (Johnston) NC

On the Neuse River, it was founded in 1770 and named for Colonel John Smith (1687–1777) who owned the land on which the town was built. As they entered Smithfield in April 1865 after some skirmishing, General Sherman's troops learned that General Robert E. Lee had surrendered two days previously, at a place in Virginia called Appomattox Court House. A Southern woman, hearing the shouting, told her children, "Now father will come home."

Smithfield (Isle of Wight) VA

Was founded in 1662 on land owned by settler Arthur Smith. There was fighting here in August 1862 and January 1864, and a Federal gunboat, the *Smith Briggs*, was captured and burned.

Smithfield (Wetzel) WV

Was first settled in 1796 and later named for local merchant and storekeeper Henry Smith. Skirmishing took place in February and September 1863, and June and August 1864.

Smithsburg (Washington) MD

Was founded in 1813 by Christopher Smith (1750–1821), for whom it was named. A hospital was set up here after the battle of Antietam. There was also skirmishing in early July 1863 after Gettysburg, when it was occupied by Union cavalry and shelled by General Stuart's artillery from South Mountain.

Smithville (Clay) MO

Humphrey Smith, for whom it was named, bought the site along the Little Platte River from the local Indians and settled here in 1822. It was burned in October 1864 during General Price's Missouri raid.

Sneedville (Hancock) TN

Was named in 1855 for William H. Sneed (1812–1869), a congressman and lawyer. There was a skirmish here in October 1864.

Socorro (Socorro) NMT

Is Spanish for "help" or "assistance" and derives from an incident in 1598 when starving members of Don Juan de Onate's expedition were fed by local Indians. A Spanish mission was established here but abandoned in 1680; it was not resettled till 1817. There was fighting here in April 1862 during the Confederate invasion of New Mexico.

Somerset (Pulaski) KY

It was first settled in 1798 and called after Somerset County, New Jersey, from where some of the settlers came, in turn named after Somerset, England. Fighting here in December 1861 was followed in January 1862 by the battle of Mill Springs (q.v.). A Union supply base, it was raided in July 1862 by General John H. Morgan, who sent a mocking telegram to a Louisville newspaper editor, announcing that he had "destroyed $1,000,000 worth of government [medical, quartermaster and ordnance] stores."

Somerville (Fayette) TN

Commemorates Lieutenant Robert Somerville who was killed in 1814 at Horseshoe Bend during the Creek War. There was fighting here in November 1862, January and December 1863.

Spanish Fort (Baldwin) AL

This was originally a trading post just outside Mobile, established c.1712, and in turn under French, British and Spanish control. A fort built by the Spanish was transferred to the United States after the War of 1812. It endured a two-week siege in late March and early April 1865, before being captured following a heavy Union bombardment.

Sparta (White) TN

Sparta was one of the leading city-states of ancient Greece, whose inhabitants were known for their courage, frugality and discipline. Sparta, Tennessee, was so called in 1809, at a time when classical names were popular. Skirmishing occurred here in June and August 1862, August and November 1863 and March 1864.

Spotsylvania Court House (Spotsylvania) VA

Was named in 1720 for Alexander Spotswood (1676–1740), lieutenant governor of Virginia, 1710–1722, with a misspelled Latin suffix meaning "forest-place" or "woodlands." The fighting around here in May 1864, immediately after the battle at the Wilderness, lasted for two weeks. During it, General Ulysses S. Grant informed chief of staff General Henry W. Halleck in Washington that he proposed "to fight it out on this line if it takes all summer." Among those killed were Union Generals James C. Rice, John Sedgwick and Thomas G. Stevenson, while Confederate General Abner M. Perrin was also killed and Junius Daniel mortally wounded.

Springfield (Sangamon) IL

Established in 1821 on the Sangamon River, it took its name from Spring Creek on the land of the first resident, Elisha Kelly. It became the state capital of Illinois in 1837 and was the home of Abraham Lincoln, 1837–1861, and his burial place. Like Chicago, it was a demobilization rendezvous point for Illinois troops in 1865.

Springfield (Hampden) MA

Was founded on the Connecticut River by William Pynchon in 1636 and named after his birthplace in Essex, England. The Springfield Arsenal, which had been manufacturing weapons for the U.S. Army since 1794, became the major small-arms manufacturer in the North after the loss of the Harpers Ferry Arsenal in 1861. The Smith & Wesson Co., Ames & Co. and the Springfield Arms Co., run by James Warner, were also located here.

Springfield (Greene) MO

Was first settled in 1829. The origin of the name is uncertain: it may derive from the former home of one of the first residents; or have been so called by John Polk Campbell, an early settler, because of a field on a hill and a spring under it. The jail was used briefly as a U.S. military prison in 1861. After the battle of Wilson's Creek (q.v.) in August 1861, also sometimes referred to as Springfield, it was occupied by Confederates, but the garrison was routed in October 1861 following "Zagonyi's Charge," when Federal cavalry led by Major Charles Zagonyi charged into the town. A Confederate attempt to recapture it in January 1863 was unsuccessful.

Stanardsville (Greene) VA

Robert Stanard (1781–1846) who gave land for the town site is remembered here. Skirmishing took place in February 1864.

Stanford (Lincoln) KY

Founded in 1786, it was called Standing Fort by the local Indians, a name which over time gradually became Stanford. There was a skirmish here in July 1863.

Staten Island NY

Settlers were granted land here in 1641 by the Dutch West India Company and Staten Island is an Anglicized form of *Staaten Eylandt*, the Dutch States General or parliament. It was the location of Fort Tompkins, Fort Wadsworth and Camp Scott. **Fort Tompkins**, begun in 1847, was named for Daniel D. Tompkins (1774–1825), governor of New York, 1807–1817, and vice-president, 1817–1825. Originally built c.1812, then rebuilt in 1847–1864, **Fort Wadsworth** was named in 1865 for General James S. Wadsworth (1807–1864), military governor of Washington in 1862, who was mortally wounded at the Wilderness. Troops from there were sent to help put down the New York draft riots in July 1863. **Camp Scott** was presumably named for General Winfield Scott (1786–1866), who was general-in-chief of the U.S. Army at the start of the Civil War, until succeeded by General George B. McClellan in November 1861. Staten Island became part of New York City in 1897.

Staunton (Augusta) VA

Was founded in 1736 and named for Rebecca Staunton (d.1755), the wife of Sir William Gooch, lieutenant governor of Virginia, 1727–1749, who gave his name to Goochland Court House (q.v.). The Ladies' Military Cap Association made not only these but all manner of military clothing. An important supply center, connected by the Virginia Central Railroad with Richmond, as well as a magnet for refugees, it was destroyed in June 1864 during General

Hunter's destructive campaign in the Shenandoah Valley.

Steubenville (Jefferson) OH
On the Ohio River, it was settled temporarily in 1765 and in 1786 became the site of Fort Steuben, named for Baron Friedrich von Steuben (1730–1794), a Prussian general who helped drill the Continental Army in the Revolutionary War. The town was laid out in 1797. There was a skirmish near here during General Morgan's raid into Ohio in July 1863. General Daniel McCook, one of the "Fighting McCooks" of Ohio, died here in July 1864 from wounds received at Kennesaw Mountain.

Stevenson (Jackson) AL
At the junction of the Memphis & Charleston and Nashville & Chattanooga Railroads, it was named in 1853 for Vernon K. Stevenson (1812–1884), founder and first president of the N. & C. Railroad. Skirmishing took place here in July and August 1862 and September 1863. General Ulysses S. Grant met General William S. Rosecrans here in October 1863 after the latter had been relieved of his command of the Army of the Cumberland following the battle of Chickamauga.

Stockbridge (Henry) GA
First settled in 1829, it was named in 1849 for Thomas Stock, the state surveyor and president of the Georgia senate. A skirmish occurred here in November 1864, at the start of General Sherman's march to the sea.

Stockton (Cedar) MO
An earlier name was Frémont, for John C. Frémont (1813–1880), the celebrated explorer, but it was renamed Stockton in 1856, in honor of Commodore Robert F. Stockton (1795–1866), who conquered California and proclaimed it a U.S. territory. There was skirmishing here in August 1862, and July and October 1863.

Stones River TN
Was named for Uriah Stone, one of its discoverers in 1766. It is an alternate name for the battle of Murfreesboro (q.v.).

Stoney's Landing (Berkeley) SC
Some 30 miles up the Cooper River from Charleston, it recalls boat-builder Theodore Stoney, a founder of the Southern Torpedo Co., which built a torpedo boat called the *David* for the Confederate Navy in 1864.

Strasburg (Shenandoah) VA
Was founded in 1761 by Petrus Stauffer (Peter Stover) who named it after Strasbourg in the German-speaking French province of Alsace. There was frequent skirmishing around here between 1862 and 1864.

Strawberry Plains (Henrico) VA
There was fighting here near the north bank of the James River in July and August 1864 during the Petersburg campaign. The presence of wild strawberries accounts for the name.

Sturgeon (Boone) MO
Was named for Isaac H. Sturgeon, a superintendent of the St. Louis, Kansas City & North Missouri Railroad. There was a skirmish here in February 1865.

Suffolk (♦) VA
When first settled on the Nansemond River in 1720 it was called Constant's Warehouse, for John Constant. It was renamed after the English county of Suffolk when it was established in 1742. It was besieged by General Longstreet's Confederates, April-May 1863, but proved too strongly defended to capture.

Sullivan's Island SC
Off the South Carolina coast near Charleston, it was originally called O'Sullivan's Island, for Florence O'Sullivan, captain of the first English ship to bring settlers here in 1670, and later surveyor general of South Carolina. It was the site of **Fort Moultrie**, at the entrance to Charleston Harbor, begun in 1776 and rebuilt several times, lastly in 1828–1834. Originally called Fort Sullivan, it was renamed for General William Moultrie (1730–1805), who served in the Revolutionary War. The garrison from here was transferred to Fort Sumter, and it was taken over and fortified by state forces in December 1860. It engaged Federal monitors in November 1863, when the USS *Lehigh* was badly damaged and ran aground before escaping. It was not occupied by the Federals till February 1865 when Charleston fell.

Summersville (Nicholas) WV

Founded in 1824 on Peters Creek, it was named for Judge Lewis Summers (1778–1843). Fighting took place here in August 1861 and July 1862.

Sutton (Braxton) WV

Was named for John D. Sutton who settled here in 1810. Originally called Suttonsville when established in 1826, it was renamed Sutton in 1837. It was burned by the Confederates in the winter of 1861, and skirmishing occurred here in August and September 1863 and August 1864.

Sweetwater (Monroe) TN

Established in the 1850s, it was so called because of its location in the Sweetwater Valley, a name in use as early as 1817 among the Cherokees who called it *Soitee Wooitee*. There was skirmishing in September and October 1862 and January 1864, and it was attacked by Confederates in February 1865.

Syracuse (Onondaga) NY

First established as a trading post c.1786 and founded in 1796, it was named Syracuse in 1824. It was so called at a time when classical place-names were popular, because its situation on Lake Onondaga was thought to resemble that of the ancient Greek city of Syracuse in present-day Sicily. The arrival of the Erie Canal in 1830 hastened its development. A saltworks established here c.1789 was an important producer of salt during the Civil War. Syracuse was a demobilization point for New York troops in 1865.

Talbott's Station (Jefferson) TN

Named for Colonel John Talbott (1801–1884), skirmishing took place here, on the East Tennessee & Virginia Railroad, at the end of December 1863. (Now called Talbott.)

Tallahassee (Leon) FL

Derives from an Apalachee word meaning "old town." Originally settled by Spaniards in 1539, it was the site of a mission for many years before becoming the territorial capital of Florida in 1824, then the state capital in 1845. The terminus of Florida's first railroad, the Tallahassee & St. Marks, from 1860 it was also the location of the Florida Military Institute. Until General Samuel Jones, commander of the Department of South Georgia and Florida, surrendered his troops here in May 1865, it remained in Confederate hands, the only state capital to do so.

Tallahatchie River MS

A branch of the Yazoo, it comes from an Indian word meaning "river of the rock." It featured in both Vicksburg campaigns, in December 1862 and January-May 1863.

Tallassee (Elmore) AL

Was first settled by the Spaniards in the 16th century. *Tallase*, a Creek word meaning "old town" or "captured town," refers to an earlier settlement. Development here began in the 1820s. A textile mill owned by Thomas Barnett (later Barnett, Micon & Co.), which made blankets, military buttons and cloth for the Confederate Quartermaster Department, was leased by the government in the fall of 1864, and machinery for making carbines was moved here from the Richmond Armory.

Tampa (Hillsborough) FL

It developed around Fort Brooke, called after its commander, Colonel George Brooke. Tampa, named in 1834, comes from a Cree word which may mean "close to it" or "near it," recorded by the Spanish as early as 1565. Blockaded and shelled in 1863, it was temporarily occupied by Federal troops, there was skirmishing in May 1864, and the salt works near here were destroyed by the U.S. Navy in July.

Taunton (Bristol) MA

Was established in 1639 on the Taunton River on land bought from the local Indians. Elizabeth Poole or Pole (1589–1654) was "a great proprietor ... a chief promoter of its settlement" and both river and town were named after her English birthplace of Taunton, Somerset. From 1656 onwards it became a center of the iron-working industry and also of shipbuilding. During the Civil War both the Taunton Locomotive Co. and William Mason built engines for Northern railroads and the latter also manufactured Springfield rifles.

Taylorsville (Spencer) KY

Was founded in 1799 by Richard Taylor (1744–1826), the father of President Zachary Taylor and grandfather of Confederate General Richard Taylor. The notorious Confederate guerrilla William C. Quantrill was fatally wounded near here in May 1865 and died the following month.

Tennessee River TN/AL/KY

Derives from a Cherokee word possibly meaning "river with the big bend." The surrender of Fort Henry (q.v.) to Union forces in February 1862, and their victory at Shiloh in April were two of the important events which took place on or near the Tennessee River. In October 1864 Federal transports and gunboats were captured and burned by General N. Bedford Forrest during a raid into West Tennessee. The Union Army of the Tennessee, in existence for most of the war, had some famous commanders, including Generals Ulysses S. Grant, William T. Sherman and James B. McPherson.

Thomaston (Upson) GA

Named for General Jett Thomas (1776–1817), who built the state capitol at Milledgeville in 1807 and served in the War of 1812, Thomaston dates from the 1820s. The Newsom Hospital, named for Ella K. Newsom, the "Florence Nightingale of the Southern Army," was located here. The town was raided by Union cavalry in April 1865.

Thomasville (Thomas) GA

Was also named for General Thomas. Some Union prisoners were transferred here from Blackshear in December 1864 at a time when they were being moved about because of the threat from General William T. Sherman.

Thompson's Station (Williamson) TN

On the Tennessee & Alabama Railroad, this was named in 1856 for Dr. Elijah Thompson (1805–1871), a planter and state legislator who gave the land for the town site. It was the scene of an engagement in March 1863, when Union infantry were forced to surrender. There was further skirmishing later that month and at the beginning of May. Confederate General Earl Van Dorn, who had commanded troops in the fighting, was assassinated a few days later at his headquarters by a local citizen, who alleged he had "violated the sanctity of his home."

Tipton (Moniteau) MO

In 1858 William Tipton Seely (or Seeley), an Englishman, gave land and laid out the town which was named for him. General John C. Frémont, who commanded the Western Department in July-November 1861, set up his headquarters in the Rose Hill Seminary for Girls. There was fighting here in October 1863.

Tiptonville (Lake) TN

On the Mississippi River, took its name from Jacob Tipton who was killed in 1791 in a battle with Indians; it was established in 1857. The Confederate garrisons, both here and at Island No. 10, surrendered to General Pope's troops, supported by Flag Officer Foote's flotilla, in April 1862 after an operation lasting a month.

Tishomingo Creek (Tishomingo) MS

Was a Chickasaw word meaning "warrior chief." Just to the north of Brice's Crossroads and Guntown (q.v.), alternate names for the battle fought here in June 1864, it was a triumph for Confederate General N. Bedford Forrest, who captured artillery, wagons and supplies and drove defeated Federals back in the direction of Memphis.

Tombigbee River MS/AL

Comes from Choctaw words meaning "coffin makers," ones who disposed of the dead. Commodore Ebenezer Farrand, CSN, surrendered the last of the Mobile Squadron here on the Tombigbee in May 1865.

Tompkinsville (Monroe) KY

Developed around a store built in 1809 and named for Daniel D. Tompkins (1774–1825), vice-president under James Monroe, 1817–1825. It was captured by General John H. Morgan in July 1862 during his first Kentucky raid.

Tom's Brook (Shenandoah) VA

A local stream, named Tom's Creek after an early settler's cabin, later became Tom's Brook, the name given to this town in the Shenandoah Valley. There was skirmishing here in June 1862 during General Jackson's Valley campaign. The engagement in October 1864, during General Sheridan's campaign in the Valley, when General Early's Confederate cavalry was routed and put to flight, became known to the Federals as the

"Woodstock Races," from the adjacent town of Woodstock.

Totopotomoy Creek (Hanover) VA

A branch of the Pamunkey River, it was named for a 17th century Indian chief who was friendly to the British. There was an indecisive engagement here, lasting three days, at the end of May 1864, just prior to the disastrous Federal assaults at Cold Harbor.

Trenton (Mercer) NJ

Was first settled by English Quakers on the Delaware River in 1679 and established in 1714 when William Trent (1655?-1724), a Philadelphia merchant, bought 800 acres from the son of the original settler, Mahlon Stacy, and laid out what was originally called Trent's Town. It subsequently became the state capital. The battle of Trenton (1776), an early American victory in the Revolutionary War, caused the name to be repeated elsewhere. Norman Wiard's Ordnance Works made rifled steel cannon here in 1861, the first ever in the United States. The state armory, located here, made rifled muskets for its troops, as did James T. Hodge and Addison M. Burt. New Jersey troops were mustered out here in 1865.

Trenton (Gibson) TN

Named after the battle of Trenton, it was established in 1824. It was captured by General Forrest's cavalry in December 1862, and there was more fighting here in April and June 1863.

Triune (Williamson) TN

Means "three in one" or the "trinity." It saw considerable military activity, with skirmishing in December 1862, March and June 1863, August 1864 and February 1865.

Troy (Rensselaer) NY

Was established on the Hudson River and named in 1789 after the ancient city in Asia Minor. It became a major center of the iron and steel industry, and during the Civil War local mills produced the plates for the USS *Monitor*, while the Troy Iron & Nail Factory of Henry Burden & Sons turned out horseshoes for the Union cavalry and horse artillery, using a machine patented by Burden in 1835. Rioting against the draft occurred here in July 1863, though on nothing like the scale seen in New York.

Tulip (Dallas) AR

First settled in 1828, its name probably derives from nearby Tulip Ridge. It was laid out in 1845. The Arkansas Military Institute, established in 1850, closed in 1861 when the cadets joined the 3rd Arkansas Infantry. There was skirmishing here in October 1863.

Tullahoma (Franklin) TN

Is a Muskogee word, from *tulla*, probably meaning "town," and *homa*, "red." It was settled by 1850 on the site of an Indian village. After the battle of Murfreesboro or Stones River, General Bragg was here in early 1863. A Richmond newspaper painted an unflattering picture: "The headquarters of an army are situated among ... a few trim cottages and a great many empty and rotten casks.... Add that there is not a hotel ... a saloon ... a bath house ... and that there is a depot, several commissary and quartermaster's offices, and a lively assortment of camps, and the daguerreotype is complete." There was fighting around the town in June, which was evacuated by the Confederates as they withdrew across the Tennessee River towards Chattanooga, and it was occupied by the Federals at the beginning of July. There was a Confederate raid on the Nashville & Chattanooga Railroad near here in March 1864.

Tunica (West Feliciana) LA

From the name of an Indian tribe, it was once a boat landing on the east bank of the Mississippi. It was called Tunica Village in 1820 and Tunica P.O. in 1853. Fighting occurred here at Tunica Bend in November 1863 and April 1864.

Tupelo (Lee) MS

A settlement known as Harrisburg, named for Judge W.R. Harris in 1848, was abandoned in 1859 when the Mobile & Ohio Railroad built its line two miles further east. The new station was called Gum Pond, later changed to *Tupelo*, a Creek word for the black gum trees which supplied the timber for the houses of the new settlement.

It was occupied by Confederate forces in June 1862, and there was a Federal raid on the M. & O. near here in December. There was fighting in May 1863, and it was the scene of a two-day battle in July 1864. General John B. Hood arrived here in January 1865 with the remnants of his Army of Tennessee.

Tuscaloosa (Tuscaloosa) AL

Was founded on the site of an Indian trading post on the Black Warrior River in 1816 and named for the legendary Indian chief *Tuscaloosa*, "black warrior," who was killed in a battle with the Spanish in 1540. It was the state capital, 1826–1846.

Bryce Hospital, built c.1853 and named for Dr. Peter Bryce, its superintendent, was located here. In late 1861 an abandoned papermill was converted into a military prison for men brought from Richmond, Montgomery and Pensacola; they were joined in March 1862 by prisoners captured at Fort Donelson and it was in use till 1863. Tuscaloosa became crowded with refugees, among them Joseph Davis, Jefferson Davis's elder brother. The University of Alabama, turned into a military college in 1860, remained open during the war but was largely destroyed by General Croxton's cavalry in April 1865, as was the Tannehill Ironworks, which had provided iron for the Confederate arsenal and navy yard at Selma.

Tuscumbia (Colbert) AL

On the Tennessee River, it was founded in 1817 and named in 1822 for *Tashka-Ambi*, "warrior who kills," a Cherokee chief. It was occupied by Federal troops in April 1862 and there was skirmishing later that month. There was fighting here in February and April 1863 and it was captured by Federal cavalry that month. General Hood's Army of Tennessee arrived here in October 1864.

Tuscumbia (Miller) MO

Founded in 1817, it was named in 1822 for Tuscumbia, Alabama, and laid out on land given by brothers J.P. and J.B. Harrison in the late 1830s. It was the scene of fighting in December 1864.

Tyler (Smith) TX

Was laid out in 1846 and named for John Tyler (1790–1862), tenth president of the United States, 1841–1845, who had recently signed the bill which admitted Texas as a state. The firm of Briscoe & Short, the most important producer of weapons in Texas, was purchased by the Confederate government in 1863 for $100,000. Using machinery from Little Rock, Arkansas, it was expanded to create the largest armory in the Trans-Mississippi Department, employing c.200 people and producing rifles of various models for Texas troops for the rest of the war, among them copies of the British Enfield, and an ammunition factory. It also became a center for refugees, chiefly from Louisiana.

Union (Newton) MS

Numerous towns and villages were called Union, usually implying union of the states. Union, Mississippi, settled in 1829, was burned by General Sherman's troops in April 1863 and there was further skirmishing in February 1864.

Union City (Obion) TN

Was captured by the Federals in March 1862, then by Confederate forces in December. More fighting occurred here in July and December 1863, and March and September 1864.

Union Springs (Bullock) AL

First settled in 1835, it was established by 1844. Its name derives from the presence of twenty-seven springs. It was the terminus of the uncompleted Mobile & Girard Railroad, and St. Mary's Hospital was moved here from La Grange, Georgia, in August 1864, before being transferred to Meridian, Mississippi, in November. Thomas H. Watts, the last Confederate governor of Alabama, was arrested here by Union troops in May 1865.

Upperville (Fauquier) VA

A name indicative of its geographical location, it was founded in the 1790s. There was skirmishing here in June and December 1863, and February 1864.

Utica (Oneida) NY

Settlement by Dutch and German immigrants began here on the Mohawk River c.1773. It was founded in 1797 and named after the ancient Phoenician city on the North African coast, in present-day Tunisia. It started to develop following the opening of the Erie Canal (1825). During the Civil War Rogers & Spencer made revolvers and Eliphalet Remington & Sons' Armory was also located here.

Valverde (Socorro) NMT

Was named for Antonio Valverde y Cosio, the acting Spanish governor of the territory, 1717–1722. A town founded in 1819 but later deserted because of Indian attacks was in ruins in 1846. There was an engagement here in February 1862 during General Sibley's invasion of New Mexico Territory, resulting in a Confederate victory.

Van Buren (Crawford) AR

When settled in 1818 on the Arkansas River it was called Phillips Landing, in honor of local landowner Thomas Phillips. It was renamed in 1838, one of several towns named for Martin Van Buren (1782–1862), eighth president of the United States, 1837–1841. The Daughters of the South, a volunteer aid society, made clothing for Arkansas troops, though fighting here in December 1862 resulted in the Confederates being driven out.

Varnell's Station (Whitfield) GA

M.P. Varnell, an early railroad agent, gave his name to this depot on the Western & Atlantic Railroad, the scene of fighting in May 1864 in the opening stages of the Atlanta campaign. (Now called Varnell.)

Vermilionville (Lafayette) LA

Takes its name from the Vermilion River, which derives from the red pigment used by the Indians as war paint; it was founded in 1824. There was skirmishing here in November 1863. (Renamed Lafayette, for the Marquis de La Fayette, in 1884.)

Vicksburg (Warren) MS

Began in 1791 as a Spanish fort on the Mississippi called *Nogales*, Spanish for the walnut trees which grew here. The Rev. Newitt Vick (1766–1819), a Methodist minister from Virginia, came here in 1814 to establish a mission. He also bought land to lay out a city but died before development could begin. His son-in-law continued with it and named it Vicksburg for him in 1825.

"Vicksburg is the key. The war can never be brought to a close until the key is in our pocket," declared President Lincoln, while President Davis acknowledged that "Vicksburg is the nailhead that [holds] the South's two halves together." Attempts to capture it began with bombardments by Federal gunboats as early as May-July 1862. After the first overland Vicksburg campaign, October-December 1862, a siege lasting 47 days began in mid–May 1863 and ended in early July, causing much hardship and suffering to both the garrison and the inhabitants. Among them was Mary Ann Loughborough who later wrote: "Caves were the fashion — the rage — over besieged Vicksburg. I sat at the mouth of the cave ... watching the brilliant display of fireworks ... as [the shells] exploded in the air."

During the siege, two Confederate generals, Martin E. Green and Isham W. Garrott, were killed by sharpshooters in June 1863. A coded message sent to garrison commander General John C. Pemberton, probably by General John G. Walker, commander of the Texas infantry division in the Trans-Mississippi, and only recently deciphered, saying, "You can expect no help from this side of the river," emphasizes the hopelessness of the situation. The surrender of Vicksburg — "the Gibraltar of the Confederacy" — on Independence Day, 1863, immediately after General Lee's defeat at Gettysburg, was a triumph for General Ulysses S. Grant and a disaster for the South, opening up the whole of the Mississippi to the Union and splitting the Confederacy in two.

Vidalia (Concordia) LA

Was established on the Mississippi in 1801 and named for Don José Vidal, an 18th century Spanish district governor, who gave land for public buildings. It was attacked by Confederate forces in September 1863, and further skirmishing took place in February and July 1864.

Vienna (Fairfax) VA

Originally called Ayr, from a house of that name owned by Scotsman John Hunter, it was renamed in the 1850s after Vienna, New York. There was fighting here in June 1861 on the Loudoun & Hampshire Railroad which was being repaired, when Confederates ambushed and captured a train. There was further skirmishing in July, November and December 1861 and in September 1862.

Waco (McLennan) TX

This is thought to derive from *Tawakoni*, a Caddo village on the Brazos River, meaning "river bend among red sand hills." It was established in 1849, and laid out on the site of a previous settlement destroyed by Indians. The Waco Manufacturing Co. was producing cotton and woolen materials as well as flour and corn meal for the Southern war effort in December 1863. There was also a cotton mill, machinery for which was brought through the blockade by Bayliss Earle. Refugees from Louisiana came to live here during the war.

Wardensville (Hardy) WV

Was on the site of Fort Warden, built in 1750 and burned by Indians in 1758. Wardensville was named for its builder, Jacob Warden, and established in 1832. There was skirmishing here in May and December 1862.

Ward's Island NY

This island in the East river, New York, was named for Jasper and Bartholomew Ward who owned it after the Revolutionary War. In 1860 it had a population of 772. It housed Confederate prisoners in barracks in 1864 and possibly also in 1863.

Warrensburg (Johnson) MO

Was named in 1836 for Martin W. Warren (1763–1852), a Revolutionary War soldier and farmer who had settled in the area three years previously. It saw considerable military activity, with skirmishing in October, November 1861, March, April and June 1862, and July and September 1864.

Warrenton (Warren) MO

When it was established c.1835 it was one of a number of places named in honor of General Joseph Warren (1741–1775), who was killed at Bunker Hill. There was a skirmish here in October 1864.

Warrenton (Fauquier) VA

Also named for General Warren, it was established in 1810. The Army of the Potomac, now commanded by General Ambrose E. Burnside, was concentrated here in early November 1862. There was skirmishing later that month and in December; also in May, September and October 1863 and January 1864.

Warrenton Junction (Fauquier) VA

Again named for General Warren, it was on the Orange & Alexandria Railroad and the scene of skirmishing in October 1862 and May 1863.

Warrenton Springs (Fauquier) VA

Also known as White Sulphur Springs, this was a fashionable ante-bellum watering place, attracting large numbers of people from many states. It witnessed fighting in August 1862 and skirmishing in October 1863.

Warsaw (Benton) MO

On the Osage River, it was named after Warsaw, the capital of Poland, and laid out in 1837. Federal stores here were destroyed by Confederates in November 1861, and there was skirmishing in April 1862 and October 1863.

Warsaw (Duplin) NC

Was so called after Thaddeus D. Love, a train conductor, came to live here in 1838 and became known jokingly as "Thaddeus of Warsaw," from the popular novel of that name by Jane Porter (1803). It was the scene of skirmishing in July 1863.

Wartburg (Morgan) TN

Settled in 1845 by German and Swiss immigrants, it took its name from Wartburg in Germany. There was fighting here in June 1863.

Wartrace (Bedford) TN

Was so called because it was on the trace (trail) followed by Indian war parties. Skirmishing occurred here in April 1862 and October 1863.

Washington (Hempstead) AR

Numerous towns, cities and counties were named for George Washington (1732–1799), first president of the United States, 1789–1797. Settled after 1824, this served as the state capital, 1863–1865, after the fall of Little Rock, becoming an important center, crowded with refugees. There were skirmishes here in May 1864 and March 1865.

Washington DC

The new Federal capital was a planned city, laid out on the banks of the Potomac in 1791–1800, to the designs of French-born architect

Pierre Charles L'Enfant, and named for President George Washington. By 1860 it had a population which included some 50,000 white residents, around 9,200 free blacks and 1,770 slaves. Unlike Richmond, the future Confederate capital, it was not well served by railroads. Only one line, a branch of the Baltimore & Ohio, ran to the city of Baltimore, though later a link with Alexandria was constructed by the U.S. Military Railroad.

The Civil War transformed Washington from a sleepy political backwater into a major command, supply, training and rehabilitation center. The streets swarmed with soldiers, both able-bodied and wounded, ambulances, supply and forage wagons, and thieves and opportunists of all kinds flocked here.

The war changed Washington in other ways too. "A whole army of brazen courtesans and 'painted Jezebels' has invaded the city, who ply their trade by advertisement in the newspapers and by public exhibition in the streets," noted the correspondent of the London *Times* in 1863. By then there were some 450 bordellos and 7,000 prostitutes offering what were popularly known as "horizontal refreshments." Several blocks on the south side of Pennsylvania Avenue consisted entirely of houses of ill repute and soldiers told of the "gay old time" they had when visiting the city.

The capital also abounded in spies. Several Confederate spy rings operated at different times, the first and best-known one managed by Rose O. Greenhow, a wealthy widow, whose activities were not curtailed by house arrest and subsequent imprisonment in the Old Capitol Prison in January 1862. Others were run by Captain Thomas N. Conrad, Frank Stringfellow, and former Shakespearean actor James Harrison.

To protect it from attack, a ring of forts was built around the city. Their construction, under the direction of General John G. Barnard of the Corps of Engineers, began in May 1861 and there were eventually more than 60 of them, manned by 23,000 troops. Forts built on the heights of Arlington, immediately opposite Washington, were known as the Arlington Lines. Unlike Vicksburg, Petersburg or Richmond, Washington was never besieged and only once seriously threatened, in July 1864 during General Early's attempted raid on the city.

Other military installations included the Washington Navy Yard, established on the Anacostia River in 1799, the Marine Barracks, and the Arsenal, built in 1803, which blew up in June 1864, killing and injuring a number of workers. The Federal Penitentiary, constructed in 1826, was also used an annex to the Arsenal during the war.

Built as a temporary substitute for the Capitol destroyed in the War of 1812, the Old Capitol Prison, though very dilapidated, housed both Confederate soldiers and spies like Mrs. Greenhow and Belle Boyd; its most notorious inmate was Captain Henry Wirz, the commandant of Andersonville prison camp, who was executed here in November 1865. An annex was called Carroll Prison. The Washington County Jail, built in 1830, was also used to house prisoners of war.

Like Richmond, wartime Washington contained many military hospitals. The largest was the Lincoln Hospital which took Confederate wounded. Others included Armory Square, Campbell, Carver, Douglas, Finley, Harewood, Mount Pleasant, Stanton and the United States Naval Hospital. Louisa M. Alcott, one of many volunteer nurses, was at Union Hospital, Georgetown, in December 1862 when the wounded from Fredericksburg began arriving. A Sanitary Fair held in March 1864 to raise funds for the U.S. Sanitary Commission was visited by President Lincoln, who praised the women of America for "their conduct during this war."

On two consecutive days in May 1865 an estimated 150,000 veterans of General Meade's Army of the Potomac and General Sherman's Army of the West (the Cumberland, the Ohio and the Tennessee), "the greatest assemblage of soldiers and equipment the nation had ever known," marched down Pennsylvania Avenue in a Grand Review by President Andrew Johnson and his cabinet, General Ulysses S. Grant and other dignitaries; it did not include any black troops, who then made up ten per cent of the Union Army.

Washington (Beaufort) NC

Was founded by Colonel James Bonner on the Pamlico-Tar River estuary in 1771, and in 1776 became one of the first towns in America to be named for George Washington. It was occupied by Union troops from March 1862 to

April 1864, and besieged by Confederates in March-April 1863. There was fighting at Hill's Point, where the USS *Louisiana* was sunk by Confederate guns in April 1863. The town was burned by Federal troops in 1864.

Washington (Washington) TX

First settled in 1821, it was founded in 1835 as Washington-on-the-Brazos and was briefly the capital of the new Republic of Texas. It went into decline in the 1850s, though the Brazos Manufacturing Co. near here, producing woolen and cotton goods, and the Washington Iron Manufacturing Co. owned by W.W. Bell, T.J. Jackson and Wilson Bell, and producing pig and bar iron, were operating in December 1863.

Waterbury (New Haven) CT

Established on the Naugatuck River in 1674, it was named in 1686 on account of the "abundant waters." It became a center of the brass industry in the 19th century, firms like the Scovill Manufacturing Co. making military buttons.

Waterford (Loudoun) VA

Was established by a Pennsylvania Quaker c.1733. By the 1790s it was known as Waterford because some of the settlers came from that Irish town. There was skirmishing here in August and December 1862, and August 1863.

Waterloo (Fauquier) VA

A number of places in America were named after the Belgian village where Napoleon was finally defeated in 1815. This one, on the Rappahannock, was already in existence by 1749 and was renamed some time after the battle. The Swartz Woolen Mills here made cloth for Virginia troops and there was a skirmish in November 1862.

Watervliet (Albany) NY

On the Hudson River, it was founded in 1788 and named in 1816. *Watervliet* derives from a Dutch word meaning "flowing stream" or "water-brook." The United States Arsenal, established here in 1813, manufactured guns and ammunition for the Union armies.

Waverly (Lafayette) MO

On the Missouri River, was laid out in 1845 and named Waverly in 1848, a reflection of the popularity in America of Sir Walter Scott's famous Waverley novels, published from 1814 onwards. There was fighting here in June 1863.

Waxahachie (Ellis) TX

Comes from an Indian word meaning "cow (or buffalo) creek." The gunpowder mill established near here in 1862 by William Rowen was destroyed by an explosion and fire in April 1863, which killed him and an employee.

Wayne Court House (Wayne) VA

A number of places were named for General "Mad Anthony" Wayne (1745–1796), who served in the Revolutionary War. A skirmish occurred here in August 1861.

Waynesboro (Burke) GA

Laid out in 1783 and also named for General Wayne. In two days of fighting in late November 1864, during Sherman's march, General Wheeler's cavalry was able to thwart a Union attempt to destroy a nearby railroad bridge, but driven off in further action along the Augusta & Savannah Railroad in early December.

Waynesboro (♦) VA

Originally called Teesville for Joseph Tees, who had a land grant in 1736 from King George II, it was renamed in 1801 for General Wayne. The Waynesboro Military Academy closed when the Civil War broke out and the cadets enlisted in the Confederate Army. Fighting occurred here in June and September 1864, in March 1865 when the remains of General Early's Confederates were overwhelmed during the last part of General Sheridan's Shenandoah Valley campaign, and in May when William H. Harman, a general of state militia, was killed when trying to rally his demoralized troops.

Waynesville (Pulaski) MO

Was laid out in 1839 and also named for General Wayne. Skirmishing occurred here in May 1862, August and October 1863, September and November 1864 and as late as May 1865.

Weldon (Halifax) NC

The Weldon family bought land here on the Roanoke River in 1752 and planted an orchard, causing the place to be known as Weldon's Orchard or Weldon's Landing. The coming of the

Roanoke Canal, and later the Seaboard & Roanoke, the Petersburg & Weldon, and the Wilmington & Weldon Railroads all hastened its development. These last two provided a vital supply line between the blockade-running port of Wilmington and Petersburg, and ultimately Richmond, and several attempts were made by the Federals to capture and destroy the Weldon Railroad.

Wellington (Lafayette) MO

On the Missouri River, was laid out in 1837 and named for Arthur Wellesley, Duke of Wellington (1769–1852), the victor of Waterloo. There was fighting here in June and August 1863, and Federals also operated around here in July 1864.

Wentzville (St. Charles) MO

Was founded in 1855 as a depot on the St. Louis, Kansas City & North Missouri Railroad and named for Erasmus L. Wentz, the chief engineer. There was a skirmish here in July 1861.

West Point (Troup) GA

Was established in 1825 on the site of a trading post called Franklin. It is one of a number of examples of locational names. This acquired its present one in 1832 because it was at the westernmost point on the Chattahoochee River, on the Georgia/Alabama state line. The Reid Hospital was located here. The town was captured by General Wilson's cavalry in April 1865. Kate Cumming, a former Confederate nurse, saw it briefly the following month and wrote: "Every way the eye turned was ruin and desolation. The depot and warehouse were a pile of blackened bricks."

West Point (Clay) MS

The site, north-west of Columbus, was sold to James Robertson by two Indians in 1844. There was a skirmish in February 1864 and St. Mary's Hospital was moved here from Meridian, Mississippi, in December.

West Point (Orange) NY

There had been a military post on the west bank of the Hudson River in upstate New York since 1778. The United States Military Academy, originally founded here in 1802 as a school of engineering, contributed more than a thousand general officers to both sides in the Civil War.

West Point (King William) VA

This derives from a personal name rather than its location. Originally named for John West, governor of Virginia, 1635–1637, then renamed Delaware for Thomas West, Baron de La Warre, who became governor of Virginia in 1610, it became West Point again when the Richmond & York River Railroad was completed in 1861. Near the meeting of the Pamunkey and York Rivers, it was the scene of an engagement in May 1862 during the Peninsula campaign, otherwise known as Barhamsville or Eltham's Landing (q.v.). There was more fighting in April 1863, and it was briefly occupied by the Federals the following month.

Westport (Jackson) MO

Now part of Kansas City, it was laid out in 1833 and so called because of its location near the Missouri River. The battle fought here in October 1864, the largest west of the Mississippi, has been called the "Gettysburg of the West" and also resulted in a Confederate defeat.

Wetumpka (Elmore) AL

On the Coosa River, the name comes from a Creek word meaning "waterfall" or "tumbling water." Settled after the Creek War of 1813–1814, it was established by 1834. The site of the Southern Military Academy, skirmishing occurred here in April and May 1865.

Wheeling (Ohio) WV

Known to the Delawares as *Weeling*, meaning "place of the skull," a site of decapitations, it was first settled in 1769 on land at the junction of Wheeling Creek and the Ohio River by Colonel Ebenezer Zane. Laid out as Zanesburg in 1794, it was renamed Wheeling in 1806. An important trading post till the 1850s, by the time of the Civil War it had become a commercial and industrial hub.

A center of Unionist activity in western Virginia, opposition to secession led to a series of pro–Union meetings and conventions here, April-November 1861, the appointment of Francis H. Pierpont as provisional governor, and the formation of the new state of West Virginia, with Wheeling as the state capital, 1863–1870.

The jail and the Athenaeum building were both used to house Confederate prisoners in 1863–1865. West Virginia troops were mustered out here in 1865.

White House Landing (King William) VA

On the Pamunkey River, it took its name from the White House, owned by William H.F. ("Rooney") Lee, Robert E. Lee's second eldest son. It was the site of General McClellan's headquarters in May and June 1862 during the Peninsula campaign, and General Philip H. Sheridan was here in May and June 1864.

White Oak Swamp (Charles City) VA

Partly a branch of the Chickahominy, it takes its name from the presence of white oak trees, fairly common in the eastern United States. The last but one of the Seven Days' battles in the Peninsular campaign at the end of June 1862 took place here, with fierce fighting among tangled undergrowth. The Confederates were initially successful, but sustained heavy casualties and the Federals were able to withdraw to Malvern Hill (q.v.).

White Plains (Brunswick) VA

Was possibly named after White Plains, New York, the site of a battle in the Revolutionary War (1776), which derived from the white balsam which grew there. There was skirmishing near here in September 1863 and October 1864.

Wilderness (Orange) VA

A chaotic, three-day battle was fought in this area of dense woodland known as the Wilderness in May 1864, with heavy losses on both sides and no definite outcome. Union General Alexander Hays was killed and James S. Wadsworth mortally wounded. Confederate General John M. Jones was also killed and Leroy A. Stafford mortally wounded. Both Micah Jenkins and James Longstreet were accidentally shot by their own men, almost exactly a year after "Stonewall" Jackson's wounding; Jenkins' wound was fatal. Afterwards, volunteer nurse Cornelia Hancock came here and worked tirelessly among the wounded.

Wilkesboro (Wilkes) NC

Named for John Wilkes (1727–1797), a British Member of Parliament and American sympathizer, to whom John Wilkes Booth, President Lincoln's assassin, was apparently related, it was founded in 1800. There was a skirmish here in March 1865 during General Sherman's campaign in the Carolinas.

Williamsburg (Whitley) KY

Dating from 1818, it was originally called Whitley Court House, for Colonel William Whitley (1749–1813), a renowned Indian fighter, then Williamsburg. A skirmish occurred here in July 1863.

Williamsburg (♦) VA

Between the York and James Rivers, it was first settled in 1633 and named Williamsburg for King William III (1650–1702), when it became the colonial and state capital, 1699–1780. One of the first Confederate hospitals was established in a female seminary in May 1861 by Letitia Tyler Semple, daughter of former President Tyler. There was a battle here in May 1862, when Colonel Christopher Mott of the 19th Mississippi, "an accomplished soldier, model gentleman and devoted patriot" and recommended for promotion to general, was killed; it was occupied by Federal troops the next day. A Confederate attempt to recapture it in September failed, but there was further skirmishing here in March and April 1863 and February 1865.

Williamsport (Washington) MD

Was founded in 1786 on the banks of the Potomac River by Revolutionary War General Otho H. Williams (1747–1794), for whom it was named. Because of its location, it was considered as a possible site for the new Federal capital in 1790. There was skirmishing here in September and October 1862, and more fighting in July 1863 and July and August 1864. (Now a suburb of Hagerstown.)

Williston (Barnwell) SC

Founded in the early 19th century, it was named for Robert Willis, a plantation owner and member of a prominent local family. There was a skirmish here in February 1865 during General Sherman's drive through the Carolinas.

Wilmington (New Castle) DE

At the junction of the Delaware and Christina

Rivers, it was first established in 1638. Captured by the Dutch in 1655, then by the British, it was named Wilmington in 1739, in honor of the British politician, Spencer Compton, Earl of Wilmington (1673–1743). The mills of E.I. Du Pont de Nemours & Co., founded near here in 1802, were the largest suppliers of gunpowder to the Union Army and Navy. Some survivors from Andersonville were photographed in June 1865 at Geer's Hospital (called after Chaplain J.J. Geer of the 183rd Ohio). Delaware troops were mustered out here.

Wilmington (New Hanover) NC

Was established on the Cape Fear River in 1730 and also named for the Earl of Wilmington in 1734. Two ironclads for use in coastal waters were built at the naval station in 1862–1864, possibly by Berry & Bros. and J.L. Cassidy & Sons, and three torpedo boats were also constructed but accidentally destroyed by fire. Froelich & Estivan's Confederate States Arms Factory manufactured swords, cavalry sabers and bayonets, as well as rifles and pistols; O.S. Baldwin made uniforms for state troops; and James Wilson produced accoutrements and saddles. There was also a naval hospital here. It became a major port for blockade runners which brought not only essential supplies and weapons for the Confederacy, but also yellow fever from Nassau in 1862, claiming hundreds of lives. The town, crowded with refugees, was evacuated by the Confederates in February 1865, following the fall of Fort Fisher.

Wilson's Creek (Greene) MO

James Wilson was a settler who in the 1820s married three Delaware women, then a white woman in St. Louis, before returning to establish a farm on the creek, a tributary of the White River, which bears his name. The battle fought here in August 1861, the second significant one of the Civil War and the largest in Missouri, was a victory for the South. It was described by one soldier as "a purty mean-faught fite." The Union commander, General Nathaniel Lyon, was killed and became the North's first military hero. It is also known as the battle of Springfield (q.v.).

Winchester (Clark) KY

Established in 1782, it was named after Winchester, Virginia, the home of its founder, John Baker. There was skirmishing near here in July 1863, and General Morgan's cavalry, driven out of Mount Sterling in June 1864, retreated here.

Winchester (Franklin) TN

Established in 1809, it was named for James Winchester (1752–1826), the first speaker in the Tennessee Legislature and a brigadier general in the War of 1812. There was considerable military action here, with skirmishing in May, June 1862, July, September and November 1863, and guerrilla activity in May 1864.

Winchester (♦) VA

Was founded in 1744 and named Winchester in 1752 after the cathedral city in Hampshire, England. During the Civil War it changed hands several times. The Frederick County Jail was used as a Confederate military prison in 1862–1864. Huge numbers of stragglers from General Lee's army, perhaps as many as 15,000, "laggards broken down in body or skulkers broken down in spirit," were assembled here in September 1862 during the Antietam campaign, before being returned to their commands.

Three battles—First, Second and Third Winchester—were fought here, in May 1862, during General Jackson's Valley campaign, in June 1863, during the Gettysburg campaign, and in September 1864, during General Sheridan's Valley campaign. In the third battle, also known as Opequon Creek (q.v.), Union General David A. Russell was killed and James A. Mulligan mortally wounded, while Confederate losses included Generals Robert E. Rodes and Archibald C. Godwin. Two others died near here from their wounds—General James J. Pettigrew in July 1863, and General Stephen D. Ramseur in October 1864.

Windsor (Bertie) NC

On the Cashie River, it was named after the famous English town and royal castle in Berkshire and founded in 1722. There was a skirmish here in January 1864.

Windsor (Windsor) VT

It was named in 1761, probably after Windsor, Connecticut, also called after Windsor, England. Lamson, Goodnow & Yale and Robbins & Lawrence made Springfield rifle-muskets for the Union Army at this town on the Connecticut River.

Woodbury (Cannon) TN

Named for Levi Woodbury (1789–1851), secretary of the Navy, 1831–1834, and secretary of the Treasury, 1834–1837, under Andrew Jackson, and secretary of the Treasury, 1837–1841, under Martin Van Buren. There was fighting here in January 1863.

Woodstock (Shenandoah) VA

Originally called Mullerstadt, for German settler Jacob Muller, it was renamed in 1761 after Woodstock, Maine, which derived from the small English town of Woodstock, Oxfordshire. There was fighting here in May, June 1862, February 1863 and September 1864. The fight at Tom's Brook (q.v.) became known as the "Woodstock Races."

Woodville (Marshall) AL

Was settled c.1815 and named for Richard and Annie Wood who were early inhabitants. It was the scene of fighting in June and August 1862, and January 1864.

Wooster (Wayne) OH

Named for General David Wooster (1711–1777), who died fighting in the Revolutionary War, it was laid out in 1808 by John Bever, William Henry and Joseph Larwill. It was the scene of a draft riot in July 1863.

Worcester (Worcester) MA

Was permanently established on the Blackstone River in 1713 after two previous settlements had failed, and probably named after the English cathedral city of Worcester. The construction of the Blackstone Canal in 1828, linking it with Providence, Rhode Island, speeded its development. It was the site of the Highland Military Academy, opened in 1857, which trained officers for the United States Army. Charles H. Ballard also manufactured carbines here.

Wytheville (Wythe) VA

Was named Wytheville by 1839, for George Wythe (1726–1806), a distinguished Virginia judge and the first law professor in the United States. Some rifles and carbines were made here for the Confederate Army by the firm of J.B. Barrett, and the mines nearby were the most important source of lead for the Confederacy. They were threatened by a Federal expedition in July 1863, and finally captured and destroyed in December 1864 by troops under General George Stoneman, who also went on to destroy the salt works at Saltville. There was more fighting here in April 1865.

Yazoo City (Yazoo) MS

On the Yazoo River, a tributary of the Mississippi, this became Yazoo City in 1839. River and city were called after the Yazoo tribe (Chickasaws or Choctaws). General Sherman's Yazoo Expedition in December 1862 was an unsuccessful attempt to take the Chickasaw Bluffs during the first Vicksburg campaign. The short-lived CSS *Arkansas* was completed at the naval station here and other gunboats were also built, but they were destroyed when the Federals captured Yazoo City in July 1863. They re-occupied it in February 1864 but abandoned it after fighting here in March.

Yellow Tavern (Henrico) VA

This was an abandoned stagecoach inn, six miles north of Richmond on the Brooke turnpike. General J.E.B. Stuart was mortally wounded in a cavalry engagement here in May 1864, during General Sheridan's raid and died in Richmond the following day.

Yellville (Marion) AR

It was named in 1844 for Colonel Archibald Yell (1797–1847), the second governor of Arkansas, 1840–1844, who was killed in the Mexican War. There was skirmishing here in June 1862.

Yemassee (Hampton) SC

The fighting at Pocotaligo (q.v.) in October 1862 is also known as Yemassee, which took its name from that tribe of Indians.

Yonkers (Westchester) NY

The site on the Hudson River was originally acquired by the Dutch West India Co. in 1639. Adriaen Van der Donck, who received a land grant in 1646, was a *jonkheer* or squire, hence Yonkers, which was founded in 1788. The Starr Arms Co. owned by Eben Starr made large numbers of revolvers for the Union Army and

Navy here, and also at Binghamton and Morrisania.

York (York) PA

Was first settled in 1735 and laid out in 1741 on land owned by Richard, Thomas and John Penn, sons of William Penn. The derivation is uncertain, but it may have been named for the Duke of York (1633–1701), later King James II, who was a friend and associate of both their father and grandfather, Admiral Sir William Penn. It was captured briefly by the Confederates in June 1863.

Yorktown (York) VA

Was first settled at the mouth of the York River in 1631 and named for King Charles I (1600–1649), who had been Duke of York before succeeding to the throne in 1625. The present town was established in 1691. It was besieged by General George B. McClellan, April-May 1862, at the start of the Peninsula campaign.

Appendix 1:
United States Census of 1860

The following table shows the population of places from the Eighth United States Census (1860), the last one to count whites, free coloreds and slaves together in one total. The 1860 Census was fairly complete for most Northern states, but a limited number of places in Southern states were listed. The problem was remedied by the 1870 Census, which included not only new data but also 1860 populations for places not previously listed. The table is supplemented by this information from the 1870 Census.

Place	Pop.	Place	Pop.	Place	Pop.
Abbeville, SC	592	Barbourville, KY	230	Brooksville, KY	262
Adairsville, GA	333	Bardstown, KY	536	Brownsville, TX	2,734
Albany, GA	1,618	Bastrop, TX	1,107	Brunswick, GA	825
Albany, KY	222	Batesville, AR	670	Brunswick, MO	3,589
Albany, NY	62,367	Baton Rouge, LA	5,428	Buckhannon, WV	427
Albuquerque, NMT	1,203	Beaufort, NC	1,610	Cahaba, AL	1,920
Alexandria, LA	1,461	Berryville, VA	356	Cairo, IL	2,188
Alexandria, VA	12,654	Bethlehem, PA	2,866	Calhoun, GA	1913
Alton, IL	6,332	Binghamton, NY	8,325	Camden, AR	2,219
Altoona, PA	3,591	Blackshear, GA	319	Camden, SC	1,621
Anderson, TX	677	Blountville, TN	2,723	Canton, MS	780
Apalachicola, FL	1,904	Bolivar, TN	1,510	Cape Girardeau, MO	2,663
Arkadelphia, AR	817	Bolivar Heights, WV	1,130	Carlisle, PA	5,664
Arkansas Post, AR	295	Bonham, TX	477	Carrollton, AR	186
Arrow Rock, MO	2,742	Booneville, KY	121	Carrollton, MO	738
Ashland, VA	148	Boonsboro, MD	3,949	Cassville, GA	639
Ashley, MO	992	Boston, MA	177,840	Chambersburg, PA	2,222
Atchison, KS	2,616	Brandenburg, KY	618	Charles Town, WV	1,376
Athens, GA	3,848	Brandon, MS	867	Charleston, IL	2,218
Athens, TN	678	Brattleboro, VT	3,855	Charleston, MO	273
Atlanta, GA	9,554	Bridgeport, CT	13,299	Charleston, SC	40,522
Augusta, GA	12,493	Bristol, RI	5,271	Charleston, TN	796
Austin, TX	3,494	Bristol, TN	624	Charleston, WV	1,520
Baltimore, MD	212,418	Brookhaven, MS	996	Charlotte, NC	2,265
Barboursville, WV	339	Brooklyn, NY	266,661	Chattanooga, TN	2,545

Chester, PA	4,631	Fairburn, GA	298	Hartford, CT	29,152
Chicago, IL	109,260	Fairmont, WV	704	Helena, AR	1,551
Chicopee, MA	7,261	Falmouth, KY	315	Hickman, KY	1,006
Cincinnati, OH	161,044	Farmington, TN	985	Hillsborough, NC	751
Cleveland, TN	2,460	Farmville, VA	1,536	Holden, MO	59
Clifton, TN	866	Fayette, MO	647	Holly Springs, MS	2,987
Clinton, GA	11	Fayetteville, AR	967	Hopefield, AR	154
Clinton, MS	289	Fayetteville, NC	4,790	Hopkinsville, KY	2,289
Cold Spring, NY	2,770	Fayetteville, TN	2,507	Houston, TX	4,845
Columbia, MO	3,207	Fernandina, FL	1,390	Humboldt, TN	1,268
Columbia, SC	8,059	Fitchburg, MA	7,805	Huntington, IN	4,606
Columbia, TN	5,396	Florence, AL	1,395	Huntsville, AL	3,634
Columbus, GA	9,621	Forsyth, GA	1,441	Huntsville, AR	251
Columbus, KY	963	Frankfort, KY	3,702	Huntsville, TX	939
Columbus, MS	3,308	Franklin, MO	2,419	Independence, MO	3,164
Columbus, OH	18,554	Frederick, MD	8,142	Indianapolis, IN	18,611
Concord, NH	10,896	Fredericksburg, VA	5,022	Indianola, TX	1,150
Corpus Christi, TX	175	Fredericktown, MO	255	Ironton, MO	386
Corydon, IN	462	Front Royal, VA	412	Irvine, KY	234
Covington, KY	16,471	Funkstown, MD	2,550	Jackson, MS	3,199
Crawford, AL	187	Gainesville, FL	269	Jackson, TN	2,407
Crittenden, KY	290	Gallatin, TN	2,020	Jacksonville, FL	2,118
Cubero, NMT	486	Galveston, TX	7,307	Jasper, TN	1,466
Cumberland, MD	2,040	Gettysburg, PA	2,390	Jefferson, MD	1,749
Cynthiana, KY	1,237	Ghent, KY	366	Jefferson, TX	988
Dallas, GA	1,033	Glasgow, MO	1,035	Jefferson City, MO	3,082
Dalton, GA	4,264	Glenville, WV	398	Jeffersonville, IN	6,328
Danville, KY	4,962	Goldsboro, NC	885	Keokuk, IA	8,136
Danville, MO	1,995	Grafton, WV	891	Keytesville, MO	1,752
Dardanelle, AR	1,601	Granby, MO	2,327	Kingsport, TN	509
Darien, GA	570	Grand Gulf, MS	158	Kingston, TN	1,517
Decatur, GA	916	Greencastle, PA	1,399	Kinston, NC	1,333
Detroit, MI	45,619	Greeneville, TN	1,094	Kirksville, MO	658
Donaldsonville, LA	11,484	Greenville, NC	828	Knoxville, TN	3,704
Dover, DE	5,617	Greenville, SC	1,518	La Fayette, GA	689
Dover, NH	8,502	Griffin, GA	2,855	La Grange, GA	4,465
Dover, TN	1,384	Hagerstown, MD	10,139	La Grange, TN	3,620
Dumfries, VA	171	Hamilton, OH	7,233	Lamar, MO	673
Dyersburg, TN	1,258	Hampton, VA	1,848	Lancaster, KY	721
Eagleville, TN	957	Hancock, MD	1,975	Laredo, TX	1,256
Eatonton, GA	2,009	Hanover, PA	1,630	Lavaca, TX	526
Edenton, NC	1,544	Harpers Ferry, WV	1,339	Lawrence, KS	1,645
Edmonton, KY	70	Harrisburg, PA	13,405	Lawrenceburg, TN	850
Elizabeth City, NC	1,798	Harrison, OH	1,343	Lebanon, KY	953
Elizabethtown, KY	556	Harrisonburg, VA	1,023	Lebanon, MO	1,169
Elmira, NY	8,682	Harrisonville, MO	675	Lebanon, TN	2,598
Emmitsburg, MD	3,119	Harrodsburg, KY	1,668	Lewisburg, WV	969

City	Population	City	Population	City	Population
Lexington, KY	9,521	Munfordville, KY	192	Raleigh, NC	4,780
Lexington, MO	4,122	Murfreesboro, TN	2,861	Raymond, MS	558
Lexington, VA	2,135	Nashville, TN	16,988	Reading, PA	23,162
Liberty, MO	2,405	Natchez, MS	6,612	Resaca, GA	777
Little Rock, AR	3,727	Naugatuck, CT	2,590	Richmond, KY	845
Livingston, TN	268	Neosho, MO	1,622	Richmond, MO	3,123
London, KY	235	New Bern, NC	5,432	Richmond, VA	37,910
Louisa, KY	255	New Haven, CT	39,267	Ringgold, GA	1,158
Louisville, GA	611	New Madrid, MO	610	Ripley, MS	683
Louisville, KY	68,033	New Market, VA	1,422	Rocheport, MO	735
Lynchburg, VA	6,853	New Orleans, LA	168,675	Rockville, MD	5,415
Macon, GA	8,247	New York City, NY	805,658	Rogersville, TN	2,289
Macon, MO	837	Newark, NJ	71,941	Rolla, MO	1,439
Madison, WI	6,611	Newburgh, IN	999	Rome, GA	4,010
Manchester, NH	20,107	Newnan, GA	2,546	Romney, WV	559
Mansfield, CT	1,697	Norfolk, CT	1,803	Rumsey, KY	373
Marianna, FL	440	Norfolk, VA	14,620	Russellville, KY	1,089
Marietta, GA	2,680	Norwich, CT	14,048	Rutland, VT	7,577
Marion, VA	445	Occoquan, VA	273	St. Albans, VT	3,637
Marshall, MO	1,779	Opelousas, LA	786	St. Augustine, FL	1,914
Marshfield, MO	408	Orangeburg, SC	897	St. Francisville, MO	455
Martinsburg, WV	3,364	Osceola, MO	2,077	St. Louis, MO	160,773
Maryville, TN	1,600	Owensboro, KY	2,308	St. Marks, FL	79
Mayfield, KY	556	Ozark, MO	119	Salem, MO	269
Maynardville, TN	188	Paducah, KY	4,590	Salisbury, NC	2,420
Maysville, KY	4,106	Palmetto, GA	1,526	San Antonio, TX	8,235
McMinnville, TN	825	Palmyra, MO	1,999	Santa Fe, NMT	4,635
Memphis, TN	22,623	Paris, KY	1,440	Savannah, GA	22,292
Mercersburg, PA	897	Paterson, NJ	19,586	Savannah, TN	1,308
Miami, MO	2,643	Pensacola, FL	2,876	Schaghticoke, NY	2,929
Middletown, CT	3,438	Petersburg, VA	18,266	Scottsville, KY	2,520
Middletown, MD	2,818	Philadelphia, PA	565,529	Searcy, AR	621
Milledgeville, GA	2,480	Phoenixville, PA	4,886	Selma, AL	3,177
Milton, FL	1,815	Pine Bluff, AR	1,396	Sevierville, TN	799
Mobile, AL	29,258	Pittsburgh, PA	49,217	Seymour, CT	546
Montgomery, AL	8,843	Plaquemine, LA	1,663	Sharpsburg, MD	2,469
Monticello, FL	1,083	Plattsburgh, NY	3,648	Shelbyville, TN	2,092
Morehead City, NC	316	Plymouth, NC	872	Shepherdstown, WV	1,219
Morganfield, KY	460	Pocahontas, TN	217	Shepherdsville, KY	305
Morgantown, WV	741	Pomeroy, OH	6,480	Shohola, PA	672
Morrisania, NY	4,517	Port Gibson, MS	1,453	Shreveport, LA	2,190
Morton, MS	2,036	Portland, ME	26,341	Simpsonville, KY	170
Moscow, TN	2,151	Portsmouth, NH	9,335	Smithfield, VA	777
Mound City, IL	898	Portsmouth, VA	9,496	Sneedville, TN	195
Mount Ida, AR	76	Prairie Grove, AR	2,585	Socorro, NMT	523
Mount Jackson, VA	1,316	Prattville, AL	3,260	Somerset, KY	662
Mount Sterling, KY	754	Providence, RI	50,666	Somerville, TN	4,193

Sparta, TN	452	Upperville, VA	398	Westport, MO	1,195
Springfield, IL	9,320	Utica, NY	22,529	Wheeling, WV	14,083
Springfield, MA	15,199	Valverde, NMT	90	Williamsburg, KY	125
Stanford, KY	479	Van Buren, AR	969	Williamsburg, VA	1,111
Staunton, VA	3,875	Vermilionville, LA	498	Williamsport, MD	3,527
Steubenville, OH	6,154	Vicksburg, MS	4,591	Wilmington, DE	21,258
Strasburg, VA	1,583	Warrensburg, MO	1,080	Wilmington, NC	9,552
Suffolk, VA	1,395	Warrenton, MO	480	Winchester, KY	1,142
Syracuse, NY	28,119	Warrenton, VA	604	Winchester, TN	2,314
Tallahassee, FL	1,932	Wartburg, TN	895	Winchester, VA	4,392
Taunton, MA	15,376	Washington, AR	480	Windsor, NC	315
Tom's Brook, VA	598	Washington, DC	61,122	Windsor, VT	1,669
Trenton, NJ	17,228	Washington, NC	1,599	Woodstock, VA	2,113
Trenton, TN	4,993	Washington, TX	1,000	Wooster, OH	3,361
Troy, NY	39,235	Waterbury, CT	10,004	Worcester, MA	24,960
Tuscaloosa, AL	3,989	Waterford, VA	429	Wytheville, VA	1,111
Tuscumbia, MO	77	Watervliet, NY	6,229	Yellville, AR	170
Tyler, TX	1,024	Waynesboro, GA	307	Yonkers, NY	11,848
Union City, TN	1,125	Waynesboro, VA	457	York, PA	8,605

Appendix 2: Towns by State

Alabama
Athens
Barton's Station
Blountsville
Bridgeport
Brierfield
Cahaba
Camp Anderson
Camp Beauregard
Camp Buckner
Camp Curry
Camp Forney
Camp Goldthwaite
Camp Memminger
Camp Moore
Camp Shorter
Camp Watts
Camp Withers
Castle Morgan
Cedar Bluff
Cherokee Station
Citronelle
Columbiana
Crawford
Dauphin Island
Decatur
Ebenezer Church
Elyton
Florence
Fort Barker
Fort Gaines
Fort Huger
Fort Morgan
Fort Mouton
Fort Tracy
Gadsden
Gainesville
Girard
Guntersville
Huntsville
Irondale
Leighton
Lowndesboro
Maplesville
Mobile
Montevallo
Montgomery
Moulton
Mount Vernon
Nanna Hubba Bluff
Northport
Prattville
Randolph
Russellville
Selma
Spanish Fort
Stevenson
Tallassee
Tennessee River
Tombigbee River
Tuscaloosa
Tuscumbia
Union Springs
Wetumpka
Woodville

Arkansas
Arkadelphia
Arkansas Post
Arkansas River
Batesville
Benton
Camden
Camp Bragg
Camp Jackson
Camp McIntosh
Camp Nelson
Camp Stephens
Camp Walker
Carrollton
Chalk Bluff
Cotton Plant
Dardanelle
Elkhorn Tavern
Fayetteville
Fort Curtis
Fort Hindman
Fort Smith
Helena
Hopefield
Huntsville
Jacksonport
Jenkins' Ferry
Jenny Lind
Little Rock
Madison
Marianna
Mississippi River
Monticello
Mount Ida
Napoleon
Pea Ridge
Pine Bluff
Pocahontas
Poison Springs
Prairie Grove
Quitman
Rockport
Roseville
Searcy
Tulip
Van Buren
Washington
Yellville

Connecticut
Bridgeport
Fort Griswold
Fort Trumbull
Hartford
Hazardville
Mansfield
Middletown
Mystic
Naugatuck
New Haven
Norfolk
Norwich
Seymour
Waterbury

Delaware
Camp Brandywine
Camp Smithers
Dover
Fort Delaware

Pea Patch Island
Wilmington

District of Columbia
Camp Barclay
Camp Barker
Camp Barry
Camp Berry
Camp Brightwood
Camp Cameron
Camp Doubleday
Camp Fenton
Camp Franklin
Camp Fry
Camp Ingalls
Camp Morris
Camp Sprague
Camp Stoneman
Fort Baker
Fort Barnard
Fort Bayard
Fort Bennett
Fort Berry
Fort Carroll
Fort Cass
Fort C. F. Smith
Fort Chaplin
Fort Corcoran
Fort Craig
Fort Davis
Fort De Russy
Fort Du Pont
Fort Ethan Allan
Fort Gaines
Fort Greble
Fort Haggerty
Fort Jackson
Fort Kearny
Fort Lincoln
Fort Mahan
Fort McPherson
Fort Meigs
Fort Morton
Fort Reno
Fort Reynolds
Fort Richardson

Fort Ricketts
Fort Runyon
Fort Saratoga
Fort Scott
Fort Slemmer
Fort Slocum
Fort Snyder
Fort Stanton
Fort Stevens
Fort Strong
Fort Thayer
Fort Tillinghast
Fort Totten
Fort Wagner
Fort Whipple
Fort Woodbury
Giesboro Point
Washington

Florida
Amelia Island
Apalachicola
Baldwin
Blountstown
Camp Chalmers
Camp Cobb
Camp Cooper
Camp Finegan
Camp Jackson
Camp Langford
Camp Lay
Camp Leon
Camp Mary Davis
Camp Miller
Camp Milton
Cedar Key
Fort Barrancas
Fort Brooke
Fort Butler
Fort Clinch
Fort Gadsden
Fort Marion
Fort McRee
Fort Myers
Fort Pickens
Fort Steele
Fort Ward

Fort Zachary Taylor
Gainesville
Homosassa Springs
Jacksonville
Magnolia Springs
Marianna
Milton
Monticello
Natural Bridge
New Smyrna
Olustee
Pensacola
St. Andrews Bay
St. Augustine
St. Marks
Santa Rosa Island
Tallahassee
Tampa

Georgia
Abbeville
Acworth
Adairsville
Albany
Allatoona
Americus
Andersonville
Athens
Atlanta
Augusta
Barnesville
Big Shanty
Blackshear
Brunswick
Calhoun
Camp Brown
Camp Davidson
Camp Hampton
Camp Lawton
Camp McDonald
Camp Milner
Camp Oglethorpe
Camp Randolph
Camp Sumter
Cartersville
Cassville
Catoosa Station

Chattahoochee River
Chickamauga Creek
Clinton
Cockspur Island
Columbus
Covington
Dallas
Dalton
Darien
Decatur
Eatonton
Fairburn
Forsyth
Fort Attaway
Fort Bartow
Fort Boggs
Fort Brown
Fort Hardeman
Fort Hood
Fort Jackson
Fort James Jackson
Fort McAllister
Fort Mercer
Fort Norton
Fort Oglethorpe
Fort Pulaski
Fort Stovall
Fort Tattnall
Fort Tyler
Fort Walker
Gordon
Griffin
Griswoldville
Irwinville
Jonesboro
Kennesaw Mountain
Kingston
La Fayette
La Grange
Louisville
Lovejoy's Station
Lumpkin's Station
Macon
Madison
Marietta
Milledgeville
Neal Dow Station

New Hope Church
Newnan
Oostanaula River
Palmetto
Peachtree Creek
Pine Mountain
Resaca
Ringgold
Rome
Rossville
Roswell
Rough and Ready Station
Saffold
Sandersville
Savannah
Stockbridge
Thomaston
Thomasville
Varnell's Station
Waynesboro
West Point

Illinois
Alton
Cairo
Camp Bissell
Camp Butler
Camp Douglas
Camp Fry
Camp Grant
Camp Hammond
Camp Houghtaling
Camp Kane
Camp Lyon
Camp Mather
Camp McClernand
Camp Taylor
Camp Yates
Charleston
Chicago
Fort Armstrong
Fort Prentiss
Mound City
Rock Island
Springfield

Indian Territory
Cabin Creek
Camp Armstrong
Doaksville
Fort Arbuckle
Fort Cobb
Fort Coffee
Fort Davis
Fort Gibson
Fort McCulloch
Fort Towson
Fort Washita
Fort Wayne
Honey Springs
Pryor's Creek

Indiana
Camp Anderson
Camp Bridgeland
Camp Carrington
Camp Colfax
Camp Emerson
Camp Frémont
Camp Heffren
Camp Jackson
Camp Joe Holt
Camp Lewis
Camp Morris
Camp Morton
Camp Noble
Camp Reynolds
Camp Robinson
Camp Rose
Camp Stillwell
Camp Streight
Camp Sullivan
Corydon
Huntington
Indianapolis
Jeffersonville
Newburgh
Pekin

Iowa
Camp Burnside
Camp Ellsworth
Camp Frémont
Camp Halleck
Camp Herron
Camp Joe Holt
Camp Kinsman
Camp Kirkwood
Camp Lauman
Camp McClellan
Camp McKean
Camp Rankin
Camp Tuttle
Keokuk

Kansas
Atchison
Baxter Springs
Camp Ben Butler
Camp Hunter
Fort Blair
Fort Larned
Fort Leavenworth
Fort Lincoln
Fort Montgomery
Fort Riley
Fort Scott
Fort Zarah
Lawrence
Marais des Cygnes River
Paola

Kentucky
Albany
Barbourville
Bardstown
Booneville
Bowling Green
Brandenburg
Brooksville
Burkesville
Camp Alcorn
Camp Allen
Camp Anderson
Camp Andrew Johnson
Camp Beauregard
Camp Boone
Camp Boyle
Camp Buell
Camp Burnham
Camp Burnside
Camp Crittenden
Camp Dick Robinson
Camp Dumont
Camp Gilbert
Camp Kenton
Camp King
Camp Moore
Camp Nelson
Camp Nevin
Camp Pope
Camp Sigel
Camp Wickliffe
Columbus
Covington
Crittenden
Cumberland River
Cynthiana
Danville
Edmonton
Elizabethtown
Falmouth
Fort Anderson
Fort Beauregard
Fort Bishop
Fort Boyle
Fort C.F. Smith
Fort Clark
Fort DeWolf
Fort Duffield
Fort Elstner
Fort Engle
Fort Heiman
Fort Hill
Fort Holt
Fort Horton
Fort Jones
Fort Karnasch
Fort Lytle
Fort Mitchel
Fort Philpot
Fort St. Clair Morton
Fort Sands
Fort Saunders
Fort Southworth

Frankfort
Ghent
Glasgow
Harrodsburg
Henderson
Hickman
Hodgenville
Hopkinsville
Irvine
Jamestown
Lancaster
Lawrenceburg
Lebanon
Lexington
Logan's Crossroads
London
Louisa
Louisville
Manchester
Mayfield
Maysville
Mill Springs
Morganfield
Mount Sterling
Munfordville
New Haven
Owensboro
Paducah
Paintsville
Paris
Perryville
Prestonsburg
Richmond
Rumsey
Russellville
Salyersville
Saratoga
Scottsville
Shepherdsville
Simpsonville
Somerset
Stanford
Taylorsville
Tennessee River
Tompkinsville
Williamsburg
Winchester

Louisiana
Alexandria
Atchafalaya River
Avery Island
Baton Rouge
Berwick
Camp Benjamin
Camp Boggs
Camp Breaux
Camp Clark
Camp Lovell
Camp Moore
Camp Pratt
Cloutierville
Donaldsonville
Fort Beauregard
Fort Bisland
Fort Buchanan
Fort Buhlow
Fort Butler
Fort De Russy
Fort Jackson
Fort Livingston
Fort Macomb
Fort Pike
Fort Quitman
Fort Randolph
Fort St Philip
Fort Williams
Fort Wood
Grand Coteau
Grande Terre Island
Gretna
Hard Times Landing
Jackson
Jeanerette
Lake Pontchartrain
Madisonville
Mansfield
Mansura
Mississippi River
Moreauville
Morganza
Napoleonville
Natchitoches
New Orleans
Opelousas
Pattersonville
Petites Coquilles Island
Plaquemine
Port Hudson
Red River
Sabine Crossroads
St. Martinville
Shreveport
Tunica
Vermilionville
Vidalia

Maine
Camp Berry
Camp Mason
Fort Knox
Fort McClary
Fort Popham
Fort Preble
Portland

Maryland
Antietam
Antietam Creek
Baltimore
Boonsboro
Camp Bradford
Camp Cadwalader
Camp Casey
Camp Heintzelman
Camp Hicks
Camp Hoffman
Camp Stanton
Cumberland
Emmitsburg
Fort Foote
Fort Frederick
Fort Mansfield
Fort McHenry
Fort Simmons
Fort Sumner
Frederick
Funkstown
Hagerstown
Hancock
Jefferson
Keedysville
Magnolia Station
Middletown
Pikesville
Point Lookout
Point of Rocks
Poolesville
Potomac River
Rockville
Sharpsburg
Smithsburg
Williamsport

Massachusetts
Boston
Camp Andrew
Camp Cameron
Camp Lander
Camp Meigs
Camp Scott
Camp Stanton
Camp Wightman
Chicopee
Fitchburg
Fort Rodman
Fort Warren
George's Island
Long Island
Springfield
Taunton
Worcester

Michigan
Camp Banks
Camp Blair
Camp Butler
Camp Lyon
Camp Williams
Detroit
Fort Mackinac
Mackinac Island

Mississippi
Aberdeen
Baldwyn
Big Black River
Biloxi

Bolton Depot
Booneville
Brandon
Brice's Crossroads
Brookhaven
Byhalia
Camp Davis
Camp Fisk
Camp Hawley
Camp Pettus
Camp Tupper
Canton
Chickasaw Bluffs
Clinton
Coffeeville
Columbus
Corinth
Edwards' Depot
Egypt Station
Ellisville
Fort Garrott
Fort Massachusetts
Fort Pemberton
Fort Pettus
Fort Twiggs
Fort Wade
Glendale
Grand Gulf
Greenville
Greenwood
Guntown
Hazlehurst
Hernando
Holly Springs
Houston
Iuka
Jacinto
Jackson
Kossuth
Lamar
Marietta
Marion Station
Meridian
Mississippi River
Morton
Mount Pleasant
Natchez
New Albany
Newton Station
Okolona
Oxford
Pontotoc
Port Gibson
Prentiss
Raymond
Rienzi
Ripley
Satartia
Ship Island
Tallahatchie River
Tishomingo Creek
Tombigbee River
Tupelo
Union
Vicksburg
West Point
Yazoo City

Missouri
Arrow Rock
Ashley
Athens
Belmont
Bloomfield
Boonville
Breckinridge
Brunswick
Butler
Camp Ben McCulloch
Camp Cavender
Camp Cole
Camp Gamble
Camp Jackson
Camp Jennison
Camp Totten
Camp Vest
Cape Girardeau
Carrollton
Carthage
Caruthersville
Centralia
Charleston
Clarkton
Columbia
Cuba
Danville
Doniphan
Farmington
Fayette
Fort Bankhead
Fort Davidson
Fort Lyon
Fort Mulligan
Fort Thompson
Fort Wyman
Franklin
Fredericktown
Fulton
Glasgow
Granby
Harrisonville
Hartville
Hermann
Holden
Hornersville
Houston
Humansville
Hunnewell
Huntsville
Independence
Ironton
Island No. 10
Jefferson City
Keytesville
Kirksville
Knobnoster
Lamar
Lebanon
Lexington
Liberty
Lone Jack
Longwood
Macon
Marshall
Marshfield
Martinsburg
Miami
Mississippi River
Monroe Station
Neosho
Nevada
New Madrid
Newtonia
Osceola
Ozark
Palmyra
Papinsville
Parkville
Plattsburg
Poplar Bluff
Quincy
Raytown
Richmond
Rocheport
Rolla
St. Francisville
St. James
St. Louis
Salem
Sedalia
Shelbina
Sibley
Sikeston
Smithville
Springfield
Stockton
Sturgeon
Tipton
Tuscumbia
Warrensburg
Warrenton
Warsaw
Waverly
Waynesville
Wellington
Wentzville
Westport
Wilson's Creek

New Hampshire
Camp Fry
Concord
Dover
Manchester
Portsmouth

New Jersey
Camp Olden
Camp Vredenburgh
Newark
Paterson
Trenton

New Mexico Territory
Albuquerque
Camp Connelly
Cubero
Fort Breckinridge
Fort Craig
Fort Cummings
Fort Fillmore
Fort Marcy
Fort Stanton
Fort Thorn
Fort Union
Fort Wingate
Glorieta Pass
Peralta
Santa Fe
Socorro
Valverde

New York
Albany
Astoria
Bedloe's Island
Binghamton
Brooklyn
Camp Astor
Camp Scott
Camp Scroggs
Castle Williams
Cold Spring
David's Island
Ellis Island
Elmira
Fort Columbus
Fort Hamilton
Fort Lafayette
Fort Schuyler
Fort Slocum
Fort Tompkins
Fort Totten
Fort Wadsworth
Fort Wood
Governors' Island
Hart's Island
Ilion
Morrisania
New York City
Plattsburgh
Riker's Island
Schaghticoke
Staten Island
Syracuse
Troy
Utica
Ward's Island
Watervliet
West Point
Yonkers

North Carolina
Asheville
Averasboro
Beaufort
Bentonville
Bogue Island
Boone
Camp Amory
Camp Anderson
Camp Badger
Camp Branch
Camp Burgwyn
Camp Claassen
Camp Clingman
Camp Ellis
Camp Fisher
Camp French
Camp Gaston
Camp Gatlin
Camp Hill
Camp Holmes
Camp Jourdan
Camp Lamb
Camp Leventhorpe
Camp Palmer
Camp Pender
Camp Randolph
Camp Ransom
Camp Robertson
Camp Rogers
Camp Vance
Camp Whiting
Camp Wyatt
Cape Fear River
Chapel Hill
Charlotte
Durham Station
Edenton
Elizabeth City
Fayetteville
Fort Amory
Fort Anderson
Fort Bartow
Fort Blanchard
Fort Branch
Fort Campbell
Fort Caswell
Fort Clark
Fort Davis
Fort Ellis
Fort Fisher
Fort Gaston
Fort Hatteras
Fort Huger
Fort Johnston
Fort Lamb
Fort Macon
Fort Spinola
Fort Stevenson
Goldsboro
Greensboro
Greenville
Hamilton
Hatteras Island
Hertford
Hillsborough
Hookerton
Jacksonville
Jamestown
Kenansville
Kinston
Morehead City
Morganton
Morrisville
Mount Olive Station
New Bern
Oak Island
Pikeville
Plymouth
Pollacksville
Raleigh
Roanoke Island
Rockingham
Salem
Salisbury
Shelton Laurel
Smithfield
Warsaw
Washington
Weldon
Wilkesboro
Wilmington
Windsor

Ohio
Buffington Island
Camp Ammen
Camp Andrews
Camp Buckingham
Camp Chase
Camp Dennison
Camp Goddard
Camp Harrison
Camp Latty
Camp Meigs
Camp Thomas
Camp Tod
Camp Wade
Camp Wallace
Cincinnati
Columbus
Fort Johnson
Hamilton
Harrison
Hockingport
Johnson's Island
Lake Erie
Ohio River
Pomeroy
Salineville

Steubenville
Wooster

Pennsylvania
Altoona
Bethlehem
Camp Cadwalader
Camp Copeland
Camp Curtin
Camp Letterman
Camp Meigs
Camp N.P. Banks
Camp William Penn
Carlisle
Chambersburg
Chester
Fayetteville
Fort Mifflin
Gettysburg
Greencastle
Hanover
Harrisburg
Mercersburg
Mud Island
Philadelphia
Phoenixville
Pittsburgh
Reading
Shohola
York

Rhode Island
Bristol
Camp Arnold
Camp Bliss
Camp Burnside
Camp Hallett
Providence

South Carolina
Abbeville
Aiken
Barnwell
Beaufort
Blackville
Bluffton
Camden

Camp Asylum
Camp Maxcy Gregg
Camp Saxton
Camp Sorghum
Castle Pinckney
Charleston
Cheraw
Chesterfield
Cokesbury
Columbia
Florence
Fort Beauregard
Fort Bull
Fort Gregg
Fort Howell
Fort Lamar
Fort Moultrie
Fort Pemberton
Fort Ripley
Fort Seward
Fort Shaw
Fort Sherman
Fort Sumter
Fort Trenholm
Fort Wagner
Fort Walker
Fort Welles
Graniteville
Greenville
Hilton Head Island
James Island
John's Island
Mars Bluff
Mitchelville
Morris Island
Orangeburg
Pocotaligo
Port Royal
Port Royal Island
St. Phillip's Island
Saluda
Secessionville
Shute's Folly Island
Stoney's Landing
Sullivan's Island
Williston
Yemassee

Tennessee
Athens
Bean's Station
Beersheba Springs
Blountville
Bolivar
Bristol
Camp Boone
Camp Bradley
Camp Breckinridge
Camp Cheatham
Camp Fiske
Camp Harker
Camp Junaluska
Camp Quarles
Camp Shaefer
Camp Sill
Camp Trousdale
Campbell's Station
Celina
Charleston
Chattanooga
Chewalla
Clarksville
Cleveland
Clifton
Columbia
Cumberland River
Dandridge
Decherd
Dover
Ducktown
Dyersburg
Eagleville
Farmington
Fayetteville
Fort Bruce
Fort Byington
Fort Cameron
Fort Comstock
Fort Dickerson
Fort Donelson
Fort Gillem
Fort Granger
Fort Harker
Fort Harris
Fort Henry

Fort McCook
Fort Mihalotzy
Fort Pickering
Fort Pillow
Fort Rosecrans
Fort Sanders
Fort Sheridan
Fort Sherman
Fort Wood
Fort Wright
Franklin
Gallatin
Gatlinburg
Germantown
Grand Junction
Greeneville
Hartsville
Hatchie River
Henderson's Station
Humboldt
Jacksboro
Jackson
Jasper
Johnsonville
Jonesborough
Kingsport
Kingston
Knoxville
La Grange
Lawrenceburg
Lebanon
Lenoir's Station
Lexington
Livingston
Lookout Mountain
Loudon
Lynchburg
Lynnville
Maryville
Maynardville
McMinnville
Memphis
Mifflin
Missionary Ridge
Mississippi River
Monterey
Morristown

180 • Appendix 2

Moscow
Murfreesboro
Nashville
Old Hen and Chickens Island
Palmyra
Pelham
Philadelphia
Pittsburg Landing
Pocahontas
Pulaski
Rogersville
Russellville
Rutledge
Savannah
Sevierville
Shelbyville
Shiloh
Sneedville
Somerville
Sparta
Stones River
Sweetwater
Talbott's Station
Tennessee River
Thompson's Station
Tiptonville
Trenton
Triune
Tullahoma
Union City
Wartburg
Wartrace
Winchester
Woodbury

Texas

Alleyton
Anderson
Aransas
Austin
Bastrop
Beaumont
Bellville
Bonham
Brownsville
Camp Austin
Camp Barnard Bee
Camp Bartow
Camp Bass
Camp Bee
Camp Belknap
Camp Brunson
Camp Burnett
Camp Carter
Camp Charles Russell
Camp Clark
Camp Collier
Camp Crump
Camp Daly
Camp Darnell
Camp Davis
Camp Flournoy
Camp Ford
Camp Gould
Camp Groce
Camp Hébert
Camp Henry McCulloch
Camp Hood
Camp Hubbard
Camp Hudson
Camp Jackson
Camp Jefferson Davis
Camp Kyle
Camp Lubbock
Camp Maxey
Camp McCulloch
Camp McLeod
Camp Parsons
Camp Pickett
Camp Raguet
Camp Reeves
Camp Roberts
Camp Robertson
Camp Rugely
Camp Rusk
Camp Sellers
Camp Semmes
Camp Sherman
Camp Sibley
Camp Sidney Johnston
Camp Slaughter
Camp Sulakowski
Camp Van Dorn
Camp Verde
Camp Waul
Camp Webb
Camp Wharton
Cedar Springs
Corpus Christi
Corsicana
Dallas
Fort Bankhead
Fort Belknap
Fort Bliss
Fort Brown
Fort Chadbourne
Fort Chambers
Fort Clark
Fort Davis
Fort Duncan
Fort Ewell
Fort Gates
Fort Griffin
Fort Hebert
Fort Inge
Fort Jackson
Fort Leaton
Fort Magruder
Fort Marcy
Fort Martin Scott
Fort Mason
Fort McIntosh
Fort McKavett
Fort Moore
Fort Murrah
Fort Quitman
Fort Ringgold
Fort Scurry
Fort Sidney Sherman
Fort Stockton
Gainesville
Galveston
Galveston Island
Gilmer
Hearne
Hempstead
Houston
Huntsville
Indianola
Jefferson
La Grange
Lancaster
Laredo
Lavaca
Marshall
Matagorda
Millican
Mustang Island
Paint Rock
Palestine
Plentitude
Rusk
Sabine Pass
Salado
San Antonio
San Marcos
Tyler
Waco
Washington
Waxahachie

Vermont

Brattleboro
Camp Baxter
Rutland
St. Albans
Windsor

Virginia

Abingdon
Aldie
Alexandria
Amelia Court House
Amelia Springs
Annandale
Appomattox Court House
Appomattox River
Appomattox Station
Aquia Creek
Arlington
Ashland
Atlee's Station

Barhamsville
Beaver Dam Creek
Beaver Dam Station
Belle Grove
Belle Isle
Bellona
Berryville
Bethesda Church
Beverly Ford
Big Bethel
Blacksburg
Brandy Station
Brown's Island
Buchanan
Bull Run Creek
Burkeville Junction
Camp Andrews
Camp Averell
Camp Barton
Camp Beall
Camp Benton
Camp Butler
Camp Carondelet
Camp Cass
Camp Du Pont
Camp Fisher
Camp Griffin
Camp Grinnell
Camp Hamilton
Camp Howard
Camp Jackson
Camp Keyes
Camp Lee
Camp Mansfield
Camp Marion
Camp Maury
Camp Nicholls
Camp Pickens
Camp Quantico
Camp Upton
Camp Whitwell
Camp Winfield
  Scott
Cedar Creek
Cedar Mountain
Centreville
Chancellorsville
Chantilly
Charlottesville
Chatham
Chickahominy River
City Point
Clarksville
Cloyd's Mountain
Cold Harbor
Covington
Craney Island
Culpeper Court
  House
Danville
Dayton
Dinwiddie Court
  House
Dranesville
Drewry's Bluff
Dublin
Dumfries
Eltham's Landing
Enon Church
Fairfax Court House
Fairfax Station
Falls Church
Falmouth
Farmville
Five Forks
Fort Abbott
Fort Alexander Hays
Fort Banks
Fort Blaisdell
Fort Boykin
Fort Bross
Fort Burnham
Fort Clifton
Fort Collier
Fort Conahey
Fort Craig
Fort Dahlgren
Fort Davis
Fort Dix
Fort Early
Fort Edward Johnson
Fort Ellsworth
Fort Emory
Fort Evans
Fort Farnsworth
Fort Gilmer
Fort Gregg
Fort Halleck
Fort Haskell
Fort Hoke
Fort Huger
Fort Johnson
Fort Lee
Fort Lewis O. Morris
Fort Lyon
Fort Magruder
Fort Mahone
Fort Marcy
Fort McCausland
Fort McClellan
Fort McGilvery
Fort McMahon
Fort Meikle
Fort Monroe
Fort Morton
Fort Munson
Fort Myer
Fort Nelson
Fort Norfolk
Fort O'Rourke
Fort Patrick Kelly
Fort Porter
Fort Powhatan
Fort Prescott
Fort Ramsay
Fort Rice
Fort Sedgwick
Fort Seward
Fort Stedman
Fort Taylor
Fort Tracy
Fort Urmston
Fort Wadsworth
Fort Ward
Fort Washington
Fort Wead
Fort Weed
Fort Welch
Fort Wheaton
Fort Whitworth
Fort Willard
Fort Williams
Fort Wool
Fort Worth
Franklin
Fredericksburg
Front Royal
Gaines' Mill
Gainesville
Germanna Ford
Gloucester Court
  House
Gloucester Point
Goochland Court
  House
Gordonsville
Guiney's Station
Hampton
Hanover Court
  House
Hanovertown
Harrisonburg
Harrison's Landing
Haw's Shop
Haymarket
Henrico
Herndon Station
Hopewell
Hungary Station
James River
Jarratt's Station
Jericho Mill
Jetersville
Jonesville
Kelly's Ford
Kernstown
King and Queen
  Court House
Lexington
Louisa Court House
Lovettsville
Lynchburg
Malvern Hill
Manassas
Manassas Junction
Marion
McDowell
Meade's Station

Mechanicsville
Middleburg
Middletown
Mount Jackson
New Baltimore
New Market
Newport News
Newtown
Norfolk
North Anna River
Oak Grove
Occoquan
Opequon Creek
Orange Court House
Petersburg
Philomont
Piedmont
Pittsylvania Court
   House
Port Walthall
   Junction
Portsmouth
Potomac River
Powhatan
Prince George
   Court House
Princess Anne
   Court House
Purcellville
Raccoon Ford
Rapidan River
Rapidan Station
Rappahannock River
Rappahannock
   Station

Richmond
Roanoke Station
Sailor's Creek
Saltville
Smithfield
Spotsylvania Court
   House
Stanardsville
Staunton
Strasburg
Strawberry Plains
Suffolk
Tom's Brook
Totopotomoy Creek
Upperville
Vienna
Warrenton
Warrenton Junction
Warrenton Springs
Waterford
Waterloo
Wayne Court House
Waynesboro
West Point
White House Land-
   ing
White Oak Swamp
White Plains
Wilderness
Williamsburg
Winchester
Woodstock
Wytheville
Yellow Tavern
Yorktown

West Virginia

Barboursville
Beverly
Bolivar Heights
Buckhannon
Bunker Hill
Burlington
Burning Springs
Camp Allegheny
Camp Bartow
Camp Garnett
Carnifix Ferry
Charles Town
Charleston
Cheat Mountain
Corrick's Ford
Darkesville
Elizabeth
Fairmont
Falling Waters
Fayetteville
Fort Boreman
Fort Mulligan
Fort Pickens
Fort Scammon
Franklin
Glenville
Grafton
Halltown
Hamlin
Harpers Ferry
Huttonsville
Kabletown
Kearneysville
Lewisburg

Martinsburg
Moorefield
Morgantown
Petersburg
Peytona
Philippi
Piedmont
Potomac River
Princeton
Ravenswood
Rich Mountain
Romney
Rowlesburg
Shepherdstown
Smithfield
Summersville
Sutton
Wardensville
Wheeling

Wisconsin

Camp Barstow
Camp Bragg
Camp Harvey
Camp Randall
Camp Reno
Camp Salomon
Camp Scott
Camp Washburn
Camp Wood
Fort Crawford
Madison

Bibliography

Abate, Frank R., ed. *American Places Dictionary: A Guide to 45,000 Populated Places, Natural Features, and Other Places in the United States.* 4 vols. Detroit, MI: Omnigraphics, Inc., 1994.
Allardice, Bruce S. *More Generals in Gray.* Baton Rouge: Louisiana State University Press, 1995.
The American Civil War. A Centennial Exhibition. Washington, DC: Library of Congress, 1961.
Andrews, J. Cutler. *The South Reports the Civil War.* Pittsburgh: University of Pittsburgh Press, 1985 [1970].
Baillie, Laureen, ed. *American Biographical Index*; 3rd ed. 10 vols. Munich: K. G. Saur, 2007.
Beers, Henry P. *The Confederacy: A Guide to the Archives of the Government of the Confederate States of America.* 1968. Reprint, Washington, DC: National Archives and Records Administration, 1998.
Bishop, J. Leander. *A History of American Manufactures.* 3 vols. 1868. Reprint, New York, NY: Johnson Reprint Corporation, 1967.
Black, Robert C. *The Railroads of the Confederacy.* 1952. Reprint, Chapel Hill: The University of North Carolina Press, 1998.
Blair, Jayne E. *The Essential Civil War: A Handbook to the Battles, Armies, Navies and Commanders.* Jefferson, NC: McFarland & Co., Inc., 2006.
Boatner, Mark M. *Cassell's Biographical Dictionary of the American Civil War 1861–1865.* 1959. Reprint, London: Cassell & Co., 1973.
Bowman, John S., ed. *The Civil War Almanac.* New York, NY: Gallery Books, 1983.
_____. *Encyclopedia of the Civil War.* London: Bison Books Ltd., 1992.
Brown, Dee. *The Galvanized Yankees.* 1963. Reprint, Lincoln: University of Nebraska Press, 1986.
Chambers World Gazetteer: An A-Z of Geographical Information; 5th ed. Edinburgh: W. & R. Chambers Ltd; Cambridge: Cambridge University Press, 1988.
Clark, Victor S. *History of Manufactures in the United States.* Vol. II, 1860–1893. New York, NY: Peter Smith, 1949.
Conrad, James L. *The Young Lions: Confederate Cadets at War.* Mechanicsburg, PA: Stackpole Books, 1997.
Cooling, Benjamin F., and Walton H. Owen. *Mr. Lincoln's Forts: A Guide to the Civil War Defenses of Washington*; rev. ed. Lanham, MD: Scarecrow Press, Inc., 2010.
Crews, C. Daniel. *A Storm in the Land: Southern Moravians and the Civil War.* Winston-Salem, NC: Moravian Archives, 1997.
Cumming, Kate. *Kate: The Journal of a Confederate Nurse*; ed. by Richard B. Harwell. Baton Rouge: Louisiana State University Press, 1998. Originally published as *A Journal of Hospital Life in the Confederate Army of Tennessee*, 1866.
Cunningham, H.H. *Doctors in Gray: The Confederate Medical Service*; 2nd ed. 1960. Reprint, Baton Rouge: Louisiana State University Press, 1993.
Daily Telegraph. "Library Return 145 Years Late," April 16, 2009.
_____. "Note of Desperation to Confederates Finally Deciphered," December 27, 2010.
De Blij, H.J., ed. *Atlas of the United States.* New York, NY: Oxford University Press, Inc., 2006.
Edwards, William B. *Civil War Guns.* Harrisburg, PA: The Stackpole Co., 1962.
Espenshade, Abraham H. *Pennsylvania Place Names.* State College: Pennsylvania State College, 1925.

Faust, Patricia L., ed. *Historical Times Illustrated Encyclopedia of the Civil War.* 1986. Reprint, New York, NY: HarperPerennial, 1991.
Field, Ron. *American Civil War Fortifications. 2, Land and Field Fortifications.* Botley, Oxford: Osprey Publishing, 2005.
_____. *American Civil War Fortifications. 3, The Mississippi and River Forts.* Botley, Oxford: Osprey Publishing, 2007.
_____. *The Confederate Army 1861–65. 1, South Carolina & Mississippi.* Botley, Oxford: Osprey Publishing, 2005.
_____. *The Confederate Army 1861–65. 2, Florida, Alabama & Georgia.* Botley, Oxford: Osprey Publishing, 2005.
_____. *The Confederate Army 1861–65. 3, Louisiana & Texas.* Botley, Oxford: Osprey Publishing, 2006.
_____. *The Confederate Army 1861–65. 4, Virginia & Arkansas.* Botley, Oxford: Osprey Publishing, 2006.
_____. *The Confederate Army 1861–65. 5, Tennessee & North Carolina.* Botley, Oxford: Osprey Publishing, 2007.
_____. *The Confederate Army 1861–65. 6, Missouri, Kentucky & Maryland.* Botley, Oxford: Osprey Publishing, 2008.
_____. *Forts of the American Frontier 1820–91. The Southern Plains and Southwest.* Botley, Oxford: Osprey Publishing, 2006.
Gannett, Henry. *The Origin of Certain Place Names in the United States*; 2nd ed. 1905. Reprint, Baltimore, MD: Genealogical Publishing Co., Inc., 1977.
Gelbert, Doug. *Civil War Sites, Memorials, Museums and Library Collections: A State-by-State Guidebook to Places Open to the Public.* Jefferson, NC: McFarland & Co., Inc., 1997.
A Guide to Civil War Maps in the National Archives; rev. ed. Washington, DC: National Archives & Records Administration, 1986.
Hanson, Raus M. *Virginia Place Names: Derivations, Historical Uses.* Verona, VA: McClure Press, 1969.
Harder, Kelsie B., ed. *Illustrated Dictionary of Place Names, United States and Canada.* New York: Van Nostrand Reinhold Co., 1976.
Historical Statistics of the United States: Earliest Times to the Present. Millennial edition. Vol. I, Part A. Population. New York: Cambridge University Press, 2006.
Hobson, Archie, ed. *The Cambridge Gazetteer of the United States and Canada.* New York: Cambridge University Press, 1995.
Hodges, Robert R., Jr. *American Civil War Railroad Tactics.* Botley, Oxford: Osprey Publishing, 2009.
Holberton, William B. *Homeward Bound: The Demobilization of the Union and Confederate Armies, 1865–1866.* Mechanicsburg, PA: Stackpole Books, 2001.
Huden, John C. *Indian Place Names of New England.* New York: Museum of the American Indian. Heye Foundation, 1962.
Johnson, Robert U., and Clarence C. Buel, eds. *Battles and Leaders of the Civil War.* 4 vols. 1887. Reprint, Secaucus, NJ: Castle, nd.
Jones, Terry L. *Historical Dictionary of the Civil War.* 2 vols. Lanham, MD: Scarecrow Press, Inc., 2002.
Kane, Joseph N. *The American Counties*; 3rd ed. Metuchen, NJ: Scarecrow Press, Inc., 1972.
Katcher, Philip. *Brassey's Almanac: The American Civil War.* London: Brassey's, 2003.
Kennett, Lee. *Marching through Georgia: The Story of Soldiers and Civilians during Sherman's Campaign.* New York: HarperCollins Publishers, Inc., 1995.
Kenny, Hamill. *West Virginia Place Names: Their Origin and Meaning.* Piedmont, WV: The Place Name Press, 1945.
Konstam, Angus. *American Civil War Fortifications. 1, Coastal Brick and Stone Forts.* Botley, Oxford: Osprey Publishing, 2003.
_____. *Confederate Ironclad 1861–65.* Botley, Oxford: Osprey Publishing, 2001.
Lawliss, Chuck. *The Civil War Sourcebook: A Traveler's Guide.* New York, NY: Harmony Books, 1991.
Long, E.B., and Barbara Long. *The Civil War Day by Day: An Almanac 1861–1865.* New York: Da Capo Press, Inc., 1971.
Longacre, Edward G. *Mounted Raids of the Civil War.* 1975. Reprint, Lincoln: University of Nebraska Press, 1994.
Lonn, Ella. *Salt as a Factor in the Confederacy.* 1933. Reprint, University: University of Alabama Press, 1965.
Lyman, Darryl. *Civil War Quotations.* Conshohocken, PA: Combined Books, Inc., 1995.

Massey, Mary E. *Refugee Life in the Confederacy*. 1964. Reprint, Baton Rouge: Louisiana State University Press, 2001.

_____. *Women in the Civil War*. Lincoln: University of Nebraska Press, 1994. First published as *Bonnet Brigades*, 1966.

McPherson, James M., ed. *The Atlas of the Civil War*. New York: Macmillan, 1994.

Miller, Francis T., ed. *The Photographic History of the Civil War*. 5 vols. 1911. Reprint, Secaucus, NJ: Blue & Grey Press, 1987.

Munden, Kenneth W., and Henry P. Beers. *Guide to Federal Archives Relating to the Civil War*. Washington, DC: National Archives & Records Service, 1962.

Names in South Carolina, vol. X, winter 1963; vol. XVII, winter 1970. Columbia: Department of English, University of South Carolina.

Overman, William D. *Ohio Town Names*. Akron, OH: Atlantic Press, 1958.

Population of the United States in 1860; compiled from ... the Eighth Census. Washington, DC: Government Printing Office, 1864.

Preliminary Report of the Eighth Census 1860. Washington, DC: Government Printing Office, 1862.

Pursell, John W. *Why Do they Call it Topeka? How Places Got their Names*. New York, NY: Citadel Press, 1995.

Read, William A. "Louisiana Place-Names of Indian Origin," *Louisiana State University Bulletin*, vol. xix, no. 2, February 1927.

Reps, John W. *Bird's Eye Views: Historic Lithographs of North American Cities*. New York: Princeton Architectural Press, 1998.

Ripley, Warren. *Artillery and Ammunition of the Civil War*. New York: Van Nostrand Reinhold Co., 1970.

Roberts, Robert B. *Encyclopedia of Historic Forts: The Military, Pioneer and Trading Posts of the United States*. New York: Macmillan Publishing Co., 1988.

Roller, David C., and Robert W. Twyman, eds. *The Encyclopedia of Southern History*. Baton Rouge: Louisiana State University Press, 1979.

Sherr, Lynn, and Jurate Kazickas. *The American Woman's Gazetteer*. New York: Bantam Books, Inc., 1976.

Shirk, George H. *Oklahoma Place Names*. Norman: University of Oklahoma Press, 1965.

Speer, Lonnie R. *Portals to Hell: Military Prisons of the Civil War*. Mechanicsburg, PA: Stackpole Books, 1997.

Statistics of the Population of the United States ... compiled from the Ninth Census, 1870. Washington, DC: Government Printing Office, 1872.

Stephenson, Richard W., comp. *Civil War Maps: An Annotated List of Maps and Atlases in Map Collections in the Library of Congress*. Washington, DC: Library of Congress, 1961.

Stewart, George R. *A Concise Dictionary of American Place-Names*. New York: Oxford University Press, Inc., 1970.

_____. *Names on the Land: A Historical Account of Place-naming in the United States*. New York: Random House, 1945.

Still, William N., Jr., ed. *The Confederate Navy: The Ships, Men and Organization, 1861–65*. London: Conway Maritime Press, 1997.

_____. *Confederate Shipbuilding*. 1969. Reprint, Columbia: University of South Carolina Press, 1987.

Taylor, Robert A. *Rebel Storehouse: Florida's Contribution to the Confederacy*. Tuscaloosa: University of Alabama Press, 2003.

Trollope, Anthony. *North America*. 1862. Reprint, Folkstone, Kent: Dawsons, 1968.

Trowbridge, John T. *The Desolate South 1865–1866*; ed. by Gordon Carroll. New York, NY: Duel, Sloan & Pearce; Boston, MA: Little, Brown & Co., 1956. Originally published as *The South: A Tour of Its Battlefields and Ruined Cities*, 1866.

Vandiver, Frank E. *Ploughshares into Swords: Josiah Gorgas and Confederate Ordnance*. 1952. Reprint, College Station: Texas A & M University Press, 1994.

Waitt, Robert W., Jr. *Confederate Military Hospitals in Richmond*. 1964. Reprint, Richmond, VA: Richmond Independence Bicentennial Commission, 1979.

Warner, Ezra J. *Generals in Blue: Lives of the Union Commanders*. Baton Rouge: Louisiana State University Press, 1964.

_____. *Generals in Gray: Lives of the Confederate Commanders*. 1959. Reprint, Baton Rouge: Louisiana State University Press, 1992.

Weber, Thomas. *The Northern Railroads in the Civil War.* New York: Columbia University, 1952.
Webster's New Biographical Dictionary. Springfield, MA: Merriam-Webster Inc., 1988.
Webster's New Geographical Dictionary. Springfield, MA: G. & C. Merriam Co., 1972.
Who Was Who in America: Historical Volume, 1607–1896. Chicago: Marquis Who's Who, 1963.
Winsor, Bill. *Texas in the Confederacy: Military Installations, Economy and People.* Hillsboro, TX: Hill Jr. College Press, 1978.
Wolk, Allan. *The Naming of America.* Nashville, TN: Thomas Nelson, Inc., 1977
Works Progress Administration Federal Writers' Project. (*American Guide Series*).
_____. *Alabama. A Guide to the Deep South.* 1941. Reprint, New York: Hastings House, 1949.
_____. *Arkansas. A Guide to the State.* 1941. Reprint, New York: Hastings House, 1948 [1941].
_____. *Connecticut. A Guide to its Roads, Lore and People.* Boston: Houghton Mifflin Co., 1938.
_____. *Florida. A Guide to the Southernmost State.* New York: Oxford University Press, 1939.
_____. *Georgia. A Guide to its Towns and Countryside.* Athens: University of Georgia Press, 1940.
_____. *Illinois. A Descriptive and Historical Guide.* Chicago: A. C. McClurg & Co., 1939.
_____. *Indiana. A Guide to the Hoosier State.* New York: Oxford University Press, 1941.
_____. *Iowa. A Guide to the Hawkeye State.* 1938. Reprint, New York: Hastings House, 1949.
_____. *Kansas. A Guide to the Sunflower State.* 1939. Reprint, New York: Hastings House, 1949.
_____. *Kentucky. A Guide to the Bluegrass State.* 1939. Reprint, New York: Hastings House, 1954.
_____. *Louisiana. A Guide to the State.* 1941. Reprint, New York: Hastings House, 1949.
_____. *Maine. A Guide "Down East."* Boston: Houghton Mifflin Co., 1937.
_____. *Maryland. A Guide to the Old Line State.* New York: Oxford University Press, 1940.
_____. *Massachusetts. A Guide to its Places and People.* Boston: Houghton Mifflin Co., 1937.
_____. *Mississippi. A Guide to the Magnolia State.* 1938. Reprint, New York: Hastings House, 1949.
_____. *Missouri. A Guide to the "Show Me" State*; rev. ed. 1941. Reprint, New York: Hastings House, 1954.
_____. *New Mexico. A Guide to the Colorful State.* 1940. Reprint, New York: Hastings House, 1953.
_____. *New York. A Guide to the Empire State.* New York: Oxford University Press, 1940.
_____. *North Carolina. A Guide to the Old North State.* Chapel Hill: University of North Carolina Press, 1939.
_____. *The Ohio Guide.* New York: Oxford University Press, 1940.
_____. *Pennsylvania. A Guide to the Keystone State.* New York: Oxford University Press, 1940.
_____. *South Carolina. A Guide to the Palmetto State.* New York: Oxford University Press, 1941.
_____. *Tennessee. A Guide to the State.* 1939. Reprint, New York: Hastings House, 1949.
_____. *Texas. A Guide to the Lone Star State.* New York: Hastings House, 1940.
_____. *Virginia. A Guide to the Old Dominion.* New York: Oxford University Press, 1940.
_____. *West Virginia. A Guide to the Mountain State.* New York: Oxford University Press, 1941.
_____. *Wisconsin. A Guide to the Badger State.* 1941. Reprint, New York: Hastings House, 1954.
_____. *The WPA Guide to New York City.* 1939. Reprint, New York: Pantheon Books, 1982.

www.ingramcontent.com/pod-product-compliance
Ingram Content Group UK Ltd.
Pitfield, Milton Keynes, MK11 3LW, UK
UKHW050523150426
5217IPUK00026B/1775